THOMSON
COURSE TECHNOLOGY

Professional ◦ Trade ◦ Reference

HOW to Be a DJ

DJ Chuck Fresh

Important: Thomson Course Technology PTR cannot provide hardware or software support. Please contact the appropriate manufacturer's technical support line or Web site for assistance.

Thomson Course Technology PTR and the author have attempted throughout this book to distinguish proprietary trademarks from descriptive terms by following the capitalization style used by the manufacturer.

Information contained in this book has been obtained by Thomson Course Technology PTR from sources believed to be reliable. However, because of the possibility of human or mechanical error by our sources, Thomson Course Technology PTR, or others, the Publisher does not guarantee the accuracy, adequacy, or completeness of any information and is not responsible for any errors or omissions or the results obtained from use of such information. Readers should be particularly aware of the fact that the Internet is an ever-changing entity. Some facts may have changed since this book went to press.

Educational facilities, companies, and organizations interested in multiple copies or licensing of this book should contact the publisher for quantity discount information. Training manuals, CD-ROMs, and portions of this book are also available individually or can be tailored for specific needs.

ISBN: 1-59200-509-8
Library of Congress Catalog Card Number: 2004106603
Printed in the United States of America
04 05 06 07 08 BH 10 9 8 7 6 5 4 3 2 1

THOMSON

COURSE TECHNOLOGY

Professional ■ Trade ■ Reference

Thomson Course Technology PTR,
a division of Thomson Course Technology
25 Thomson Place
Boston, MA 02210
http://www.courseptr.com

SVP, Thomson Course Technology PTR:
Andy Shafran

Publisher:
Stacy L. Hiquet

Senior Marketing Manager:
Sarah O'Donnell

Marketing Manager:
Heather Hurley

Manager of Editorial Services:
Heather Talbot

Senior Editor/Acquisitions Editor:
Mark Garvey

Associate Marketing Managers:
Kristin Eisenzopf and
Sarah Dubois

Developmental/Project/ Copy Editor:
Brian Proffitt

Technical Reviewer:
Chad Carrier

Course Technology PTR Market Coordinator:
Elizabeth Furbish

Interior Layout Tech:
Shawn Morningstar

Cover Designer:
Mike Tanamachi

Indexer:
Kelly Talbot

Proofreader:
Dan Foster

Dedication

This book is dedicated to:

DJ Richie Huber for teaching me the ropes

DJ Suzy Fresh for reminding me there is more to life than just being a DJ

DJ Joseph Montalvo for his eternal optimism and dedication

DJ Kokopeli Dan for showing me that Karaoke is sort of fun

DJ Post Modern Pam for her lifelong friendship and explaining how radio really works

Pat Jr., Bobby, and the boys at Pat's Music in Philly for putting up with all my stupid questions over the years

And Rockin' Ron Capps, Jammin' Julie Grove, Tony "White Lightning" Deremer, Ronny Fresh, Robby Fresh, Def Masta Homey Fresh (Chris Bennett), Stew Shocka, Digital DJ Louie, Eddie Jordan, Lisa G, Mike Staff, Bob Palio, "Spring Water", and all the thousands of customers, managers, and DJs I've worked with over the years for their support and for making it fun.

About the Author

Chuck Fresh has 20 years' experience as a private party, nightclub and bar, and radio DJ and currently works as a nightclub consultant. Fresh has been featured in numerous DJ and nightclub magazines, including *Nightclub and Bar Magazine*, and he is the author of *Make Some Noise*, *Wild Party Contests*, and *A DJ's Guide to Latin Music*. Fresh now resides in Melbourne, Florida, and is a nationally recognized voiceover talent. He also runs Bar Marketing, LLC and The DJ Resource, providing party games and promotional services to nightclubs, bars, and DJs all over the world.

Contents at a Glance

Contents

3 Becoming a Mobile DJ 77

4 Mobile and Club DJ Equipment   125

5 All About The Music   167

6 Performance DJs 205

9 The Digital Domain   259

Introduction

Everyone always asked me if it mattered.

"Does what you say to the crowd matter?" "Does it matter if you can beatmix well?" "Do my scratching skills matter?" "Do the games you play at private affairs or the promotions you do at clubs matter?" And the number one "matter" question: "Does the music really matter?"

Typically, if you're a bedroom DJ, nothing really matters, although it's more fun to play songs you like rather than music that systematically fits into the technical aspects of what you're trying to do. If you're a radio DJ, the music doesn't really matter, because you won't be choosing it, and you won't have a clue how your audience responds to it anyway. If you're a nightclub DJ, it absolutely matters, but only early in the night before people have had enough alcohol or drugs to forget the difference. And if you're a mobile private party DJ, it depends on the crowd, and your answer will always be different. Some crowds would respond to you banging two sticks together on the microphone, and others wouldn't dance if you held a large cannon to their butts with a shaky trigger finger.

For more than fifteen years of my life, I worked as a radio, club and mobile DJ. I went to bed at about 4 AM and slept until 10 AM most mornings (when not working a day job for insurance benefits). I lost touch with most of my high school friends because I was working while they were out partying.

There is one good point, now that I look back…I missed the entire *Cosby* show.

But I was having fun. I was earning money doing what I loved to do—writing and playing music. And I got to do many things most people would never dream of doing, including but not limited to acting as a pseudo-psychiatrist, relationship counselor, bouncer, director of marketing, bartender, maitre'd, camp counselor, concierge, deal broker, buyer, sales rep, sound and lighting engineer, national act producer, PC repair technician, video producer, gigolo, and other things I simply can't remember at this point.

I was building a career that would ultimately include feature magazine articles, radio commercials all over the world, a stint with a local rock band, and ultimately the creation of this book. We all make sacrifices in life, and I'd do it all over again, the same exact way.

So now you're thinking about becoming a DJ. Maybe you're already a DJ looking to advance to the next level. Or maybe you've been DJing in your bedroom and decided it's time to start making some money at this madness. The first question you must answer, as honestly as humanly possible, is which kind of DJ you truly want to be. The second question, that's much more important if you're interested in a career as a DJ, is which you'd be best at.

It's pretty common to see a DJ on MTV, in TV commercials, or in music videos doing all kinds of crazy things with records in front of an audience of screaming fans. And virtually every private affair now has a DJ rather than a live band. DJs are everywhere today. I have to admit…it's hard to believe that all these people get paid for talking, playing music and having fun! Now you can too. This book will help demystify the three different types of Disc Jockey jobs and help you fulfill your DJ dreams.

As I wandered the halls of my corporate day jobs, bleary and bloodshot eyes giving away the fact that I had a hangover and was up until at least 4 AM the night before, yet still managing to force a friendly smile, people always asked me about my "other" life as a DJ. Some of the more popular questions were, "Is it fun?" "Do you make good money?" "Do you get a lot of chicks?"

Yes, I guess, and oh, yeah! The first thing I tell folks is that it can be a huge pain in the butt to break in to this business. But once you do, you're officially involved in the multi-billion dollar entertainment industry. If you've got a few spare bucks for equipment and music, a lot of time to practice, and if you're dedicated and you have the know-how, you too can make a comfortable living at this nonsense. Yes, you can have fun while getting paid playing music for a living. And for whatever reason, chicks seem to love DJs.

Contrary to what some egocentric New York DJs will tell you, you don't need a ton of raw talent to be a successful DJ. You don't need to know music theory; how to play an instrument; how to sing or how to dance. You don't have to be born with special DNA. Many basic DJ skills can be learned from the information and diagrams in this book. You can watch and listen to those considered "successful" in their part of the DJ business for other skills. About 95 percent of this job consists of purely mechanical actions and good judgment calls, and the rest is schmoozing to get ahead. This book will teach you everything you'll need to be successful in all three of the main DJ fields.

It's been my personal experience that about three out of five existing "professional" DJs, in all three DJ fields, are immature, insecure, irresponsible idiots. They're lazy, inconsistent, and often dangerously unpredictable. I used to think it was a Northeast thing, but it's much wider than that, spanning the entire nation. Maybe it's the insecurity of the industry as a whole that forces DJs to act this way, I'm not sure. There are more backstabbing people in this field than any other field I've ever seen, surprisingly including Corporate America! Of the thousands of DJs I met early in my career, only three offered to help me learn my craft. Almost everyone is in it for themselves, and it's pretty rare to find someone who's willing to give you a hand and teach you what you need to know. Hopefully, you'll sway the odds and help repair this crazy industry.

Starting out in the DJ business can cost you about three to several thousand dollars in music and equipment, most of which will be wasted if you're not careful. Don't make the same mistakes the rest of us made. Depending on which type of DJ you choose to be, your music, equipment, and accessory needs will vary widely. You might also need tons of music, much of which you won't like (unless you actually like "The Chicken Dance"). If you're just into it for the glamour (or to make mixtapes for your friends from your bedroom), you've chosen a fun but expensive hobby.

No matter which DJ direction you choose, you'll need to invest lots of time figuring out the intricacies of your equipment as well as learning your music inside and out. Your number one priorities will be practicing with your equipment and performance, and researching new trends, music, and promotions. If you think being a DJ is just showing up at 9 PM and leaving at 2, you're in for a rude awakening! Radio DJs spend hours on something called "Show Prep." Nightclub and bar DJs must always be at the forefront of new music, so they'll spend hours listening, evaluating, and learning new songs. Mobile DJs spend several hours in the sales process, and then even more hours organizing events directly with their clients. Bad DJs don't spend nearly enough time in preparation, and it shows in their sloppy work. These bad DJs will be your first targets when looking for a job.

This book investigates the radio, club and bar, and mobile DJ fields. We'll show you what you need to do to get started and how to be successful at each. We'll explain the major advantages and disadvantages of each individual field. We'll cover Group Dynamics, contests and promotions, music, equipment, terminology, sneaky tricks, and so much more. Based on this information, you should be able to decide which field will be best for you and have a running head start over most of the other knuckleheads all competing for the same job.

Unlike most other DJ books, my goal is to get you out of your bedroom and into the real DJ world. I've shared years of not only my own personal experiences, but those of other successful DJs from various DJ fields. If you read thoroughly, pay attention to the world around you, work hard, and do a bit more than is expected of you, you too can have a great career as a professional DJ.

So do all those aforementioned things matter?

Well, yes, and no. I never had a perfect answer for that question. You'll have to figure out the right answer for your situation yourself. And that's what makes it fun....

1
BECOMING A RADIO DJ

I had dreamed about becoming a radio DJ since I was about ten years old. I used to make tapes in my bedroom with an old record player and a cassette tape recorder my grandfather gave me. I had a few records my parents bought at a garage sale and I'd play them over and over again, announcing the name and artist along with today's weather and news. I'd listen to DJs on the local radio stations and tried to copy their styles with my pre-pubescent voice. I have no idea where those tapes are but I'd bet they're hilariously terrible.

I got my first "real" radio gig at Temple University's college radio station in Ambler, Pennsylvania. It was a tiny, 5-Watt signal that barely reached to the end of the campus, but always blared loudly in the student dorms and cafeteria. I worked the weekend shifts, so I got to bring my own music and say whatever I wanted. Some of the skits my friends and I did on that station would make Howard Stern look tame by comparison!

I did that for a semester or two and got tired of it. I later joined Temple's "real" FM radio station, WRTI in Philadelphia, as a reporter for a program called "Lifestyles." I did a few reports on campus events and activities, and decided then I didn't want to be a reporter. Music was much more fun for me. Since WRTI was an all-jazz station then, I packed up my headphones and tried not to let the door hit me where the good Lord split me.

A few years later, I got the radio bug again, and managed to find a gig at a community radio station while doing nights as a nightclub DJ. I did Friday mornings from 7 until noon, playing a preset list of Top 40 and soft rock songs on "carts" (tapes that look like an old eight-track tape, if you've ever seen one of those). I was always half asleep because I worked a big club on Thursday nights until 2AM then partied until 3 or 4AM. I recorded pretty poor demo tapes and shotgunned them out to everyone I could. Good thing most unsolicited demo tapes go directly into the trash.

While working at a big nightclub in New Jersey with several radio personalities, I finally got a break. I filled in part-time on a small commercial station in Trenton, New Jersey as a co-host on a show that played "Post Modern" music (alternative rock). When I finally got a part-time job offer at that station, they told me I'd have to give up my nightclub gigs because they were a "conflict of interest." Since I was already in my mid-twenties, married with a baby, and making five times more cash at the nightclubs, I had to turn down the radio gig. There was my dream, right in front of me, but the timing was all wrong. Easy come, easy go.

So that's my radio story. But if you're single and carefree, and you dig traveling all over the country while living on microwaved foods, there's nothing like the rush you'll feel when you meet adoring fans who tell you they never miss your show.

My advice to someone entering the radio field is to make sure this is exactly what you want to do for a living, and make sure you're young enough before all the "adult" problems (bills, mortgage, kids, etc) take over. Forget new cars and fancy clothes—prepare to live in almost poverty level conditions indefinitely. Don't count on having a single circle of lifetime friends, because you'll probably have to start in a tiny market where no one would ever want to live, and you'll have to move all over the country at the drop of a hat to take on better opportunities. Leave your ego at home because you will get fired and laid off frequently. But if it's truly what you have your heart set on, go all out and do whatever you need to do to break in. Spend all the time, effort, and money you can into producing a killer demo tape, which I'll cover later in this chapter. Eventually, someone will open the door for you and you, too, will get an opportunity of a lifetime.

This section offers a brief analysis on the radio business, your options, and an introduction to basic radio terminology. For a much more in-depth description of the business, great tips on how to land your first on-air job and a great success story, definitely get your hands on a copy of Mike Staff's *How To Become A Radio DJ* (available at www.djbook.com)—it's mandatory reading if you're dead serious about a job in the radio industry. Mike's book even comes with a sample demo tape that he used to get his radio job, so you know it works.

What's Involved

For the most part, being a typical radio jock can be the most rewarding DJ job, due to the local fame it may produce for you. All you have to do is play the music some program or music director has already chosen for you and make some announcements that are already written for you. Once in a while, you might even get to "ad lib" (say something funny or entirely original that you came up with) to show people that you actually have a personality... but don't count on it.

A successful radio DJ does much more than play preselected music and make prefabricated announcements. The successful DJ must be quick-witted, innovative, and a visionary with plenty of patience and a very tough skin, because equipment does fail and strange situations call for quick and smart fixes. Many DJs will choose to specialize in a specific musical genre. They have their own personal and consistent approach or "shtick."

Most successful DJs have built a reputation of being totally obnoxious and/or very respected in the industry, and because of this, they are allowed much more leeway than the typical radio DJ. These people are constantly preparing for their next show. They're always thinking about things they can do or say on the air that will keep listeners tuned in day in and day out. They have professional production teams that help them get great guests and promote wild contests. Unfortunately, it usually takes years of experience and frustration to get to this level. Many successful DJs have been fired several times for pushing the envelope only to be recognized and rewarded years later for their successful intuition. For a good true-life story, read *Private Parts* by Howard Stern, or rent the movie of the same name.

Since the norm for radio DJs is only one person on the air at any given time, this job can get lonely, especially when you're starting out on overnight or weekend shifts when the daytime office staff is gone. You won't get the interaction or immediate feedback you'll get at clubs or private affairs, so you'll never really know if your audience is digging your show. If you're lucky and you land a job that's not at some small town all-news station, the station may send you out to host nightclub contests and events, broadcast live from concerts and special events, and maybe even interview singers and bands. That's when this job gets really cool (and profitable).

You'll have to learn how to use some pretty complex computer equipment, and you'll need to know how to use it well. Fortunately, most radio stations are computerized, which takes a lot of the manual labor away from this job. In the old days, I had to locate music "carts," which would or would not be where they were supposed to be (depending on how nice the prior DJ was), fill in program logs by hand, locate the commercials and public service announcements, and be in two places at once as I tried to run from one side of the studio to the other side to hit the two switches I needed to hit for an Emergency Broadcast Service test. Some gymnasts would have envied that feat!

You still may have to do two or three things simultaneously, such as pre-record your next segment, record a telephone call, and adjust the volume, but it's much easier today with the computer automation offered by modern on-air systems. But it's still not foolproof. You will make mistakes. And when you screw something up, thousands of people will hear it. Fortunately, they can't see you sweat.

Since the Federal Communications Commission (FCC) regulates radio stations, there are many more rules in this DJ discipline than in any of the others. Although some radio programs seem to get away with murder, it's usually not exactly as wild as it may seem sometimes. Most of what goes on in radio is pre-scripted and well within established decency limits. You've got to be careful what you say and do over public-access airways, or you could be fired, fined, or even sued. Most of the shock radio programs are still feeling the shockwaves generated by the new censorship microscope generated as a result of Janet Jackson's Super Bowl incident. The FCC does not monitor every single radio broadcast because they simply do not have the budget or manpower to do this. FCC disciplinary actions are largely the result of a formal complaint filed by some lone loser who has nothing better to do than listen to radio hosts they hate.

The Challenges of Radio

Unfortunately, a paid shift on your local commercial radio station is usually the hardest DJ job to get. More and more radio stations are finding it cheaper to buy nationally syndicated shows rather than produce their own, so opportunities for radio DJs could shrink in the coming decade. Due to relaxed Federal Communications Commission (FCC) station ownership rules, many radio stations are now part of multi-station corporate conglomerates. These big radio conglomerates are usually publicly traded companies who are overly worried about enhancing shareholder value and not angering their sponsors in an effort to maximize stock prices. These conglomerates have begun to consolidate operations and the overall creativity of radio is waning. The local aspect of radio broadcasting is also beginning to disappear.

Radio is in the process of evolving to survive. With the advent of CD writers, multiple CD changers, and portable MP3 players, more and more people are tuning out the radio and tuning in their own favorite programming. You could say that folks are becoming their own DJs. But radio won't go down without a fight. Multi-million dollar consulting firms are working their butts off trying to find new ways to keep you tuned to that commercial-laden FM dial. And that's a good thing if you've got your sights set on radio.

The major downside to this career is that this is the least stable of all DJ jobs, since low ratings can force stations to make seemingly random format changes and get rid of DJs overnight. You then may have to move all over the country before you can get a job in your home market several years down the road.

You'll usually have to start in a tiny market somewhere in the boonies making minimum wage or less. Average small market pay is in the neighborhood of $15,000-30,000 a year. Some mobile DJs can make this in a few months! Early in your radio career, plan to live at poverty level, get familiar with the unemployment line, and know where your local bus station is.

If you're lucky enough to graduate to a mid- to large-size market, you could earn as much as $50,000 to $100,000 a year depending on your shift, your popularity, and the situation. The radio DJs that get to do private appearances on behalf of the radio station (which is where your real money is made) usually earn about $100-$150 an hour for a two-hour appearance. This can add up to some big comfortable bucks quickly.

Radio shifts are also becoming more and more scarce. Why? Simple supply and demand. There are only a certain amount of commercial FM radio station frequencies available and they're quickly being bought by large media conglomerates that are consolidating resources to maximize profits. This means that the supply of radio shifts is shrinking while the demand for radio jobs is increasing. Most people I know who were in radio have moved on to something more lucrative like sales, audio production, and a wide array of other things. They've grown older and their responsibilities and obligations have grown more complex, usually requiring more money than most radio jocks earn.

Don't let this discourage you—there will always be opportunities in radio for the next big morning DJ who can drum up more ratings than the last person. If you're up to the challenge, you can learn how to become a radio DJ and chase down this dream.

Skills Needed

In the old days, you had to have a strong booming "God-like" voice to be in radio. You've probably noticed by listening to your local station that you don't need a deep voice to be in radio these days. There are some pretty wimpy sounding dudes on the air, even in major markets! Years ago, due to limitations of radio broadcasting technology, only folks who were deep voiced and very well enunciated were hired as broadcasters. That's why when you hear old radio broadcast recordings, the announcers sounded so fake or "over the top"—they were trying to be heard! Today, most radio stations use electronic processing equipment to compensate for those wimpy voices, so you don't really need a radio voice. What you will need, however, is a radio "delivery." This is a combination of a very positive-sounding personality, emphasis on the right words, and non-mumbling enunciation.

Don't worry—these skills can be learned, and easily faked if necessary. No one is in a great mood and has a "smile in their voice" twenty-four hours a day. All you have to do is listen to your local broadcasters closely and attentively, and you'll notice they all have something in common—that radio delivery! Record your favorite stations on a tape or CD, and fast forward to the breaks where the DJ speaks. Listen to the breaks and the DJ's delivery carefully. Then practice repeating their words in your own voice, but enunciate the words exactly like they do. It'll seem really strange at first, but you'll get used to it, and before you know it, you too will be ordering Mc Donald's drive-thru with your new radio delivery.

Being extremely organized and synchronized is critical to a radio station's operation. Songs must fill a certain span of time and commercials have to be aired at specific times. Although it's becoming very rare, some DJs must field phone calls and requests from interested listeners to develop a loyal audience. There are also legal obligations you must fulfill, like hourly station identifications. Radio disc jockeys must be able to coordinate both time and audience constraints while on the air.

Fortunately, computerized on-air systems take care of most of these things for you. Computers can speed up or slow down music without changing the overall "pitch" of the music, making these changes virtually unnoticeable. It's now possible to program music and commercials to the exact second. All you'll have to do is make sure your announcements fit neatly into the prescribed times of the breaks, and that's the tough part that comes with practice and experience. Usually, an experienced program or promotions director will write the announcements for you, so they'll know almost exactly how long it should take to read that particular announcement. But I still hear DJs mess this up because they're too quick or too slow.

You'll need to be quick on your feet, always ready to cover those inevitable mistakes, or to create fun radio on a whim. I remember an incident where a record started to skip while it was playing on the air. I didn't have another song queued up, so I jumped on the microphone and made up this a short freestyle rap while I queued up another record. I called my little performance the "Busta Nut Remix" during the next break. This type of quickness comes naturally to some people, but can be learned through your experience and listening to the experiences of others in the business.

There are no schools or videos or books that can realistically introduce you to everything you'll need to know to become a successful DJ. What you really need to do is get your basic experience for a couple of years in a real radio station, wherever you can get it, and then move up to a station that's willing to promote you. For true radio success, you'll need a winning idea or concept, and a program director or station manager who believes in you and who's not afraid to take chances in order to improve the station's ratings. You need to be a key factor in increasing station ratings. These positions are the most coveted positions in radio, so you'll have to develop patience as you search for your perfect gig and prepare to pounce.

The Ratings

All radio stations live or die by the Arbitron Radio Market Ratings Survey. If ratings are up, the station can charge more for its advertising and everyone is happy. If ratings fall, heads start to roll. And the finger pointing usually is directed at the low man on the totem pole: you, Mr. or Ms. DJ. Somehow, it's your fault that people aren't listening as much as they used to. It doesn't matter that management tells you exactly what to play and say, it's still somehow always the DJ that gets the boot first.

You should have some knowledge of how the rating system works. Basically, it's all simple statistics. Several million randomly chosen people are contacted and paid by the ratings service to complete a seven-day "Radio Diary" for a certain period of time, which is a detailed list of every single station that person listened to, including start and stop times, and listening locations (home, work, car, etc.). Several pieces of comparative demographic information are also collected in the diary, such as age, gender, employment status, socioeconomic data, ethnicity, etc. All this information is then compiled and calculated using complex statistical formulas to develop an estimation of the total number of people listening to a particular station at a particular time. Reports are generated showing breakdowns by age, gender, time of day ("Daypart"), and stations listened to. These quarterly reports are collectively known as "The Ratings."

Radio stations review the overall "Rating" (the percent of all listeners in the radio station's broadcast area listening to the station during a certain time period) and the overall "Share" (the percent of one station's total estimated listening audience). These numbers are broken down further into "AQH" or "Average Quarter Hour" Persons, Ratings, and Shares, and "Cume" Persons and Ratings. These ratings are broken down even further by age, gender, and other demographic and psychographic details. If you're interested, these measurements are described in detail on Arbitron's Web site (www.arbitron.com).

Statistically speaking, one survey (person) may count for as many as several thousand people's listening habits. Some baggy pants hip-hop bling-bling knucklehead down the street from you just might be influencing your favorite classical radio station to change formats! Fortunately, the "law of large numbers" tames silly blips like this and the whole survey comes out relatively accurate (within a certain slim "margin of error") when all the surveys have been compiled.

People or relatives of people who are employed by media or marketing agencies are asked to exclude themselves from the surveys, because they could obviously skew the results in a manner that might make their employer look more favorable.

Types of Radio Jobs

There are quite a few types of on-air radio DJ positions including music DJs, talk show DJs, sports announcers, sports reporters, traffic reporters, news announcers, and news reporters. Additionally, there are tons of support jobs, such as producers, engineers, sales representatives, program directors, music directors, promotions and marketing people, event DJs, and other fun jobs that radio stations need to be successful.

Music DJs

The most visible radio job is obviously the music DJ, the average DJ heard on various music formats all over your AM and FM dials. They occasionally mention promotional station announcements during music-based programs. This particular DJ job requires the least amount of thought and planning, since most of your announcements are written for you, and all the music you'll play was most likely picked a week or two in advance. Most music radio DJs are little more than glorified mixing board operators (known as "board ops").

This is also the most profitable type of DJ, since these are the folks who get tapped to broadcast special events live on the radio, affording you tons of public exposure along with a healthy paycheck that's in addition to your normal radio pay. These special events will command an hourly fee that's probably five times what your normal hourly fee will be; and this is how successful radio DJs earn most of their money.

You'll be expected to show up about an hour before your shift starts, primarily so the prior DJ and your boss know you're there. You'll sit around and twiddle your thumbs and drink lots of soda or coffee and make nice nice with the receptionist if it's during office hours, since a music DJ doesn't really have much in the way of show preparation. About three to five minutes before your shift begins, the prior DJ will step out from behind the console, pack his or her stuff up, and let you know you're up after this song or set. Since things are usually automated, this could occur ten to fifteen minutes prior to the end of the other DJ's show. If you're following someone who's voice tracking (pre-recording a local radio show from another location so that it sounds like it's a genuine local broadcast) or a remote syndicated broadcast (a pre-recorded show that runs nationally), you'll sit in even earlier. Hopefully, you'll enjoy the show.

You'll plug your headphones into the board, and your shift begins. You'll take a look at the program log on the computer, and you'll know exactly what songs are coming up, and when you'll be expected to break in with banter, promotional announcements, news, weather, or sports. Typically, most daytime music DJ shifts run four hours, but can run five or six hours during weekends or overnights.

"Drive time" DJs, the DJs who host shows during the AM and PM before and after work hours while people are driving to or from work, tend to be the most popular DJs at the station. Typically, they're given much more freedom than the other on-air personalities on the station. They may get to host contests, skits, "phony phone calls," and even ad lib here and there. These shifts require much more preparation time, but the pay and recognition can be exponentially more than a typical DJ receives.

Talk Show DJs

Talk shows are the most difficult DJ job. You don't have the crutch of music to lean on—you are the entertainment! Talk shows require several hours of preparation. You'll need to thoroughly research your topics so you know exactly what you're talking about. It's impossible to be captivating if you don't know which facets of your topic are interesting and worthy of discussion. You'll need to track down guests and arrange their participation, hopefully scheduling them down to the exact minute you need them. You'll need to figure out the full flow of your show, and then guide it along that flow, carefully tailoring all digressions back to the main subject matter. Most prominent talk-show DJs, like Howard Stern or Rush Limbaugh, have entire staffs dedicated to show preparation.

You'll need to arrive at the station very early, hours before your shift, so you can fine tune today's topics. You'll verify that guests have arrived, and any experts scheduled to telephone in aren't caught up in their busy schedules and haven't forgotten about you.

When you go on, you'll do a monologue presenting your topic, citing your research and findings along with your personal opinions about the topic, hoping to generate interest and telephone calls from people who wholeheartedly agree with your opinions and fiercely oppose your point of view. You must remain fair at all times, always offering and encouraging both sides of every story. You'll usually have the assistance of an engineer or screener who'll try to get the gist of what people who have called in before you actually talk to them, so you're somewhat prepared to handle them live on the air. Normally, your show will have a digital delay of several seconds just in case some knucklehead spouts off certain four letter words or other fun things that's better suited for a bar and could get you and the radio station in trouble.

Whether your topic is sports, relationships, politics, current events, the occult, or whatever, your talk show will ebb and flow, going through parts that are less interesting than others. It's your job to keep things on course, providing compelling points of view and humor where applicable. Bring lots of bottled water to avoid dry mouth.

Sports Announcers

Sports Announcers are folks that live, eat, and breathe sports. They know every player on every pro and college team in every sport. They can tell you how many points someone scored during a certain game two years ago, and can recite someone's most recent batting average. Sportscasters have a mind for numbers and statistics and an incredible memory. What a great job for a sports fan—getting paid to talk about the love of your life! These jobs are tough to come by. Most folks hone their skills by announcing play by plays for high schools, small college, or community teams.

A sports announcer usually gets a seat at an event in a special area designated for "the press," usually known as the "press box." This area usually has a perfect view of the entire playing field so he or she can comment on every play. Sports announcers are expected to show up early before a game, and hopefully score some interviews with key players, coaches, or managers that can provide some "color" before, during, and after the game. The announcer typically does the "play by play" announcing, following the plays and describing them as clearly as possible, keeping in mind that his or her audience cannot see what's actually taking place. Sports announcers paint a picture of the event in progress.

In most professional sports broadcasts, a second announcer is employed, known as "color" announcers. Color announcers are the folks that add a little extra spice to sporting broadcasts in between plays or when the play starts to lull. For example, color announcers like John Madden in football and Tim McCarver in baseball are the guys who provide the interesting and often surprising little tidbits of information that make most sportscasts entertaining. They've usually got a license to use a sense of humor and have some fun with the broadcast.

Sports Reporters

Sports Reporters are the less glorious version of the Sports Announcer, since they may not get to attend the games. Typically, sports reporters have a few short minutes to summarize the highlights of several games in several sports, sliding in a few sound bites here and there if they're lucky. Sports (and news) casters can get a lot of up to the minute information over the wire (specialized subscription-based news feeds available at many radio stations) and the Internet.

Traffic Reporters

While some TV traffic reporters might get to fly in helicopters reporting on traffic problems first hand, most radio traffic reporters usually work for a commercial traffic reporting service. They are typically confined to a cozy desk as they call in their traffic reports while someone else discovers where the problems spots are. Since traffic reports are generally given during AM and PM "Drive Times" (the most listened to dayparts, since people are stuck in their cars during their commute), and since DJs during these shifts have a bit more latitude to ad lib, you may actually get a chance to participate in some clever unscripted on-air banter.

Some say being a traffic reporter is a great way to begin a career as a radio DJ. While it is a way to get on-air experience and get your name noticed, you won't learn the board operation skills or typical radio station political skills you'll need to survive. And your voice always sounds very different over the telephone, so people won't readily recognize your true radio voice. If you've got your sights set on an on-air position, becoming a traffic reporter is no more than a toe in the door and a job to hold you over until you get a real radio break.

Newscasters

If you love current events, become a newscaster. But remember, a newscaster only reports the news objectively, citing actual facts from the news reports, known by some in the industry as "the news wire," or simply "the wire". A newscaster should not offer a personal point of view. In contrast, a talk show host can be subjective, meaning he or she can offer different points of view or personal commentary.

Unless you're a newscaster on an all-news station, a newscaster only gets a few minutes an hour to read all of his or her news stories. If you're lucky, you'll get to talk about the weather too, that can buy you a few more moments of precious on-air time. News reports usually are limited to AM and PM drive-time broadcasts, when the most people are listening.

News Reporters

A news reporter is a trained journalist sent to the site of the action. He or she looks for witnesses and comments from police and other individuals who have first hand knowledge of the events that created the story. In addition to being a responsible journalist, you'll need to have a news-like delivery. You'll have to sound captivating, never boring, even if the news is boring.

The few remaining news-only stations have reporter jobs similar to those in television. You'll spend a lot of time going on "location" (physically going to the location where the news is happening). The reporter gathers all the key facts, including any relevant supporting and opposing views so the story is shown in the fairest means possible, then compiles a short summary which becomes the news report. The news report is then recorded in the station's studio or in a mobile studio for insertion into the newscast at a later time. There are certain incidents that warrant live reports, meaning you'll be live on the air with very limited time to gather information or rehearse your story. Don't worry, live reports are usually saved for more experienced reporters.

National Public Radio (NPR) offers a different type of radio reporter job. Since they're commercial-free, they can go much more in depth with their stories, affording some really neat opportunities that you just can't get away with in traditional commercial radio or television.

Other Radio Jobs

There are also other radio jobs that most folks tend to "fall into" while they're waiting for an on-air break. The truth is that most people who had their sights set on an on-air career finally decide that food and shelter are necessities rather than priorities, and graciously accept a non-broadcasting position at the station. They still get to be part of the team, and they get to escape the nine to five corporate trap most of us fall into. Most radio jobs are relatively loose regarding hours and location, with performance being evaluated based on results rather than attendance. And since most radio folks are inherently creative, radio jobs can be lots of fun with daily practical jokes and a light-hearted office attitude.

Most aspiring and retiring DJs eventually find their way into the radio sales department at some point during their careers. These commission-based jobs can be very lucrative to folks blessed with a great attitude and a drive to succeed. Radio sales reps can have a tremendous amount of "unaccountable responsibility" with their clients, meaning they can pretty much run the entire campaign any way they see fit with virtually no repercussions if things don't work out. Since the sales rep is an agent of the station, most advertisers think the sales rep is some kind of marketing genius. I've seen some automobile dealers give free reign to some sales reps, letting them act as *de facto* directors of marketing. The rep would choose the advertiser's budget, schedule, and completely write and voice the actual commercial! Most radio sales reps are present at all of their clients' major sales and events, and usually become part of the advertiser's inner circle of family and friends. There are very few other jobs that can afford this type of exposure and unaccountable responsibility.

Show producers are usually hired to run large scale sports, talk, and news programs, along with specialty music programming. They're responsible for booking guests, arranging and scheduling interviews, and compiling data and information that eventually becomes part of the main DJ's program. A good producer is an invaluable part of a winning show's team. Some folks thrive on being the catalyst rather than the star in the spotlight. If this is you, you might want to think "producer" as a long term goal.

Production engineers are the folks who produce radio commercials and other pre-recorded announcements. They've got access to the most important part of a radio station facility—the production studios! You'll be the master of the station with thousands of dollars in equipment at your disposal and hundreds of tracks of digital blank space waiting for you to add music, sound effects, voice, and your own magic that will hopefully create a winning program or radio commercial.

You'll need experience running all kinds of special effect generators through a mixing board that can have a hundred individual channels. There's cutting, splicing, remixing and editing that can all be done digitally with a click of a mouse. In the old days, we used reel-to-reel tapes with razor blades! To create our edits, we would actually mark the tape with chalk or crayon, then slice the tape with a razor blade, then carefully tape the two remaining sections together, hoping the tape would hold until we could transfer our work on to a recordable cart. That method was insanely problematic and time consuming. Today's digital computer based editing systems allow you to cut, copy and paste segments together in virtually unlimited ways, always allowing you to "undo" your last few edits if it doesn't sound right. With manual splicing, you only got one chance. If you cut and taped the tape in too many places, it started to get weak and eventually popped apart, forcing you to start from scratch.

Station managers/general managers are the *de facto* supreme leaders of the station, ultimately responsible for programming, music, ratings, personnel and sales. GMs rarely get involved in the hiring or firing process, so you won't have to deal with these guys. They're usually not as approachable as program directors or music directors, since they're responsible for the higher-up business tasks of running a radio station.

Program directors (PDs) are the people who are in charge of the general direction of a radio station, similar to the captain of a ship. They hire and fire the DJs, choose the music the station plays, and initiate the promotions that the station runs. Many program directors were on-air DJs at one point in their career, so they know the DJ job and what's expected, as well as all the sneaky tricks you'll try to pull as you become more experienced. This is a person you'll want to become friendly with as soon as you can. But always remember that he or she is your boss.

In larger radio markets and stations, some program directors delegate the music programming to a music director, or MD. These people choose every song the station will play and when those songs will be played. Their goal is to create the most captivating and popular mix of music within the station's format in an effort to retail listeners longer, so their ratings rise and the sales department can charge more for advertising. Today, corporate conglomerates have the ultimate decision of which of their stations play what, and they send their direction to the MDs at the station level. You'll usually have to follow their list exactly song-for-song during your shift.

Finally, promotions and marketing people are every station's underpaid and overworked group of employees. They're the people who travel all over the broadcasting area during evening and weekend hours to help promote sales and special events. They're the folks that come up with the flyers, handouts, games, and giveaways at every station event. Many of these positions are held by college interns, and it does provide real and valuable experience in the industry.

Talking the Talk: Radio Terminology

Regardless of which type of radio DJ you want to be, and how you decide to get to wherever you're going, you'll have to know your stuff so you know what you're talking about when thousands of your listeners tune-in to your program for their information. You'll have to study current events and current trends. You'll need to stay completely relevant at all times, and there's no room for slacking.

The first step to beginning your broadcasting career is research. In addition to having familiarity with the station's format and existing personalities, you should know some important radio industry terminology. You never know who you'll run into in a social setting or at a station promotion—if an engineer happens to be the program director's best friend, and you're at least minimally familiar with some basic radio terms, you'll sound much more interesting and experienced than someone who doesn't have a clue. The first rule of sales is familiarity—and you're essentially selling yourself and your knowledge when applying for a radio job. These terms may come up during a job interview, or during a conversation in which you're networking with other radio types, so it's best if you know what they're talking about and how to properly respond.

The whole radio transmission process is pretty complicated and difficult to understand unless you're an electronic physicist. I've spoken with several radio engineers and I'm still not really sure how it all works. But I can share the basics, which might be enough to start any engineer to happily discuss his understanding with you. Most engineers are pretty lonely souls, so they're happy to have someone who speaks their language.

Basically, the "frequency" of the radio transmission is established through electromagnetic carrier waves. The carrier waves ultimately determine which number on the AM or FM dial the transmission a listener will need to tune to hear the accompanying audio frequency waves. If your carrier waves are broadcasting on 102.1 megahertz (MHz), your radio will pick up that transmission on 102.1 on any standard FM radio dial. The carrier waves themselves are inaudible (nearly silent). The audio frequency waves, consisting of the sound produced by the music and voice signals captured and transmitted by the radio station, are combined with those carrier waves in a process known as "modulation."

Once the carrier waves and the frequency waves have been modulated, they are then electronically amplified and transmitted (broadcasted) to your radio. Your radio receiver receives the modulated broadcast from the station indicated by the carrier waves, then decodes the two signals in a process called "demodulation," which completes the broadcast loop and produces what we actually hear on the radio. It's really much more complicated than this, but that explanation should at least get you by. There are plenty of books and information available on the Internet or at your local library if you're truly interested in this topic, but you won't really need to know more than this unless you decide to become a radio engineer.

"AM" stands for "Amplitude Modulation." Essentially, the strength of an audio frequency wave varies by the intensity of the note that stimulates it. The resulting sound wave is measured by its height, or "amplitude." It's an older, actually more efficient transmission technology that's been replaced by FM and digital solutions. The advantage of AM over FM is that its longer wave (or "cycle") allows it to travel further without being absorbed by the atmosphere. AM consists of the radio band somewhere between 540 and 1710 Kilohertz (KHz, or thousands of Hertz).

The frequency range of reproduced sound on AM radio stations generally begins at about 100 Hz and is limited to 5 KHz by the Federal Communications Commission (FCC) in an effort to reduce noise and interference. To put that in perspective, the music CD has a frequency that roughly matches the average range of human hearing, which is from 20 Hz to 20 KHz. That's why AM transmissions sound so shallow and tinny—the lower end (bass) and upper end (treble) are cut off the signal before it's transmitted.

Interestingly enough, AM sound technology is what's still used for most telephone and television broadcast systems. An important downside to AM signals is that they can be very noisy, subject to interference from motors and thunderstorms.

On the other side of the radio dial, you've got the "FM" frequencies. FM means "Frequency Modulation," and resides between 88.1-107.9 Megahertz (MHz, or million Hertz) on your radio dial. This method employs an emphasis on a higher rate of oscillation, or a higher "frequency," resulting in better sound. Similar to digital audio technology, the more times per second a sound is reproduced (or "sampled"), the more closely it resembles the actual sound. FM also affords stereo broadcasts, which is really a combination of two "sideband" broadcasts (one for the left channel, one for the right channel), which are very close in frequency. The downside of an FM broadcast is that it doesn't quite have the reach of an AM broadcast due to its shorter waves (cycles), so you need more raw power to push the signal further.

FM stations generally broadcast their audio signals with a frequency range of 50 Hertz (Hz) to 15 kiloHertz (kHz, or thousands of Hertz cycles), with its limits being set by FCC regulations. Again, a music CD ranges from 20 Hz on the lower end (bass) to 20 KHz on the high end (treble), so you can see why an FM broadcast will never be as accurate as a CD. FM has a higher "signal to noise" ratio than AM, which means there is cleaner sound (less hiss and noise).

"Broadcast power" is the number of physical electrical watts that the transmitter is allowed to produce, which is one of the factors that directly affects how far the signal will reach. Most major market FM stations broadcast at about 50,000 watts, which is enough to reach about a 75-mile radius in most flat areas. Your radio receiver only needs to receive about one single watt to clearly demodulate a broadcast. Since radio transmissions travel in a straight line, their signals are transmitted from broadcast towers, which are at the highest possible location in the area. This helps the modulated broadcast signal travel further by avoiding being absorbed by buildings, people, and anything else that may block its path. Broadcast antennas (usually called "broadcast towers") are also "directional;" meaning that a radio station could determine in which direction to aim its broadcast for optimum receipt of their signal. The FCC ultimately rules on allowable signal strength, allowable broadcast tower height, and in which direction the signal shall be broadcast in an effort to avoid interfering signals from stations close together on the radio dial.

"The Board" is the heart of any broadcast facility. Basically, it's simply an electronic mixing board that controls the volume and destination of each of your sound making units. Boards consist of many channels, anywhere from three stereo channels to over twenty stereo channels. One channel of the board is allocated for each microphone, CD player, or other electronic sound-producing element. Each channel has its own individual volume setting, which must be properly adjusted to avoid "over-modulating" the signal (playing it too loud causing a distorted and unpleasant sound).

The Harris Corporation BMXdigital board. Reprinted with permission from Harris Corporation.

Most radio DJ boards have three main settings for each channel; "program," "aux," and "cue." You must assign each channel the proper setting to make it perform the way you want it to. The "program" setting is the one that is broadcast over the air. Any channel assigned to "program" with its volume over zero will go out over the air, so be careful not to send more than one signal over the air at one time! The "Aux" is usually attached to a studio monitor and is used to listen to a song or commercial in the studio only. Channels set on "aux" will not go out over the air. Finally, the "cue" position is used to cue a song up in your headphones only. There are several board manufacturers, but most radio boards are fairly similar in functionality. The best way to learn how to operate a board is to sit with an experienced DJ and just watch closely.

Smaller low budget college and community radio stations still use either industrial CD or Sony Minidisc players to play their music, announcements, and commercials. Newer and larger radio stations have a computer that's specially built to play these elements directly from its hard drive (or from another networked computer). Some smaller, older stations still use "cart" machines, which originated sometime in the 1950s. The cartridges, known as "carts," kind of look like old eight-track tapes, if you've ever seen one. They're large plastic cassettes that have a continuous tape with a start/stop strip in their leader tape. Most cart machines are outfitted with a set of remote control buttons that are usually mounted in a convenient location so the DJ won't have to move while speaking and queuing up the next element of his or her show. Another neat functionality of carts is that they automatically re-queue to the starting point, so you shouldn't have to rewind or search for the start point. Be careful, I've had older carts that were so worn out that they missed the queue points.

Newer commercial radio stations use automated computer programs, which is essentially a computer with the music and commercials loaded to its hard drive. Mike Lowe, program director of WLRQ-FM, a Clear Channel station in Melbourne, Florida, told me their station, along with most other Clear Channel stations, use the PSI Prophet NextGen system. It's a pretty cool computer program that graphically shows every song, commercial, promo, and break in a vertically arranged timeline that's displayed on a computer monitor so you know exactly what's coming up during your program. Lowe says they're very easy to use and very functional.

Like anything else, equipment failures happen, so you've got to get to know all of these machines well. This will help you know what to do or who to call in the event that they do fail. And always have a backup plan just in case.

Most commercial radio stations "break" for commercials twice an hour in thirty-minute intervals. If you're listening to the radio and a station breaks for commercials, you'll usually hear that most stations in your market tend to all break for commercials at about the same time, usually at 10 minutes past the hour and again at 40 past the hour. It's kind of an unwritten agreement so stations don't lose listeners due to commercial advertisements. Most breaks occur at about ten before the hour and twenty past the hour. These breaks can be called "Commercial Breaks," "Stop Sets," or "Stop Downs," with the terminology typically depending on the age of your program director.

A "segue" (pronounced SEG-way) is merely the transition between songs, or a transition between a song and some other element of your show. During a segue when you're expected to actually talk, you'll typically announce your name, and perhaps mention an upcoming station promotion. Sometimes you'll mention the artists that are about to be played after commercial messages. The most important thing is that your segues are "tight," which means there's no quiet space or "dead air" in between your transitions. In commercial radio, your segues will be predetermined almost to the exact second by your program director. There's usually not much freedom for creativity due to the tight controls in commercial radio.

"Dead air" is the worst possible thing that can happen in radio. This phenomenon occurs when there is no audible sound on the air, usually as a result of a human or mechanical screw up. Most listeners tune away when there's dead air, probably to see if their radio is still working. You can imagine what that will do to your show's ratings!

"Backselling" or "back announcing" is talking about a song you've just played in a positive light in an effort to inspire listeners to purchase the CD. Record companies expect radio DJs to do this, but radio stations rarely allow the DJ the time to actually do it. In a backsell, you would mention the artist, song title, and the CD the song is on. Check with your program director to see what the deal is at your station. Whatever you do, even if told by a representative of the record label, don't break station rules, or you will end up getting fired.

A "talk-up" or "ramp" is just as it sounds; you're talking over the music in the "intro" (the instrumental beginning) of a song up until it ramps up to where the singing starts ("the post"), or during the "outtro" (the instrumental ending or ending fade of a song). Every song has a different intro and outtro length, and some songs don't have intros or outtros at all, so you'll really need to practice getting your timing perfect in various time lengths. Most professional promotional CDs have the intro length noted directly on the CD. Newer automated radio stations note the intros time along with a countdown timer right on the computer screen. Older radio stations usually have an adjustable countdown timer so you'll know exactly how long you have to talk. You would look at the record or CD, and hopefully someone noted the intro time on the cover somewhere. You'd then manually set the countdown timer to that number of seconds, then hit the start button on the timer as soon as you start playing the song and talking. That's right—you'll have to do two things at once. Just remember, never talk over the singing!

"Radio Liners" are an informal promotion or a live commercial about a station event or a public service announcement. Liners are usually played during a segue between songs or between a song and a commercial. These fancy, studio produced promotional announcements are responsible for replacing live DJ breaks and announcements in many cases. Mobile and club DJs call these "DJ Drops."

A "Station Identification" or "Legal I.D." must be broadcasted once an hour, typically within five minutes before or after the hour changes. The FCC requires that all commercial radio stations announce their call letters (or station ID) along with the physical location of their broadcast. This will sound something like "You're listening to WYWY, 98 Point 9 in Orlando."

Some radio stations require their DJs to take telephone calls from listeners (either requests or responses to on-air contests) and play them on the air. These calls are answered while you're playing music or commercials, and are recorded off the air just in case someone uses profanity. You'll then fit the recorded calls into your program during a segue. When you get really good at this, you can make it sound like you've just picked up the phone and are talking live on the air!

A "Spot" is another name for a radio commercial. Spots are usually 15, 30, or 60 seconds long and played in groups of four or more.

"Slander" is the mortal radio sin that could get you fired or even sued. It is publicly saying something in an effort to injure another's reputation ("libel" is written defamation). For example, you use someone's real name on the air and say (even jokingly) that he or she is embezzling money from his or her employer, and it's not true. That person can complain to your boss, which will probably get you fired. That person then has the right to haul you into court and make things even more miserable for you. Regardless if the statement is true or false, if they can prove that they were injured by the statement itself, you could end up in a whole lot of trouble. Even if you say something untrue that even slightly hints at a hidden meaning—that too can be actionable. And don't think you can hide behind someone else either. A defense of saying that someone else said it first won't fly in a court of law. If you're the person they heard say the statement, you're the one who's going down.

Fortunately, it seems that celebrities are usually exempt from this type of lawsuit as long as you can prove that you are telling the truth, or that you have said your words without malicious intent. If you make up a blatant lie about a celebrity that is intended to harm the celebrity's reputation, you will get sued. Shock radio guys say some silly things, but it's usually under the well understood guise of comedic intent, where their reputations are very well known for saying wildly false things, so the listener obviously knows the shock jock is simply joking around. The whole issue is pretty fuzzy, so use a lot of caution. A good rule of thumb is to know and trust your source and still double check it; or don't chance saying anything that makes you a target.

How to Begin Your Career as a Radio DJ

Now that you've got the basics down, there are a number of different ways to begin getting real world experience to prepare for your career as a radio DJ. Unlike becoming a mobile or club DJ, you just can't wake up and decide that you'll go out and get a radio DJ job. There are fewer positions than ever, and competition is very fierce. Most commercial radio stations won't take a chance on someone with no real radio broadcasting experience. It's a really rude Catch-22; how are you supposed to get experience when no one will let you in the door? Here are a few of the more effective ways in which you can get that all-important real-world experience.

College Internships

Although college looks great on your resume and can help you get an edge in the experience department, a college degree is not necessary to get a job as a radio DJ. Radio station managers will probably prefer someone with at least some real hands-on experience over a college grad with no experience.

Many colleges have a small radio station and offer courses in radio and TV broadcasting. Some even offer full degree programs, usually as a subset of their communications program. Know that the variation of courses and resources vary widely among colleges. I went to a school that had really antiquated equipment that did not at all prepare me for a state-of-the-art commercial station. Some schools have really cool modern studios. Yet other schools may have no real facilities and will try to teach you using videos, props, and textbooks. I recommend always opting for the college with real studio facilities, if you have a choice.

The best part about attending college is that they offer radio internship opportunities at real commercial radio stations. This is absolutely the best way to get your foot in the door of a local radio station, all while earning college credits toward graduation. You'll get to know the promotions and marketing people first hand, and you've got an opportunity to meet the program director if you really want to. Interns get first-hand experience in observing how a real commercial radio station operates. Once the folks at the station see you around and get to know you, you've pretty much got free reign to go hang out wherever you can (on your own time) to observe the on-air studio, production facilities, business office, and any other area you're interested in. If you're lucky enough to befriend the on-air DJs, you'll get to learn how the board works, and you may get opportunities to speak on-air during promotions or breaks, affording you that priceless on-air experience. Note that these opportunities are obviously the exception and not the rule.

It's important to understand that most internships are not paid positions, and are definitely not designed to give you on-air experience. They're primarily used to aid sales, marketing, and promotions functions to lighten the load of their overburdened staff. Expect to do some heavy photocopying, filing, faxing, answering telephone calls and e-mails, sealing envelopes, sweeping floors, making coffee, and anything else your mentors ask you to do. The interns who go above the call of duty and use their initiative to do a little extra are the interns who stand out, and are usually afforded the better perquisites ("perks"). Favorite interns may get to hang out with air personalities backstage at concerts, or do silly things on-air during a morning or evening drive-time show.

Interns who befriend production staff get the incredibly valuable benefit of the production engineer's assistance in creating their all important demo or "air-check" tape or CD. Your demo is more important than your résumé in this business! You'll be able to listen to other successful DJ's demos, as well as observe the packaging and other little tricks that helps (or hurts) prospective on-air talent.

Finally, since an intern is already "in the door," you may get first notice of any permanent positions that become available. Some interns are hired on the spot, before jobs are even posted.

Other Ways to Gain On-Air Experience

If you're not a college student, there are other ways to gain valuable radio experience.

Local Cable TV

Many local cable TV providers have radio stations that broadcast on their local-access cable TV channels. You can volunteer to help out on these shows, or even get your own show. This is a great way to "learn the board" and learn how real radio stations operate. While I was living in Fairfax County, Virginia, working for Time Life Music, I decided to take the Radio Broadcasting 101 course they offered at the time. The course was a prerequisite for hosting your own radio show on their WEBR radio station broadcasted over their cable network of over 275,000 households in Northern Virginia. They had a nice-sized radio broadcasting studio on their premises with relatively modern equipment. Every Saturday morning, six other radio wannabes and myself learned the basics of radio while gaining valuable on-air experience during our training. For our final exam, we had to create our own 30-minute radio broadcast complete with music and pre-approved promotional announcements. The course was very informative and lots of fun. We were awarded a certificate at the end of the course that designated us as "qualified radio broadcasters."

LPFM Stations

One of the latest developments in the radio business is the creation of Low Power FM (LPFM) radio stations, which are usually non-profit, religious, or educational institutions that broadcast a fairly weak signal (about a mile or two in diameter) solely for local events. These stations are all over the place now, creating even more on-air, internship, and volunteer opportunities.

In my home town of Melbourne, Florida, there's a LPFM station known as "C-93 FM," branding themselves as "Today's Hottest Hits and More." They basically broadcast top-40 music from some beachfront studio, sort of competing with the local Cumulus-owned Top-40 station in our area. They do nightclub appearances and promotions, and appear to operate in a manner that's surprisingly very similar to a commercial radio station. This particular LPFM station advertises that it's always looking for new faces for various station positions, including on-air shifts. If you scour your local area, you too will probably find a LPFM station looking for help. It's a great place to get your feet wet and learn as you're making mistakes.

Internet Broadcasting

Rolling a bit lower on the broadcast experience credibility scale, we arrive at Internet broadcasting. With the popularity of today's broadband Internet connections, anyone with above average computer skills can set up their own personal live or pre-recorded "webcast." There are several websites that make it fairly easy for you to actually create a radio show and broadcast it live all over the world via the Internet. You'll obviously need a broadband connection, a sound card, a microphone hooked into your sound card, and a bunch of audio files encoded to the popular MP3 format to make this work.

When it was still free, I messed around with a fairly easy to use Internet radio site called "Live 365" at live365.com. With their free software, you can actually broadcast your show live using your microphone and computer. This is an awesome way to see what everyone else is doing while you practice your show and get your own delivery down. Plus, it's a real, live station—so you never know if someone important is tuning in!

They'll even tell you how many people are listening to your show. I spent a good five hours on a show one night and managed to get 10 listeners. Boy was I proud! Today, Live 365 charges a fairly reasonable monthly fee for broadcasters to help offset the cost of music licensing fees. For free webcasting and to listen to thousands of live webcasts, visit AOL's Shoutcast at www.shoutcast.com.

Webcasting is a great way to practice your radio skills, and it's a pretty cool hobby, but it's not really considered to be resume-worthy radio experience. The main problem that program directors will find with webcasting is that there are no rules, so you're not really getting radio training. Also, you can use a cheap sound card and any free MP3 player, both of which are rarely found in real commercial radio settings.

Broadcast Schools

Hands-on experience guided by experienced professionals is the easiest way to learn about any career, but not always the best way to get a job. There are scores of Broadcast Schools or Radio Schools that offer "radio training." Just like with college programs, these programs vary considerably in the quality of instruction and studio equipment. And some of these broadcast schools can cost more than an entire college semester! Many of these schools offer "job placement assistance." Unfortunately, they often use the same help wanted listings as everyone else in the industry. Not to mention you're competing with your current classmates as well as prior graduates who may still be unemployed. Before enrolling in one of these programs, check with your local Better Business Bureau to see if there's anything shady going on.

Your "Demo" Tape

Just like you'll need a résumé to get a traditional job, you'll need a professionally produced demo tape to get anywhere in this business. This tape will feature your voice and your personality exactly as it would sound if you were to be awarded a job at the radio station you're interested in. This is often referred to as an "air-check." If you're applying for a newscaster position, your demo will be your newscast. For a music format, it's what you say between songs or at the end of a music set before going to a commercial break. For talk radio, flap your gums about something interesting but not too controversial. You don't want to scare the station into thinking you're an uncontrollable psycho.

You'll need to say some stuff about the songs you're playing, and read some stuff about the station's current promotions. Listen to the station for clues on how things flow from song to song and program to program. Tape some of the promotional announcements, then read them yourself on to your demo. Check their web site for a "what's happening" link and get to know what they're doing. If the station isn't in your market, you can check their web site for a live broadcast link. You could even find a chat room in the city where the station is, then ask the locals what you need to know. You could also offer to pay someone to tape the station for you. Do your homework so you can talk the talk! Just like in the business world, nothing turns radio station management off more than someone who knows nothing about their business.

Unfortunately, many new people in the radio business must have their demo tapes recorded in a production studio. The problem most radio station employers have with studio demo tapes is that they'll probably know it was made in a studio, and virtually anyone can produce a great demo tape in a studio. The true question is if that person can do what they did on their demo tape behind a live microphone broadcasting to thousands of people. Many people choke under pressure. And there's no rewind button on live radio.

Before doing your demo tape, practice, practice, and practice again. Although this may sound embarrassing, use a tape recorder or digital recorder at home to get your delivery down perfect. You can even hook a cheap mixer up to a VHS VCR and record two to six full hours (SP or SLP speed) of your show as you practice. Write down everything you're going to say at first. This is radio—people can't see what you're doing! Play the tapes back and honestly critique yourself. Then have others objectively critique your tape—ask them to be brutally honest. Figure out what could be better or tighter, and then go try it again. You will want to be completely sure you can do an effective job when you're live and under pressure.

Using scripts always helps. You could record your local radio talent to get a feel for what they say and do, which is probably the best thing to do since you'll get a feel for how the station's programming flows. Transcribe some of the DJ breaks and rehearse them yourself. You can throw in a few fun things too, to show you actually have a personality. One of the mini-scripts I wrote for my demo went as follows:

> "Ninety Seven Five, W-P-S-T. Chuck Fresh bringing you the most slammin' jams in the Delaware Valley every night from seven 'til midnight. The P-S-T request lines are open at 1-888-97-5-WPST from Pennsylvania or 609-97-5-WPST from Jersey. Gimme a buzz with your favorite PST tune and we'll see if we can't get it on... the tune, that is... unless you're a really hot babe, and maybe you and I can, uh, never mind... Join me, Chuck Fresh, at the PST party at Radio USA in Princeton this Thursday from five til seven. I'll have all kinds of PST stuff to give away, including a shot at two tickets to see Jon Bon Jovi live at Radio USA on the 29th! But you gotta be there to win. That's PST live at Radio USA at the Princeton Marriott on Route 1 this Thursday from five 'til seven. More great PST music coming up, including all new Aerosmith and our top 9 at 9, next on 97-5 P-S-T."

Obviously, you should write your own script for your real demo, but feel free to borrow my shtick as you're practicing.

Keep your demo to two or three minutes tops. Put your absolute best stuff first—don't try to build to a climax, or you'll risk having the stop button pressed quickly. Program directors are usually very busy, so you've got to show them that you can be clever, serious, silly and appropriate in various situations very quickly. Keep the music sections short—play just a few seconds of the intro and/or end of each song. They want to hear you; they've already heard the music a million or more times! If you're talking over a song's musical intro, cut the music shortly after you've finished speaking. Good demos keep rolling continuously, breaking each section on a beat so it seems like one continuous program. It's also good to include a commercial to show that you've got some production expertise. Copy and re-record some commercials that the station is currently running, or write your own to show your imagination.

Back in the old days, a big pet peeve of program directors (PD) was waiting for the "leader tape" on cassette tapes to pass, forcing them to find the beginning of your demo. If you're still using tapes, cue it up and have it ready to go the second they press the play button. Use a 10-minute cassette so you don't scare the PD into thinking you've sent a 60- or 90-minute demo! You can get the 10-minute cassettes at your local musician's store or on the Internet. Don't use noise reduction in case they're playing the tape on an old deck without it, or you'll risk sounding like you're speaking with your hands over your mouth. If you're recording your demo directly on to a CD, it's better to break each of your segments into separate tracks if you can, with no gaps between the tracks. Most of today's CD recording software will give you an option to eliminate the typical two second gap between songs or tracks so it all flows together smoothly.

Spend a few extra bucks to professionally label your demo cassette or CD with your name and your phone number. Try not to handwrite your information on the media or the sleeve—a professional look will further enhance your chances of getting hired because you'll look like your taking this very seriously. There are many computer programs that will produce attractive CD or cassette labels. If your demo doesn't produce any good leads after a few months, do it over from scratch. Make it better. Update your songs and banter. Include some new skits. Most aspiring DJs are constantly revising their demo tapes.

Most importantly, be yourself. Be natural. When you're finally on the air, this is what will prevail; so let them know who you really are!

If you're going after a CHR (contemporary hits radio), Hot AC (adult contemporary), or your basic Urban or Top-40 station, use only the most appropriate and current music and news to show that you're relevant. Don't think you're going to teach them a lesson by including new or different music they're not playing. They probably have a reason why they're not playing those songs, and you don't want to rock the boat before you've had a chance to get on it. Check the latest *Billboard* magazine charts under each specific category—many local newspapers usually print the top ten songs in each category weekly.

Music Formats

You'll need to thoroughly understand each of the music formats before creating your demo tape for a specific station. I've listed a few individual formats below, and the types of more popular artists you'd expect to hear on each format. The main music formats are as follows:

- AC
- Hot AC
- Alternative
- CHR/Pop
- CHR/Rhythmic
- Christian
- Country
- Latin
- Rock
- Active Rock
- Smooth Jazz
- Triple A
- Urban
- Urban AC

CHR Radio

On a "CHR" formatted radio station (also known loosely as "Top 40"), you'd hear artists like these:

Usher

Linkin Park

Jessica Simpson

Britney Spears

OutKast

Beyoncé

Sean Paul

Jay Z

Evanescence

Janet Jackson

Hot AC

On a "HOT AC" station, it's sometimes difficult to tell the difference between this format and CHR. Think of Hot AC this way—it's kind of like CHR with more rock and less rap. Expect to hear artists like these:

Sheryl Crow

Matchbox 20

Sarah McLaughlin

Nickelback

Jessica Simpson

OutKast

Melissa Etheridge

Janet Jackson

Urban

On an Urban station, they cater to the flava of young people into artists like:

Ludacris

Usher

Jay Z

Chingy

Beyoncé

Juvenile

Sean Paul

Nelly

R. Kelly

Alicia Keys

For current charts or for an example of what music fits into what category, visit www.randr.com or pick up a recent copy of *Billboard* magazine.

FCC Obscenity/Indecency Standards

It is a violation of federal law to broadcast "obscene" programming at any time. It is also a violation of federal law to broadcast "indecent" programming during certain hours. The Federal Communications Commission (FCC) has the responsibility to enforce the laws that govern our nation's publicly accessible broadcasts. The FCC may revoke a station's license, impose a substantial monetary fine, withhold or place conditions on the renewal of a broadcast license, or issue a warning for the broadcast of obscene or indecent material.

According to the FCC, "obscene" speech is not protected by the First Amendment and cannot be broadcast at any time. To be obscene, material must meet a three-prong test:

* An average person, applying contemporary community standards, must find that the material, as a whole, appeals to the prurient interest;

* The material must depict or describe, in a patently offensive way, sexual conduct specifically defined by applicable law; and

* The material, taken as a whole, must lack serious literary, artistic, political, or scientific value.

The FCC has defined "indecent" programming as programming that contains patently offensive sexual or excretory references that do not rise to the level of obscenity. Indecent programming may, however, be restricted in order to avoid its broadcast during times of the day when there is a reasonable risk that children may be in the audience, which has been defined as between 6 a.m. and 10 p.m.

Most radio stations no longer take chances when they think there's a potential for nastiness. A company called Eventide produces broadcast delay units, which some broadcasters refer to as a "delay" or a "panic button." These digital components can time shift a broadcast up to 40 seconds without ever having dead air. If the delay is used, it simply skips ahead in time, from one second to the full delay, leaving the potentially damaging remark off the air. The unit then re-stretches the broadcast digitally, so the delay is built up once again. This gives a program director or station manager a few moments to think and ultimately block a comment they think would get them in trouble from going out over the air.

The Eventide BD500
Broadcast Delay Unit.

The FCC investigates all claims can complaints about really nasty stuff that's said on the air, so just don't do it. In making indecency determinations, context is key! The FCC staff must analyze what was actually said during the broadcast, the meaning of what was said, and the context in which it was stated. Specifically, there's no "excrement" or graphic sex talk allowed on the air, ever. You will get fired, and the station could lose its license. For more information about FCC indecency enforcement actions, see their web site at http://www.fcc.gov/eb/broadcast/opi.html.

Marketing Yourself

When you're done your schooling or internship, get yourself a sweet résumé and press kit together. Clearly list all your qualifications, related experience, and education. Write a killer cover letter that tells your prospective employer what qualities and dedication you can bring to the radio station. If you're not good at writing, spend a few bucks and have a professional agency help you with your cover letter.

Get yourself a professional press-photo headshot done (usually in black and white). You can go to your local mall or photographer to get a professional one done. This will make you appear to be a true professional and give you an edge over other candidates.

Learn everything you can learn about the radio station before you apply for the job. Know who owns the station. Know the names of the people who run the station. Know the station's format and playlist. Know things about their existing on-air personalities. Know subtle facts about the artists they're playing if it's a music station. All this information is easily available if you take the time and effort to look for it. Use the Internet to visit the station's web site, or call the station for their press kit.

When you finally get the interview for the job of your dreams, be prepared for it! Go over your notes and have someone quiz you on the information. Get plenty of rest the night before. Wake up early the day of your interview, and eat a good meal. Ease up on the coffee—it may make you nervous. Don't be late. Wear a business suit for goodness sake; this is a real interview with a real business! If I sound like your freakin' mother, good! Take your interview dead seriously and let the people who are interviewing you know you take it very seriously.

Frankly, radio is one of the toughest businesses to break into. But if it's something you really want, don't give up. Keep your chin up and keep trying. If you're prepared and you take it very seriously, chances are you'll break in sooner or later in a small market somewhere. You may not make more than minimum wage your first year, so be ready to adjust your lifestyle if necessary. It will be worth it in the long run.

Job Outlook

Big communications conglomerates like Cumulus Radio and Clear Channel are buying most of the worthwhile radio stations in an effort to consolidate resources to maximize profits. It's a really smart move on the corporate part, making really rich people even more wealthy, but bad news for aspiring radio DJs. They're actually hiring DJs to pre-record announcements for several simultaneous shifts in different markets, known in the industry as "Voice Tracking." An engineer or computer then mixes those announcements with music later—often for several different stations at once. An entire four hour shift can be recorded in perfect CD quality, along with pre-recorded crossfades and sound effects, in less than an hour, and up to two weeks in advance.

Radio DJs all over the country are scrambling to keep their jobs and new commercial radio DJ shifts are becoming much harder to come by.

However, new subscription-based national satellite radio technologies are now emerging that will compete against traditional broadcast radio. Since they're new, they'll have to be fiercely creative to generate interest in their services, which could make radio fun again as the medium is reinvented.

Satellite radio services such as XM and Sirius are slowly but surely building their subscription bases, and most new car manufacturers are now including one or more of these satellite bands in their new vehicles either as a standard accessory or an option. It's only a matter of time before these services become a major player in the radio industry. Unfortunately, due to the nature of satellite radio technology, all of their shows are national, so there's no job multiplicity offered by redundant local outlets. And most of their studios are consolidated into their national studios in New York or somewhere else, meaning you'd have to relocate if you scored a job with one of these entities.

Nokia produces cell phones with FM radio receivers that can display something called "Visual Radio." With the Nokia radio, users can view the title and artist of a song playing, view upcoming concert dates, participate in promotions and easily purchase ring tones or other content from their favorite artists.

Digital radio stations are already in Canada, England, and Germany, and there's talk about an American upgrade in a few years. These cool new transmitters deliver compact-disc quality audio signals to radio receivers along with new wireless data services such as station, song and artist identification, stock and news information, local traffic and weather, and much more. This could open up a whole new world of frequencies and possibilities. And that's when the opportunities and fun will really begin.

Real-World Experiences

Here are some valuable real-world experiences that may help inspire you, or possibly deflate your radio dreams! Keep an open mind, because this is an arena where there are no hard and fast rules. Your mileage may vary.

Mike Staff

WRIF's Mike Staff, author of "How to Become a Radio DJ: A Guide to Breaking and Entering."

Mike Staff got the job of his dreams at the station he grew up with, WRIF in Detroit, Michigan. He does middays on the weekends from 10AM 'til 3 PM.

When Mike isn't busy rockin' the streets of the Motor City, he occupies his time running his two businesses. One of which is MS Productions, a Mobile DJ business specializing in weddings and parties. "I really enjoy working weddings because of the great people I've met," says Mike. Mike Staff provides elegant entertainment with state of the art sound and lights, and an unsurpassable professionalism that is sometimes hard to find in the mobile DJ industry. Hundreds of Detroit area brides and grooms rave about Mike's DJ services.

Mike Staff's other business is promoting his self-published book, *How to Become a Radio DJ: A Guide to Breaking and Entering*. This is a step by step, multi-media presentation that details exactly what it takes to break into the radio business. The foundation of the program is Mike's highly acclaimed book, as well as two audio cassette tapes, The Mindset of Successful DJ's and Creating a Winning Audition Tape. Mike Staff's program has now been sold in nine countries and in almost every state in the U.S. "One of the things that bring me the most enjoyment is helping people get into radio," says Mike. "The radio business has been *very* good to me and I really want to help other people experience the same success."

Lisa G

WRED's Lisa G.

Lisa G works middays on WRED FM in Portland, Maine and runs a production company called "Lisa G Productions." Lisa told me her mother ran a modeling agency and decided to do some radio advertising. Lisa accompanied mom to a radio station and ended up writing and voicing her spot. Not too long after that, Lisa brought a tape of the spot in to the program director at the same station who hired her on the spot.

Lisa advises radio newbies with hopes of becoming an on-air personality to try and get a non-broadcasting part time job at any radio station, even a tiny AM station, to be sure you have what it takes to have a presence on air. You can spend four years in school and know how to run everything from the board to the transmitter but that does not make you a good on-air personality. Bottom line: you either have it or you don't.

Lisa also advises that radio is a cut-throat business. "There are many egos involved and it is a very past paced environment. You need to be able to think on your feet and juggle five things at once. It's not a business for the timid."

Dave Mann

Dave Mann retired from radio after 28 years to form Dave Mann Inc., a voiceover company in Tampa Florida. While in radio, Mann won two Billboard "DJ of the Year" awards while in Jacksonville and Tampa.

Mann got into radio after his senior year in high school after completing courses in the morning of his senior year at a vocational tech school in Gary, Indiana. He just went in and asked to see the Program Director at the local radio station, and after a small audition, he was put on Saturday and Sunday mornings. From there, he went on to several markets while also trying to build a professional baseball career. Radio eventually won the career battle, and Mann stayed in the radio game until he was 47.

"I never chose the music I played unless I was told I could drop or add a song for time purposes. In fact, at many stations if you decide to choose your own music... you will be fired immediately."

Mann advises people getting into radio to learn the production department very well. "DJ's by and large will be almost totally eliminated in ten years except for large profile morning shows, but someone will always have to read commercials and produce them. Remember to use radio as only a stepping stone to someday having your own company or being in syndication for tracking. If you think it is a stable lifetime job like General Motors... you are sadly mistaken."

Jon "Rock 'n' Roll" Anthony

Jon "Rock 'n' Roll" Anthony got his first Radio Job in 1972 through a childhood friend who was working at a gospel station in Birmingham, Alabama. Anthony was in the 11th grade. His career included positions as the Production Director for WFLZ-FM "93.3 FLZ," "News Radio 970 WFLA-AM," and WSSR-FM "Star 95.7" Tampa. He currently does voice tracking for Atlanta's "Cool 105.7" weekdays from 8pm-1am.

Anthony advises new DJs entering the radio field to keep your content clean, and to be patient. Do anything asked of you, even if it's beyond reason. If you make a mistake, forget about it, but get it right the next time. Most importantly, Anthony stresses to always be nice to listeners on the request line. You never know who's on the other end.

When asked "Who chooses the music you play?," Anthony answers, "The program directors, music directors, and other people involved with your station across the country. 99% of all DJ's simply play the tunes in the order they're programmed. Request lines are basically used for research purposes."

Denise Kelly

Denise Kelly from Tampa, Florida works for Cox Radio doing traffic for four stations and a weekend shift. She's been in the business over ten years now. Her first job in radio was Market Research (telemarketing). Kelly was in high school at the time and her sister worked at the station, and got her in the door.

Kelly advises new recruits to "get your foot in the door any way you can." Promotions departments, any type of internships are great ways to start. Once you're in the door, Kelly insists that you learn everything you can about every department as quickly as you can.

Mel "Toxic" Taylor

Mel "Toxic" Taylor got his first radio by taking his college tapes to a brand new Philadelphia radio station. They were looking for new on air talent, and he was hired on the spot, which is a pretty amazing feat considering Philadelphia is a top five market. When asked what major market radio DJs earn these days, Taylor estimates that "Due to cutbacks and the economies of voice-tracking, pay scales have inched down over the years. An average afternoon DJ salary in Philadelphia is now about $45-65k per year."

Taylor advises new radio DJs to understand that traditional radio stations are but one place to look for work. Internet and satellite radio will provide many new "radio" opportunities in the future.

Michael Lowe

Michael Lowe is the Program Director of WLRQ in Melbourne, Florida. Lowe got his first job while doing college radio at UCF in Orlando. When asked "Who chooses the music you play?," Lowe answered, "I do. I'm the PD. We do consult with our Regional VP of Program Director, but the final decision is mine."

2
BECOMING A NIGHTCLUB OR BAR DJ

Working as a club DJ, you've got to deal with drunks and work in the dark. But you get to pick all the music, you program the whole night, and you MC the entire show. And when it all goes right, it can make you feel pretty darn good. This is why I made the switch from radio to clubs early in my DJ career. I couldn't deal with some knucklehead telling me to play some boring slow song twice an hour; I wanted to choose my own music that I knew would make my audience go wild. I was proud to be a club or bar jock. You're the on-air personality, you're the music director, and you are the promotions director all rolled up into one. Add all three positions to your résumé!

Getting My Start

I started doing small bars for free with a friend right after high school. My first paid solo gig was spinning "oldies" music at a popular ice cream parlor for the entire summer on South Street in Philadelphia. I didn't have equipment when the owner offered me the job, so I went to an appliance store and bought a small home stereo setup with two Technics belt-driven turntables and a cheap microphone I bought at Sam Goody. My setup sounded like crap, but it got the job done. The ice cream parlor had a second level that was well lit and visible to the street through a huge glass window. For some strange reason, I felt the need to jump on top of the counter and start lip-syncing Elvis. Everyone on the street stopped and watched, then applauded when I was done acting like a moron. Fortunately, I was never inspired to do that again. But that was the beginning of my nightclub and bar experience.

DJ Chuck Fresh workin'
the mix.

Coming Up in Philly

I got a job working for a retired radio DJ named Shawn Michael, who ran a small DJ company and had a couple of medium sized backwoods suburban bars. I was in heaven—I could play and say whatever I wanted, and I got paid for it! This is when I started developing original promotions and got my reputation as the local "bad boy." My first real bar account was a place called "Yesterdays" in downtown Philadelphia. I had to play oldies music (again) on really bad turntables with records that were scratched beyond belief. Shawn provided all the records, some of which appeared to be original issues of oldies hits that would probably be worth some big bucks in better condition. I gasped as Shawn showed me a "secret" of how to get his records to sound better. He would get a glass of seltzer and a napkin, and actually wet down the record with the napkin before playing it. And for some strange reason that I still cannot comprehend, it made the records sound less scratchy! The bar was always crowded, and it was a great place to learn the basics of DJing in a bar situation.

After complaining about playing oldies, Shawn promoted me to a larger account, Casa Maria, a Mexican cantina-restaurant with a small bar and an even smaller dance floor located in King of Prussia, Pennsylvania, a well-known and busy Philadelphia suburb. I finally got to try my beatmatching skills in front of a live crowd! This was much more fun for me than oldies nights. I worked there for about six months until I heard about an opening at a hotel based bar called Touché.

My audition for Touché was at one of their sister clubs called "Polo Bay" in center city Philadelphia. A DJ named Mel Toxic explained that these bars had a unique system of controlling crowds through a psychologically inspired program called "The Format." This format controlled the songs we played as well as the lighting programs that corresponded with the music. Sets were broken down into "A" through "F" sets, with A sets being more mellow, non-danceable cocktail hour type music; and progressed to the F set, which were "Fun" songs intended for prime time sets in the club. The entire night was pre-programmed in a set rotation. The music was provided for all the DJs, with every record clearly labeled with the A through F moniker. There was no mixing needed, because the format usually precluded DJs from choosing records that were mixable.

After displaying the basic skills of reading the letters A through F and following the instructions of the written manual that was prominently displayed in every DJ booth in all of their clubs, I was hired for Thursday happy hours at Touché.

Man, I was the king. My first real club! I went out and bought new clothes, and practiced my "format" skills for an entire week.

I arrived an hour early for my shift at Touché the next Thursday night. I was responsible for turning the entire sound and lighting system on, which may sound simple, but trust me—in most bar and club situations, it's a disaster. Nothing is properly labeled, there are no instructions, and the first time you see it, this equipment looks like it was forcefully removed from an alien spacecraft and dropped haphazardly into the DJ booth. Nightclub and bar systems grow almost organically, with more and more components being added to the original plan so nothing appears to make sense. Eventually, I found the power switches for the amplifiers, and fired them up. The mixer didn't have an on/off switch, so the red power light was already in the "on" position. The turntables were easy enough to turn on.

Next problem—the entire sound and lighting system was "zoned," meaning it had separate volume and intensity controls for each part of the room. I wasn't aware of the differences at the time, so I instinctively turned them all up about half way. Five o'clock rolled around, and I put my first "A" set record on, according to my format book. The music boomed through the club, and I thought it sounded great. All the sudden, the manager comes flying over the bar in a panic and jumped in the booth, correcting all the volumes. I didn't realize the zone levels were part of the format. The music was too loud in the office and at the bar, overpowering people so they couldn't hear each other. Whoops! Eventually, I figured the system out over my first few shifts, and got pretty good at it. After my first month, I was responsible for training some new DJs.

I met the regional manager, who apparently liked my style (I followed his rules), and he offered me a summer position at a larger property called "Polo Bay" at the New Jersey shore. The two-hour commute was brutal, especially after working a day job. I did that bar for a summer, and got pretty tight with Julie Grove, my manager.

Going Euro in Jersey

At the end of the summer, Julie was offered a general manager position at a new free-standing club called "M-Street" in Voorhees, New Jersey. The original concept stated that this bar was supposed to be a "European style dance club," where all we played was high-energy Euro house and techno. I happened to be Julie's favorite DJ, so she hired me as the head resident for the new club. I got to pick my shifts first, and was responsible for hiring all the other DJs. I was also responsible for purchasing and programming the entire music library, which was a pretty heavy responsibility. Due to certain corporate politics, I was practically forced to hire a certain connected DJ I had bad feelings about, who avoided the format and trash-talked all the other DJs, including me. This problem is typical in this business. Egos tend to reign superior to common sense, as you'll probably find out for yourself.

Overall, my M-Street experience was fantastic. I got to run various promotions and write and record my own radio commercials, which was the basis for my subsequent career in radio production. I created a massively successful Tuesday night, which is virtually impossible in this business, which ultimately created enough buzz and profits to allow the club to be sold for a healthy profit, leaving me out of a job. The guys who bought it had their own DJs. The club eventually changed its name, then went out of business a year or so later, as most nightclubs typically become stale and die in a short time

Working in Atlantis

During my resident tenure at M-Street, I branched out to several other nightclubs both on my own and through another very successful DJ service called East Coast Entertainment run by Bob Palio. He had an account called Club Atlantis, which was a huge multilevel nightclub attached to a banquet hall in Bensalem, Pennsylvania. This place had an insane sound and intelligent light system installed and maintained by one of the smartest people in the industry. In addition to its normal client base, weddings would always dump into this club, which kept it very busy. Its biggest night was Sunday night, which was one of the premiere nights in the Philadelphia area. Everyone who was anyone went to Club Atlantis on Sunday nights. It was considered an honor to work at Atlantis on Sundays, and I had my eye set on getting that night. Eventually, after about six months of helping to build their Thursday and Friday nights, the existing Sunday night DJ said something stupid to the owner of the club and was fired immediately. They offered the coveted Sunday night shift to me. I was already working six nights a week at four different clubs, and my girlfriend was about to kill me. But this was way too cool to pass up.

CHAPTER 2

This was it—the highlight of my DJ career! I had finally made it, and it felt like I had just recorded a hit single and become famous overnight. I spent a fortune on new records, and rocked that house every Sunday night for about three years. I was featured in a three page spread in *Nightclub and Bar* Magazine. I was mentioned in the local newspapers and in the club's radio ads. Hell, I even had a "fan club"! I was exactly where I wanted to be in my career. Everyone I knew came out on my first Sunday night for my debut, and it was an incredible event that I'll never forget.

Atlantis had an amazing DJ booth. It was raised way up in the air at the end of a long catwalk with sliding Plexiglas windows across the entire front of the booth, which spanned the entire width of their huge dance floor. To the far right of the booth, there was a monster lighting panel that controlled every set of lights in the bar. They had Intellibeams, Emulators, Dataflash strobes, fog machines, bubble machines, 1000-Watt spotlights—everything that was dope, def, and funky at the time, they had it. The Atlantis lighting system was no less than awesome. What really freaked me out was that the sound and light guy hooked everything up through X10 modules that he could actually control from his *cell phone*! I saw him do it. Near the light panel, there was a sliding Plexiglas window that was accessible to customers, and a secret hidden door that led to a passage behind the main bar. The owner actually lived at the club, so you could sometimes see him running around in the back hallway in his undies late at night. Towards the center of this DJ booth, they had two Technics 1200 turntables, a Denon dual CD deck, and a modified Urei 1620 mixer that somehow removed the microphone input from the tape out feed so you could make mixtapes without talking on them. To the far left of the booth, there was a huge rack of amplifiers, crossovers, equalizers, compressors and limiters that looked like an LED lightshow in itself. Behind this rack, there was a 10 foot by 10 foot secret room, where all kinds of legendary unmentionable things happened during my tenure at this club.

Believe it or not, I became bored with that situation. The crowds were fickle, and didn't respond well to new music. They seemed to want to hear the same exact songs week after week for two years! I hadn't received a raise or bonus for all my hard work, because everyone considered it an "honor" to DJ Sunday nights. "What do you need more money for? You've got all the women you can handle!" I was already exceeding what everyone else in my area was doing business-wise, and I had outgrown the glory. It was time to get while the getting was good, so I left Atlantis and created my own DJ service with a guy named Joe Montalvo.

Minding My Own Business

Our DJ service was the most kick-butt service in the Philly area. Not only did clients get a multitalented DJ, we offered additional services that allowed us to charge higher rates. We added promotions planning, club calendars, flyer design services, video services, Club TV slide shows, radio commercials, routine maintenance, and even sound and light installations. I created and hosted mind-blowing games like the Three Way Kissing Contest, Plungerball, and The Shuffle Golf Challenge that created cult-like followings. All this stuff made my company an invaluable asset to my clubs.

As I was training new DJs to work for me, I found that many beginners have the misconception that they'll need to become the next big scratcher or trance mixmaster who will work on the international circuit. The truth is that relatively few clubs will support this type of DJ. Most mainstream bars and clubs are looking for an entertaining DJ rather than some mixmaster who refuses to speak on a microphone. There's nothing stranger than clearing the dance floor and having everyone stare at you while playing obscure remixes or songs they've never heard before. Most small to mid-sized bars and clubs not in New York, Los Angeles, Chicago, or Miami seem to prefer more of a well-rounded, mobile DJ type entertainer.

It can look really cool to scratch records in front of a crowd of screaming fans. I even won a scratching contest back in the day. But let's think about the whole scratching thing for a minute. Record scratching is nearly impossible to dance to unless the DJ is really, really good at doing it live so that it sounds like an extension or remix of the original song. But in most mainstream clubs, your average customer will get pissed off because they think you're ruining the song they've heard on the radio 50 times that week—the version without your scratching. In reality, the persona of the "scratcher" or "mixmaster" is overrated. And even though some of these people get all the MTV coverage, there aren't many clubs that will hire that type of DJ. Don't get me wrong —it's extremely cool to do a quick scratch once in a while just for fun, but don't get caught up in it as a way of life. It's a myth that you have to be a great scratcher to be a successful DJ. You can count on your fingers the number of scratchers actually making a living being a DJ, compared to the thousands of other non-scratching DJs earning a comfortable living.

But don't be disappointed—you can still beatmix, scratch occasionally, have fun, and make a comfortable living in a small or mainstream club.

Working as a Club DJ

A mainstream nightclub DJ has five main responsibilities:

* You have to be the voice of your venue. It's your job to set the tone and the mood of the night while promoting upcoming events. You have to remind people where they are, who you are, and why they need to keep coming back for more.

* You have to be one of the primary customer service contacts. A DJ is usually a focal point in a club or bar. You're stationary, easy to find, and usually accessible. People look to you to tell them where the restrooms are, or what kind of music or entertainment your bar features.

* You have to figure out a music program. Considering both the clientele of your room and your boss's desired target market, you've got to choose the right songs that will keep these people in your room and fit the specified program. This can become quite a balancing act.

* You have to effectively mix that music. This is the hardest part: you've got to do all of the above, plus choose your next few songs and smoothly mix them once every three or four minutes.

* You must do everything in your power to preserve your bar's liquor license. A liquor license allows the bar to legally sell liquor and beer according to state regulations, which is how most clubs make most of their revenue. If you physically harm someone or do something that's flagrantly obscene or illegal as an agent of the bar, you could put your bar's liquor license in jeopardy.

Most "resident" club DJs (the term given to the club's "permanent" DJs) tend to make more money than average radio DJs for a number of reasons. You'll usually need to invest in all of your own music, effectively making you the music director during your shift. You'll also need to take the time to plan and execute all promotions, making you the promotions manager too. And you'll directly interact with the customers as a sort of a customer service ambassador, so you've got to look good and be positive. It's a job that's much more involved than it looks.

Most club and bar DJs don't earn as much as mobile DJs, mainly because they don't have to purchase and carry all that heavy sound equipment. And since you're consistently working week after week, you'll exchange your stability for a lower hourly rate. It's kind of like a quantity discount. Most professional club DJs make anywhere from $20 to $50 an hour depending on their business skills, their reputation, the size of the room, and the size of the market. If you pick up three or four five-hour shifts every week, you can live fairly comfortably with a lot of spare time. If you become a big name in the big city circuit, you could make up to $10,000 a shift!

In the following sections, I've outlined the most important things to know about being a nightclub or bar DJ. You too will learn to be a "master of human behavior that's influenced by alcohol." The whole complicated bar and club industry will begin to make sense to you. Get ready for all the secret tools you'll need to become the top of this industry's next wave of club and bar DJs. Successful DJs are already comparable to rock stars, or as one of my old managers used to call us, "lifeguards" (because chicks swarmed around us). They'll be multitalented individuals who can effectively program, mix beats, and MC a crowd getting them high on nothing more than your programming.

You'll learn about programming music for any type of crowd, and how to push the line and get the "wow" factor. There's nothing like the rush of hearing your crowd scream in joy when you say something cool or play a hot song. You just can't get that in a radio studio! I'll also touch on proper speaking techniques, annunciation, pronunciation, voice projection, and what you should and should not say and how to say it without getting in trouble. And I'll suggest techniques for opening up direct communications between you and the people who sign your checks, outside promoters, cooperative businesses, and even your local liquor purveyors.

It's important to remember that nightclubs and bars exist only because they earn money selling beer and drinks. Anything you can do to help them sell more booze will help you keep your job, and increase your earning potential in the long run.

Once your local club owners and managers start hearing about you, more job openings will appear. You'll also begin to build a small celebrity base. Your following will grow, making you even more marketable. And the path this book suggests will also prepare you for life after DJing. You can prepare for a career in nightclub promotions, record promotions, sales, radio, public speaking, TV or a whole lot more.

Entertainment Theory

You've decided to become a club or bar disc jockey for a number of reasons: money, fame, love of music, desire to meet people, or whatever. Many DJs don't realize that they are now involved in one of the world's largest industries, the entertainment business. We are getting paid to entertain. "Entertain" has many definitions, including enthrall, delight, amuse; it's usually more than methodically playing the same exact song one after another every night like a pre-recorded CD. DJs entertain through a combination of the right music mix, a glowing personality, and something unexpected once in a while. This is not an easy thing to do, since it borrows from several completely unrelated disciplines.

Successful music programming relies on your ability to tune into the psychological makeup of your crowd, and it's a knack learned from trial and error. It's not necessarily choosing the hottest song of the day; it's choosing the best music for your particular crowd. You'll need to learn how to pick up the subtle hints that'll tell you everything you need to know. Age, gender, ethnicity, dress, mannerisms, accent, hairstyles, shoes, nails, bling bling—all of these conscious fashion decisions and inherent demographic traits will begin to paint a mental image after a while, and you'll surprise yourself by developing the ability to look at a crowd and know just what would make them rock.

The physical act of mixing the music—creating seamless transitions and combining songs—is an artform. It is a very difficult skill to master. It's also incredibly enjoyable in the right situation, when you fall into that "zone," where everything else seems to disappear and all you're left with is the mix. It's almost like a high! But, to be perfectly honest, I've found that most average people don't notice or don't appreciate this skill. Sure, it's nice to keep a continuous flow on a dance floor, but the more I experimented with "anti-mixing" (purposefully breaking up the monotony of a seamless beat), the more I learned the music programming was much more important. So many club DJs favor the mix over the song, forgoing a better song simply because "it won't mix" with the current record. It took me several years to figure that one out.

And then there's the art of public speaking—the ability to command a crowd with nothing more than your presence, your voice, and a few smartly chosen words. Club DJs who talk too much are incredibly annoying, mainly because all they're spouting off is some unimportant word-barf simply because they like to hear their own voices. But on the other hand, club DJs who don't talk at all are missing an incredible opportunity. Even the highest paid trance and techno DJs say a few things into the microphone to get the crowd hyped! It's noticing the time when the excitement in the room is just about ready to explode, then shouting something painfully cliché, like "Somebody scream!" And the room erupts in a scream that can be heard for three miles. It's the right words at the right time that can instantly raise your value.

Finally, there's the fine act of crowd manipulation. With a little practice and some basic research, you can make crowds behave almost any way you want to. You can make them happy. You could make them sad. You might incite a riot! Believe it or not, many emotions can be controlled largely with nothing more than your choice in music. Add a few other sneaky tricks from the magic bag you're hopefully filling as you read this book, and you too can become the next puppet master.

To be really successful in this business you must comprehend the underlying nature of people. Remember this simple concept, and you will be guaranteed success and longevity: the bar and club business comprises the entire social lives of thousands of people all over the world. In our paranoid world where it's harder and harder to meet people in everyday situations, people turn to bars and nightclubs in search of new friends and that elusive mythical soul mate. All of their current friends go there routinely. The local bar or club is the most important part of their existence. It doesn't matter if the person in question is old, young, rich, poor, an executive, a janitor, black, white, blue, or green. They represent a long-term fixed income for bar owners, and subsequently, for their DJs. Moreover, they are all people. They are all *customers*. And dammit, this place *is* their social life. This seemingly insignificant fact gives you all kinds of power.

CHAPTER 2

To reach the level of a master DJ, you must become more than a human jukebox—you need to become a true entertainer. You'll have a command of all of the above disciplines. It comes naturally to some lucky peeps, and unfortunately takes years of practice and research for the rest of us.

Bands vs DJs

And ever since the DJ has come on to the scene, there's always been an unspoken riff between DJs and bands. You'll probably run into this situation at some point in your DJ career, so I'd be remiss if I didn't get you ready for it. I was so befuddled by this invisible riff that I actually joined a band to see what the big deal was all about. For a short time, I was a singer in a rock band called "Kiss The Red" that performed in small bars in and around Princeton, New Jersey in the late 1990s. I got the first-hand scoop on why bands hate DJs.

Bands have been around for thousands and thousands of years, since our ancestors were cavemen. They've got a bit of a head start on the DJ thing, which began on a tiny scale sometime in the 1950s.

Their main argument is that they work a hundred times harder than DJs, because they must spend years first learning how to play an instrument or sing, and even more time learning every word, note, chord, and chorus in upwards of hundreds of songs throughout their careers. Unfortunately for them, most of those songs get old and backlisted, meaning they don't actively perform them any longer because the response to those songs is weak. A DJ can pick up a studio duplicate of the song that's been recorded by the artist who made it popular and heard millions of times on the radio, and play that exact replica at any time with absolutely no notice or practice.

A band's real argument is that they are physically performing the songs, providing a much higher level of entertainment than any DJ could provide. In most cases, they've got us there. Most DJs sit around like a lump and simply press buttons, providing as much entertainment as a barstool. Some newer digital jukeboxes are actually more entertaining than some DJs I've seen. But you can beat this argument with an interactive show, some well-timed clever announcements, games and contests, and an entertaining presence.

Bands by nature have at least three people and sometimes up to twenty if they have a complex horn section, so there are many more people who must get paid. This is where we DJs really have it over the bands. Many bars and clubs choose DJs to replace expensive bands, simply because the band isn't pulling its weight and earning a profit for the bar.

Bands do get more chicks. As a DJ, I managed to do pretty well with the ladies. But band guys beat DJs exponentially. When I was singing with Kiss The Red, I got more chicks, and much better looking chicks than I ever got as a DJ! And it's not just the singer—the drummer got his share too, and he never said a word. There's something about the apparent star power of a musician. The emotions and movements generated during a band's performance seem to raise some kind of inner love instinct in women.

Most professional bands are pretty cool and are a pleasure to work with. It's the smaller, newer bands that are a pain in the ass, mainly because they're insecure and see you as a threat to their livelihood. When band members don't greet you warmly, don't sweat it. They're probably afraid of you.

Your DJ Name

Obviously, working in a young, hip, fast-paced industry like the nightclub and bar business requires nice trendy clothes, usually of a popular designer flavor. You'll also need a cool attitude, even if you've never been considered to be a cool person. Don't worry, you can fake it. Remember, this is the entertainment business, so some acting is a requirement.

Once you've got your dress and attitude squared away, it's time to figure out a dope, def, and funky DJ name that's hopefully more relevant than those previous adjectives.

I got stuck with "DJ Chuck Fresh" in the mid 80s, and it just doesn't make sense to mess with it now. Many old schoolers initially thought I ripped off Doug E. Fresh, an old school rapper with a hit called "The Show." But that's simply not true. I was fumbling through the name decision process when I was trying to figure out who I was going to be. I was Chuck Rock, Chuck Young, Def Masta Homey Ock, and even Corey Foxx for a while. A co-worker at a department store and I were joking about DJ names one night, and she called me "DJ Fresh." There it was—"DJ Chuck Fresh"! It was perfect. I was always being fresh, both in a nasty and nouveau way. I wrote it down to see how it looked in print, and the rest is history.

"DJ Stewart Shocka" got his DJ name from his parents' recollection of his childhood days. For some strange inexplicable reason, Stew used to call records "shockas" as a youth. His father told the story frequently, so the "Shocka" thing kind of stuck with him.

Does this guy look like his name could be "DJ Chuck Fresh?"

WHAT'S IN A NAME?

Does your DJ name really matter? In the full scope of things, not really. "DJ Paul Oakenfold" is a terrible DJ name, but he's one of the hottest DJs in the world. "DJ Swedish Egil" is even worse, but he's got his own worldwide radio show. A clever DJ name like "DJ T-Ice" may help you get noticed more quickly, which might allow you to become successful faster than someone with a name like "DJ Thurmond A. Weisberg."

"DJ J-Mo" used to be "DJ Joe Money," until my friends and I realized he never had any money when it came to picking up the bar tab. Capitalizing off the J-Lo thing, we changed his name to "DJ J-Mo." He's still fighting us on it, but we'll win eventually. The power of repetition can be frightening.

Your real name may not fit into the "cool" motif. For instance, my real name would be "DJ Chuck Graudins." Obviously, my real name just doesn't have a flow to it. So unless you were blessed with a really cool name, you'll probably need to come up with a "handle," or your own DJ name.

Over the years, I've heard some really cool names like DJ Bad Boy Joe, DJ Psycho Bitch, DJ J-Mo, DJ Less Than Zero, DJ Shocka, DJ White Lightning, and the Wireless DJ. I've also heard my share of really lame names like DJ Walt Seal, DJ Bruce, DJ Simple, and even DJ Bob. Do yourself a favor—get together with your friends and coworkers, and think long and hard and try to come up with something cool. Your DJ name tells a story about your personality, not to mention it might stick with you forever. Once you create a reputation under a certain DJ name, you probably won't want to start all over again from scratch.

There are several ways to create your own, killer DJ name. Most of us already have nicknames given to us as children. If your nickname happens to rhyme with something cool, you could come up with a clever rhyming twist. Some people simply use their first name with an "E" sound on the end along with the first initial of their last name, but only if it rhymes with the letter E, such as "Bobby G" or "Mikey T." A name like "Bobby F" doesn't sound as smooth as the "Bobby G" thing. You could borrow a popular current phrase, but remember that most current phrases quickly become old and overused. Some pretty cool names come from obscure things, such as feelings, emotions, intangible items, medical conditions, science, technical terms, religion, and even literary mistakes. And it's always easy to reword or rearrange a popular artist or DJ name so that it's different enough not to confuse people.

Preparing to Play Live

If it's your first night at a new club, naturally you'll probably be a bit nervous. Here are some suggestions you can use to chill out and make your first night much smoother.

Getting the Lay of the Land

Know the club, and know the people who go there. Go to the club several weeks ahead of time and listen to the DJ and the music. Make sure you're there on the night you're scheduled to play so you'll know what's expected of you. Listen to the songs, and take notes. You can later use these notes to figure out your own custom programming. Pay attention to exactly when the DJ plays the hot songs and remember that. Note the response on the dance floor. Every club and night has its own individual personality, so you'll want to rock the house before you rock the boat on your first night. Know what I mean?

See if you can get in the club early one night, maybe on an off night. Get to know the feel of the equipment. Get used to the quirks. Make sure there's a "booth monitor" or a "monitor speaker" in the DJ booth, and make sure it works. Sound travels relatively slowly, so there can often be a delay in the time from when your CD or record player puts out the sound information to the time when your ears pick it up or your feet feel the bass drum from speakers that are a couple hundred feet away. This fraction of a second delay can totally trash your mixes. A monitor speaker helps by letting you hear the master program in "real time" without the delay. Know how the sound works in the room. It's going to be different when you're playing with bodies in the house, but at least you'll have some experience to go with.

Use the information from your research to plan out your first night. Know the sets you're going to play, and at what time you plan to play them. If you can, practice these sets several times before you get to the club. Most importantly, know the music. Don't think you can bring a brand new record to the club and break it live for the first time without previewing it. There can be all kinds of strangeness like skips, dropouts and unexpected four letter words that could get you in trouble when you wing it.

Bring some extra cartridges and needles if you're working with turntables. Carry a CD cleaner if you're playing CDs. And don't forget to bring your headset. I've never worked at a club that had its own headset—mainly because DJs often sweat on them. If you forget your headset, you're going to have one hell of a time mixing well! I've done it a few times—it was always a very interesting experience.

Make sure you look at the mixer to see how the prior DJ left you set up. Check the cross fader and any assignable switches. Some DJs even change the way the mixer is wired if they're bringing in their own equipment. There's nothing more unnerving than pushing the play button with a room full of people and no sound comes out!

Your First Night

You'll come in to your DJ booth about 15-30 minutes early. You'll get all your CDs or records into your booth and set yourself up. You'll then spot check and test all the equipment to make sure that when you play music, something's coming out. If you're the first person on, you'll probably need to fire up all the amplifiers and lights. If you're not sure how to do this, find the manager and ask. Many booths have a required order of turning things on so you won't damage anything.

Next, you'll basically warm up by playing some recurrent music (music that was popular six months to two years ago). I'd break out all my new stuff to get a feel for how it sounds in the room. Since no one really danced during the first 30-45 minutes of the night no matter what I played, I took this time to practice some new mix sets. Try to stay away from the most popular floor-packing songs early in the night; save those for your prime time hours when the room is busy and people are packed on the dance floor.
I thought about including sample song lists in this section, but clubs and bars are so varied by location, clientele, and current music trends that it would be virtually impossible to compile a list that would be relevant to every situation. Here's where you'll have to do your own research—listen to DJs at other clubs, and on mix shows on your local radio station. If you're lucky enough to have a small music store in your area that caters specifically to DJs, they'll be a tremendous help in pointing you in the right direction. Props out to Pat's Music in Philadelphia for saving my ass several times in my clueless early days.

If you're following another DJ's shift, ask him (or her) what songs he or she has played in the last hour or so. You'll look like a fool if you're playing a song the previous DJ just played! You can play a really hot song the last DJ played, but wait at least two hours have passed before you do it. That's usually enough time to make it acceptable for a crowd to hear any song a second time.

Throughout the night, you'll be looking around the room "reading the crowd." You'll know if you're on the right track by watching people tap their fingers or shake their feet to the beat of the song. See if they're singing along with the music. Note if they're staring blankly into space. And when you hit the play button on that killer song when the floor is packed and the crowd screams in joy, you'll feel like God for a second or two; you might just get chills! These are subtle clues that can answer many of your music programming questions.

IF YOU SCREW UP

If you botch a mix or two, don't sweat it. Believe it or not, most customers won't even notice unless it's pathetically bad. If it's sounding like a freight train in a china shop, you may be in trouble. Just finish it quickly and move on to a better mix next time. If you're mixing and you notice your next song is coming in off-beat, cut the volume back and try again. If you're out of time, line up your slam and let 'er rip. *Never apologize.* More on the beatmixing thing later.

Watch your nerves. In my early days, I sometimes made the mistake of taking the needle off the record that I just mixed into, leaving a very eerie silence. I've also mistakenly hit the tonearm of the turntable, making a god-awful scratching noise. Settle down and go with the flow. Don't let these mistakes get you down—laugh about them! Be prepared for these mistakes by knowing what could happen and what you can do to make it all look like it's part of your show when they do happen.

Your goal is to set the pace of the night. You'll work your crowd up into a frenzy, then bring them down a bit, then pump them right back up again. This flow will keep your night from seeming monotonous and will make people realize how good you really are. By creatively programming your music and events, you'll be able to increase bar sales and make yourself look better. Timing is everything. You'll begin to feel the timing the more you do this, as long as you're paying attention.

Performing at Free-Standing Clubs

Although the "DJ Culture" hype would have you think all club DJs work in these tremendously large and glamorous nightclubs in New York City or Miami's South Beach where drug-induced people dance wildly to anything, it's really mostly BS. I'd estimate that two percent or less of the thousands of club DJs all over the nation and the world have those dream gigs. The other 98 percent of us work at smaller clubs and bars where relatively sober folks won't dance to anything they haven't heard a hundred or more times before on the radio. Even at the big free-standing clubs I worked, every time I played a new song, even if my mix was perfectly flawless and seamless, as soon as the crowd realized they didn't know the song, the dance floor thinned considerably. This was incredibly frustrating! As I was coming up, everyone told me club DJs were supposed to be the trend setters who made new songs popular. In most cases, unfortunately, that's simply not true. A free-standing club is a building that's nothing more than a nightclub. Its self supported, and its only goal is to jam as many people into it as the law will allow. A hotel-based club is considered to be a perq for hotel guests. Hotel-based clubs focus on making the hotel guests comfortable, and everything else (including profitability) is secondary.

It's mostly all about the music and the mix at most free-standing nightclubs and bars. You, as the DJ, are the king (or queen), and you can usually play whatever you want whenever you want to, obviously in an effort to keep people dancing, drinking, telling their friends about the great time they had, and coming back.

A TYPICAL FREE-STANDING CLUB NIGHT

In many areas, nightclubs and bars are legally forced to close at 2 or 3 AM. And most "clubbers" won't go out before 10 PM, so you've got about three or four hours tops to do your magic. Here's the typical flow of a night in a free-standing club that's open from 9 PM to 2 AM.

8 PM: Arrive at the club. Turn all systems on. If it's not already on, turn on the mixer first, then amplifiers (to avoid the nasty huge mixer power-up "pop" sound that can damage speakers). Get all your CDs and/or records organized so you know where everything is. Get yourself a coffee, tea, or drink, and make a final dash to the restrooms, because you may not be able to leave once your show starts.

8:30 PM: Begin to play your first song at a very low level. As you get to know the bartenders and servers, they'll appreciate you playing music that they like to listen to. It'll score you some extra points if they like you, because they interact with the manager much more frequently than you do. Most bar staffs hang out before and after their shifts, and it's always better if they like you.

9:00 PM: This is it—the doors have been unlocked and your club is officially open. It's kind of eerie those first few moments, because no one ever shows up before 9:30 PM. You sit there and wonder if anyone at all is going to show up! You can keep playing music the bar staff likes until you've got a tangible real crowd. I used the first hour or so to learn new music.

10:00 PM: By now, some of the older fringe of your crowd has started to enter the bar. They can't hang out as long as the younger people, so they're out earlier to avoid falling asleep at the bar. You'll also get the beginnings of any group or bachelorette parties. All these early fringe people will usually dance, but only to songs they know. If you play songs that you'd normally consider older, you can create what I used to call a "base dance floor." As other people straggle in, they'll see people dancing already, and it usually feeds on itself to create a more crowded dance floor.

10:17 PM: I almost called my first CD "10:17 PM," because this was always the "magic" time when the dance floor would convert from a base dance floor to my "real" dance floor. No matter what I was playing, most people in my clubs weren't ready to dance before 10:17 PM. The truly strange part of this was that it didn't matter which night it was, or where my clubs were—10:17 PM seemed to be consistent across them all! There was no apparent common factor. I'd be in West Chester, Pennsylvania on Wednesday night, 80 miles away from Princeton, with almost no chance of anyone overlapping, but the dancing didn't begin at either bar until 10:17 PM.

From **10:17 PM** through **11:00 PM**, you'll gradually raise the volume as you continue to build the dance floor with "recurrent" hits (big songs from the last year or two), saving your new heavy hitters for the "prime time" hours.

11:00 PM: Now entering Prime Time (from 11:00 PM until 1:00 AM), you'll begin to bust out your really popular stuff. It's best to engineer your flow to represent a roller coaster ride—starting with a huge hit, then playing some new, up-and-coming stuff, maybe a few big recurrents, then hitting them with another huge hit. To keep things interesting, I recommend performing a complete cycle every 45 minutes or so.

In some clubs, the owners like when you play slow songs between your sets. This allows the guys who can't dance a chance to ask a girl to dance. When the dance is over, he'll usually offer to buy her a drink, which increases bar sales. Also, when people are dancing all night, they can't be buying drinks at the bar at the same time! A natural break every so often allows the bar to make some extra money, so it's good to thin the dance floor a few times a night. In other clubs, they may want you to keep the energy up all night long because their bars are busy enough. Check with your owner or manager to see what they'd like you to do.

CHAPTER 2

1:00 AM: By this time, most of your initial older crowd has already left, and the existing crowd is beginning to dwindle. Most folks have had a healthy amount to drink, swallow, smoke, or snort by now, so this is the time when you can play music your crowd isn't familiar with. Their inhibitions are almost nil, so they'll dance to just about anything at this point. You've got about a half hour to go nuts and try all those mixes you've been dying to try.

1:30 AM: Most bars will make you offer "Last Call at the bar" (a customer's last chance to order drinks) at around 30 minutes prior to officially closing the doors. This signals the bartenders to wrap things up, close out all checks, and take any last minute beverage orders. Your job is usually to wind the remaining crowd down by keeping them dancing and happy. This is also usually the time most fights break out in clubs, so many clubs will recommend that you play a few slow songs to chill the atmosphere a bit. Other clubs keep pumpin' until the absolute last second. Check and see what the deal is at your bar.

These self-sufficient clubs usually have their own built-in permanent sound and lighting systems. Since their main focus is running a club, their sound and light shows are usually much cooler and more sophisticated than the sound and lights in other types of bars and clubs. You'll need to learn how to operate these systems quickly. Usually, the manager has a basic understanding of what's what. If you're lucky enough to have a "light man" to operate your lights, he or she can usually help you figure out the sound equipment too. The best way to learn is to have another DJ, hopefully not the one you're about to replace, show you the basic operations in a live situation, meaning when the club is open and operating. This way, you'll be introduced to how the flow typically works in this venue, as well as the recommended volume levels as they progress throughout the night.

Performing in Hotel Clubs

Free-Standing clubs don't have the inherent limitations of hotel-based clubs. In the Marriott and Hilton properties I worked, the hotel customer always came first (Figure 2.3). Hotel crowds can be incredibly fun if there's a large group traveling together on business. They're away from home, their partners or spouses are hundreds or thousands of miles away, so they won't be as shy and reserved as they might normally act in a corporate situation. I've seen the most conservative looking people get a few drinks in them and do things that you'd only see in the movies.

But, unfortunately, the average hotel customer is usually a boring middle aged pot-bellied male business traveler wearing a bad suit and an even worse tie who is traveling alone, so he has no power base, and he has absolutely no idea what real nightclub customers desire. He's the moron who will personally guarantee that if you play some slow paced classic rock song at midnight while the entire dance floor is slammed with young hotties dancing to the latest hip-hop hit, the place will go crazy. And since the club manager is a hotel employee, he or she has to step in and tell you to play that crap that'll clear your dance floor and make you look like an idiot DJ. When you ask Mr. Hotel Guest Moron why he's not dancing, he'll typically reply, "Dance? I didn't want to dance to it. I just wanted to hear it." Before you throw the CD case at Mr. Moron's head, remember, he's a hotel customer, and if you piss him off, you'll probably lose your job. If this guy walked into a free-standing club, you could probably have a waitress pour a drink on his head with little to no repercussion.

A TYPICAL HOTEL BAR NIGHT

5:00 PM: Most small bars and hotel bars have a phenomenon called "happy hour" that usually lasts more than one hour following a typical work day. Drinks may be two for one in an effort to attract an after work crowd that might usually head straight home. Typically, most hotel bars open at noon, and there's probably some knucklehead who's on his eighth beer by the time happy hour begins. You're walking in with your CDs and all your gear, and before you have a chance to put your gear down, he jumps off his barstool and asks you, "So, whatcha got? Got any Jimmy Buffet in there?" All the sudden, this poor lonely sap is your best friend. As he casts a blind eye to your tip jar, he continues to bombard you with requests, probably because he's finally found someone to talk to. You want to tell him to screw off, but you remember you work in a hotel bar, and hotel guests are a priority, so you bite your tongue and kindly explain to him that you're in the very important process of setting up and you'll be with him in a moment.

Depending on the bar, you'll usually play some classic and contemporary rock songs, maybe some oldies, and a touch of R&B. And a solid block of Jimmy Buffett's greatest hits is always cool during happy hour.

6:00 PM: Your new best friend has ordered his next two beers from your DJ booth, while talking your ear off about something you really don't care about. Some cute women start to enter the bar for an after work martini. Your best friend finally decides to head back to the bar. No one is ready to dance yet, but the bar is starting to fill.

Better DJs are prepared with an arsenal of fun props and games like Shuffle Golf, Pro Thumb Wrestling, Trivia, Shocking Roulette, The Bar Wheel, and other fun interactive games that corporate types love to play. This warms the crowd up to the room, and entices them to buy another drink or two and stick around to see what kind of fun you've got up your sleeve next.

7:00 PM: By now, your former best friend and some women have had enough to drink so they feel comfortable dancing. They'll ask you to "Play something I can dance to" and "Can you pick it up a little?" When you affirm their request and ask what songs they had in mind, they come up blank and try to sing it to you. "You know, that songs that goes 'La Dee Da Dee Lee La BOOM', can you play that one?" You rack your brain for a minute or two, trying to figure out what the hell she's talking about. Then it comes to you—it wasn't "La Dee Da Dee, it was Ladi Dadi Lo Ladi!" You manage to find the song, pop it on, bring up the volume on your microphone, and announce that this song is out to [your requestor's first name]. Expect most happy hour clients to ask you incredibly silly questions.

8:00 PM: Now we're in the "transition period." Here's when the old crowd fizzles out and the late-night crowd starts to trickle in. Unless you've had an incredible Happy Hour shift and they're still raring to go, you may have to suffer with an empty dance floor once again. Normally, the resident or late night DJ begins his or her shift at 9:00 PM, so they don't want you to play a song they plan to play. You'll effectively be starting over again, trying to build energy from scratch.

9:00 PM: The DJs have completed their shift change, and you are either headed home or beginning your show. Your crowd is still in its transition period, so you've got about an hour or so to warm up. A few happy hour leftovers might be dancing, but chances are they're winding down and getting ready to leave soon. I'd fart around with the sound and lights, and listen to the bartenders bitch about what lousy tippers happy hour people are.

10:17 PM: There's that mysterious time, and... BOOM, right on the money—again! A substantial crowd materializes on the dance floor, just like in the free-standing club. If the hotel doesn't have a strict music programming format, you're free to spin your magic. I used the same successful rollercoaster format with a few twists. In hotels, you've got less hard-core dancers and more people who just want to be entertained. Hotel bar crowds afford you the luxury of being able to dig deep into your disco, rock, or oldies collection to throw an occasional curveball—a song they never expected to hear in your bar. I'd throw three, four, five, sometimes ten of those old hit songs in the mix, and the crowd always screamed as soon as those songs hit the speakers.

11:00 PM: You're in your prime time. Bustin' out dope jams for the masses, keeping the energy high. Your bar manager will come and hang out in the DJ booth, probably because he or she is bored, or because since most DJ booths are slightly elevated, they've got a better view of the room from your perspective. You'll rock on until about midnight, because hotel clubs tend to thin our earlier because hotel guests are notoriously sleepy. This is also about the time your more idiotic bar managers will begin to walk around the room pointing a strange device in the air in several different directions. This can resemble a drunk mime show, and it's pretty humorous to watch. He's either pretty wasted, or he's actually measuring the sound levels in the room using a device called a "decibel meter" or "sound level meter." Many hotels have developed acceptable noise standards for most public areas in an effort to lengthen the life of their sound equipment, and to avoid becoming a nuisance to other people in the hotel. Some hotel clubs are built as an afterthought, meaning the club could have been retrofitted at some point during its career. Retrofitted clubs are typically built directly underneath hotel rooms, so expect guests to complain more often.

12:00 AM: Your room will thin considerably, leaving you with the younger folks and the really drunk other people who are, unfortunately, probably hotel guests. Fortunately, I had a door on my DJ booth that I'd close shortly after midnight to avoid all the just plain stupid requests I'd get from these people after midnight. Your manager is probably exhausted because he or she's probably been there since 10:00 AM, so they probably won't care what you do at this point. You can usually get away with just about anything after midnight at a hotel bar or club.

Radio USA DJ booth at the
Princeton Marriott

Hotel club sound systems are usually less complicated and neater than free-standing club systems, usually because the hotel's purchasing department probably overpaid some hotel contractor an obscene amount of money to set up their sound and light systems. To build up their billable hours, some installation firms take their time in setting things up and labeling everything so these systems are virtually foolproof. This can be a really good thing for a new, inexperienced DJ.

Hotel clubs and bars are typically open early, so their after-work crowds have somewhere to relax and enjoy a few overpriced drinks and appetizers. The bar manager usually turns on the sound system when he or she is setting things up early in the afternoon, so that's already done for you by the time you walk in for your "happy hour" (early evening) shift. If they don't have one of those subscription based looping electronic music systems, such as Muzak, they'll typically grab a CD from somewhere, insert it into the deck, and play it on loop mode until you get there.

Fortunately, there are usually two shifts a night at some hotel bars and clubs—one for the happy hour DJ, and one for the late night DJ. This adds quite a few potential DJ shifts in your area, perfect for training new DJs. And happy hour crowds are a little easier to work with than picky, hard-core clubbers. Most hotel clubs employ a "DJ Service," a company that provides subcontracted DJs so the club doesn't have to hire them as employees. The DJ Service charges the hotel a weekly entertainment fee, and is responsible for auditioning, hiring, and firing DJs. Most DJs who work for a DJ service are younger people trying to break into the business.

Hotel clubs rarely afford you the luxury of doing whatever you want, because they feel whatever nastiness you do may reflect poorly on the club, the hotel, and ultimately the company that's managing an entire portfolio of hotels. You probably won't be able to play those nasty new hip hop songs that spout off bad words, if you can play any hip hop at all. Depending on the micromanaging aptitude of the hotel bar manager, and his or her boss, and his or her boss, and his or her boss (get the drift?), there may be all kinds of funky written (and purposely unwritten) rules you'll have to follow. It can be a head trip!

Performing in Smaller Bars

Most smaller bars have a tiny DJ area, if you're lucky, or they'll just retrofit you into an inconvenient corner somewhere (hopefully not in the path of the dartboard) next to a makeshift dance floor. Hey— you're lucky to have the gig! Most smaller bars don't really need DJs, but you should never admit that. It takes a really good salesman to get this gig, and that's why you'll find 40-60 year old DJs spinning at many small bars. Those old guys need time off occasionally, probably to attend a friend's funeral or have a colonoscopy, so they'll need backup DJs, and that's where you new guys come in. Small bars are a great place to practice your skills while earning some money to buy music.

Know that in most bar situations, when it comes to entertainment, the band is always king. Many bars that feature entertainment hire bands for their big nights. Bar owners think a band provides a more dynamic looking form of entertainment, since there are multiple people all doing stuff while they're on stage. It is fun to watch, especially when the band is good at working the crowd. By contrast, an average bar DJ presses a few buttons and leafs through music once every three or four minutes, then stands around staring into space while the song is playing. It's your job to prove that you too can be a dynamic form of entertainment that's even more captivating than a band. This takes time, practice, experience, imagination, and props. More on this later.

Small bars usually require the DJ to bring his or her own sound systems as a condition of employment. Most of these bars don't feel it's a worthwhile investment to purchase and install a permanent sound system, unless they see that their bar is doing significantly better with a DJ. If they use bands, most bands bring their own sound systems anyway. You will need to know the basics about setting up and troubleshooting DJ equipment, because it will be your responsibility in this situation.

Here's how a typical night would go when performing in a small bar. For illustration sake, let's assume you're doing "band breaks," which means you'll perform 20-30 minutes an hour when the band is off stage taking a break. This is a fairly common situation in smaller bars, and I've got experiences on both sides of this situation as a DJ and as a band member, so I'm one of the few folks who actually understands the dynamics between these two entities.

You'll need to learn and rehearse using a large library of four-letter expletives. You'll soon see why.

A TYPICAL SMALL BAR NIGHT

8:00 PM: You'll roll up with your car full of equipment and unload everything in the bar. Bartenders and servers are working like drones, busy setting up their stations. They may nod their heads to acknowledge your presence, but don't take it personally if they don't. A really tinny sounding jukebox is playing some bad classic rock at an unpleasant volume. You'll set up your equipment, get your music oriented, test everything to make sure it works, then hunt around for someone who knows how to turn that damn jukebox off. When no one 'fesses up, you subtly trip over the jukebox's power cord, and begin to play your own version of classic rock, which avoids pissing off that 50-something bartender who wouldn't tell you how to turn the damn jukebox off in the first place.

9:00 PM: You're all set and ready to rock the house. All of a sudden some long-haired strung-out hippie-looking dudes stroll in carrying guitars and other equipment. They completely ignore you as they find their way to the stage. The bartenders immediately acknowledge their presence and practically jump over the bar to shake the hippies' hands. You're feeling slighted, but don't. Remember, the band is king in these small bars. You recall that this is a stepping stone to a bigger free-standing bar or club gig, and you chill and think, "No problem, that's cool." Under your breath, you utter certain choice four-letter words.

10:17 PM: People are beginning to dance, and you're feeling great about it. You did it—you found the sweet spot! You're feverishly rummaging through your records or CDs trying to line up the next four or five songs that'll guarantee a packed dance floor, when all the sudden, "THUMP, THUMP, THUMP!" What the… "THUMP THUMP THUMP!" It's the band's brainless drummer, beginning to do his "sound check." What would you expect from a guy who hits things with sticks for a living? In his defense, his thumping is actually a necessary procedure, since this is a critical stage where the band's soundman has to "mike" the drums so they sound good during the band's performance. But damn—the least the drummer could do is play in time to the song you're playing! Their system is usually ten or more times more powerful than your puny little portable DJ system that the punk bartender has been telling you to turn down over the past half hour, so your music is drowned out by that "THUMP, THUMP, THUMP." Your dance floor dissipates. You become depressed and utter even more nasty choice four-letter words. Don't sweat it—you'll get your chance to rock the house later. Consider this your warm-up time.

10:30 PM: In your nicest, most professional tone possible, you get to introduce the band. Hopefully, they've made nice and given you a list of the music they plan to play (a "set list") so you won't play the same songs they plan to play. You kick back, turn your volumes to zero, and head to the bar for a 30 to 40 minute break, during which you can attempt in vain to convince that annoying bartender to respect you at least half as much as he respects the band. It's not a bad gig when you think about it. You've got most of the night to hang out with your friends or friendly customers, and you're getting paid for it! You think about sneaking back behind your rig and slightly raising your microphone level so this "SHREEEK" comes over the system ("feedback") that drives the band nuts because they think it's their system, but your common sense takes over and you just laugh about it. With bands that were really jerks, I would grab a wireless microphone and sing along softly but way off-key from somewhere they couldn't see me. And once in a while, I'd thump the microphone out of time, which drove the drummer completely berserk. But that was wrong, and I don't recommend you do it. It was hilarious, though…

11:15 PM: Now's your time to shine. The band has stopped playing and said, "We'll be back in a few minutes." There's a deafening silence in the bar. Most professional bands will usually give the DJ a signal that they're going off after the next song, so you can introduce yourself and say something clever like, "Let's give it up for this awesome band, Mike's Headache! They'll be back in a few, but while we're waiting, let's get on that dance floor!" But some of these band knuckleheads just don't care. Typically, you'll be finishing up your business in the bathroom and have to make a mad dash to your DJ rig. Many more dirty four-letter words come to even the most religious minds. Hopefully, you've already cued up a song so you can immediately raise the volume and begin your set. The band has warmed up the crowd, so these folks are ready to dance! You don't have to play the same type of music the band plays—most people will enjoy plain old dance music that's relevant to their age and ethnic group. When you become proficient at reading a crowd, you'll know exactly what to play, and your crowd will love you for it. Your dance floor will be exponentially more crowded than anything the band could generate. The band will sit and sulk and give you dirty looks from across the room. And five minutes before they come on for their next set, "THUMP, THUMP, THUMP…"

12:00 PM: You'll introduce the band once again, and here comes your second paid break. This time, you're feeling much more confident, since you had the crowd eating out of your hands. You had a full dance floor, and this band can only manage to get four of their groupies dancing. In many cases, especially during weeknight gigs, your shift is over. But you've got to hang out just in case something goes wrong with the band. You've been promoted to backup man. What the hell—you're getting paid for it, so kick back and enjoy.

12:45 PM: The crowd has thinned considerably, especially during weeknights. The band is done, and they're beginning to place their equipment squarely in the middle of the dance floor as they disassemble their rig, making it impossible for anyone to dance. Since the band is king, they can often decide when the night is over. A smart bar owner or manager will see this and prevent it from happening, since there might be several more beer and drink sales if people hang around and dance a little longer. But many bar managers are either drunk themselves or have brains the size of peanuts. Just throw something on and practice your beatmixing skills. Remember, you're still on the clock until the manager decides to close the bar.

CHAPTER 2

Performing in Adult Clubs

An Adult Club, also known as a "Gentlemen's Club," is a bar where scantily dressed female dancers gyrate their bodies while stripping down to not much more than a G-string bikini trying to earn cash tips from lonely or horny or lonely and horny men. The dancers typically "tip out" or pay the DJ, and also "pay the house" for the privilege of performing there. The bar function is entirely separate, and more removed from a DJ job in this situation. During my DJ career, I spent a few weeks working for an adult club in Philadelphia. I was offered a better position at a real club, so I was forced to cut my adult club experience short. Marc Pears, known in the adult club industry as "DJ Marky Mark," has about 15 years experience in the trade, and offers his tips here.

Back before 9/11, Pears used to earn thousands of dollars in tips per six to eight hour shift while working in some of the largest and most prominent adult bars in Manhattan. The economy subsequently tanked, as did his earnings. It's still a very comfortable living, according to Pears, but only if you're a true professional and you don't get caught up in all the craziness that exists in this business.

A TYPICAL ADULT CLUB SHIFT

12:00 PM: The lunch crowd starts to filter in. Depending on where you are, you'll usually see a broad mixture of white collar workers, blue collar workers, ages, and ethnicities. What's amazing is that all of these guys are pounding beers during their lunch hour, knowing they've got to get back to work! But that's not your concern. Your dancers will stop by to say hello and sign in with you. They might ask if you have a new song you could play for them during your shift, and you'll coolly and casually reply, "I'll see if I can get that on for you baby." You'll announce that Tiffany and Desiree are now coming to the main stage, and Candy is arriving at the second stage. You might be instructed to promote private table or couch dances, where a gentlemen pays ten to twenty dollars for a private three-minute dance. You'll play three short songs, then announce that Chocolate and Peaches are now moving to the main stage, Angel is coming to the second stage, and Tiffany, Desiree and Candy are now available for table dances. You'll continue this rotation over and over again, ensuring that there are always girls on the stage for the gentlemen customers to watch.

3:00 PM: You're amazed because some of your lunch crowd is still friggin' here! The blue collar construction worker who's shelling out twenties like they're candy enables you to finally understand why it takes five years and millions of dollars to fix an expressway. Whatever. Since the crowd has thinned, the girls are standing around, bored out of their skulls. Some come up to you to chat to kill some time. They'll ask you if you have a girlfriend, or if you're married. They'll ask what you thought of their performance. You'll ask "Bubbles" for her real name, and compliment her on how pretty her real name is, and how she strangely reminds you of a beautiful girl you once knew. If she's buying your crap and thinks you're an all right guy, she'll segue into telling you all about her abusive boyfriend that stole her credit cards and cheated on her with some other bitch dancer from another club. You listen and empathize, calling him a "rat bastard." You act genuinely surprised at "how anyone could possibly treat a beautiful flower like you with such disrespect." She gives you a hug, firmly pressing her silicon implants against your chest, and walks away smiling. Another satisfied customer.

5:00 PM: The blue-collar construction guy is drunk off his ass, and decides he needs to go check in. Hopefully, someone has called for a ride, or if he snuck out, he'll fall asleep in his truck before he takes to the road. The after work crowd starts to stumble in after a hard day at the office. Some will play it cool and go to the pool tables while watching these heavenly dancers out of the corner of their eyes. Others hide at the pool tables because they're too cheap to tip the dancers at the bar. Several new dancers have arrived for the after work shift, and you're responsible for working them in to your existing rotation. You've decided that Misty and Coco are to go on the main stage next, and Cinnamon has offered to give you twenty dollars if you keep her off stage because she wants to spend some extra time with some of her regular customers. After you graciously accept her cash, you smoothly tell her that you need her for the rotation right now, but depending on how many girls come in, you may be able to keep her off stage later if she goes on just this once.

6:00 PM: The late night DJ arrives and the shift change occurs. The daytime DJ passes on his rotation schedule to the night DJ, but only after making sure he's been tipped out by all the girls from his shift. A "feature act" is scheduled to perform tonight—"Silicon Sally," a nationally known porn star, will do two shows tonight. The manager is feverishly running around trying to prepare things while all the regular girls are giving him a dirty look. The late night DJ is usually more experienced and knows how to handle feature acts along with the typical dancer nonsense. He slips in virtually unnoticed, and the show goes on.

8:00 PM: The room is pretty busy now, and the level of anticipation for Silicone Sally is high. Sally's tour manager (usually her boyfriend *du jour*) has given you her music on a dirty, scratched CD. He instructs you to "Just play it the way it is. You won't need to make any introductions, because nationally known voice talent Chuck Fresh already recorded it on the disc." You curse me out for a moment, then decide that it's cool either because people might think that's your voice announcing the talent, or because you get to take a paid break. The lights come down, and the introduction begins. Silky Silicone Sally stalks then slithers on to the stage. The lights go bright as day as Sally's standing in the center of the stage with the brim of her sombrero reaching out nearly as far as her 48 double Ds. The crowd goes wild. Her show continues for fifteen minutes or so, and she sticks around to sign autographs and sell obscenely priced instant photographs with the customers. You slip back into your normal rotation for the next two hours until the silicone princess's next scheduled performance.

9:00 PM: The manager calls the DJ booth and says it's time for "Up Time." This means you get all the girls to line up offstage, and you'll then introduce them one at a time. Hopefully, you've learned their names and you can say something flattering about each of them as they strut across the bar. This is similar to a fashion show, but instead of showing off fashions, you're showing off your girls to all the customers. It's kind of a dumb routine and all the girls hate it, but many managers will ask you to do Up Time.

10:17 PM: Nothing spectacular ever happens at 10:17 PM in an adult club. Rock on and continue with your rotation until the wee hours of the morning.

CHAPTER 2

Women who work in adult clubs are master manipulators. They're actresses, doing everything they can do with their bodies and minds to get as much money out of men as possible. And the DJ is no exception. Pears says that you've got to come in strong from the beginning, and never let your guard down. You don't have to be a hardcase, but you've got to let these girls know that you're there to work and not to socialize like the customers the dancers are used to. You're the boss—you pick the rotation, you choose the music, and that's that. Pears also recommends that you be extremely organized. Create written lists for dancer rotations so there are no discrepancies—everything should be recorded in black and white.

Many new adult club DJs fall into the tender trap and are sweet-talked out of tips. And all these girls talk to each other—once one of them has screwed you over, you're pretty much permanently labeled as a loser. The girls have respect for professional DJs, and they'll test you any chance they get.

This job requires the least DJ training. Adult club or bar DJs don't need to concern themselves with beatmixing, scratching, or maintaining a dance floor. You're not the headlining entertainer, and you'll rarely ever be noticed by customers. You're part of the background operation. Your primary function is scheduling the dancers, and playing music that helps them get into their groove a little better. This job is more similar to that of a radio station DJ, only there are no commercial breaks, and you choose all the music. The sound and lighting equipment is part of a permanent installation, so you won't need to concern yourself with that either. However, you will need to deal with dancer attitudes, rampant illogical and unpredictable female emotions, and P.M.S. first hand, which can make any other DJ problems pale by comparison.

You'll be responsible for getting two to sixty dancers into a "rotation." This means you're responsible for arranging who performs when and where they'll be performing. Depending on the club, you may have several separate stages you'll have to manage. You'll announce on the microphone which girl is coming up on each of the stages, and you'll then rotate them every three songs (or roughly every nine minutes). Typically, you'll randomly pick who you want to dance on the main stage first. Some clubs have two girls perform on one stage simultaneously, and other clubs have smaller stages that can only accommodate one girl at a time. Depending on the shift you're working and the number of girls present, these rotations can vary widely. Most clubs have unwritten rules that take a while to understand, but are fairly simple once you get it.

And then there are the exceptions. Some girls hate dancing on the stages for a number of reasons, so they'll actually try to tip you to skip them in the stage rotation. If you've got a large number of dancers, you can usually skip a dancer or two and enjoy the additional cash. But if you've got a small pool of girls, you'll probably piss her off when you tell her you can't skip her in the rotation because you need her on stage. Not only do you lose those extra bucks, but now you've got a chick bad-mouthing you! In some of the more tightly run clubs, if a girl doesn't report to the stage during her rotation, she can be fined or fired. The difficulty of your job is determined by the level of cooperation of the management team. There's always the issue of the owner's favorite girls, who can do no wrong. They'll always make things miserable for you by skirting the rules with no penalty. Eventually, you'll learn how to deal with these exceptions, and how to say the right things at the right times to make your job as smooth as possible.

Each of these girls is required to "tip you out," meaning they all are required to give you a minimum dollar amount paid from their tips. Depending how much they like you and how well they did on their shift, some of the more generous girls can provide a quite lucrative bonus. Some of these dancers can get lucky and hook up with an intoxicated wealthy dude that'll spoil them with tips that can reach thousands of dollars in one shift! In some clubs, you'll have to troll around yourself and try to collect from each of these girls at the end of your shift. In better clubs, the "house mom" (an older, more responsible, usually retired dancer who looks after the girls) will do this for you. The average major-market minimum tip-out is ten to twenty dollars per dancer, plus whatever else they want to throw in.

What's best about this particular industry is the sheer number of shifts that must be filled. Some of these bars are open 24 hours a day, seven days a week! This provides oodles of DJ job opportunities. Typically, shifts are broken down into six or eight hour shifts. It's a lot of time on your feet, but you'll be pretty busy so it'll seem to pass quickly.

The most important thing you can possibly do is *memorize all the dancer's names* as quickly as possible. This will give you tons of the respect you'll need to be successful in this industry.

Performing in After Hours Clubs

Due to "grandfather clauses" of liquor license laws, bars that have had liquor licenses since the beginning of time are allowed to continue to use those licenses subject to their original terms, which may or may not match the current laws. Most of the time, older licenses have later closing times than newer licenses. If all bars in your state are required to close at 2:00 AM, a bar with an old liquor license can skip the earlier closing and stay open until the time issued on his or her old liquor license after invoking its grandfather clause. Obviously, drinking age and other laws cannot be superceded by an old liquor license; only its closing time. Some after hours bars without a liquor license are restricted to soda, juice, water, and coffee sales.

After hours bars are typically housed in dirty, dark, old rooms. They don't have to look pretty due to simple supply and demand. There are very few after hours bars, so they've got the luxury of always turning a profit with little to no promotional expenses. Many people call after hours bars "last chance saloons," since most single folks go to these bars because they failed to hook up at the last bar they were hanging out at that was forced to close at 2:00 AM.

These bars typically begin as wannabe real nightclubs, but don't make it in the mainstream. So they've settled for the after hours thing. I've seen after hours clubs located in old warehouses, strip malls, VFW lodges, and a number of other scattered places.

Performing in an after hours club is fairly easy, since your audience is already charged up from the last place. All you'll need to do is bust out the funky jams, chase the roaches out of your DJ booth, and start rockin' the house. Your shift will usually start an hour or two before the big clubs dump out so you've got time to warm up. Since you're already starting late at night, these shifts don't usually run over three or four hours. Most of these clubs get their big hits right about at the legal club closing time and then for a solid hour afterwards. Since you don't need to build, just hit your people with the latest and most popular jams.

Typical Club and Bar Equipment

If you're providing your own equipment for a bar or club account, you may want to use equipment that's a bit more durable that traditional wedding DJ equipment. If you're scheduled for multiple nights, chances are you're going to leave your equipment in the room. Even if you specifically state that you don't want other people to use it when you're not there, some knucklehead bartender who's a wannabe DJ is going to fire it up and unscientifically test its durability. In my experience, bar and club equipment tends to get beat up much more than regular mobile DJ equipment. You're usually using it several nights a week, and it often gets used as furniture and drink stands by wilder crowds.

If you're lucky enough to get a club account that has its own sound system, do your homework and know the club's equipment. Remember that if your system sounds like crap, people are going to look at you like it's your fault. You'll need to know the basic physics of sound before you can truly understand any components.

The most important element of the physical sound system used in a dance club is the bass. Bass is like a magnet to the dance floor—people seem to find it easier to dance when they can feel the bass in their feet. Invest in a separate bass bin and a separate amplifier if you're providing the equipment for your club account; and be sure to ask for sufficient bass if your club provides the sound system.

There are tons of resources on the Internet, and there are salespeople at your local sound equipment vendor who can give you some excellent tips on the best amplification equipment for your room. Make sure you don't undercut the sound needs of your room. Requirements are based on the type of music you're going to play at your club, the size of the room, the shape of the room, and the amount of people you'll expect on a busy night. Big clubs have all this information calculated using complex geometric formulas implemented by professional sound installation companies.

Let's start from top to bottom, beginning with the equipment you'll need to know how to use first hand, and ending with a quick review of supporting equipment that's usually there and needs little to no adjustment. We'll go more in depth with these components in a later chapter.

Turntables and CD Players

The first line of equipment is the component that actually plays the music. If your bar is still living in the 70s and using vinyl, you'll probably find a pair of old, dirty, direct-drive turntables. These turntables hold their speed much better than the cheaper belt drive turntables. Since you'll be adjusting speed, the consistency is important. I like the good old original Technics 1200s turntables, which fortunately have been the industry standard for a few decades (Figure 2.4). They've got an amazing durability record and a really fast response time, and their heavy weight and adjustable tonearms help to avoid skipping. They're a pleasure to use if you spin vinyl.

Technics' world famous 1200 turntable (SL-1210M5G).

If your bar is set up to use Compact Discs, I like Denon dual CD players (Figure 2.5). They're as reliable as CD players get. Like most professional turntables, Denon pro CD players have speed (pitch) adjustment controls that you'll need when you beatmix. You can manually set cue points, which is a big help when beatmixing or playing songs with unusually long or non-danceable introductions.

Denon's DN-D9000 Dual
CD deck.

Some newer clubs have gone fully digital, using a specially engineered computer and a program like PCDJ. All the music should already be loaded into the computer, and there's usually a CD drive that can read any music that's not already there. These systems can be very awkward to use depending on the software and external controllers provided. DJ RAK (Figure 2.6) builds terrific digital systems with controllers that are very similar to Denon's CD controllers, which makes these digital DJ systems much easier to use.

The DJ RAK Digital DJ System.

It's important to know that all kinds of mishaps can occur regardless of your choice of media, whether they're spinning discs of plastic, metal, or vinyl. Turntable ground connectors can fall off, producing a really nasty and annoying hum that's amplified through your system. Needles clog with dust, producing a strange muffled sound if the needle doesn't just slide across the record. Vinyl or plastic records get scratched and skip, especially if you're messing around with scratching. CD players can skip if your discs are dirty, or if the unit is bumped or shaken. I've even seen a CD player have a computer-like crash, where it needed to be turned off and reset. Your responsibility is to cover your ass and be ready for these problems not if they happen, but when they happen. Get into the practice of carrying spare cartridges and needles and even spare CD players if you have the means. Unlike most jobs, if something goes wrong while you're DJing in front of hundreds or even thousands of people, the silence will let everyone know something is wrong. And most crowds are merciless. They'll let out a "boo" that can be heard for miles around, making you feel three inches tall.

Mixers, Headphones, Speakers, and Amps

A "mixer" is a standalone unit that combines the electronic music signals from your music components and delivers that signal to the amplifier for amplification (Figure 2.7). One of my favorite mixers is the Urei 1620, which I still use, but unfortunately is discontinued and no longer made. This unit has no on or off switch, and I've left one on for over five continuous years. It looks pretty beat up, but it has never overheated, never made crackling sounds when raising or lowering volumes using its smooth-as-butter knobs—nothing but freakin' perfection.

The Rane Electronics
MP2016 Rotary Mixer.

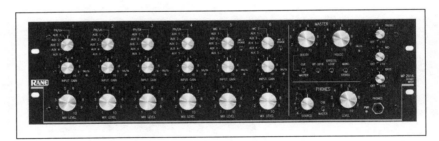

Some DJs like individual sliders with a cross fader, and others (usually old schoolers like myself) like knobs. I believe knobs give you better control with a single adjustment, rather than forcing you to adjust separate gain or volume controls. I prefer individual controls because most CDs are "cut" (recorded) at different volumes. With my individual level controls, I can compensate for this difference in volume immediately. If you plan to work in a bar that plays heavy dance music, you may prefer a mixer with a cross fader, which is a single slider that automatically brings the volume of one channel of music down while bringing the new song in. Many DJs prefer the cross fader. There's not much of a difference in the resulting sound, and crowds don't care what you use. It all depends what you learned with or what style of mixing you want to pursue.

You're going to need a headphone or a headset for cueing up and mixing upcoming songs. Back in the day, DJ Rich Huber showed me how to chop an old Radio Shack stereo headset in half and make two single cup headsets. He liked those because they rested nicely between his shoulder and ear. These cups were also the loudest, most bass responsive headphone I could find at the time. There are a bunch of specially designed DJ headsets available on the market today that are as good as or better than our chopped headsets.

The mixer sends a processed electronic signal through wires to your amplifier (or to a "cross-over," if you have multiple amplifiers). If your boss has cut corners and doesn't have the proper amplifiers and speakers for the room, chances are that sooner or later, in the middle of that unexpected killer night when the bar's on track to set new sales records, that amplifier is gonna crash. And who is everyone going to look at? Who's the manager going to blame? *You.* Been there, done that. All amplifiers are built with a specific power rating in mind. While engineers typically expect you to abide by conservative engineering rules and play clean, controlled sounds through their amplifiers, in reality an eternal conflict exists. The energy of a room (or their level of hearing loss) always seems to tell DJs to make things louder, pushing their amplifiers to and beyond recommended limits. And that's when problems occur.

Speakers are the hapless losers in this equation. They sit quietly hanging in a corner somewhere, and just take all the abuse the amplifier hands them. Hopefully, the sound engineer has installed sound limiters, or has correctly installed speakers with expectations that greatly exceed the potential RMS power of the amplifier. I've "blown" several speakers by applying too much amplifier power and actually cracking the paper or urethane "cone" attached to the magnet, which is the unit that vibrates and ultimately produces sounds we hear. I've even "smoked" a speaker—the cone actually caught fire briefly one night! Wasn't my bad (that time), the sound guy installed the wrong cone into the custom cabinet.

We'll get into the physics of sound and sound equipment a little later. You'll really need to understand the basics of how it all works to get the best possible performance. Don't worry, I've made it as fun and understandable as possible.

Lights and Special Effects

Crowd energy is an obvious phenomenon brought about by not so obvious means. It's the positive feeling you notice when you walk into a room and you decide that you like what you feel, so it makes you want to stay there longer. But it's not just you; everyone else seems to be upbeat and happy too, although no one can quite explain why they feel that way. It's almost as if someone cast a magical spell over everyone in the room! All bars and clubs strive to create this energy, and the most successful bars have plenty of it consistently.

Like sound, correctly placed lights can create all kinds of subliminal energy in a room. This kind of energy feeds off itself and creates even more energy. Light energy makes your job easier and adds to your success. To illustrate, imagine a plain room with four walls and some light bulbs hanging from the ceiling. Pretty boring. Now make those lights flash on and off. Add color to the lights while they're flashing. Now add some subtle and sinister movements to those lights so they're dashing and darting all over the room. Add some flashes from a strobe. Can you see the difference? All the sudden the room is alive and full of energy.

It's amazing how something as simple as blinking colored lights adds a degree of energy to your room. If you're fortunate enough to work in a club that has "intelligent" (computer controlled) lighting, you've got a whole new set of really wild tools that will help your show become even better. If you're providing the equipment for your club, pick up a few cheap moving lights to help energize your show. You can get some smaller fixtures for as little as $100 a piece. I recall a nightclub in Philadelphia instructing their bouncers to wave their flashlights over the dance floor to create a cheap laser-like effect. It looked kind of cool when the lights were lowered.

Strobes are the only form of lighting you have to be careful with. I've had people complain that they were prone to epileptic seizures with the use of strobe lights. I've kept this in mind, and now I voluntarily curb my use of strobes. I use them for very short blasts only during songs that have pronounced drum roll type effects.

All special effects, including strobes and other intelligent high-powered lights, tend to lose their dramatic effect if overused. They also burn high temperature halogen bulbs that are expensive and a pain to replace. Make sure you use these sparingly, but don't hesitate to incorporate them into your show.

Some major clubs have huge "intelligent light" shows run by a special programmable controller that hopefully has some cool presets already programmed. Intelligent lighting has fixtures that you can program to change color, direction, gobo, beam size, and brightness. Running intelligent lighting on random presets is anti-intelligent. Folks who spend thousands of dollars on intelligent lights and don't use them intelligently are silly. If you run into any, ask them to send me a check so I can sit around and do nothing too.

High End systems has some insane new products including their DL1 digital light. That bad boy isn't just a plain old intelligent light, it can actually project captured video images. With a little fog, it can project three dimensional images of several colors simultaneously. There are new innovations in this field all the time.

Other clubs might use a dedicated computer using software like Martin's Light Jockey programs. Busy clubs with a good budget will usually hire a separate person who gets paid to operate these lights. If you're not lucky enough to get your own "light man," you can usually get someone at the bar or an off duty DJ to help you run your lights for free during prime time if you ask them nicely and show them the basics.

The DL1 Digital Light.

There are several special effects available created specifically to enhance light shows. "Fog" is the most important and popular special effect. Oil or water based fog kind of hangs out in the air and reflects the light beams, so it appears there's a laser-like continuous three-dimensional beam shooting across your room. Intelligent lighting can produce hologram-type effects with enough fog.

Bubbles are the next most popular special effect. Lights shine on the bubbles as they fall from tubes in the ceiling creating an almost diamond sparking effect. The problem with bubbles is that they can be extremely slippery, causing an insurance nightmare for a club owner. I understand there are now non-slip bubble formulas, which is very cool, although I can't imagine how that's possible.

Some clubs have built in snow machines that shoot either plain white confetti, or some kind of foamy substance. Similar to bubbles, snow machines produce a cool effect when combined with different colored and patterned lights.

Foam parties have been and will continue to be the darlings of the Spring Break type crowds who don't mind jumping into a pool of suds to dance and frolic. Lighting effects are often shined into the foam, creating some really interesting lines.

Kabuki confetti launchers, although not really lights or lighting effects, also is a cool special effect that should be mentioned. Manual and automatic launchers shoot a stream of string confetti or traditional confetti across the dance floor, usually emphasized by a light show. The firing of these carbon dioxide launchers is usually controlled by the DJ.

Using Video

The latest DJ innovation is the incorporation of video into the show. Due to the widespread availability of inexpensive LCD or DLP projectors and plasma screen monitors, DJs are now able to run promotional messages and show digital photographs of the guests or featured artists almost instantly during their shows. Many bars fail to see the potential of these in-house marketing tools, and opt to leave the channel set to some sports or news network.

Several companies now produce videos made especially for bar and club situations. The same companies that produce promotional CD compilations also produce DVD compilations with the video versions of popular songs. There are "ambient videos," which are nothing more than colors and shapes screaming across your video screens that resemble a bad acid trip. There are historical video segments that are also in the ambient category that show silly things like those historical train crashes and rocket launch mishaps. And digital DJs have something called a "Visualizer," which creates pretty cool colorful patterns that follow the beats of a song. Some bars actually have installed video cameras that allow you to watch yourself dancing on a huge projection screen. Gnarly.

Like lighting, video is a special effect. It's not as "in your face" as lighting, but video can be instrumental in showing people a good time. And like any special effect, overuse of the same exact effect kills the desired reaction.

There's actually an entire branch of nightclub and bar DJs who use primarily video known as Video Jockeys, or "VJs." A VJ manipulates video similar to the way that a DJ mixes records, only they've got an additional sense to excite. Now that Pioneer Electronics offers a unit that can play DVDs with pitch (speed) control, it's actually possible to beatmix videos for the first time in history.

CHAPTER 2

Bar Games and Special Promotions

In reality, the DJs who people talk about and get the big paying gigsusually aren't master mixers or great scratchers—they're the DJs who put on a full interactive show. They host compelling and often crazy contests and promotions that get everyone involved. Reading a crowd and then creating, producing, and executing relevant contests and promotions is probably the most difficult challenge a club DJ faces. You can practice mixing and scratching in your bedroom until your fingers fall off. But there's only one way to figure out what people will respond to—and that's by trial and error. Those who took chances and failed occasionally learned what works and how to make what works even cooler. If your goal is to become the next legendary nightclub or bar DJ, prepare to spend a lot of time being embarrassed by things that don't work out. Learn from your mistakes, and realize the eventual payoff can be immense.

I've hosted contests and promotions that ranged from lame corporate-sponsored events to avant-garde frenzies that I created and promoted myself. While working my clubs and researching others all over the country, I realized that the most successful promotions and contests were the ones walking a fine line between political correctness and reckless disregard for society. There really is no authority on contests and promotions. There are a few companies that dabble in it, providing promotions in conjunction with large corporate sponsors who are worried about public relations. But there are not many people that I've met or heard of that can effectively complete the following business specific tasks:

* Totally relate to the clientele of a specific room. You must spend a lot of time with your guests to really know what's going on.

* Analyze what's going on in your room. Listen to the comments. Leave your DJ booth once in a while and get involved in customer conversations. If your customers don't talk about their likes or dislikes, then you solicit issues. Ask leading questions like "Do you like this music?", or "Do you think this promotion will work well in this bar?"

* Evaluate local dynamics and competition from a customer's point of view. Get into their heads and their friends' heads. Hang out with them. Go where they go. Do what they do. Learn what really makes them tick.

* Recognize the total potentiality of a room. Analyze all the factors of success in your room and in all your competitors' rooms, then figure out a strategy by which you can combine all the winning factors in your own room and kick their butts.

* Develop a formal strategy for improvement based on the above findings. It's not easy to do. But if you're successful, you've just graduated from DJ to DJ/consultant, and you've got one hell of an addition to your resume and promotional pack.

Every town has its hot clubs. And every hot club has at least one specific big night (two or more if they're smart). That big night was probably created via a dynamic of internal and external promotion combined with an element of word of mouth that amplified the initial investment. Something big happened at that place, and whatever it was, everyone had a need to talk about it. Sometimes one huge event on a certain night is all you need as a catalyst for a successful night, as long as you're ready to follow it up with equal coolness.

It's common knowledge that in everyday conversation, most people feel a need to tell a story. It makes us feel important. It makes us feel needed. And if it's a really good story, it often elevates our social standing. You, as a DJ and crowd leader, can have people amplify whatever message you want to send.

The hype and spin you devise that's successfully vocally transmitted to the families, friends and coworkers of your customers is collectively known as "the buzz."

Unfortunately, the same dynamic applies in a converse situation. If your club has held several half-assed events that totally sucked, or even worse, done nothing at all for an extended period of time, you may already be labeled as the bar to avoid. At this point, in most cases, it's time to close the bar's doors for a few weeks, change the bar's name and wallpaper, slap on some new paint, lick your wounds, and do it the right way next time.

Whether you're in the black or kissing the red, know that you'll need to consistently make a lot of noise to achieve and continue success in this business.

With all that said, I've included some fun bar games that adults of drinking age and older can participate in. You may need to recruit some assistants and maybe some extra security for some of these games. Some require big bucks, some are free, and some might even earn you a buck or two. Some of these contests and promotions are great for their entertainment value. They can also be good at breaking the ice and getting people together. Some are a bit more risqué than your run-of-the-mill promotion, so you've got to choose if being politically correct is more important to your employer than making money. Make sure you've had that conversation with your boss before you go and pull any of this stuff off. In most cases, the bar manager will develop and pay for promotions, but they'll always appreciate your input.

First things first. You'll need to a boatload of numbered raffle tickets, which will be used to randomly select participants for various contests and promotions. I recommend getting tickets with space on the back for the contestant's name and address. This can be used to verify the identity of the person who is called to participate so there's no ticket swapping, and more importantly, you could use these names to build and update your mailing list for future marketing and promotions.

The Law

Definitely review your own state's laws and regulations before going gung-ho with some of the Adult contests in this book, or you could get in trouble. Some states are a little more lenient than others when deciding what they'll permit in venues authorized for liquor consumption.

Georgia happens to be one of the tougher states, and might be a good basis to determine what you can and can't do until you've had a chance to review your own laws. We've pulled this right from Georgia's liquor laws of 2001, section 3-3-41.

> A. No person shall perform on licensed premises acts of or acts which constitute or simulate:
>
> 1. Sexual intercourse, masturbation, sodomy, bestiality, oral copulation, flagellation, or any sexual acts which are prohibited by law;
>
> 2. The touching, caressing, or fondling of the breast, buttocks, anus, or genitals; or
>
> 3. The displaying of any portion of the female breast below the top of the areola or the displaying of any portion of any person's pubic hair, anus, cleft of the buttocks, vulva, or genitals.

CHAPTER 2

B. No person shall use on licensed premises artificial devices or inanimate objects to perform, simulate, or depict any of the prohibited conduct or activities described in subsection (a) of this Code section.

C. It shall be unlawful for any person to show, display, or exhibit, on licensed premises, any film, still picture, electronic reproduction, or any other visual reproduction or image of any act or conduct described in subsection (A) or (B).

It shall be unlawful for any operator to employ, encourage, permit, or assist any person to engage in any conduct or activity in violation of this article. The violation of any provision of this article by the operator of any licensed premises shall constitute grounds for the suspension and revocation of any and all alcoholic beverage licenses issued to such operator. Any person who violates any provision of this article shall be guilty of a misdemeanor of a high and aggravated nature.

Ouch! That means you could be arrested and thrown in the slammer for being naughty. What's worse, the owner or manager could be arrested too, which might not reflect upon you in a positive way. Know the rules, and don't take silly chances.

The Five-Step Plan for Successful Promotions

Here's a "primer" that may help explain more clearly what's important in executing successful events. One of my companies, Bar Marketing, has shared this with thousands of bars and nightclubs all over the world, so it's important that you, as a DJ, know what I'm telling people.

Promotions won't usually work well at a dance-only club. Since most clubs are not dance-only clubs, you'll have more opportunities as a working DJ to implement promotions. They're not meant to completely dominate a night, only to provide a fun break from dancing. In a dance-only club, all you'll be worried about is providing a constant beat.

Most normal folks are inherently lazy and incredibly boring. The reason they watch TV and movies is to achieve the kind of stimulation that the real world, including most bars, just can't provide. And with all this terrorism crap, pyrotechnics fires, and stampede scares, things are even worse. This may explain why some people have shifted their disposable income to different types of entertainment and away from our bars. We know how to solve these problems and bring these lazy folks back, and we're going to share this information with you in a five-step plan that you can implement immediately.

Step One: Market Wisely, Market Well

Even if you've got the best, biggest, wildest, most expensive promotion in the world, no one's going to come to your party if they haven't heard about it. You can and should alert people in many ways. Marketing can be expensive, but so is any other worthwhile investment.

You must let your potential guest know what's happening or what's coming up via flyers, or radio and newspaper advertising if you can afford it. Unless you've got a great creative team working for you, don't let the radio station or newspaper design your ad—they're often too busy to devote the time and resources necessary to create great advertising. Plus, since they do it for free, they have no incentive to create great ads for you or their other hundreds of advertisers all competing for space. It's definitely worthwhile to hire an outside firm who's getting paid to create your ads.

Invest in grass-roots marketing to get your message directly to the people to reinforce your paid advertising. You should always have your friends, family, staff, DJs, and other paid promoters distribute flyers and general word of mouth well in advance of your promotions.

If you're planning a big public party, always send press releases to let your local radio and TV stations and newspapers know what's going on, because your wild promotions are newsworthy! Many folks don't realize that newspapers are always looking for stories to fill their empty space, and a well crafted press release makes their job much easier. Call the newspaper yourself and find out the name and contact information for the most appropriate reporter, then mail, email, or fax your press release directly to that person.

Be sure that you keep in mind that by generating press, you're creating an image for your club in the public's mind. If you're doing pretty wild stuff, you may get labeled as the local rebel, and some busybodies with nothing better to do may get upset and try to cause some political trouble for you. In many cases, it's good to be the bad boy of your market, as long as you control the spin. Carefully craft your press releases to show that you're promoting innocent fun. The worst thing you can do is let that spin get out of control. Don't get labeled as a drug infested mob hangout where people are routinely murdered!

Step Two: Choose Relevant Promotions

People have seen and heard about wet t-shirt contests for well over thirty years. You would thing it would be boring and way overdone, but for whatever reason, these contests still attract one heck of a crowd! Figure out what makes your crowd tick. Is it sex, money, humor, or all of the above? Create contests and promotions that push your customers' buttons, and keep pushing the limit to keep things interesting.

Step Three: Create and Maintain Excitement

When you've chosen a great promotion, choose a complimentary reward or giveaway, and promote the hell out of it! To keep your costs contained, in addition to tapping your local Anheuser Busch rep's deep promotional pockets, solicit and work with other local complimentary businesses, such as malls, auto dealerships, sporting goods stores, electronics stores, travel agencies, music stores, and anyone else who has half a brain and understands the power of cross promoting to your captive audience. Offer something big, flashy, and almost unbelievable to the winners of your contests. I've seen bars give away exotic trips, shopping sprees, and even cars, trucks, boats and motorcycles.

It's also important to keep the excitement fresh. Don't run any single promotion longer than three or four weeks at the most. The best promotions can be completed in one single night, often within the space of 30 minutes when planned, practiced, and executed properly. People will get tired of things quickly, so always keep things moving.

Step Four: Add the Entertainment Factor

As with any promotion, the key element should always be entertainment. This requires preparation, practice, and sometimes requires an artificial boost via staged events. There is absolutely nothing wrong with soliciting or hiring a bunch of professional actors or models to participate in your promotions, especially the wilder ones! Normal people tend to do normal, boring things, if you can get them involved at all. Inherently, we're voyeurs as a society. So give the people what they want—give them a show!

Bar Marketing is assembling a crew of actors and actresses who will get paid to participate in wild promotions at clubs and bars all over the country. Tons of people are looking to break in to show business, and you can help them add things to their resumes. You too can follow our example by taking classified ads in your local newspaper stating something like:

> **WANTED**: Actors and Actresses for Wild Nightclub Promotions. Earn money while competing for large cash prizes. Must be 21 or older. Call Mark at 555-5555.

And in a sneaky but valiant effort to boost your DJ salary, we've been telling bar managers and owners to "never skimp on an MC." He or she is the person who can make or break your promotion, no matter how well it was planned! Find someone who's good looking, glowing, extremely quick witted and just oozing personality. I definitely recommend auditioning and hiring a professional for any promotion. Hopefully, you are that professional.

Step Five: Follow It Up

Make sure the radio stations and newspapers are talking about what happened. Show pictures on your website or flyers of real people doing crazy things. Shoot videotape and play it on your monitors. Reinforce the fun people had by proving how much fun they had. Use these steps during any promotion any night of the week, and watch how sales and attendance increase during your shifts!

The Games

Now, for the good stuff. One of my books titled "Make Some Noise" has over 200 fun bar contests and promotions. I've included a few of the more relevant ones here to aid you in your conquest to become the coolest, most innovative, most interactive, highest paid nightclub and bar DJ in your area. They're also perfect for many types of private parties. Have fun with these—I did!

The Shuffle Golf Challenge

If you or your pals are golfers, this is an incredibly fun and challenging contest for you (Figure 2.9). My bar manager, the legendary Ronny Capps, and I were walking through the Nightclub and Bar show in Las Vegas and we noticed two never-ending legs dressed in a teeny tiny little miniskirt putting a golf ball on what looked like a shuffleboard mat. Of course, we had to stop and investigate this matter. We found Shuffle Golf to be simply a cross between shuffleboard and putting without a cup. You use a golf putter to putt a ball into the scoring areas.

It's not really golf, so you don't have to be a great golfer to do well at this game. There's no brute physical strength required to be successful, so there's no advantage for males or intimidation for females. And we created a twist so that there's an advantage to getting the lowest score, so it was actually cool to lose. This was the perfect happy hour promotion!

The Shuffle Golf Challenge

We did this at a bar every Thursday at 7:00 PM, usually a dead time for us—until we started this contest! At least 50 people came to our bar every week for a chance to win up to $500 in cash, and most of them brought two or more friends or coworkers with them. Although Ron Capps was largely responsible for taking a chance with the implementation of this contest, I was elevated from a DJ to a "hero."

We left the Shuffle Golf mat available for people to practice hours before the actual contest, which created an even better buildup. The amazing thing was that no one really got good at this game, no matter how long they practiced! Since there's no real cup, there's no way to perfectly putt the ball so it stops in a certain area. Even in real golf, a putt into a cup would probably overshoot the cup in most situations if the cup were flat.

Announce that numbered tickets would be given out about 15 minutes prior to the competition. You could have a scantily dressed hottie chose up to 20 contestants at random. And to avoid anyone feeling like a loser, you could offer a special prize or drawing for those who hold a ticket but do not get to play. Consolation prizes might include leftover beer or liquor giveaways. Everyone felt like a winner.

At playtime, whoop up the crowd to get everyone excited, announcing your top prize. Read the few rules and procedures of play.

The Shuffle Golf mat, produced by the Shuffle Golf Company in Colorado (www.shufflegolf.com), has two sets of playing areas, one that's in a square formation, and the other that's more naturally curved. Both areas are separated by point values, meaning that if the ball stops in that area, the contestant is awarded the number of points in that particular area. I didn't notice much of a difference in higher scores one way or the other, playing about 50 games in each direction over two years.

Allow each contestant to putt 5 plain old golf balls from anywhere behind either of the set of numbers on the special Shuffle Golf carpet in an effort to score as many points as possible out of a potential perfect score of 50, or a potentially terrible negative score of -2 to as little as -25, depending which way you're playing.

In the event a ball lands on a line between two point areas, the some predetermined "official" (usually the bar manager) should make the final and indisputable point call depending on what area he or she determines the most surface area of the golf ball is in. If the ball lands between the green and a point area, the official makes a judgment whether or not points are allowed, again, based on where the most surface area of the ball is. If it seems too close to call, allow the higher point total by default.

Let everyone take their turn at putting. If someone beats your current high score—ours started at 23 points (a number some golfer in our bar said was a reasonable goal to start with), and got as high as 37 over the two years I was involved with this contest—you can award a $250 grand prize. If no one beats the high score, simply award a lesser cash prize to the highest score that week. I have never seen anyone score more than three 10 point scores, although theoretically it is possible to hit all five into the 10 point area. But don't bet the house on it—we've seen weirder things happen! Start low and try it for a few weeks to see how your crowd does.

The overall lowest score of the week qualifies for what we affectionately called "The Beer Zone." The lowest score always won a free beer of his or her choice. So even if someone's score really sucked, we made it fun to lose (after we made fun of that contestant). Try this—you won't believe the fierce competition over that coveted beer!

We added a few neat things to our traditional competition that made the popularity of this promotion explode. We borrowed one from a TV game show called the "Daily Double." We'd pre-select and mark one of the chosen numbered tickets at random. When the MC called that person, we announced that this was "Today's Daily Double!," and we played some funky music to enhance this part of the contest. Anything this person won, if they won anything, would be doubled. This enables you to advertise that you are awarding up to twice the normal prize money! (We were burned only once in 52 weeks, having to shell out an extra $50, and never an extra beer.) The added pressure of this situation usually causes people to choke.

In our competition, we usually removed the balls immediately after they stopped and their scores were counted. Some people prefer to leave the balls on the playing area, and not counting the points until all five balls have been putted. The latter method allows the contestant to knock previously putted balls into or out of point areas. Although we don't have much experience with leaving the balls in the playing area, we did not see much variance in point totals, since the balls had an equal chance of being knocked into another point area or out of the point areas altogether. Note that is virtually impossible to score 50 points if you leave the balls in the playing area, simply because the small, round, red 10 point area is too small to realistically contain more than two or three balls.

A big part of the Shuffle Golf Challenge is a powerful host. Have him or her tease your crowd before the contest starts so that your guests will beg to participate. And during the contest, do a play-by-play while promoting upcoming events. We recommend a $100 cash prize for one-time winners, with the $250 prize available if someone beats the high score. Token prizes such as cool t-shirts or hats for second and third place are a nice touch.

An even better way to boost the popularity of this contest is to create your own "Masters Tournament," complete with a large prize and a green jacket for the champ. Once every quarter, we would invite all the weekly winners back to compete for the quarterly championship, where we'd offer some type of incremental prize, like a trip to a famous golf course complete with accommodations and greens fees. In a bar or club situation, it's a terrific way to encourage repeat visits. Obviously, your contestants will invite their friends and co-workers, creating several small parties.

You'll need the Shuffle Golf playing carpet that you can rent for about $200 for a few hours, or I'd buy one because I'm sure you and your guests will all want to play this again at your next parties. You can order these at www.barmarketing.com. You'll also need a putter and five golf balls.

Here are some cool variations you can use to keep things exciting:

❊ **Shuffle Golf Ball Drop**. This removes the perceived benefit of letting people line their shots up by putting the ball from anywhere behind the white line separating the numbers from the green area. We'd have a hot chick drop the ball, and the contestant would have to putt from wherever the ball lands. This adds some serious sex appeal to this contest.

❊ **Shuffle Golf Bumpers**. This requires a set of 3" wide wood bumpers that surround the target point areas, and contestants are allowed to bounce their balls into the point areas. We don't have much experience with this mode of play, but we did notice that playing with the bumpers would probably have led to higher point totals, since the balls would bounce off them and roll back into point areas rather than falling off the mat completely. In our method of play, we used to call any balls that hit the bumper "dead and out of play."

❊ **Shuffle Golf Obstacles**. We've added obstacles on the playing field that make this game even more difficult! We'd use bowling pins, hockey pucks, beer bottles, or whatever we had lying around the room. Balls were allowed to ricochet off the obstacles into the point areas.

❊ **Crazy Shuffle Golf**. This involves using your choice of four or five regular golf balls, plus one bonus ball, a "joke" golf ball. The joke ball is one of those "unputtable" golf balls that wiggles unnaturally all over the mat.

❊ **Twister Golf**. I was really bored early one night at a nightclub in Princeton, NJ. As I was smacking golf balls around the room with the putter forcing the bartenders to duck for cover, I dug into my bag of tricks and found an old Twister playing mat that was in pretty good shape. Then the light bulb lit—let's try to figure out a game called "Twister Golf!" I set up a mini putting green on the stage, and placed the Twister Mat next to the putting area. I had my assistant spin the Twister once for each foot to determine what my putting stance would be, and that's where the fun begins. It's golf with a twist! This game is played in a manner very similar to the Twister game itself, but the spinner is used to determine the position of the feet only. The spinner is used twice; once for the left foot and once for the right foot. Each foot must be placed on the color that the contestant spins for that foot. This leads to some very interesting putting stances! We gave prizes to the person who sank the most consecutive putts from his or her randomly selected stance. This is a nice promotion that can be done with golfers and non-golfers, since the playing field is leveled. If you take a golfer out of his natural stance, you take away most of his or her edge.

❊ **Twister Shuffle Golf**. Here is a variation on our wildly popular Twister Golf (see above). Instead of having the perceived benefit of putting from your normal stance, make your contestants spin a Twister wheel, then place their feet on the appropriately colored dots on the Twister mat. Your contestants will be forced to putt in weird positions, such as Right Foot Red and Left Foot Green. This will totally mess everyone up, but it's funny to watch! Let these folks place the ball anywhere behind the first set of numbers.

Thumb Wrestling Championships

So mud wrestling, arm wrestling and sumo wrestling might be a little much for your crowd. Here's something you can get the average Joe to do! You can even put men against women in this contest. The object is to find the ultimate thumb wrestler in your room.

Start with two, four or eight groups of two contestants to keep things simple. Just like most of us did when we were kids, have your contestants interlock their right hands with their thumbs exposed and ready to go. They touch thumbs to the opposite sides of the other person's hand three times, then come out wrestling! The object is to manage to hold the other person's thumb down for a count of three, using only your thumb. The only rule is that they must all keep their hands flat on the table. Separate each semifinal by about 20-30 minutes to build up the excitement of your final competition.

At the finals, stop the music and incite all kinds of fanfare. Mention that you have a really cool prize for the official thumb wrestling champion. If you've got the budget or a hot looking lady available, have her act as a model or "ring girl" to present the winner with a printed winner banner and a small trophy. Silly over-indulgence in ceremony is what makes this contest really fun.

The Couch Potato Olympics

Many typical men spend most of their time off with their butts in a recliner or on a couch, so here's an opportunity to let them show you that they haven't been wasting time! The Couch Potato Olympics lets big burly men (or women) show you just how talented they've become with a series of interesting events, including:

- **The Remote Control Relay**. Contestants are asked to search a typical VCR tape or DVD and pause on a predetermined randomly located scene from a movie, such as someone smiling, someone crying, an explosion, or a favorite scene from your favorite movie or chick flick. The tapes are rewound to the beginning before each contestant begins. We liked to use the fake orgasm scene from *When Harry Met Sally*, but you can use anything your little heart desires.

- **Trail Mix Masher**. Each contestant must completely finish a typical bag of trail mix, down to the last crumbs in the bag before advancing to the next event. You can substitute chips, pretzels, or even peanut butter sandwiches if you're the cruel type. Make sure your contestant is not allergic to peanuts!

- **Beer Guzzler**. After downing the salty trail mix, the contestant must completely drink a large bottle of beer (if of legal drinking age, otherwise you can substitute non-alcoholic beer or seltzer). We used the "oil can" version of Fosters beer, or a 45-ounce Colt 45 for fun.

- **Audible Dynamics**. After the beer and trail mix, your contestant must produce a single audible burp, and one single audible fart. Silent but deadly farts do not count. Have your contestant bounce around on the couch to "shake it up" before he or she does this for dramatic effect. We handed our contestants a wireless microphone for the big sound! If the contestant could not produce the desired sound within one minute, he or she was disqualified.

❋ **Trash Can Shooter**. We'd give our contestants a copy of Sports Illustrated or Playboy Magazine and ask them to rip a page out, ball it up, and toss it into a standard sized office trash basket about ten feet away. The contestant must make three successful baskets and then proceed. If the contestant used the entire magazine without successfully making a basket, he or she was disqualified.

❋ **Scavenger Hunt**. Finally, our contestants were instructed to hunt around the cushions of the couch without removing them and collect exactly one dollar in change to tip the pizza boy. We usually used mostly dimes, nickels and pennies to make it a bit more difficult and placed about four dollars in change where the contestants could easily reach it.

All these activities must be completed without the contestant removing his butt from the couch! With multiple couches, the first couch potato to complete all the events wins. With a single couch, the contestant who completes all the tasks in the shortest amount of time wins.

Sometimes, you need some quick and easy stuff that you can do on a whim with little to no preparation. Some of the following contests might be enough to make you look god-like when executed at the right time in the right manner. These contests are easy, but the timing and execution are the skills it will take time to acquire.

Closest Birthday

Ask for anyone celebrating a birthday today, and reward them with a prize. Chances are they're in the bar with a group of their friends, so they'll hoot and holler and make all kinds of fuss when you announce this, making you look even cooler. If there are no current birthdays, ask for someone who has a birthday tomorrow or had a birthday yesterday. Still no takers? Find the person with the closest to today's date and give them a prize. Birthdays are one of the big reasons some people come to a party, so it's always good to bring additional attention to them. Be prepared to issue multiple prizes.

Shortest Man

If it's early in the night, this works better if you have a measuring tape and physically measure each of your contestants out of the spotlight rather than stopping everything to measure them together. Short people have a tendency to get all pissy if you poke fun at them in public. If it's late at night and they've had a few drinks, then you can do it in front of everyone. Award a better than average prize to the poor schmuck and he'll feel six feet tall.

Shortest Woman

This variation is similar to the shortest man contest, but women don't take is as bad, so it's not nearly as brutal.

Tallest Woman

Men dig this. We've always wondered why very tall women always wear 3" heels making them ridiculously taller. Line up your volunteers and measure them without shoes.

Baldest Man

Men hate this. We've even counted the number of hairs left on people's head—that's usually hilarious!

Biggest Ears

Everyone with big ears hates this contest, but it's a very funny game. Use a ruler to measure from the top of the ear to the bottom of the earlobe, or the total width of the ear. Award a nice prize to encourage participation. We usually offer $10.00 an ear.

Stupid Trivia

We hate traditional trivia because it's so darn overplayed and boring. So we came up with a twist that works extremely well, similar to what Jay Leno now does on the *Tonight Show* (although we did this long before Jay tried it). Stupid trivia consists of normally obvious questions and answers that sometimes just aren't all that obvious! This game is a complete hoot because it makes everyone look equally silly. Sample questions include the following:

> How long did the Hundred Years War last? (116 years)
>
> Which country makes Panama hats? (Ecuador)
>
> From which animal do we get catgut? (Sheep or Horses)
>
> In which month do Russians celebrate the October Revolution? (November)
>
> What is a camel's hair brush made of? (Squirrel Fur)
>
> What was King George VI's first name? (Albert)
>
> What country created French Fries? (The U.S.)
>
> What color is a purple finch? (Crimson)
>
> Where are Chinese gooseberries from? (New Zealand)
>
> What is the color of the black box in a commercial airplane? (Orange)

See? Not so simple, eh? You can come up with several other Stupid Trivia questions from trivia books or games, or simply by watching the news or reading tabloids.

Frozen T-Shirts

Here's a great game we've borrowed from our Mexican friends who helped us party during Spring Break! Take 5 to 10 plain white t-shirts, and soak them well in water. Without totally wringing them out, fold them into a small square and place them in a freezer for a couple of hours before the start of the contest. When your contest starts, give each participant a frozen t-shirt square and award prizes to the first person who can unfold the t-shirt and put it on. Frozen boxer shorts are even more fun. We now have a special four person t-shirt, where there are actually four holes for heads. All four people must work together to unfreeze the t-shirt and wear it.

Balloon Stuffer

Another easy contest that's lots of fun. Have four or five people stuff small 4″ balloons under their shirts. Whoever can stuff the most unbroken balloons under their shirt in a certain period of time, usually 30 to 60 seconds, wins.

Baby Bottle Beer Sucking

Baby Bottle Beer Sucking is one of the oldest Spring Break promos in the book, but we're still amazed at the number of people who have never heard of this. It's an easy promotion where you can involve a whole bunch of people all at once. The whole thing takes less than three minutes, but gets the crowd energized. And this contest is very inexpensive to run, and you can do it anywhere. We've even pulled this contest off in bars without entertainment.

You'll need about a dozen cheap plastic baby bottles that you can get at any discount store, enough non-alcoholic beer to fill them all, a pair of scissors, and some towels. Fill a bunch of baby bottles with the non-alcoholic beer. We've seen this done with real beer (not mentioning any names here) only to later find that it was a direct violation of that state's liquor control laws (whoops)! You should enlarge all of the holes of the nipples with a pair of scissors so that this contest will not take forever. Line up your contestants together. The first to completely finish the entire bottle without spilling wins the prize. Keep the towels close in case there's a mess. Have someone designated as a judge in case there's a close call.

Your cost: about $30 for empty baby bottles and some beer. Good prizes for this contest include cash, gift certificates, or a large baby bottle! Let your contestants keep the baby bottles too. It's very amusing to see that most of your contestants will use the baby bottle for their beer during the rest of your party. Makes for some good pictures!

Get Leid

At some point during the party, distribute plastic or silk Hawaiian leis all over the room. Don't explain why you're doing this. Later that night, have your host announce that the person who "gets the most leis" within the next 2 minutes wins a prize.

Effectively Marketing Yourself

Being a successful DJ involves running a successful business. If you decide that this is the field for you, you've got to do your homework. Get yourself a professional looking headshot, resume and cover letter. Get help if you need it. Club and bar owners are business people, and they will respect your professional attitude. Before you go for your interview, prepare by following these simple steps.

Shop your market. Go to the bars that are doing well on the night you want to take over. Watch what they're doing. Listen to the music. Watch the DJ. Pay attention to his or her timing. Talk to the people who go there, and outright ask them why they are there.

Pick your target audience. Talk to some people in that group and ask them what they'd like to see a DJ do. You would be amazed at how many people would skip that stupid TV show (in many cases, this is your #1 competition) and make that trip to your bar if you've got something going on that gives them something to talk about. People want to live like they're part of those TV shows, and you'll soon have the power to make that happen.

Make a plan. Write your entire promotional idea and a plan of execution down, make it look professional, include a generous budget, and present it to your club's owners and/or management. Don't forget to allow it sufficient time (at least eight weeks) to grow without killing it. You wouldn't pull a tree out of the ground before it had a chance to sprout roots, would you?

Convince the manager or owner to hire a Master DJ/MC: *You*. You're the person that's going to make things happen. Tell them that this is where many of the best plans fail. Bars and clubs will spend the extra advertising and promotions dough, but won't bother to hire the right people to implement it.

To make a dead night a good one, they'll need good bartenders and waitresses, and definitely a "Master DJ." Include your resume, and don't be afraid to cite any additional skills from other non-DJ related jobs that make you look even more responsible.

Find the local promoters or DJ services. In smaller markets, there a bunch of "DJ services" that provide DJs for a series of clubs. In some bigger cities, these guys are known as "promoters." Both of these types have the responsibility of choosing the right DJs for that particular club, or they'll lose the contract. You won't make as much cash working for one of these guys since they'll take a big cut off the top, but it's a sweet way for a new DJ to break in and get his or her name well known.

Get some professional equipment at home, and practice your ass off. It's all going to come down to your audition and your performance, so it's important for you to feel as comfortable as possible. The best way to do this is to get yourself a set of DJ equipment that's identical to the one they use in the club you want to solicit.. Whichever way you choose to spin, make sure you practice enough to operate these bad boys with your eyes closed.

Remember that a "MASTER DJ" isn't necessarily a "mixmaster" or record scratcher. Club managers and owners know these people can mix an amazing music set, but they also realize that most mixmasters have the personality of a goldfish and will do absolutely nothing for their sales or promotions. You should strive to be a complete entertainer. You'll have to become an experienced MC. If you don't have that experience, watch and learn from the masters in your area. You'll have to be extremely outgoing, quick on your feet, and virtually fearless. You'll also need to be extremely friendly, which is a very important tool in building a night. Many customers feel special if the DJ pays attention to them, especially if the DJ mentions the customer's name on the microphone during his or her show. This makes people want to come back.

Teach them that Master DJs don't come cheap. They may have to spend two to three times their normal DJ wages to acquire one of them. Initially, they may not think this is worth it, but convince them to watch their books. They'll see long-term gains. Remind them that if a DJ lacks personality, they're paying an expensive human jukebox.

Venues you might want to target as a bar or club DJ include but are in no means limited to:

* Adult clubs
* After hours bars
* Ice cream parlors
* Retail stores
* Music stores
* Tanning salons
* Shopping malls
* Free standing clubs
* Private clubs (Moose Club, American Legion, etc)
* Hotel clubs
* Roller skating rinks
* Bowling alleys
* Outdoor bars

Always do some sniffing around to try to find out why the prior DJ left. He or she might have been doing something that the manager or owner didn't like, and you wouldn't want to repeat that history for obvious reasons.

Finally, all DJs should have a contract. I've found that the bar and club business is full of fly-by-night operators who seem to have created a new sport called "bill dodging." I've lost thousands of dollars in unpaid radio commercials and consulting fees, and I know DJs who have lost equipment and their entire music collections, which is even more painful to replace than equipment. Always cover your butt, no matter how cool you think the bar owner is. As a matter of fact, it's the "cool" ones you have to look out for most of all—they're often sneaky guys that can sell a blind man a pair of glasses and convince him he can see out of them. A contract will let him know that you're no dummy, and it will lessen the chances that he'll take advantage of you.

Adding Credibility to Your Show

Anyone who's anybody knows the first step to becoming a somebody is acting like you already are a somebody. Fake it till you make it! You've got to rise above the rest of the little people. Since little people readily identify pop stars as real celebrities and radio DJs as pseudo-celebrities, you are hereby permitted to borrow a bit of flair from both industries to aid your cause.

Your first step is making your show sound official. This can be done by adding professionally produced radio-type introductions and pre-recorded periodic segues, similar to what you hear on your local radio stations. A company I'm affiliated with called The DJ Resource produces a product called Custom DJ Drops that sound exactly like radio liners, featuring your DJ name and anything else you might want to say.

Your next step is making your show look official. Professionally designed logos, business cards, flyers and posters promoting you and your show will go a long way in making you look like you're for real. Some DJs offer their own mix CDs with a professionally produced label. Although that's probably not legal in most cases, it looks really cool. Request sheets with your logo imprinted on them are also a cool touch. And people love to get free stuff. Pens, hats, embroidered shirts, bags, bottle openers, key chains, laser pointers, and anything else with your name, logo, telephone number and website on them will be snatched up quickly, further branding your company and increasing your popularity. Make sure you always have plenty of business cards and literature available for people to book you at other clubs and parties.

Finally, you'll need to *be* official. This is the most difficult thing to define, not to mention achieve. Being official is basically deciding to become a "career DJ," and subsequently taking your job very seriously rather than approaching it as an optional part-time hobby. You'll either need to hire a real agent, or act as your own agent. An agent is responsible for promoting you in an almost insane manner, something that can be really weird to do if you're representing yourself. He or she will send professionally written press releases to the local newspapers letting them know when and where you're playing, trying to build your name to celebrity status. A good agent continuously tries to get you auditions at bigger and better nightclubs, and sends your demo discs out to every radio station that plays mixes in the nation. Your agent will professionally negotiate your contract terms and fees for playing out. Professional agents are paid a percentage of everything you earn, so the more they can get for your services, the bigger their cut. Never pay an agent to promote you in advance, because that's not how agents work. If he or she is asking for up front money, it's probably a scam.

Notice that I've thrown the words "professional" and "professionally" quite redundantly around in the previous paragraphs. Going "professional" means that you've hired someone who actually produces or does audio, print, or whatever for a living. Amateur or self-designed wares and procedures usually look amateur, and trust me, looking amateur will hurt your reputation. First impressions, especially poor ones, may last a lifetime, and could ruin your chances of redeeming yourself in the future when you finally decide to take my advice and hire professionals. From what I can recall, my first demo packages were self-created pieces of garbage that I wouldn't give to my worst enemy today. They probably supplied many bar managers with packing material, or worse, a good laugh. If you've got the means, definitely hire a professional and spend a few dollars and do whatever you decide to do the right way.

In some bars and clubs where you're expected to be more interactive, you can also do cool radio type things like quoting Billboard chart positions, delivering celebrity facts and gossip, and also dropping customers' names. Customers will think that you're broadcasting live on the air, which adds subliminal credibility to your show. Always mention your name before and after song sets and contests, just like they do on the radio. Don't forget that the key benefit here is self-promotion. You're trying to sell yourself as a master level DJ, somebody that has no fear and makes things happen.

Cover Letter

Here's a sample cover letter that you can borrow and modify to solicit your own potential clients. Be sure to include all the extra services you can offer.

Today's Date

Owner's Full Name
Club Name
Club Street Address
City, State, Zip Code

Dear Owner,

Thank you for the opportunity to provide Disc Jockey Entertainment Services in your bar. We're excited about the opportunity to help increase your sales with fun, interactive entertainment that will increase attendance and repeat visits.

[Our DJ Company] has a tremendous amount of bar games and props including the all new Bar Wheel, where people spin the wheel for a prize or a funny task; the Inflatable Cash Cube, where your customers grab all the coupons and fake money they can in 15 seconds to trade for prizes such as drinks or t-shirts; and The Shuffle Golf Challenge, where we invite people to try and putt five balls to win up to $500 that we'll provide ourselves!

Obviously, we've got the hottest rock, country, disco, dance, oldies and hip-hop collection in the area. Anything you or your customers would like, we've got it all. And the music format is always entirely up to you. If there's a certain type of music you don't want played, just let us know and it's outta here.

Unlike most other DJs, from the minute our show starts to the end of our show, there's always high energy fun.

We also offer something called "In-House TV," where you can use your existing TVs to advertise your specials and promotions when there are no good sports to watch. You can actually EARN MONEY by selling as many of your 20 digital slides as you wish to other businesses, like car dealers, tanning salons, taxi or limo services, beer distributors, liquor companies, etc. for as much as you think you can get for them, and YOU KEEP THE PROFITS! Please let me know if you'd like more information on this exciting new development.

Please don't hesitate to contact me directly should you have any questions about our services. I'd be happy to meet with you at your convenience to discuss your entertainment plans.

Thank you for your time,

[Your Name]
[Your Telephone Number]
[Your Website]

The Contract

I've included a sample nightclub and bar contract so you can familiarize yourself with some of the more common terms, inclusions and exceptions. Do not simply copy this contract and use it as your own, because your particular situation and the laws in your state may be different, and you may mistakenly omit or include something that should or shouldn't be there. It's well worth a couple hundred bucks in attorney fees to have a lawyer draw up an agreement that specifically fits your plan.

[YOUR COMPANY HERE] SERVICE AGREEMENT

This is a formal agreement between [BAR OR CLUB NAME HERE], the purchaser of Disc Jockey entertainment, and [YOUR COMPANY HERE], the provider of Disc Jockey entertainment, for the services described below.

Name of Venue:

Venue D.B.A. Name if applicable:

Address of Venue:

This agreement shall be active for six months from the date of its execution, and is renewable up to thirty days prior to its expiration.

Please indicate days entertainment is required at the above location from [YOUR COMPANY HERE]:

Monday Tuesday Wednesday Thursday Friday Saturday Sunday

Start Time for each day:

End Time for each day:

Entertainment fee agreed upon is [PRICE PER NIGHT—use a total price per night rather than an hourly fee, so if the bar closes early, you still get paid for the whole night. It's fair because you would have to be there regardless] for a total weekly fee of [PRICE PER NIGHT x number of nights].

All payments should be made payable to "[YOUR COMPANY HERE]" and you agree to remit payments within 14 days of the date printed on the invoice. In the event of non-payment, [YOUR COMPANY HERE] retains the right to immediately cancel any and all scheduled future performances and this agreement and pursue collection efforts through collection agencies and/or the appropriate local courts. Purchaser will be responsible for all court fees, legal fees, and collection costs incurred in collection efforts. Purchaser shall be charged $30 for each returned check plus a $10 service charge for each collection notice. Past-due balances will incur interest at the rate of 2% for each month in which the balance is outstanding.

The Purchaser reserves the right to control the manner, means and details of the performance of services by [YOUR COMPANY HERE] via a written event planner or music request list prior to the event. Without a written planner or request list, [YOUR COMPANY HERE] shall attempt to play Purchaser's and Purchaser's guests' music requests but shall not be held responsible if certain selections are unavailable. [YOUR COMPANY HERE] reserves the right to censor music requests that may be considered offensive or inappropriate for the venue and its audience. [YOUR COMPANY HERE] reserves the right to choose the sequence of songs played for the preference of the majority and the flow of the event.

This agreement to perform shall be excused by detention of personnel by sickness, accidents, riots, strikes, epidemics, acts of God, or any other legitimate condition beyond [YOUR COMPANY HERE]'s control. If such circumstances arise, all reasonable efforts will be made to find comparable replacement entertainment at the agreed upon fees. Should [YOUR COMPANY HERE] be unable to procure a qualified replacement, Purchaser shall receive a credit or full refund of all prepaid fees for the scheduled performance that was excused. Purchaser agrees that in all such circumstances, [YOUR COMPANY HERE]'s liability shall be exclusively limited to refunding any fees prepaid for the missed scheduled performance, and that [YOUR COMPANY HERE] shall not be liable for indirect or consequential damages arising from any breach of contract.

Purchaser will take reasonable steps to protect [YOUR COMPANY HERE] personnel, equipment and music before, during and after all scheduled performances. In the event of circumstances deemed by [YOUR COMPANY HERE] or its entertainers to present a threat or implied threat of injury or harm to our staff or any equipment, [YOUR COMPANY HERE] reserves the right to cease performance and contact authorities immediately. If the Purchaser is able to resolve the threatening situation in a reasonable amount of time (maximum of 15 minutes from initial notice), [YOUR COMPANY HERE] shall resume performance in accordance with the original terms of this agreement. Purchaser shall be responsible for payment in full, regardless of whether the situation is resolved or whether entertainer resumes performance.

In order to prevent equipment damage or liability arising from accidental injury to any individual attending this performance, [YOUR COMPANY HERE] reserves the right to deny any guest access to the sound system, music recordings, or other equipment. In the event of injuries or damages resulting from insufficient protection on Purchaser's part, Purchaser will be responsible for paying for all of [YOUR COMPANY HERE]'s resulting costs (including insurance deductibles, medical treatment, and repair or replacement of damaged music and equipment) that are not reimbursed by insurance.

Purchaser shall provide [YOUR COMPANY HERE] with safe and appropriate working conditions. This includes, but is not limited to, sufficient space next to the dance floor (if any) for [YOUR COMPANY HERE]'s setup(s); a 120-volt electric outlet (3-prong grounded with at least 15 amps available) from a reliable power source near the set-up area; additional electric outlets on individual and separate circuits for lighting (if contracted for); facilities that completely cover and protect [YOUR COMPANY HERE]'s equipment from adverse weather conditions (direct sunlight, rain, excessive winds, leaks, excessive heat, humidity, etc.); crowd control if warranted; and free parking. Purchaser accepts full responsibility and is liable for any damages, injuries or delays that occur as a result of failure to comply with any or all of these provisions.

Except as otherwise noted below, [YOUR COMPANY HERE] will provide all of the equipment that it needs to fulfill this agreement. In any event, [YOUR COMPANY HERE] will not be responsible for any failures in or caused by equipment that is not provided by [YOUR COMPANY HERE].

Purchaser shall pay any charges imposed by the venue. These charges may include, but are not limited to, parking, use of electric power, ASCAP/BMI/SESAC entertainment fees.

This agreement cannot be canceled except by mutual written consent of both the Purchaser and [YOUR COMPANY HERE]. If cancellation is initiated by the Purchaser in writing and agreed to by [YOUR COMPANY HERE] in writing, Purchaser will be required to pay any unpaid costs already incurred by [YOUR COMPANY HERE], but not more than the total fee agreed upon.

Purchaser agrees to defend, indemnify, assume liability for and hold [YOUR COMPANY HERE] harmless from any and all claims, demands, damages, losses, suits, proceedings, penalties, expenses or other liabilities including attorney fees and court costs, arising out of or resulting from the performance of this contract, regardless of the basis (except for gross negligence on the part of [YOUR COMPANY HERE])

Purchaser may not transfer this contract to another party without the prior written consent of [YOUR COMPANY HERE].

CHAPTER 2

This agreement is not binding until received and signed by [YOUR COMPANY HERE]. Any changes must be written and signed by both the Purchaser and [YOUR COMPANY HERE]. Oral agreements are non-binding. The latest contract supersedes all previous contracts between Purchaser and [YOUR COMPANY HERE] for the event listed above. If any clause in this agreement is found to be illegal, the rest of the agreement shall remain in force.

I have read and agree to all terms as written in this contract. By signing this agreement, I affirm that I have legally binding authority as an owner or agent of the purchaser to enter into this agreement.

Signature

Printed Name

Title

Date

3

BECOMING A MOBILE DJ

Introduction

Bruce Keslar, president of the National Association of Mobile Entertainers, estimates that there are over fifty thousand mobile DJs in the U.S. and Canada. That makes this branch of the DJ industry by far the largest and most prominent. This also means this is where you will face the most competition.

DJ Joseph Montalvo from Spinners Entertainment.

Mobile DJs perform at the widest varieties of events, such as weddings, anniversaries, birthday parties, corporate affairs, block parties, reunions, Bar and Bat mitzvahs, etc. In addition to being the Master of Ceremonies as well as the program director, this job entails carrying and installing a portable or "mobile" sound system. So you're not only the MC and PD, you're also an engineer, all at the same time! At first, it can seem like an overwhelming amount of responsibility. But it's a really cool rush when you're finally able to pull it all off without blinking.

If you're a good salesperson, or liar, this is definitely the field with the best opportunities to get paid DJ work quickly without having to pay your dues. Since it's awkward to invite potential customers to watch you perform at someone else's wedding reception or private party, because they are "private" affairs, you could fool people into thinking you've "been doing weddings for twenty years now." I love when thirty-something year old DJs tell me that—I find it amazing that they did their first weddings at ten or eleven years old. The point is if a potential customer did not ask the right questions, she might never know that you had never performed in public. These types of deceptions happen all the time in this business. Fortunately, they don't all turn out bad.

The mobile DJ field is also the best avenue to make decent money in the long run. A typical experienced wedding DJ can earn anywhere from $500 to $1,500 a gig! When you get good, you can run your business from pure referrals, effectively reducing your marketing costs to almost nothing, and that's when you really start making the bucks. Since most mobile gigs occur on the weekends, you'll need to be in two places at once in order to grow your business into a business, rather than just being a job. Most successful mobile DJs eventually branch out and hire subcontractors to work for them so their company can do multiple jobs on a single day. You can also cross-market your customers into all kinds of things like digital pictures, video projection, videography, props, party favors, invitations, games, dancers, lights, Karaoke, and various other profitable nonsense which can add even more profit to your bottom line.

Since there are more private parties than anything else, this is the easiest way to break into the DJ field. Some friend, relative, co-worker, acquaintance, whatever, is always throwing a small party, and you can always volunteer to be its DJ to gain some valuable experience. Many new DJs throw parties themselves just so they have a reason to DJ. If you can't purchase the equipment yourself, you can easily get a job with an established DJ company with little to no investment. They'll often provide the equipment and the music. You can learn while making your mistakes there, then starting your own thing later, like most of the DJs I know did.

Now for the bad news. It will cost you several thousand bucks to get started in this field, because you'll need to purchase your own sound system and music. Over the past four or five years, many computer savvy DJs escaped the huge expense of purchasing a music library and simply borrowed their music from online music sharing sites such as the original Napster and KaZaa. With CD writers now below $100 and blank discs costing about forty cents each, a new DJ could theoretically build his or her entire library for well under $200. It's important to realize that this practice is a direct violation of copyright law. I remember building my first collection (legally) over several years for a cost in excess of $5,000, and then rebuilding for another ridiculous amount when I decided to convert from vinyl to CDs. It's not cheap.

There is also much more responsibility in this DJ field. Again, you're responsible for music, announcements, and the whole darn sound system, not to mention marketing, advertising, public relations, billing, purchasing, collections, event coordination, insurance, blah, blah, blah. If you can't walk and chew gum, this may not be the field for you. Here's what's involved.

There are the logistics of physically moving and installing an entire sound system, and sometimes even a lighting system. That system must be properly set up within a certain allowable time frame. And a backup sound system must be quickly available and actually exist—"vaporware" backup sound systems, although great for easing a worried party host's mind, won't help you in a bad spot.

Banquet halls often require that DJs carry liability insurance in case a customer injures themselves on your equipment. People could trip on non-taped speaker wires or power cords. I've even heard of speaker stands tipping over and injuring people.

You'll need a much larger music library than a club DJ, because you won't know what to expect. Weddings and other types of private parties attract friends and family from across all socioeconomic borders, so you'd better have a little something for everyone. More importantly, you'll need many hours of research just learning all these songs.

Mobile DJs also provide many hours of unpaid consultations leading up to the date of the affair. Before a wedding reception, you've got to track your bride down for the order of the events, the song lists, and the names of anyone being announced.

There's also the issue of the sheer pressure of performing at someone's once-in-a-lifetime affair. Many times you'll know very little about your customer's guests, and sometimes they will not respond or dance to your actions no matter what. This can get pretty stressful at times.

Performing at Wedding Receptions

Weddings aren't necessarily the most prevalent mobile Disc Jockey event, but they are the largest subset of the *professional* mobile DJ market. Most people in their right mind would not take a chance on an amateur bedroom DJ for a once in a lifetime affair. There are thousands of weddings per year that require the services of a professional DJ. And with the alarmingly high divorce rate, many people are getting married for the second or third time, further increasing the pool of potential weddings.

For hundreds of years, live performers or bands were the traditional entertainment for weddings. Sometime in the 1960s or 1970s, the band bubble burst. Someone figured out that you could bring your records to a party with a couple of record players and sound just like a live radio show for a whole lot less than a band costs. Since then, many people have switched their preference from band to DJ due to a personal preference for the real song by the artist who made it famous, or merely for cost-controlling purposes. Bands usually charge much more money because there is more manpower involved. Most bands are at least four people, and those people need to get paid. A DJ can be a one-man show. Some snooty big-money folks still seem to prefer a live band, because they think it seems more "classy" than a DJ. But even this trend is showing signs of changing, as the DJ industry becomes more of a professional industry.

There is a great amount of preparation that occurs prior to a wedding reception. Since this is a "private" affair, your customer has the right to determine the overall flow of traditional wedding events, what you say and don't say, and the kind of music you will play at his or her reception regardless of your professional opinion or what her guests think.

 SECRET: Although every wedding reception is inherently different, the truth is that the flow of most traditional wedding receptions are basically a cookie-cutter approach with a few minor timing changes depending on your customer's preferences.

You'll want to come up with a standard form that addresses each individual situation. We used to call ours "The Wedding Information Form." This form lists all the names of the ushers and bridesmaids who are to be announced, plus all the special events and traditional stuff that are scheduled to take place. We used to have the bride and groom complete this at least two weeks before their reception. This way if there are any discrepancies, you've got the whole plan in their writing! I have included a sample to give you an idea of what one looks like in the Forms section of this chapter.

CHAPTER 3

Here's a sample wedding reception agenda for a typical four- or five-hour Christian or Jewish affair. Remember, there are several variations on these customs depending where in the world you are and what the customary practices of the particular religion of the families happen to be. To make things even more confusing, there are more mixed marriages than ever, where traditions from both the bride and grooms family must be entertained. Some couples choose to be painfully traditional, and others may want to avoid traditions altogether. The last thing you want to do is upset a bride on her big day, so definitely make sure you know exactly what she wants well in advance. This is why communication with your bride and groom is so incredibly vital in this business. I've also included some super-secret industry tips to help you look better and make your show run even smoother.

The Ceremony

In the event of a non-traditional or multi-traditional wedding, the ceremony usually takes place at a banquet hall or some other public facility rather than in a church. In these situations, you may be asked to provide music and/or sound reinforcement (wireless microphones, mixer, amplifier and speakers) for the ceremony. Since this is such a serious and important occasion where the actual wedding vows will take place, a perfect performance during the ceremony is always required.

You'll arrive well in advance to set up your equipment. You should position your speakers well out of the way, usually in the far back of the area where the ceremony will take place. And always properly tape your speaker cables and power cords down, because tripping the bride or one of her guests is unforgivable (and may get you sued). Usually, a banquet manager or wedding coordinator will be involved in your setup, and they have predetermined methods that will help hide unsightly wires. Especially important is making sure that any wireless microphones are positioned in a manner where there is no interference or feedback. Usually, a brand new set of batteries will preclude any issues.

Typically, you'll play elegant classical music by Handel, Vivaldi, Bach, Beethoven, and all those type of folks as the guests arrive. There are several inexpensive wedding compilation CDs that should provide all the tunes you'll need. Everything will be set in advance, so you'll have clues that will guide you when to change or kill the music. You usually won't do any announcements during the ceremony, since the priest, rabbi, or justice of the peace is the master of ceremonies. You'll hand the officiate a handheld wireless microphone or a small lapel microphone that he or she can attach to his or her clothing. When your groom arrives, you may want to attach a wireless microphone to the lapel of his tuxedo. As the ceremony proceeds, you'll hang out in the back of the room or area behind your mixer, controlling the sound levels.

When the bridal party begins to walk down the aisle, you'll play some more traditional pre-chosen classical music known as "Processional Music." My favorite processional song was Canon in D by Pachelbel. Then, it's the moment everyone has been waiting for—the beautiful, glowing bride begins to walk down the aisle escorted by her father or some other male companion. Here's where you could hit the traditional Bridal Chorus (known as "Here Comes the Bride" from the "Lohengrin" opera by Richard Wagner). It's important to realize that opera-type brides will realize that Lohengrin is an incredibly depressing play with hints of evil and sorcery—the groom is a secret knight who ultimately leaves the bride, and she dies at the end! Nice story. If confronted with this tidbit of trivia in a sales or consultation with your bride and groom, you will now know and appear much brighter than most typical DJs. Don't worry, your learned bride and groom will usually be happy to offer alternate suggestions from more cheerful acts.

Once the bride reaches the groom, the music is faded. During the actual vows, you will play no music.

When the jig is up and the bride and groom are officially hitched, they'll turn to face the audience, receive some applause, then proceed back down the aisle as husband and wife. Here's where you'll play some "Recessional Music", which is typically "The Wedding March" from "A Midsummer's Night Dream" by Mendelssohn. I'm not aware of any controversial facts about The Wedding March. You'll keep playing similar music by Bach, Beethoven, and other classical favorites until most of the guests have left the ceremony area. Hopefully, you've got a few minutes to break down your equipment and run to the reception to set things up there, if you haven't done so in advance.

Cocktail Hour

Most traditional wedding receptions have something called the "Cocktail Hour." Since most wedding ceremonies take place somewhere other than the reception hall, this time is usually used as a buffer, allowing time for the bridal party to arrive, relax, and regroup as they get ready for the next phase of their big day. All the guests who attended the ceremony also need somewhere to hang out while they wait for the reception to begin, so the bride and groom rent the reception hall an hour early. While the guests arrive, you'll play music that's mellow but not sleep inducing. Guests are arriving and becoming accustomed to the room. They're catching up with old friends or distant relatives, so you don't want to play music too loud or play anything more exciting than background music. Good choices include smooth jazz such as George Benson, Sade, or Basia. Some people prefer soft rock, big band, ethnic or even classical music. Traditionally, the bride and groom are not in the same room as you and the guests during this hour. They don't come in until their grand introductions.

You won't have to speak until the end of the cocktail hour, which almost always lasts longer than an hour.

The photographer often uses the cocktail hour to finish up bridal portraits. So just to cover your butt, make sure you've set and told everyone an absolute time that can be used for the cocktail hour. Discuss this with your bride and groom and banquet manager well ahead of time. An inexperienced DJ can quickly lose control of this situation, and the cocktail hour can end up lasting two hours. If this happens, the banquet staff will hate you because the prepared food will become cold, and everyone will have to rush everything else later. There will be less time for dancing, and you'll look like you weren't in control. Remember, your business will eventually be driven by referrals from banquet managers in addition to satisfied customers, so try to always be a professional. Communicate openly with all involved parties and broker a compromise if you must.

 SECRET: Be advised that although most professional photographers are team players who can be the source of valuable referrals for future jobs, you will run into the occasional pompous jerk who doesn't care about you or your program. Most photography packages are designed to keep the initial costs low and more attractive. They then zap brides on the back end with additional fees for photographs that weren't included in the low-priced package they initially purchased. This is where they earn their big money. I've been forcefully pushed out of the way by a photographer trying to capture a shot of a fun contest I was running. The bride, who happened to be a friend of mine, saw this and humiliated him with a public tongue lashing. I know another DJ who got into a shoving match at wedding receptions which was a complete disaster. A photographer isn't in business to make your life easier— he or she is in business to sell photographs. Know this, and try to be conscious of where the bride and groom are. Exercise common courtesy and try and stay out of the photographer's (and videographer's) way whenever you can.

CHAPTER 3

Wedding Introductions

Immediately following the Cocktail Hour, you'll be responsible for formerly introducing the bridal party. About 10-15 minutes before the end of the cocktail hour, you'll need to go hunt down your bridal party and ready them for their grand introductions. In better halls, the banquet manager or wedding coordinator will arrange this for you.

If you're doing the wedding alone without an assistant, it's a good idea to pre-record some continuous music on a CD or Minidisc so you'll have enough time to leave the room and chat with the bride and groom without having to worry about the music stopping. If you're stuck without pre-recorded music, play a CD that has the same type of cocktail music for the next two or three tracks. You've got to be careful with compilation CDs; they often shift gears radically and can produce less than stellar results. You don't want hard core rap song to follow a smooth jazz song when you're absent from the room.

Our wedding information forms asked for the correct pronunciation or phonetic spelling of everyone's name in the bridal party to avoid embarrassing mistakes. We would get everyone in the bridal party together outside the main room to go over their names one more time to make sure everything's right. We'd then give them a few tips for best photographic results. We told them to come out smiling and to be aware that everyone will be taking photographs. We also suggested that all couples should enter the room arm in arm. Using your wedding information form, you'll line the ushers and bridesmaids up exactly as they appear on the list on your wedding information form. The correct order should be on the form.

Begin your introductions by slowly fading the music and saying something like "Ladies and Gentleman, in a moment we will introduce the Bridal Party. We'll give you a moment to please find your seats." Once everyone is ready, greet the crowd, introduce yourself and the name of your DJ company, then begin to announce the bridal party.

Since the introductions are the grand entrance and the focal point of this entire affair, you should play some music that's fairly intense. My favorite introduction tracks for the bridal party at a classy type affair include Canon in D (available on a CD called "Classical Wedding Traditions" on the New Traditions label), Eric's Theme by Vangelis (from the Chariots of Fire soundtrack), or "Santorini" by Yanni (on the Live from Acropolis CD). For a younger couple who have party animals as guests, you can choose any instrumental house, trance, or techno song. "Get Ready for This" by Two Unlimited and "Children" by Robert Miles are both still fairly popular in this situation. Then, just before you introduce the bride and groom, most DJs still play an instrumental version of "The Wedding March." It sets the tone for the grand entrance and makes you look like a true professional.

Here's how traditional introductions usually go:

Parents and Grandparents

Usually the parents and grandparents will be escorted directly to their seats. If a parent or grandparent is unable to walk, they may remain at their table and simply be introduced as "Seated at his or her or their table, the grandparents of the bride, Mr. And Mrs. Nakamichi. Let's have a warm round of applause for the bride's grandparents!" Continue until all grandparents have been announced.

Ushers and Bridesmaids

You can begin this series of introductions by saying something like "Ladies and Gentlemen, it's my privilege to introduce the Bridal Party, beginning with bridesmaid Jennifer Lopez escorted by usher Sir Mixalot." You can then simply introduce the names of the bridesmaids "escorted by" the names of the ushers. It's traditional to use the full name and title (Mr., Miss, Ms. or Mrs.) of each usher and bridesmaid, but exceptions happen all the time. Ask your bride and groom what they would prefer. Depending on the bride and groom's preference, I'll either have these people report directly to their table, or have them line up along the dance floor, males on one side, females on the other. This can set up some nice video and photographic opportunities when the bride and groom finally do their first dance.

Flower Girls and/or Ring Bearer

Some weddings have little kids that walk down the aisle for no reason other than the cute factor. This gives the audience a chance to say "awwww." Suck it up and just smile. If the banquet manager hasn't shown the children where to go, it's your job to make sure they know to go where they're supposed to go. Some people like to keep the children with the bridal party, some send them directly to their tables. I like to have someone waiting for them on the opposite side of the dance floor so there's no confusion.

Maid or Matron of Honor and Best Man

These are two people chosen especially for this honor by the bride and groom, and should be treated as such. Announce them as something like: "And now I would like to introduce two very special people chosen by the bride and groom to represent them today. Please welcome the Maid of Honor ('Matron of Honor' if she is married), Ms. Tanya Thang escorted by the Best Man, Bob Abooey." Big fanfare ensues, with the big moment quickly approaching.

Bride and Groom

Here's the big moment everyone has been waiting for. I like to have the entire room stand up for this honor, plus my bride and groom usually get a kick out of this. Slap on some dramatic introduction music, and let's bring them in. You can announce them by saying something like, "Ladies and Gentlemen, if you would all please rise. It is my honor and privilege to introduce to you for the first time, the brand new Mr. and Mrs. Robert Roberts!" Everyone claps and cheers wildly.

SECRET: Instead of lining up the bridesmaids and ushers along the edge of the dance floor, there's something called a "human arch" which is supposed to bring them luck. You'll find that "luck" is a great way to get all these people to do queer things they wouldn't normally do. The bridal party lines up along either side of the dance floor, males on one side and females on the other. When the bride and groom are introduced, the ushers and bridesmaids all lift their left arms to form an archway, with the bridesmaid holding her bouquet at the top. The bride and groom then duck and scurry under the archway on their way to the center of the dance floor. Another Kodak moment for your photographer.

The Bride and Groom's First Dance

Traditionally, the dance floor is off-limits or "sacred" until the bride and groom have danced their first dance. This is why many DJs have the bride and groom dance immediately after they are introduced. The bride and groom should have selected this song way prior to their wedding date, and it should be on your wedding information form. This song should say something special about them, and most couples will have a song or two in mind. You can offer to help them select one only if they ask.

You can introduce this dance with verbiage like "Ladies and Gentlemen, Mr. and Mrs. Whatever will now dance their traditional first dance. They have selected 'Thank You' by Kiss The Red." At the end of their dance, ask the guests to give the bride and groom a warm round of applause.

Other DJs prefer to have this dance after the cake cutting. It really depends on the bride and groom's preference and adherence to tradition.

SECRET—Sometimes the song chosen for the first dance can be uncomfortably long, and some couples just don't feel comfortable staying on the dance floor all by themselves for all that time. Know in advance how long the song is, then ask your bride and groom if they want to remain on the dance floor for the entire song, or if they'd like you to fade it out a bit early. They might not realize how long five minutes are until they've actually been out in front of everyone staring at them for those five minutes. Some couples eat the attention up, and others can't stand it. Some brides and grooms dance alone for the first half of the song, and then have the DJ invite the full bridal party or all the guests to join them on the dance floor. Ask your bride and groom what their preference is.

The Blessing or Benediction

Once your bridal party is at their table, you will introduce the guest who was pre-selected (priest, reverend, rabbi, parent, friend, etc.) by name to say the blessing or benediction. You will hand this person your microphone, then step back, bow your head, and wait for him to finish. Once the blessing is complete, you will get the microphone and avoid saying "Yo yo yo—let's give it up for the blessing! Great job!" Simply walk over to the best man or whoever is proposing the toast, introduce him, and quietly sneak away once again.

There may be a rare occasion where you will be asked to give the blessing when you have basically non-religious types who feel the need they need some religion on this auspicious occasion. During one of my first few wedding receptions when I was still wet behind the ears, I got snagged at one wedding reception and was asked to do this. I didn't want to look inexperienced, so I said, "Sure! I can handle that." So I scrambled to the hallway and called one of my more religious buddies in a panic. In a few minutes, we came up with something that we felt was non-denominational yet religious sounding that went something like this:

"May the Lord bestow upon you peace, tranquility and happiness. May you both find joy and solace in each other's company. May you both walk hand in hand to the end of time and still see the spark of love in each other's eyes. We thank our God for this union, for the food we are about to eat, and for the good fortune we all have in finding all these true friends around us. Thank you Lord, Amen."

I thought it sounded good as I read it from my cocktail napkin, but I'm sure I broke all kinds of religious rules. But I appeared to be an experienced professional despite my lack of experience.

The Toast

This is traditionally the best man's duty. As a proactive entertainer, it's a good idea to let the banquet people know the toast is coming several minutes before it happens to insure that all of the guests have a full glass of champagne.

Traditionally, this is done before dinner, but we've had brides and grooms prefer this during or after dinner. The best toasts generally recall sentimental moments of the relationship of the groom and the best man, mention humorous things about the bride and the groom, and offer best wishes for the future. In addition to the best man, many families offer toasts from other family members and friends, including a toast by the maid of honor. At my wedding, I offered a toast by the groom!

Sometimes you'll run into an idiot best man who has no idea what to say and probably is completely drunk from throwing down J-ello shooters in the limousine. Check with the best man well in advance to ensure that he has his toast prepared or that he didn't forget it. I would always carry a sample toast that could easily be modified in emergencies. I've actually helped write speeches for best men at wedding receptions.

Here's a sample toast I wrote for someone (as a joke) that you probably should *never* use:

> I remember the first time I met Jack. That SOB was a poor, lonely soul with no direction. He would stare at girls and even drool at times. Once in school, his fly was down because his mind was somewhere else. I didn't tell him until later in the day, because it was too funny. And then came Jill, a wonderfully bright and pretty girl who actually took notice of Jack. She really straightened him out. I still don't know what she sees in him, but I thank God that she does see something in my friend Jack, because he bothers me much less these days. On behalf of everyone here, please allow me the honor of wishing the two of you many, many happy and healthy years together. Oh, and by the way, Jack, you're fly's undone. Please raise your glasses in honor of the new Mr. and Mrs. Hill!

Dinner Hour

Traditionally, brides budget one hour for chow time. Of the hundreds of weddings I've done, I've only seen one or two that actually lasted an hour. Count on at least an hour and 15 minutes. During this time, you'll be playing mellow jazz songs, soft ballads, and maybe some other stuff requested by the bride and groom. In some markets like most of New Jersey and eastern New York, DJs start bringing people on the dance floor during the dinner hour. In Long Island, New York, it's fairly common to see people doing the Macarena with a mouthful of soup or salad. Personally, I think this is cheesy, but a young bride will want to do exactly what she has seen others do simply because that's her "normal." Dinners should be quiet and classy. But chat with your bride and groom about this and ask them their preferences. And know CPR so you can help the bride's grandma when she chokes on a potato while doing the limbo.

During this hour, you may be invited to eat dinner also. Personally, I think this is unprofessional because you're on the clock, but it's your call. Since one of your main selling points is that you don't take breaks like bands do, I recommend eating before or after the reception. Photographers usually eat, but that's because they work eight to ten hours straight, and there's really nothing to photograph during dinner. You're only working for four or five hours, plus an hour or two to setup and break down. If you do suffer from a metabolism malfunction and you feel you need to stuff your face during dinner hour, then make sure that you discuss this with your bride in advance so she won't be charged for your meal. Some DJs actually write this into their contracts.

Parent Dances

Many DJs use the parent dances to break up the dinner hour from the remainder of the reception. Other DJs prefer to have the parent dances immediately after the bride and groom dance. We used the former since it seemed to work well as a catalyst to get people up and dancing, but it's up to you and your customer.

Traditionally, the bride will first dance with her father. If her father is not available, then she may choose to dance with some other male who she feels close to, usually the same person who "gave her away" during the wedding ceremony. In the event the bride's father has passed away, be very careful not to announce this as the Father and Daughter dance, or to invite the "bride and her father to the dance floor!" I've seen this happen, and the bride broke down in tears and left the room because her father had recently passed away. Supposedly, she had warned the DJ several times about this well in advance and again on her wedding day, but this DJ was preprogrammed into his thoughtless traditional mode. Good songs to recommend for this traditional dance include the following.

"Because You Loved Me" (Celine Dion)

"Butterfly Kisses" (Bob Carlisle)

"Daddy's Little Girl" (Paul Anka)

"Father's Eyes" (Amy Grant)

"Have I Told You Lately" (Van Morrison)

"Hero" (Mariah Carey)

"My Girl" (The Temptations)

"Stand By Me" (Ben E. King)

"Thank Heaven For Little Girls" (from the motion picture *Gigi*)

"The Wind Beneath My Wings" (Bette Midler)

"Times of Your Life" (Paul Anka)

"Unforgettable" (Nat King Cole / Natalie Cole)

"What A Wonderful World" (Louis Armstrong)

"You're The Inspiration" (Chicago)

"You Are So Beautiful" (Joe Cocker)

The groom will then follow dancing with his mother for the traditional Mother and Groom Dance. If the groom's mother is not available, he may decide to dance with the bride's mother if they're close. Otherwise, the groom will opt to skip this traditional dance.

"Because You Loved Me" (Celine Dion)

"Butterfly Kisses" (Bob Carlisle)

"Greatest Love Of All" (Whitney Houston)

"Have I Told You Lately" (Rod Stewart)

"Hero" (Mariah Carey)

"Just The Way You Are" (Billy Joel)

"Stand By Me" (Ben E. King)

"Sunrise, Sunset" (from the Fiddler On The Roof soundtrack)

"Through The Years" (Kenny Rogers)

"Unforgettable" (Nat King Cole / Natalie Cole)

"What A Wonderful World" (Louis Armstrong)

"Wind Beneath My Wings" (Bette Midler)

Wedding Party Dance

Once the parent's dance has been completed, the bride and groom may want to have the entire wedding party come to the dance floor for the wedding party dance. This dance can also take place during the bride and groom's first dance, where the bride and groom's first dance will be split 50/50, and the wedding party will be asked to join the bride and groom on the dance floor. Although any song could be used for this dance, here are the most popular requests in my experience.

"Celebration" (Kool & The Gang)

"Friends" (Elton John)

"Friends In Low Places" (Garth Brooks)

"I'll Be There for You" (Theme from "Friends")

"That's What Friends Are For" (Dionne & Friends)

"We Are Family" (Sister Sledge)

Party Time!

After the formal dances have been completed, invite everyone to join in on the dance floor. In the beginning of the reception, you'll play a lot of popular music to get everyone involved in dancing. Usually a mix of oldies and current and classic dance songs works best, but you should be open to requests and suggestions. Try to get an idea of what the bride and groom are musically into, and what they totally hate. We would send song lists to our customers and have them choose some of their favorite songs. Let them know that they should take into consideration the music preferences of their guests when choosing or eliminating song titles.

For the most part, your music program will basically be a cookie-cutter imprint of everyone else's wedding. Obviously, if your bride and groom are African-American, Hispanic, or any other nationality, your music mix should be adjusted. If you plan well enough in advance, you should be able to find the music your bride and groom and their family and friends will recognize and enjoy. We've actually invited the bride and groom to provide their own music in these situations, and they've always happily obliged, impressed because we took the time and effort to custom tailor their reception rather than impose our own cookie-cutter format.

You should play music in sets of five-eight songs throughout this period. Slow songs are huge at weddings (for all those folks who can't dance), so play lots of those. You'll probably cycle through "oldies" music;

CHAPTER 3

touch on some swing or "big band" music from the 1940s and early 1950s for the grandparents and kids who still think swing is cool; then round out by playing some disco, dance rock, maybe some country, and contemporary Top-40 music.

Again, I hate to include sample song lists for fear of DJs using them as the "official wedding song playlist," because there's no such thing. But, due to several repeated requests, I have included a sample starter list for your average American middle-of-the-road wedding. Again, I reiterate, do not become a pre-programmed DJ! No two weddings or parties or crowds will ever be exactly the same, and there is no "correct" song list that works in every situation, no matter what some lazy egocentric cheesy mustached Philadelphia DJ who has a hundred and fifty years experience tells you. Trust me, that's how being a DJ can become incredibly boring, and you'll end up hating the job. Be creative and have some fun with your music programming. Please always ask your clients what music they like. Have them write their favorites on your Wedding Info sheet, and try to build your own sets around their preferences.

Party Hour 1

The older folks will usually hit the floor first because they've gotten over the fear of not being cool. Dig deeper into the oldies and dance rock stuff to get them going, and the younger folks will gradually filter into the mix. Here are a few examples and my recollections about the reactions to each song during the first hour of a typical wedding reception.

"Love Shack", B-52s
For whatever reason, this silly song has always been my magic opener! It's got fun lyrics, it's easy to dance to, it's got energy, it's not intimidating, and it crosses several age groups. It's hard to beatmix due to its 135 BPM rock beat—I usually slam out immediately after she says "Tin roof—rusted!"

"Mony Mony", Billy Idol
This song was originally done sometime in the late 1960s by Tommy James and the Shondells, so it has some oldies power. When Billy Idol did it in the 1980s, it scored some Gen-X power, and a whole lot more energy! So you've got a really popular song that spans over 20 years of recognition! The best part is that this is a "group participation" song in some parts of the country. Right after Billy screams "Mony Mony" and pauses, your audience may shout "Get laid, get f**ked!", or "Get paid, get drunk" if they're a little more conservative. This may not be appropriate for some audiences, so hopefully they'll restrain themselves when necessary. But it's pretty exciting when it happens, and it makes you look like a party animal! I think this song is about 130 BPM.

"Runaround Sue", Dion
Here's another very popular oldie that just about everyone has heard. It's got a dance beat that older folks will appreciate, and most folks will even help sing it.

"Ain't Too Proud To Beg", Temptations
The Temptations have always been a popular group. And thanks to appearances in a few recent movies, this song has an all new popularity to it. The opening is instantly recognizable, and it seems to call people of all ages to your dance floor.

"Dancin' In The Street", Martha Reeves and the Vandellas
Another popular Motown song that'll help you meet your Motown quota. In Philly, people used to complain if we didn't play enough Motown, so we'd throw this gem in to pack the floor. A good alternative is this group's other big hit, "Heatwave."

"The Glenn Miller Medley", or Jive Bunny's "Swing The Mood"

You've got to throw something in the mix for the ancient folks, because there tends to be a "jitterbugger" at every wedding reception! The "Swing The Mood" selection is a medley of a bunch of the old Glen Miller swing songs with some popular 50s and 60s tunes mixed in (with a swing beat) for an even more popular appeal. Don't ever try to mix in or out of a swing song, or granny may hit you over the head with her purse.

"I Saw Her Standing There", The Beatles

The Beatles had a lot of hits, but not too many people could easily dance to. This is a rockin' song with a 50s feel with tons of energy that's still very popular to dance to. Everyone knows The Beatles. If you need a substitute Beatles song, you could use "I Wanna Hold Your Hand".

"Two older slow songs, like Elvis, Sinatra, Nat King Cole or Johnny Mathis

The best way to attract more people to your dance floor is to play lots of slow songs during wedding receptions. Slow songs are the easiest to dance to, since you can virtually hide in your partner's arms! And couples enjoy a nice slow dance every so often.

"Stayin' Alive", Bee Gees

This classic is instantly known by everyone from kids to senior citizens, and is definitely one of the best floor packers ever written. Its infectious beat and melody are easy to dance to at about 110 beats per minute. Play it all the way through!

"Oh What A Night" (Extended Remix), Frankie Vallie

This song made a huge comeback when it was remixed in the late 1980s, and people still respond very strongly to its unforgettable melody. The remix was about 108 beats per minute, so it mixed fairly well with "Stayin' Alive". The best place to bring this song in is when the piano hook starts.

"Dancin' Queen", Abba

Another classic Disco song that's very well known and easy to dance to. It's got a very well known piano arpeggio that starts the song that's perfect for slamming rather than beatmixing for maximum impact. I've seen many DJs skip the intro and try to mix this song, but it should be a crime because they lose some of the power of the song when they do this.

"We Are Family", Sister Sledge

Here's the ultimate family get-together and dance song! Most brides will grab everyone they can grab, even the most reluctant dancers, and drag them to the floor for this photo opportunity. It's a fun disco song at about 114 BPM. This has a memorable drum-based intro, so it's best to "slam" rather than beatmix this song also for maximum impact.

"Celebration", Kool and The Gang

Here's another must-have song, although every DJ I know hates it because he or she has heard it more times than anyone in their right mind would want to. It's got a strong, memorable drum introduction that people will instantly recognize and scream about. I think this song was somewhere around 125 BPM, but I never found it necessary to beatmix it. (Are you detecting a pattern yet?)

Two slow songs from the 80s or 90s

"When A Man Loves A Woman" by Percy Sledge, "Here and Now" by Luther Vandross, or "I Will Always Love You" by Whitney Houston would fit well in this segue.

CHAPTER 3

Party Hour 2

Now that people have become accustomed to the room, and the older folks are tired and sitting down, the middle-aged people (25-40) have had enough to drink so they should be ready to take over the dance floor now. I'd hit them with some music from their younger days and infuse some crossover recurrent hits from the past few years to get the younger crowd interested. Unless your bride asks you not to, you'll begin to bring your music programming more current in an effort to get the younger people moving towards the dance floor.

"Electric Slide", Marcia Griffiths (line dance)

This song is a terrific opener for crowd participation. You may have to teach this dance to some amateurs, so make sure you or someone else at the party can show folks how to do The Electric Slide. Most people will know this simple four step dance (three steps left, clap, three steps right, clap, three steps back, clap, bend over and shake your butt, quarter turn hop to your right, repeat sequence). Beware—in the heyday of this song, I used to get many requests *not* to play this! Make sure it's cool with your customer. I think it's been around long enough now so it's not quite as annoying.

"I Will Survive", Gloria Gaynor

Here's the ultimate female solidarity song that'll pack every single and married woman on your dance floor as they look silly mouthing the words. There is no way to mix the original version of this song, and unfortunately, all the remixes I've ever heard don't do it justice because they have abandoned the beauty and power of the original introduction in exchange for a mixable beat. Play the original version, and play the piano intro, and don't worry about mixing this song. The intro is so strong that people will immediately recognize it and run to the dance floor seconds into it.

"Copacabana" (remix dance version), Barry Manilow

Finally, one of the very few remixes that actually enhances the original song, and even makes it DJ friendly! This is a great floor-packing song that simply has party written all over it. At about 124 BPM, this will infuse a whole lot of energy into just about any party.

"Hot Hot Hot", Arrow (original mix, *not* the lame Buster Poindexter version!)

The Arrow version of this song was the original cut, and was 10 times better than the lame Buster Poindexter rip-off that became popular in the early 1990s. Arrow's version has more energy, and since he's from the islands, it has more authenticity as a Latin song. People traditionally will start a conga line when this song comes on. If they don't, you can start one yourself! Just announce something like, "Let's start a conga line!" Get the bride and/or groom out front with your wireless microphone, and hopefully people will lock their hands on to the waist of the person in front of them and dance/walk around the whole room giving other folks a chance to join the party train. We used to take the line out of the room and around the lobby just for laughs. Make sure you don't bypass the beginning of this song either, especially where the "Ole, Ole" kicks in.

"Rappers Delight", Sugar Hill Gang

Probably the most popular hip-hop song of all time with no bad words and no negative message. Folks of all creeds and colors love this song. It's a terrific introduction to any hip-hop set in a wedding setting.

"Getting Jiggy With It", Will Smith

Another immensely popular, totally non-offensive hip-hop track that'll pack your floor almost anywhere. This late 1990s hit is a terrific transition to newer music.

"Gonna Make You Sweat", CC Music Factory

Another instant classic from the early 1990s that just attracts folks to the dance floor like a magnet. Other great songs along this line are "The Power" by Snap, "Bust A Move" by Young MC, "It Takes Two" by Rob Base and DJ EZ Rock, "Ice Ice Baby" by Vanilla Ice, and "U Can't Touch This" by MC Hammer.

"Good Vibrations", Marky Mark

A powerful, super high-energy jam of about 124BPM from the early 1990s that's instantly recognizable and easy to dance to. I love the Ultimix version of this song—the original mix was very difficult to work with unless you don't ever plan on beatmixing.

"Pump Up The Jam", Technotronic

When you've got things rolling, this aerobic-music type jam will solidify your status as a dance DJ God. It's somewhere around 124BPM with lots of energy and mass appeal. Good substitutions might include "Twilight Zone" by Two Unlimited, "Move This" by Technotronic, or "Another Night" by Real McCoy.

Two slow songs from the 90s, like something by Celine Dion, Whitney Houston, or Mariah Carey

Now you're showing your customers that you actually do have music that's newer than 1980! If you've got a lot of requests for newer music, you can substitute some of today's hottest new slow jams.

"Brick House", Commodores

Now that the older folks have had a chance to rest, and it's still too early to bust out the really hot funky jams, you might want to slide back in time a bit. Brick House is a floor packer with staying power. Let the intro drums play and people will instantly recognize this song and run to the dance floor, in most cases.

"Respect", Aretha Franklin

The Queen of Soul does her thing as she belts out the other official female anthem and subliminally forces women to band together and sing out loud on your dance floor.

Party Hour 3

If it's a good bunch of people, at this point, they'll probably dance to you banging your skull on the microphone. If it's a lame crowd, you'll be pulling your hair out by now. Hopefully, you've got a jumpin' crowd that's ready for some crazy, fun, group participation music!

"Jammin'", Bob Marley

People dig reggae, mon, so throw them a bone somewhere! "Jammin'" is easily Bob Marley's most danceable and popular song.

"It Wasn't Me", Shaggy

Continuing with the pseudo-reggae feel, hit them with an insanely popular Shaggy song that'll bring you up to what most out of touch people will consider "the current decade."

"Macarena", Los Del Mar

Time for "group participation time" again! People still love this silly song with an easy accompanying line dance that folks with handicapped parking privileges could do. Basically, this dance involves standing still while shaking to the beat and putting your hands in different locations on your body. You may need to show some folks how to do it correctly, but most will know it and someone will probably volunteer to teach. Call out the moves: I think it was something like "Hand, hand, palm, palm, shoulder, shoulder, neck, neck, hip, hip, butt, butt, shake it on down, and JUMP!"

CHAPTER 3

"Believe", Cher

People wonder how she's done it, but it's still cool to play Cher songs in the 21st century! Believe is one of her all-time greatest songs, and its mass appeal should attract a pretty large dance crowd. This song has plenty of energy at about 130 BPM, and there are several good remixes and edits available.

"Drove All Night" (Hex Hector remix), Celine Dion

Celine Dion finally hit it on the nose with this song! After a string of famously popular slow songs and quite a few less popular attempts at dance music, Celine's remake of this Cyndi Lauper original combined with Hex Hector's 137 BPM remix became an instant classic will get people screaming.

"Get The Party Started", Pink

Here's a high energy party anthem that will be popular for years to come. There are several really good remixes of this song, and the radio version works well too.

"Who Let The Dogs Out", Baha Men

It was the biggest song anywhere for a long time, then it got so burned out by radio stations playing it once or twice an hour that no one ever wanted to hear it again! Fortunately, enough time has passed now that it's cool to play again. You'll find this same dilemma with many popular songs. People will joyfully scream the "woof" part of this song, again, making you look like you're running an incredibly fun party.

Two more slow songs from whatever era you think is most popular to your guests

More slow songs, please! At this point, it doesn't really matter what the slow songs are, so just throw something nice on that you think your guests will dig.

"Old Time Rock N' Roll", Bob Seger

This is a terrific song to open a dance set with! Definitely play this from the beginning; people will get extremely excited when they hear the piano come on. Turn the volume way up for the two piano riffs in the beginning, then quickly reduce it to a normal volume once Bob shouts, "JUST GET THOSE OLD RECORDS OFF THE SHELF...."

"Shout", Isley Brothers

Another classic oldie that's sure to have people singing and dancing en masse. This is a rock song that's impossible to beatmix, so don't even try it. The beginning "WEEELLLLL" is very strong too, so crank that part way up. A trick most pro DJs use is turning down the volume at the part towards the end of the song immediately after he sings "HEY HEY HEY HEY;" there's a crowd singing along with the record, but your guests will usually enjoy singing this out loud themselves. Turn up the volume when he sings, then turn off the volume when it's the crowd's turn for a really cool effect.

"Twist", Chubby Checker

I've always played this song immediately after "Shout" for some reason, and it's always done well. The Twist is one of the easiest dances that anyone can do, and most people will run to the dance floor to do it. It's still insanely popular.

"YMCA", Village People

When you're ready to bust back into the polyester era, bust out this killer group participation jam that'll be sure to have people joyfully spelling the letters Y—M—C—A with their arms and hands.

"You Shook Me All Night Long", AC/DC

It's always struck me as strange, but this song is a HUGE party song although it only hit #35 on the Billboard chart in 1980! Just like most of the best dance rock songs, you'll be stuck with yet another intro you'll simply have to play. The guitar in the beginning of this song is one of the most recognizable riffs in the music business. Back in the 90s, I used to mix that riff with the break in Tone Loc's "Wild Thing" for an incredible impact! I'd have to pitch (speed) this song up 2-4% to keep up with Wild Thing, but it seems to sound even better pitched up.

The Rest of the Party

You should have a pretty good idea of what your crowd is responding to at this point, so feel free to be creative in your mix. Typically, many of the older folks are pooped or have left by now, so you can experiment with newer music if it's cool with your bride and groom and their friends. Try to feel out your bride and groom and play what you think they'd appreciate. If they're drunk and don't care at this point because they're making their rounds collecting cash from their guests, you can play for the majority. But definitely make it a point to check in with your clients.

Make sure you've got lots of slow song sets ready to go whenever you think your crowd needs a break.

Additional Dances and Events

Sappy people like to include special spotlight dances for family or friends who are celebrating a birthday or anniversary within a week or two of the affair. You can throw these into your program whenever you feel they fit. These dances are preceded by a brief announcement on behalf of the bride and groom. All additional special dances should be solicited by or at least approved by the bride and groom.

Dollar Dance

To raise a few extra bucks, the DJ will invite people to dance with the new bride for a small fee, usually a dollar, hence the term "dollar dance." For kicks, you can establish the initial fee with an auction; the highest bidder wins the honor of the first dance. If the bride and groom decide to have a dollar dance, try to wait until the blood alcohol level is a little higher so the dance will be more profitable.

About an hour or so into your party time, you may need to take a break and emcee the following traditional events when requested by your bride and groom. These events are rarely a surprise, since they've been done at thousands of weddings for decades. Nonetheless, they're still fun.

The Bouquet Toss

Preparation for this event includes letting the bride know in advance, because she'll be busy visiting tables and doing the bride thing. You'll also want to make sure the bride's throwaway bouquet is available.

First, you will invite all the single women to the dance floor. You'll then call the bride to the dance floor. While the girls are waiting on the dance floor, you should play a fun "girl" song, like "Girls Just Want to Have Fun" by Cyndi Lauper, "It's Raining Men" by The Weather Girls, or "All I Want to Do Is Have Some Fun" by Sheryl Crow. The bride can choose anything she wants for this event.

You'll then invite the bride to stand in front of all the girls with her back facing them. Then announce that you're going to count backwards from three, and then the bride will toss her bouquet over her shoulder to the single women. You can also add some color to this event by explaining the tradition of this event. The old story goes something like this: "The single woman who catches the bouquet will be the next person to get married or have a romantic interlude."

If a young girl (under 18) catches the bouquet, you may want to have the bride choose a substitute for the last act of this tradition.

As an alternative to the bouquet toss, many brides will now personally give the bouquet to a close friend or relative as a gesture of thanks.

Removal of the Garter

After the single woman has caught the bouquet, you'll ask the bride to have a seat on a chair that you've placed on the dance floor. You'll then ask the groom to come to the dance floor. You must instruct the groom to kneel and remove the garter from the bride's leg. We would play something funny like "The Stripper" theme to accentuate this event. Everyone will hoot and holler.

Good songs for this event include the following:

> "Do Ya Think I'm Sexy" (Rod Stewart)
>
> "Girls Just Wanna Have Fun" (Cyndi Lauper)
>
> "Legs" (ZZ Top)
>
> "Pretty Woman" (Roy Orbison)
>
> "The Stripper" (Instrumental by David Rose)
>
> "You Sexy Thing" (Hot Chocolate)

Garter Toss

This is where all the guys get rowdy. After the garter has been removed and the bride has left the dance floor for her own safety, you'll then ask all the single gentlemen to come to the dance floor. During this fiasco, you should play a fun "boy" song, like "Macho Man" or "Oh Yeah." You'll then ask the groom to toss the garter over his shoulder on your count of 3. We used to tell the groom to fake the first toss and watch all the guys jump around in anticipation. We'd then remind them that this was not a football game, and that there will be a 15-yard penalty for unnecessary roughness. The groom eventually tosses the coveted garter into the crowd of testosterone, and some lucky guy will catch it or grab it off the floor under a mad rush of crazed men.

Cool songs for this event include:

> "Bad Boys" (Inner Circle)
>
> "Macho Man" (Village People)
>
> "Oh Yeah! " (Yello)

Putting the Garter Back On

You'll then ask the woman who caught the bouquet and the gentlemen who caught the garter to come to the dance floor. Have the woman sit down in the chair. The object of the last part of this activity is for the gentleman who caught the garter to place that garter on the leg of the woman who caught the bouquet. We'd play something along the lines of "The Theme to the Pink Panther" to enhance the excitement of this event. We would announce that the higher the gentleman places the garter on the woman's leg, the more luck the bride and groom will have. DJ Joseph Montalvo in Philadelphia would further announce that if he could get the garter up one leg and down the other, the bride and groom would be set for life! Another interesting thing to do here is reversing the roles; have the woman place the garter on the man's leg. Big chuckles here.

Montalvo also told me about a new twist to this event. He'll announce that he didn't like the way the man placed the garter on the woman, or that a rule was somehow broken, and he'll get the audience to agree with him for a re-do. He'll then pull out a blindfold and place it over the man's eyes. While he's blindfolding the man, the woman has snuck out of the chair and some volunteer *man* has sat in her place, rolling up his pants. Joe will have the man kneel once again, and proceed to try place the garter on the guy's leg! Once the man feels a hairy leg, he'll usually jump back and rip the blindfold off to see that his lady is now a man! Don't let him off the hook though, make him place the garter from the man's leg for "fifty more years of health, wealth and happiness for the bride and groom" for maximum impact. Obviously, you'll have to secretly tell the woman who caught the bouquet about your plan and ask her to get a male volunteer before you start this crazy event.

Fun songs to help this event along include:

"Theme From Mission Impossible"

"The Pink Panther"

"U Can't Touch This" (MC Hammer)

Cake Cutting

After the bouquet and garter ceremony, we would host the traditional cake cutting ceremony. The timing of this event can vary depending if the cake is to be served as dessert—check with the bride in advance. You as a DJ will call the bride and groom to the cake, and instruct them to cut the cake. We would play a fun song to get this thing going. You'll then host the bride feeding the groom and vice versa. Sometimes it gets messy, other times not. It's your job to do the play by play for this event, but stay out of the way so the photographer and videographer can get their shots.

Fun songs for this event include:

"Cut the Cake" (Average White Band)

"How Sweet It Is" (James Taylor)

"I Wanna Grow Old With You" (Adam Sandler)

"Love & Marriage" (Frank Sinatra)

"Peter Gunn Theme"

"Sugar, Sugar" (The Archies)

"The Bride Cuts The Cake" (Various Artists)

"When I'm 64" (The Beatles)

CHAPTER 3

Last Dance

At the end of the reception, it's a nice gesture to play a set of slow songs. For the last song, you'll want to dedicate it to the guests on behalf of the bride and groom. Mention that the bride and groom appreciate everyone sharing their special day with them. Wish the bride and groom many years of health, prosperity and happiness. Then tell everyone you have business cards available.

A few good songs for closing your gig on a positive note include:

"Always And Forever" (Heatwave)

"Closing Time" (Semisonic)

"From This Moment On" (Shania Twain & Bryan White)

"Good Riddance/Time Of Your Life" (Green Day)

"Goodnight Sweetheart" (The Spaniels)

"I've Had The Time Of My Life" (Bill Medley & Jennifer Warnes)

"Last Dance" (Donna Summer)

"New York, New York" (Frank Sinatra)

"Save The Best For Last" (Vanessa Williams)

What A Wonderful World" (Louis Armstrong)

"Wonderful Tonight" (Eric Clapton)

"You're Still The One" (Shania Twain)

Fun Wedding Events

There are a few cute and sneaky things you can do to enhance your weddings that'll hopefully get you a tip and some referrals for more work.

First, you can call the bride to center of the dance floor. Have her take a seat in a chair. Tell the groom to come up to his bride, and get down on one knee just like he was proposing to her. Then invite all the men in the house to surround the bride and groom on the dance floor. Immediately cue up "You've Lost That Lovin' Feeling" by Hall and Oates or The Righteous Brothers to the part where it says, "Baby, baby, I get down on my knees for you..." Have all the guys sing along to this song for a full-bore group participation event.

Secondly, you can have the groom stand in the center of the dance floor. Say a few kind words about how good he looks tonight. Then tell the crowd that there's an old, time-honored tradition where the bride and groom get a year of good luck for every kiss on the cheek that the groom gets, and the luck increases if they leave lipstick marks. All the chicks in the place will swarm the groom and kiss him on the cheek. This'll get big chuckles.

And finally, there's this gag that many DJs are doing now that's a hoot. You'll need to get a bunch of key blanks from your local hardware store. At some point during the reception, find the maid of honor and ask her to sneak around the room and give a key to as many women who are *not related to the groom* as she can find without the bride or groom knowing. Tell her to tell the women that the DJ will soon ask for these keys, and have her tell everyone not to tell the bride or groom. Then find the best man, and ask

him to secretly give keys to as many men as he can *who are not related to the bride*, again without letting the bride or groom know what's going on. At some point during the reception, announce that you need the groom to come to the DJ. You'll say something clever about how great it is that he's finally found the right woman
(ask for some applause), and that he's happy that he'll no longer feel the need to be with another woman. At that point, announce that you need all the ladies who have a key to the groom's "secret apartment, formerly known as 'The Love Shack,'" to return their keys at this time. All the women with keys will then walk up and drop their keys in a bucket or hand them to the groom as his new bride watches in a panic. (If the groom has a great sense of humor and you can get some unrelated men to come up at the end, it'll be even funnier!) Then comes the kicker; bring the bride up and ask her if she knew anything about the "Love Shack". Then, mention that you've heard through a mutual friend that she too had a secret apartment! Ask all the men with keys to that apartment to return them at this time. It's a great practical joke that makes everyone laugh. Make sure you get keys to as many unrelated older people as you can for an added kick (obviously, you wouldn't want to infer that the bride's father was having sexual relations with the bride).

If you're new at these things, the absolute best thing you can do is make nice with the photographer. Chances are he or she has years of experience doing these things, and he can help walk you through the timing of everything that needs to be done. Plus, it helps make his job easier since he can orchestrate the flow to catch the best photographs. And since photographers are among the first things a bride chooses when getting married, if he likes you, he may refer you to his brides, and a referral will almost always guarantee that you'll get the job.

Performing at Anniversary Parties

Anniversary parties usually rank up there with taxes, libraries, and class reunions on the boring scale. By the time someone decides to have an anniversary party, they've been married for 20 to 50 years and are obviously up in the years themselves. They'll want to hear music from their teen years, so you'll need to be well-versed in that music.

Some anniversary parties can be as complex as a wedding reception. When couples decide to "renew their vows," they're essentially replaying their wedding reception! There may be different players, or not as many people in the bridal party, but they may want to follow all the typical wedding traditions. In this event, you'll need to break out your wedding information sheets and layout your roadmap.

In my experience, I don't recall a whole lot of activity at most anniversary parties, although there were always exceptions. Many of these parties are much smaller than wedding receptions, and it's not uncommon to have these parties at smaller restaurants or at the customer's home. There's typically at cocktail hour, a dinner hour, and a few hours of dancing.

Some good songs for an anniversary party would obviously include the anniversary couple's wedding song, several songs from their era, and perhaps one or more of the following:

"Don't Know Much" (Linda Ronstadt & Aaron Neville)

"Have I Told You Lately" (Van Morrison)

"Save the Best for Last" (Vanessa Williams)

CHAPTER 3

"Through the Years" (Kenny Rogers)

"Still" (The Commodores)

"Unforgettable" (Nat King Cole)

"Wind Beneath My Wings" (Bette Midler)

"You Decorated My Life" (Kenny Rogers)

Notice that these are all "oldies," since most of your anniversary couple will be older. Young people don't usually celebrate their anniversaries until they've become older.

Performing at Class Reunions

In my experience, class reunions can really suck for DJs because there's always some miserable knucklehead asking you to turn down the music. I always wondered why reunion planners hired disc jockeys when all they really wanted was elevator music.

Most of the guests at reunions are specifically there to chat, network, and catch up with old friends. Many won't waste much time on the dance floor, but you never know. But reunion planners still hire DJs, and that helps to keep us in business. Moreover, these affairs are often booked on a weeknight, which will help to fill your off nights.

Traditionally, there's a cocktail hour, a dinner hour, and supposedly two hours for partying and announcements. There are occasionally games and contests depending on who's organizing the affair. You really don't need ice breakers for reunions, since everyone practically already knows everyone. Better reunion planners might include a few fun interactive games, and perhaps some kind of awards ceremony.

The deal here is to play songs that were popular during the four years these people were in high school. It'll take a little math to figure this out. If it's a tenth reunion, we'll count back 10 years to their graduation year, then subtract another four to figure out the first year of your music range. You'll then need to research the hottest songs during those four years, because these are the songs they grew up to. *Billboard* Magazine produces a yearbook that lists the popular songs of every year back to the beginning of popular music.

The music is usually kept at a lower volume during reunions so everyone can chat at a comfortable level. If you do get a full dance floor at some point, of course you may raise the volume slightly.

Performing at Proms and School Dances

The complete opposite of reunions are dances that occur while the students are still in school, like proms and other school dances like homecomings, dinner dances, graduation parties, and holiday parties. There aren't many DJs that concentrate on this type of party on a professional level, mainly due to the very high equipment and music requirements, not to mention high-maintenance school kids. The most important part of these dances is your music. You must be completely relevant and up to date in your music, or you will fail miserably—today's undisciplined kids are brutal. School dances demand only the newest music and the coolest club lighting effects at their dances.

But if the big show is what you want to do, and you want to bust out concert type sound with sound levels most adults cannot humanly tolerate, then this is the gig for you. Prom DJs can charge anywhere from $1,000 to $5,000 depending on your reputation, the size of your area, and the number of students attending the dance.

It's not uncommon at school dances to see six foot high full concert-like cabinets run by multiple amplifiers and accented by intelligent lighting systems that would make even the area's biggest clubs jealous. These DJs also use fog, bubble, and confetti machines during their shows.

Most school shows are full-on dance parties with little to no talking required. You can even scratch (but only if you're good at it) and students may actually appreciate it!

School dance DJs also spend a lot of time in preparation. Meetings with school administrators and prom committees are often required, and things can change up until the last minute.

Remember that school dances are always G- or PG-rated events. Even though all the rappers do it in their music, you will be strictly forbidden from using profanity on the microphone or at the event.

Also, make sure you have a contract signed by an ADULT, usually the committee chairperson who's usually a teacher or school administrator. Contracts signed by school dance committee members are unenforceable since they're usually under 18 years old and not legally able to commit to contracts.

Performing at Company Picnics, Fundraisers, and Other Corporate Affairs

I used to love doing corporate gigs because they were great money, and they were usually during the daytime hours when I had nothing else going on. Companies of all sizes routinely have going away parties, morale boosting parties, product launch celebrations, retirement dinners, and all kinds of other special events that require entertainment. In all honesty, people rarely danced at these events. They'll usually hire you to provide a sound system because it's often cheaper to hire a DJ than rent from a professional audio/visual company, plus they get a guy to run the system included. Yes, you may be a glorified public address system. Hey—if they were willing to pay, I'd play.

For corporate parties that actually want you to be a DJ, your clients will expect you to provide and emcee team building activities and interactive games. It's common to see games and contests like Potato Sack contests, water balloon tosses, the frozen multi-headed t-shirt, The Shuffle Golf Challenge, and other safe, low impact things.

Holiday parties will represent a huge boost in private party bookings for you. In the old days, you were cool playing Christmas music all night long. But in today's politically correct climate, you must play music for every other ethnic background in existence. There's a good amount of seasonal money involved in company picnics and Christmas parties, now often known as "non-denominational holiday parties" in an effort to be politically correct. You'll basically play a wide variety of music for a wide variance of age groups. There are usually company-sponsored speeches and awards thrown in that you may be asked to MC. You can also upsell your customers into various games and contests like a basketball shoot, a putting contest, and other fun stuff.

The flow of these events is always different, so there's no real preset guide you can follow. Many of these affairs will be outside parties, so you'll have to deal with weather issues. Make sure you've got a bunch of large plastic bags to cover your equipment just in case it rains. You'll have many discussions with your clients well in advance, so you'll know what's expected from you.

Performing at Bar and Bat Mitzvahs

Our company initially stayed away from Bar and Bat Mitzvahs for years simply because we didn't understand them. DJs who knew how to do these behaved like this market was a closely guarded secret, so they could avoid competition. Unfortunately, there was no book like this to help us learn about them. Eventually, we hooked up with an event coordinator who showed us how easy these events were, we started to love these parties!

There is a terrific amount of money available in this business. Customers tend to be slightly more demanding than usual at these events because, these parties can me more of a status thing for the parents rather than a celebration for kids. That's the way it was in Philadelphia and South New Jersey, your mileage may vary. In that area, people routinely throw tremendous parties that can cost between $10-$40,000 dollars.

The premise is this—when a Jewish child turns about 13 (varies in some sects), the kid is thrust into adulthood, so to speak. The boy (Bar Mitzvah) or girl (Bat Mitzvah) has a big religious service in their honor, usually followed by a huge party. Bar Mitzvah parties are similar to the Christian Communion, only they are exponentially more involved. It's normally a formal affair, and has some similarities to the wedding format. There's usually an event coordinator who will run the show, which can be a huge help to you as a DJ.

Here is a sample flow of how a typical Bar or Bat Mitzvah may go.

Cocktail Hour

Just like a wedding, these affairs often begin with a cocktail hour. Keeping in mind that the average age will be about 12, your guests probably won't be conversing nicely while sipping Martinis at the bar. You may need to play some dance music or host some small contests during the cocktail hour. Many DJs do the Karaoke thing to keep the little monsters busy. Depending on the event budget, other people may use magicians, balloon artists, face painters, jugglers or dancers during this time.

Grand Entrance

Similar to a wedding, the guest of honor is hidden in a separate room to regroup from his or her ceremony, or to take pictures. After the cocktail hour, he or she will prepare to make their grand entrance. Parents and important family members are lined up in order, using a Bar Mitzvah Info Sheet. Often, the event coordinator will announce the names with the correct Hebrew accent. If it's your duty, make sure you know how to pronounce each name properly.

As the guest of honor finally enters the room, you'll want to play something exciting. Crank up the volume. If you've got lights and smoke set up, fire them all up! Good songs for the introduction are

"O Fortuna" by Apotheosis, "Get Ready For This" by 2-Unlimited, or something else fast and punchy as dictated by your customer. Ask everyone to give the guest of honor a warm round of applause.

The Blessing of the Bread ("Motzi")

Usually right after the Grand Entrance, the traditional Motzi occurs, known as the blessing over the Challah or bread. Usually, the guest of honor (often referred to as the "Mitzvah") will do the prayer that he or she has rehearsed during this ceremony. We've also seen the rabbi or a parent recite the traditional prayers.

Chowtime

Usually the kids will scarf down their food in about five minutes and be all over you immediately following. Instead of blasting loud dance music while the adults are still filling their plates, we would usually do a low-key game or group activity to keep the kids busy for a while.

Dancing and Games

After the meal, you're free to open it up and create party madness. Since kids get bored easily, it's a good idea to play short sets of music broken up with kids games and contests, such as Huggy Bear, Coke and Pepsi, Musical Chairs, a Hula-Hoop contest, or maybe a limbo contest. Make sure you've got a bunch of prizes to give to the kids. Stuff like glow necklaces, CD singles, DVDs and videos seem to work really well.

Coke and Pepsi

Practically anyone who's been to a Bar Mitzvah has seen or played the game "Coke and Pepsi," so they'll often expect to play it. You'll set up two lines of an equal amount of people on each side of the dance floor. You'll label one side "Coke," and the other side "Pepsi." You'll play some fun music in the background—I actually made a remix of Coke and Pepsi jingles from old TV commercials. When you call "Coke" or "Pepsi," that side must run to the other side and sits on the knee of their partner. The last person to successfully sit on someone else's knee is "out," and is removed from play. The object is to find the fastest couple through elimination and award them a prize. In his book "DJ Games," Marc Pears suggests mixing things up by using other names and other things to do, like saying "Doctor Pepper" or "Seven Up," and assigning various tasks with those names. For instance, you would explain that if you call "ROOT BEER" both sides would have to run to the middle and give a "high 5" to their partner and quickly return to their spot, with the last couple to return being disqualified. Or, perhaps saying "Seven Up" means both sides must exchange places, again, with the last straggler disqualified. It's a silly but fun game that kids seem to enjoy.

Huggy Bear

"Huggy Bear" is another silly elimination game. All players are invited to the dance floor. You'll play a song and tell everyone to dance. Most people won't really dance, they'll all kind of stand in a position because they know exactly what they're supposed to do. You'll then stop the music and say a random number like "Five!", and your contestants must get into groups of that number. Whoever is not in a group with five people is "out". You keep doing this, obviously with numbers that work for the amount of contestants you have left. Obviously, you can't call "TEN!" if you've only got nine people left.

The Hora

At some point during the reception, often immediately after the Grand Entrance, your guests will form a large circle with a smaller circle inside. All the guests should be holding hands. The circles will move in opposite directions. This is the traditional Jewish dance called the Hora. During the Hora, family members may lift the guest of honor while he or she is sitting in a chair. This usually happens spontaneously and automatically, but you may have to influence it on once in a while if you're sure your customer has asked that this be done. There are several Jewish party song medleys and variations of the song "Hava Nagila" that are appropriate for the Hora.

The Candlelighting Ceremony

About two hours into the affair, the Candlelighting Ceremony is started. What happens here is about 13 or 14 family members or close friends of the Mitzvah come up to light candles on behalf of the Mitzvah. You'll want to announce the inception of this event. Sometimes you'll then hand the microphone over to the Mitzvah who will introduce the names of the persons who will be lighting the candles, and sometimes they'll want you to do it. Sometimes the Mitzvah will want the candle lighters introduced to a special song as part of the presentation. To properly organize this, you'll need all this information well in advance listed on your Bar Mitzvah Information Form, similar to the wedding information form, located in this book.

More Dancing and Stuff

You'll want to try to get everyone involved and on the dance floor. You can do this by playing a mix of songs from the 50s through today's hottest hits. Be sure to include some of the "floor packer" songs as described later in this book.

Remember that each Bar Mitzvah and Bat Mitzvah has its own personality, based upon the preferences of the family, regional customs and religious considerations.

The Grand Finale

Close to the end of the party, you'll have everyone give the Mitzvah and his or her family a large round of applause, and play a few songs in their honor. Some folks like fast songs, other might want slow songs. Check with your client.

In New York and some other areas where they really go all out for these things, they'll do a nice gesture where all the guests will applaud and thank the staff for their hard work. We're not sure who started this or why New York DJs do this, but it's not a bad idea. It's typically done later in the party, sometimes immediately following the Candlelighting ceremony so that most of the staff is out on the floor and not hiding in the kitchen.

Performing at Sweet 16s

Sweet 16s are a glorified birthday party that's similar to a Bat Mitzvah, only at less than half the price! When an average American girl reaches the age of 16, she'll expect her father to throw a big birthday bash celebrating this rite of passage. Latino girls do something called a "Quinciñera" (pronounced KEEN-SEEN-AIR-AH), which is the same thing, only done one year earlier (a "Sweet 15"). Here's how one of these affairs typically goes.

Cocktail Hour

Similar to a wedding reception, you'll have about an hour of mingling music, often in a separate room. This is sometimes called a Cocktail Hour. If the cocktail hour is in a room other than the main room, you'll need a separate sound system, or you'll need to be able to move your main system really quickly! We'd just run a single speaker into the other room if it was close enough, or we'd use our backup system in the cocktail room and break it down later in the night. Your customer should tell you the kind of music she wants during her cocktail hour. Since it's typically a bunch of teens, she'll probably ask for top-40 stuff you'd hear on the radio, saving the really good dance songs for the party hours. Upscale events usually opt for smooth jazz during this hour. The guest of honor is typically hiding in another room somewhere, preparing for her grand entrance.

Grand Entrance or Introductions

About an hour into the party, you'll ask everyone to find their seats in the main room and prepare for the grand entrance of the guest of honor. Hopefully, you've got an assistant who'll keep the music playing, or you'll have enough music cued up and ready to roll as you meet up with the Sweet 16 and her family and prepare them for their entrance. You'll usually line them up with any brothers or sisters coming in first, then any grandparents, then the Sweet 16 girl escorted by her choice of just her father, her father and mother, or some other person who's special in her life. Also, ask who will be offering the toast immediately after the first dance. Some families like to have a prayer or "benediction" offered by someone. If this is the case, it's traditionally done before the toast. It's best to have all this information written down. You should create a form similar to our Wedding Information Form found in this chapter. Make sure you ask for proper pronunciation of all names if you're not sure of anything—don't take any chances!

Have all the guests stand, then announce the guests of honor, one pair at a time, asking them to applaud each couple as they enter the main room ("Give it up for " or "Please put your hands together for...," or "Let's have a warm round of applause for...."). Finally, you'll put on a special grand entrance theme (chosen by your guest of honor in advance), and with much fanfare, you'll say something like, "Ladies and Gentlemen, it is my privilege to introduce to you our guest of honor, our Sweet 16, Miss Firstname Lastname, escorted by Mr. or Mrs. Lastname!" Everyone will clap and go nuts for about 10-15 seconds. Keep smiling.

Special Dances

Immediately following her grand entrance, you'll invite your guest of honor to dance a special slow dance, usually with her father, but it could be her grandfather, uncle, or boyfriend depending on her wishes. Occasionally, she'll dance with her father, and then a second dance with her boyfriend. If she decides to do a second dance, ask her if it's cool if you can invite the rest of the guests to join them on the dance floor halfway into the second song. It gets really boring standing around watching people dance for six to ten minutes!

The Toast

Following the first dance, you'll ease into the toast. During the first dance, check with the banquet manager to make sure he or she has provided champagne or some other non-alcoholic toasting beverage for the toast so no one is caught off guard. Ask everyone to remain standing, then introduce the person who will be offering the toast to the Sweet 16 girl (usually her father, or the person who escorted her in). This person should know he or she is giving the toast in advance, and will usually have something prepared.

If there's a meal being served, you've usually got a few minutes to dance before the meal starts, so rock the house with some of your hottest house, hip hop and/or reggae music to get things going. If there will be no formal meal, keep rockin' for six to ten songs, then play a slow song to break things up. If the parents have invited their friends, make sure you throw in some disco and oldies to keep them happy, too.

Candlelighting Ceremony

About an hour or two into the Sweet 16, you'll break for the Candle Lighting Ceremony. Almost exactly like a Bat Mitzvah, 16 family members or close friends of the Sweet-16 chick come up to light candles, all offering best wishes to the birthday girl. You can hand a wireless microphone to all the candle lighters and make them wish the guest of honor a Happy Sweet 16. The guest of honor can choose her favorite slow song, or something cheesy like "Happy Birthday Sweet Sixteen" by Neil Sedaka or "Sixteen Candles" by The Crests, that she'd like you to play during this event. After they're all done lighting the candles, it's time to party again.

You may want to toss in some fun contests or games to add to the fun of the party, but remember, these are teens a little older than Bar Mitzvah kids, so the traditional kids' games may not go over too well. I've got some really crazy stuff in one of my other books, *Wild Party Contests*, (Brevard Marketing; 2003) that would be great for a Sweet 16 party.

Performing at Other Mobile Parties

Hopefully, your marketing efforts will influence parties for a wide variety of reasons to help build your business. Some ideas you could influence might include:

Birthday Parties

Engagement Parties

Divorce Parties

Weight Loss Parties (to celebrate losing a certain amount of weight)

Job Promotion Parties

Pink Slip Parties

Retirement Parties

After Prom Parties

Graduation Parties

Housewarming Parties

Grand Opening Parties (to celebrate a business opening or expansion)

Family Reunions

Family or Company Picnics

CD or Record Release Parties

Memorial Day Parties (to kick off the summer season)

July 4th Parties

Labor Day Parties (to celebrate the end of the summer season)

Halloween Parties

New Years Eve Parties

Car Shows

Carnivals

State Fairs

You could arrange a party for just about any situation you can imagine! These types of parties tend to be less organized, a little more light hearted and fun. Basically, you'll play a broad mix of popular dance music and throw in some games and add-ons to spice things up a bit.

Obviously, during a birthday party, you would have everyone sing "Happy Birthday" sometime during the program. Some good alternative birthday celebration songs include "Birthday" by The Beatles or "Celebration" by Kool and the Gang.

New Years Eve parties are usually formal events in dress only, with the only required event being a countdown at midnight. I always arranged to have a big screen or projection television showing Times Square, New York for the official ball drop for pleasing eye candy. You could add a top-ten songs-of-the-year countdown to make your show sound more official.

Preparation for a Mobile Job

Part of the term "Mobile DJ" is the word "mobile," which means you'll be traveling to many different places with a portable set of equipment and music. I've always wanted to call mobile DJs "PJs," or Portable Jockeys, but those initials were already taken by sleepwear and might cause more confusion that they're worth.

Since no two venues are the same, you should always thoroughly investigate the place where you'll be performing ahead of time. Here's a list of questions you'll need answered well in advance.

Where is the place of the party or reception?
You'll need to know exactly where the banquet hall is. If you're not familiar with the location, get written directions and go and find it well before the day of your gig. You don't ever want to be late to a wedding reception.

CHAPTER 3

Where will you set up?

You'll need to know exactly where you're supposed to set up. Speak to the person in charge of banquets and have them show you the room and the area where you'll be performing. Familiarize yourself with the room and where the tables will be, and begin to plan your setup. Ask them where they prefer the speakers be set up to stay out of the food servers' way and for the best possible sound performance.

Where's the juice?

You'll need to know where the power outlets are. Make sure they're 110 volt service and not 220! Determine if they're on a separate circuit, or if they're on the same circuit as the dishwasher. Try to get at least 20 AMP dedicated service for sound equipment, and an entirely separate circuit if you're running lights and special effects to avoid "tripping" the circuit breaker. Power failures are not only embarrassing; they could damage your expensive equipment.

What's up with the tables?

Do you have to bring your own tables for your equipment or music? Find out in advance, or you may be spinning on the floor! Most banquet halls will provide skirted tables for the DJ, but I've seen smaller private parties at a restaurant where an unprepared DJ was forced to use chairs as tables because all the tables were being used by the guests.

Do I need coverage?

Does this hall require you to carry your own insurance? Some places require $1 million in liability insurance with documentation before you're allowed inside the room. This requirement is becoming more common. Banquet halls that have had bad experiences with amateur DJs can help avoid more bad experiences by only allowing "professional" DJs to perform, meaning those who have invested in obtaining an insurance policy.

Does fog put you in a fog?

If you carry special lighting, fog, bubbles and confetti, does the hall allow them? Some halls expressly prohibit fog because it may set their smoke detectors off. Smaller halls with lazy management teams may expressly prohibit certain types of confetti because smaller pieces can be difficult to clean up.

When can I bust in with my funky dopeness?

How early can you get into the hall to begin your setup? You'll want to get there as early as possible so you can set up in a relaxed manner. You should always do a "sound check" before the event begins to ensure each and every piece of your equipment is operating properly. Sometimes mobile equipment fails due to being knocked around in a car, van or truck, so you'll obviously need to know this in advance so you can do something to replace malfunctioning units.

Got tunes?

Make a checklist of all the music you'll need for your party, especially the special songs. There is absolutely no excuse for forgetting to bring songs specifically requested in advance by your customer. The omission of a requested song for a bride and groom's first dance could potentially ruin a wedding reception, and subsequently your reputation! I've been in a situation where the DJ forgot the bride and groom's song. Fortunately, I heard about the issue from someone in the bridal party, and I happened to have my music in my truck, so I saved his ass on this occasion. Today, with laptop computers and wireless Internet connections prolifically available, it is possible to instantly purchase and download a missing song on the Internet, but that's still no excuse for being unprepared. Another thing to watch out for is scratched or cracked records or CDs. I would always have at least one backup of all the important requested songs with me at every performance for peace of mind.

Got equipment?

Make a checklist of all the equipment you'll need, and actually go through it as your packing up your equipment for your affair. I've included an equipment checklist in this chapter. Include backup systems and an emergency toolkit.

Know your turf

Know the general area of the banquet facility, just in case you need to run out for anything. I used to map out the closest Radio Shack, Circuit City, or Best Buy just in case.

Got milk?

Bring something to drink in case you don't have time to break away. It's also a good idea to pack a snack or eat a full meal before you get to your gig.

Whoops factor

It doesn't hurt to have a change of clothes, just in case something stupid happens. I saw a DJ pee his pants once and hide behind his rig all night.

Mobile Advertising, Marketing, and Imaging

In order to make any real money in this business, you'll need to sell your services directly to the consumer. This is different from the marketing described for the Radio DJ or the Club DJ, since they're primarily involved in business-to-business marketing. Consumer marketing is an entirely different animal. When dealing with customers on this level, your main goal is to make them feel confident about you. They're trusting their very important once-in-a-lifetime affair with you, so they want to be sure they've chosen the right DJ.

You'll find that many of the larger full-time DJ companies bad mouth smaller DJ organizations by trying to discourage people from hiring a "part-time" DJ. Having worked for a larger mobile DJ company, I understand the sneaky tricks they use.

They'll mention that smaller, independent DJs may not have adequate liability insurance. A good point, but not necessarily a disqualifying feature. Unless your client is lawsuit happy, a standard business liability policy should cover any potential losses. The hall or place where they party will occur also has liability insurance, and chances are they'll be held liable for any injuries or damages that occur on their property.

They'll try to scare customers into thinking smaller DJs don't have a reliable back up system or personnel. Although larger DJ companies have several DJs available, chances are they're all working during your event since most events occur on Saturdays. And the non-working leftover guys are probably people you wouldn't want hosting your affair anyway! It's a very rare occasion where a DJ won't be able to show up to perform as scheduled. But things do happen and you should have some kind of back up plan just in case.

CHAPTER 3

They'll try to prove that their DJ service is superior by showing you a book full of glowing testimonials. Testimonials are important marketing tools, but they're not necessarily the pinnacle of trust. I've seen DJs write their own testimonials signed by friends or family who they never performed for! And people are much quicker to write a complaint letter rather than a letter of praise. Where are all the angry complaint letters they've received? Why aren't they on display too?

Personally, if I were hiring a DJ, I would consider someone who holds a 9-to-5 job a whole lot more responsible than some full-time DJ one who sleeps until 3 in the afternoon every day and works two days a week.

Regardless of your company's size, it's you and your sales materials the customer will evaluate, so you've got to make them feel comfortable enough to hand over their hard-earned cash and trust you with their affair. Marketing is simply positioning yourself in an effort to look like the best buy using purely psychological techniques. It all starts with the image you project. The following topics discuss proper marketing and imaging for your successful DJ company.

Telephone Coverage

In order to be considered as a real business, you'll have to represent yourself as a real business. The first step is to make your first point of contact, usually the telephone, sound like a real business. Our biggest advantage as a new business was that we had a toll-free 800-vanity number. People perceived us as a bigger, more responsible company since we had that 800 line. Now these toll-free numbers are everywhere and you almost have to have one to look like you're serious about the business. Make sure your 800 number "terminates" or rings into a dedicated business line that always answers with the name of your company. Modern technology will allow you to forward your calls directly to any phone. We used to forward our calls to our cell phones and advertise that we had 24-hour service.

Credit Cards

In addition to enabling impulse purchases that might not occur if you only accepted cash or checks, accepting credit cards will help people to trust your company. Most people identify businesses that accept credit cards as "real" businesses. And most people realize that if they have a problem with your services, they can "dispute" the charge and maybe not have to pay the bill. That rarely happens, but it does suck, and you probably did something silly and deserve it if it happens.

You'll need to open a business bank account plus a "merchant account" that will process the credit card transactions and ultimately deposit them into your business bank account for a small surcharge. Expect to pay the credit card company a "discount rate" of anywhere up to 4% of each sale as commission, and possibly a transaction fee for each sale. "Swiped" transactions, or transactions where the customer actually is in your office and you physically swipe the card and capture their signature authorizing the charge, are typically less risky and may get you a lower discount rate. Make sure to use the credit card logos in your promotional materials.

Contracts

You'll need to establish a formal contract to protect yourself, and to protect the customer. This is a document that promises that you will appear and perform as promised in exchange for monetary consideration, or cash. It must be written and signed by you and the customer. It should have language that specifies exactly what you're promising to do in exchange for your payment. It also protects your customer from you not showing up, and also protects you from unreasonable damages or demands. It's always best to ask a lawyer to help you create your contract. I've included a sample contract that should not be used as is, because your state laws and regulations could render it invalid. Again, spend a few bucks and have a local attorney review your contract for potential "loopholes," which are errors or omissions that could leave you open to damages.

If your customer is a "minor" (a person under the age of majority, or under 18 years of age), they do not have legal capacity or authority to enter into a contractual agreement. For example, if you contracted with a 14-year-old to perform at a school prom for $4,000, you might perform at the party. Then, when it came time for payment, the 14-year-old could legally tell you to go pound sand and skip away giggling. And there's absolutely nothing you can do about it. Make sure you've got a responsible adult available to sign the contract.

If your customer is another business rather than an individual person, make sure the person signing has the legal authority to sign on behalf of the company. If that customer faxes you a signed contract, ask them to mail you the original signed copy because some courts may not accept a fax as an original valid contract.

Your contract should ask for a deposit to reserve your company for the date and time in question. We have no problem getting at least a $150 deposit for weddings and other types of private parties. We stipulate that the balance must be paid in full prior to the day of the scheduled affair. It's up to you if you deem that deposit refundable or non-refundable. We decided that a deposit was only refundable if the client cancelled the contract more than 180 days prior to the affair. If it were any shorter of a time period, we figured we might be turning away business since we had the existing contract on file.

Referrals

Another important part of gaining a potential customer's trust is showing them all the satisfied customers you've had in the past. Ask all your customers to help you build your business by giving out your name and telephone number to any friends, family or coworkers thinking about having a party or hiring a DJ. Complimentary businesses, such as photographers, videographers, wedding coordinators, banquet managers, florists, and others will often see a potential client before a DJ will, so it's important to befriend as many of these folks as possible so they too will recommend you and give out your brochures and business cards.

Your Sales Kit

Finally, professional looking business cards, brochures and literature will show your potential customer that you are a serious, worthwhile business entity. If they perceive that you've invested money in professional printing, they're more likely to take your company seriously. Include a photograph of yourself (preferably dressed in a suit or tuxedo) in front of your setup. If the customer can see your formal dress style and a professional setup, they'll feel even more comfortable with your company.

There are a few considerations with respect to your developing your literature. Desktop publishing software has become inexpensive and widespread, allowing virtually anyone the ability to create his or

CHAPTER 3

her own brochures. If you're not a natural born writer, rather than shoot yourself in the foot with a bad brochure, have someone with some writing experience help you write your sales pitch. There are writers everywhere, and many college students that will do it for free in exchange for the experience. And have a professional designer do the layout and printing for you so it doesn't look amateur.

Try to use at least one other color in addition to black. Use full color if you can. Also try to use a thicker, higher-grade coated paper. People often notice and subconsciously appreciate things like this. Avoid colored papers, since they look unprofessional and are often hard to read.

When designing or using logos and colors, make sure that you're consistent in the use of the logo and colors. Use it on your business cards, your letterheads, your contracts, and on your brochures.

Here's what you should include in your sales kit for "warm" or solicited leads, meaning people who were recommended by someone else and have actually asked you to send them some information.

Your Personalized Cover Letter

You can use a standard form letter, but take the time to type the customer's name and address on the letter. As I shopped my competition, I noticed very few other DJs took the time to do this. This is a major rule in professional sales! Customers appreciate this and will reward you for it. Your cover letter should be relatively brief, and it must include the major sales points of your company in a bulleted format. If you want to take the extra initiative, include the sales points you previously discussed with the client.

Your Professional Brochure

This document speaks to your client about your company. You'll want something that's laid out professionally, preferably in color, with photographs of your people and equipment rather than silly meaningless stock brochures that look identical to someone else's. People will more easily make a purchase if they can actually see what they're getting. Again, include your main sales points in this brochure. Avoid things that can change quickly, like prices, music lists, and current trends so you can avoid costly reprints. Put those in your cover letter.

Copies of Recommendation Letters from Businesses and Satisfied Customers

Again, you're trying to build your customer's trust. Your services are considered a big-ticket item, so customers are naturally going to be a bit more cautious when choosing. Give them as many reasons as you can to go with your company and not someone else's.

Current Song Lists

You're going to want to show your customer how diverse you can be. Private affairs consist of a wide range of people and lifestyles, so you'll want to have at least a little something for everyone. Break your song lists into categories, such as "Oldies," "Disco," "Current," "Specialty," "Hip Hop," "Latin," etc. Go ahead and borrow the lists in this book to get you started. When you add new selections, simply add them to your lists. This will help you appear to be organized.

A Sales Agreement or Contract

You've got to cleverly ask for the sale. Don't ever send anything without asking for the sale! Try not to make this form look like a formal contract. Be creative, use your logo and lighthearted font styles while still including all the formal language. If you've got a ton of fine print, have it printed on a second sheet or on the reverse side of the contract in a lighter color. Include language that says you require an up-front deposit in order to reserve their date, how much it is, and who to make their check payable to.

A Self-Addressed, Postage Paid Envelope

Since you're already working with a warm lead, why not make it one step easier for your customer to choose you? The total cost of this is a first-class stamp plus an envelope. We saw our closes increase by 25% with this tricky method.

A Few Business Cards, And a Small Token of Your Appreciation

Include some business cards and a personalized gift like a pen or a magnet card or a wedding planner with your company's name on it. Make sure it's cheap but useful. People dig gifts—it makes them feel warm and fuzzy when you think of them.

The whole point of the sales kit is to convince the potential client to like you. It helps when they feel confident that they can respect your organization, and that you are the best person for the job. You also want to make it as easy as possible for the person to send you a check or their credit card information to close the sale.

Drumming Up Sales

Here are several ways in which you can increase your business. See what works best for you, and concentrate on making all your marketing work as well.

Targeting

When you're starting out, you'll want to try to get experience with as many types of parties and markets as possible. This way you can ultimately decide what types of parties or what kinds of people you enjoy working with the most. Choose your favorites, and then evaluate how you can best reach the people who throw those parties. If you're into proms, you'll need to hype up your cool image with posters and flyers and maybe a radio ad campaign. If you're into weddings, you'll want to exhibit at a local bridal show. If you're into trance and techno, you'll want to hang out with the local promoters who throw rave parties. Some marketing techniques will work well for one market segment and bomb on others, so you've got to identify your target.

The Internet

Websites are now a must-have form of promotion for all DJ companies. If you think about it, a website is your on-line instant brochure that's available 24 hours a day, 7 days a week. Many people do all kinds of pre-buy research on the Internet. It's the perfect compliment to your professionally designed brochures and your toll-free 800 telephone line. You can save hundreds of dollars in printing and postage by directing your customers to your website to search your song lists or photos of prior events. Websites are easily updated, and much less expensive to update than printed material. Include all the information from your sales kit. Remember to ensure that your logo and colors on your website match those on your literature! Be consistent—it'll make you look like a real company.

The key to generating sales via the Internet is being everywhere. You'll need to get yourself prominently listed in the major search engines, as well as being linked to the websites of complimentary businesses.

CHAPTER 3

Most other businesses with websites will be happy to "trade links" with your business, meaning you will place a link on your website in exchange for them placing a link on theirs. Always check up and see if they held up their part of the bargain!

Bridal Shows

If you've decided to pursue the wedding industry, Bridal Shows are probably the most important way to get your company in the mainstream. You can find out exactly what the customer is looking for, and then tell them how you can give it to him or her. You'll need to be clean shaven (especially women) and dressed well, have lots of professional literature to give away. You'll need to appear to be happy, upbeat, confident, and accessible.

It's not necessary, but it's a good idea to have a professional display unit that has a backlit logo. This really will make you look like one of the big guys—or even better than they do in most cases! We also had a TV space built into our display. We showed show specials and video and pictures of us in action. A good-looking display will attract more people to your booth and will help potential customers trust your company. My company, The DJ Resource, produces custom electronic slideshows that many DJs are now using at bridal shows.

Make sure you have all the proper promotional supplies for the bridal show. These include plenty of brochures, business cards, a clipboard, blank lead forms for potential customers who want more information or a personal meeting, and a bunch of pens.

When you finish the show, the company who put the show on will usually send you a list of all the registered visitors. You'll then mail all these people a follow up letter with a flyer or brochure, and hopefully pick up a few more gigs. If you get their phone numbers, definitely call them and follow up using the same telemarketing principals listed below.

Telemarketing

Telemarketing is tough these days, especially with new legislation and the government's "Do Not Call" list. With all the telemarketers out there, it's hard to even get past "hello" today. It can be very frustrating, and you will probably grow tired quickly. Lists of "warm" or solicited leads are legal, since you have their permission to call them, and they're usually a little easier to work with. These leads are gathered from people you've met at bridal shows, referrals from previous customers, or recommendations from other bridal vendors.

When you finally get the prospective customer on the line, the clock will be ticking and your time will be limited. You'll have to make a positive impression within the first few seconds or face the dreaded click. You'll want to engage the potential customer in a meaningful dialogue that explores exactly what that customer wants. You'll want to ask them leading questions that will get them to tell you how you should approach them.

Have your questions prepared ahead of time, written down on a list in front of you as you're making your calls. Your questions can include some of the following:

"Have you spoken to any other DJs yet? What did you like or dislike about them?"
This opens up a dialogue where you can discuss why your services are better or more advantageous than your competitor's. Try to let the customer say as much as they will before you counter with your sales pitch.

Take notes and make sure you address every one of his or her points. Create a file for this potential client with your notes so you can refer to them later when you're asking for the sale, and when you're performing at the function. Make sure you don't do what they didn't like about another company!

"What kind of music are you and your friends into?"

This lets you advertise your super-duper music collection, and also gives you a chance to get ideas as to how to expand and better your collection. Tell the client you will send them a song list of all your current music. If you don't have the music they're talking about, don't lie and say you do, or you could blow the sale if they start to discuss the artists and you don't know what you're talking about. Tell them you will get it immediately, and include it on your song lists. Chances are someone else will want that music too.

"Have you seen other DJs perform at (type of affair)? What did you think about them?"

This is the most effective market research you can do—finding out what customers actually think about your competition! Ask about volume levels, music selection, appearance, vocal ability and more. Compare and contrast this against yourself. Try to remain as positive as possible and not bad-mouth anyone; just cite the positive qualities of your operation. Take good notes here, and be ready to counter any negative points.

"Do you want lights, fog, bubbles, or confetti at your affair?"

Be ready for upsells! The more add-ons you can sell your customer, the more money you can make. Offer them complete lighting packages, party favors, fog, bubbles, and all kinds of nonsense. Mark it up to a price that's competitive with retail, so if they go to price it themselves, they'll see your price is right in line and you're not trying to rip them off.

"Can I send you a brochure and some additional information about our company?"

Always go for the kill and ask for the sale. But if they're not sure and don't want to book immediately, follow up with a brochure and a nice sales kit. People tend to read mail they're expecting. If you send it unannounced, it could get trashed as junk mail. Don't forget to ask for the sale again in your mail kit.

"Were you considering other types of entertainment, such as a band?"

This is the DJ's oldest nemesis—the "Band versus DJ Dilemma". It's your job to win this battle by offering all the reasons why a DJ is just as good as or better than a band. Stress that you're not as expensive as a band because you don't have five people to pay, you don't take breaks, and that you're able to play a much wider array of music performed by the artists that made the songs famous.

"When do you plan on making a decision about your entertainment?"

Even though most folks will just pull some random date out of their butts to answer this question, take notes and use this as a deadline. You'll have several chances to close this sale, so space them out between the present time and the date you're holding them to. Remind your potential client that dates are filling quickly, and that most reputable DJs are booked well past a year in advance.

Direct Mail

This is a nice name for the term "junk mail." You'll get a list of potential clients from a bridal shop or magazine, and you'll attempt to convert those leads into customers with a direct mail package. I worked for a company that mailed out over 10 million pieces of direct mail a year. Response is usually very low, but there are certain tricks you can use that will make this profitable for you.

Your direct mail package will be a scaled down version of your full sales kit. You may want to reduce the size of your kit to avoid higher postage costs. You'll still want to send a brochure and a cover letter that covers the advantages of choosing your company. Try to personalize the letter if you have the time and resources.

Some of the tricks used by the "pros" of direct mail in their effort to get you to open it rather than toss it include:

Hand addressing envelopes.
Studies show that envelopes with human handwriting have a better chance of being opened than pre-printed addresses or labels, because they look personal. Handwritten addresses now stand out.

Using stamps rather than bulk rate postage.
Big companies are now using cheesy looking bulk-rate stamps that have no value in an effort to make their junk mail look like they have real stamps.

Using brightly colored or oversized envelopes.
Your eye is naturally attracted to the biggest and or brightest piece in the bunch. If your package looks interesting, you've got a significantly better shot at being opened.

Using envelopes that look like important document or express delivery envelopes.
This stresses "importance". And they're usually larger than regular envelopes, so they'll stand out that way too.

Also mail your packages to local businesses in your area that support weddings or private parties, such as banquet halls or bridal shops in an effort to generate referral business and name recognition.

Lead Generation

There are many ways in which to drum up business for your mobile DJ operation. You're only limited by your imagination and your creativity. Here are a few of them:

Scan your local newspapers for engagement announcements. Send them a congratulations card with a business card inside. Follow up in a few weeks with your brochure and sales materials.

Hook up with the salespeople at your local banquet halls. Unfortunately, the trend seems to have evolved into a payola scheme in some places where you have to "pay to play." I'm not sure this is legal. Avoid places like these; there are plenty of others that do business the old-fashioned honest way.

Chat with local businesses that support weddings and private affairs and offer to exchange literature. For instance, if you hooked up with a bridal shop, you could send their brochure with your materials in exchange for them displaying your cards or brochures somewhere in their store.

Make friends with other DJ services in your area that you respect. Tell them you're available on a subcontractor basis when they're sold out. In exchange for this, you should send them your overflow business.

Contact local schools and churches and offer them an organizational discount if they use your services.

Offer to perform for free at local charity events when you have free time. This will help you get some exposure in the market.

Advertising

Advertising is a necessary evil of any business. You'll need to spend money to make money! The key is to spend it as efficiently and as effectively as possible. Most businesses re-invest anywhere from 5-20% of their earnings back into advertising in an effort to grow their business, depending on the business and its age. You'll need to consider a few things while developing your advertising plan:

What's your budget? This is probably the most important consideration. Obviously, if you're just starting out, you'll need to let people know that you are out there. New businesses must spend a disproportionate amount on advertising as part of their start-up costs. Figure out what you can afford over the next 12 months while leaving yourself with enough operating income for other expenses such as equipment, insurance, taxes, music, printing, office space, and communications charges.

Who is your market? You've got to figure out how to effectively reach your target audience, and this relies heavily on the vehicle you choose. If you want to do weddings, you can use bridal magazines. If you want to do school dances, you can use local newspapers and flyers. If you want to do everything, you'll want a nice mixture of different vehicles.

What is your capacity? You can spend thousands of dollars in an effort to bring in a large number of leads. But if you're only a one or two person operation, chances are you'll have to turn some of that business away because you can't be two places at the same time. You've got to figure this into your equation as you decide how to divide your advertising dollars.

What is your offer? You've got to give potential customers a reason to call you. What is the premise of your pitch? Do you have the most music? The best sound system? Celebrity caliber entertainers? A money saving coupon? Define your focus and sell it in your advertisement. Let people know why they need to call you.

How can they contact you? Make it easy for your potential clients to contact you. Clearly define your telephone number, your e-mail address or your office address. If they can't find you, they can't use you.

We'll cite our personal experiences with different types of advertising. Hopefully, you won't make the same mistakes we did in our early days!

Yellow Pages

We thought we would "tear up the market" by buying a quarter-page display ad in our local yellow pages, but we were dead wrong. At about $750 per month, our yellow page ads nearly bankrupted us our first year in business. Yellow page display ads are very costly, and in our experience, almost every lead that came from our yellow pages advertisement was some price-shopper who told us we were too expensive. It is important to be listed in the yellow pages in case someone mentions your company's name but doesn't have your telephone number. And now it's even worse, with multiple books in most markets. Be ready for Yellow Page salespeople will do cartwheels and show you all kinds of statistics to get you to purchase an expensive display ad.

Magazines and Newspapers

If you're doing weddings, you might want to try bridal magazines. There's nothing more targeted than a local bridal magazine, and nearly all brides pick up a free copy somewhere in their travels. If you're doing birthday parties or corporate gigs, take out a small ad in the local paper. These advertisements are known as "print" or "display" advertisements. You can buy anything from a small listing in the classified section up to the back cover of a magazine, which is usually the most expensive thing you can buy. You'll need to gauge your spending using the guidelines listed above.

You'll have choices in size and in color. Black and white ads usually will cost about half of a color one, and can be just as effective if designed well. The biggest ads aren't necessarily the most effective; it's all in the design and the positioning. Smaller ads can be much more effective than poorly designed larger ads. Use your money to hire a professional designer to create an ad you can use in several different places. Get yourself a catchy headline that will stop readers in their tracks! Make it as big and bold as you can. Remember that you're competing with all the other stories and advertisements, so do something that will catch a reader's attention. Ask for a right page position, since these are more apt to be seen that an ad on the left page.

Radio

We took a chance and used radio to promote one of our DJ companies. We had a company that specialized in "Modern Rock" music just as it was becoming mainstream, so we bought radio commercials on the two new Modern Rock stations in our area. This was a big success because this market was untapped, and since the radio station was just developing this new format, commercials were cheap.

Try to target your audience. Radio offers format separation, so you can more clearly target a market or demographic segment. We would limit our radio advertisements to evenings and weekend mornings because that's when we thought brides would be running around to bridal shops and banquet halls. This ensured that their wedding was the first thing on their mind.

Radio is usually very expensive, especially in larger markets. We've paid up to $400 per spot while testing different stations. But there are opportunities to be had. Try to work out a cooperative deal with another vendor that supplies the private party market, such as a tuxedo shop or a limo company. This way you can both split the cost of the ad and promote both of your businesses.

Do your radio advertisements yourself if you can! Radio stations will offer to write and produce a commercial for you, but chances are it will sound like all the other advertisements on the station. Stand out by creating something yourself, or by hiring a professional agency.

Television

TV is a terrific vehicle for advertising. The only problem is that you're limited to 30 seconds in most cases, and production costs are expensive. You can get some great deals with your local cable company today and advertise in a small segment of your area on networks like MTV and VH1 for as little as $20 per commercial in some areas! Make sure you don't create an advertisement that's half-assed or you could waste a lot of money. Take some time, plan it out and do it right. Make it classy.

The Internet

You can place "banner ads" on bridal websites for a small fee that can direct traffic directly to your website if you have one. The Internet is becoming more and more popular as people use it to do pre-buy research. Don't spend a lot of money on banner ads, because it's still hard to tell how many unique visitors a website gets. There's a huge difference between "hits" and "unique visitors," so shop carefully. Try to trade links rather than buying them.

Billboards

My old partner always had this dream of putting our company smack dab on the biggest billboard on I-95. Not only would it have cost us thousands of dollars to do this, we'd have to lock into a long-term contract that included a bunch of billboards in other undesirable areas. Billboards are used for two things: reminder advertisements for a big company, or a destination advertisement for somewhere along that roadway. Stay away from these until you're mega-huge.

Free Publicity

If you're doing something wild and new, chances are you can get yourself written up in the local newspapers or even on the evening news. Let your local media know what you're doing that's making all this noise by issuing a professional "Press Release."

There's a standard format for press release. They're usually no more than a page or two long, typed and not hand written, and include all the basic facts (who, what, when, where, why, and how). It will start with a headline that summarizes what you're doing, followed by the date and location of the event. Subsequent paragraphs include the actual details beginning with a summary in the first paragraph. Include your name and a way to contact you at the bottom of your release.

Many companies specialize in creating and distributing press releases to the right people. Investigate your local area for someone you feel comfortable with.

Super-Secret Marketing Tricks

Since I worked for some pretty major marketing companies during the day, I borrowed and adapted some of the gimmicks they used to make millions of dollars. These little tricks will make you tons of dough and increase your closing rate dramatically. Use them to make yourself big bucks. Invite us out for drinks on your new yacht.

Invitations

Invitations were our secret weapon—no one else was doing this before we were. As a special bonus for booking our DJ or video company, we would offer our clients invitation printing services AT COST. Most bridal shops, tuxedo joints and other companies would offer a 10-25% discount on invitation services; but we offered them at a full 40-50% discount, which was our wholesale cost. Our customers saved hundreds of dollars on their invitation orders. The best part of this deal is that it can cost you nothing. All you have to do is contact a few of the major invitation printing companies like Carlson Craft, Regency, and Birchcraft. For about $50 each, they'll set you up with a sample book, a line of credit, and a bunch of coupons you can use to defray that $50 cost. You then place the orders, and forward a copy of the invoice to your customers, so they can see exactly what they're paying. It's worth sacrificing the profit of invitation sales to build your business. Word of this deal spread like wildfire and heavily increased our referral business.

Wedding Shopper

My DJ partner was a purchasing manager during the day, so he was a professional negotiator by trade. He used those skills to enhance our DJ business by acting as a Wedding Shopper for our DJ clients. He would do the legwork involved in getting quotes from other wedding related businesses. Since we were throwing them business, they would give us a nice discount that we would pass on to our customers. We had deals with photographers, florists, limousine companies, videographers, tuxedo rental outfits, and bakeries. You can also try to strike deals with halls and bridal shops, but know that many of these services are traditionally booked much earlier in the process.

Centerpieces

Most centerpieces are made of floral arrangements, and can cost a couple hundred dollars. We happened to know some people who went to art school and did some design stuff on the side, so we enlisted their help in creating an "alternative" centerpiece. They came up with all kinds of neat faux flower arrangements, candy sculptures, pottery, and other things. People loved these alternatives! Once we even supplied a modified version of the electronic game "Simon," where you chase those stupid lights around using your memory. This was a huge hit. Again, we threw these in at cost. Your customers will appreciate the compliments they get on their centerpieces!

At weddings, it's traditional to have a small favor for your guests. Well, we took it upon ourselves to create alternative party favors. We started with small chocolates home made by one of our DJ's wives. We've also done small gag gifts like small rubber smiley faces that stick out their tongues when you squeeze them. You can find a whole bunch of neat stuff in the Oriental Trading Catalog (oriental.com). Again, we did these at cost, and people loved our imagination.

Balloon Decoration

Brides love balloon decorations! We rented a small helium tank and bought a box of balloons. At private parties other than formal weddings, we would tie a bunch of balloons to the back of the chairs in the banquet room before the guests arrived. You'd be amazed at how festive this makes a room look! This was a free service to our customers. You should check with your customer in advance to see if they have any reservations about this. Most people will totally love this add-on.

Kabuki Confetti Blasts

There's nothing more festive than confetti! A company called Kabuki from Canada makes a terrific self-contained confetti launcher that uses CO_2 cartridges and a few different types of confetti. Most of their confetti paper products are large, bright, colorful paper that's much easier to clean up than traditional confetti.

A Kabuki Confetti Blast.

Digital Imagery

We bought one of the first digital cameras on the market; so we were able to take instant digital photos of our customers live at the affair. We also carried a laptop computer and a color printer. We would have an assistant take a few photographs of the bride and groom during their first dance, or a couple photographs of the guest of honor at other types of parties. Within minutes, we'd have a full-color 8x10 photo in a frame for them! This amazed people and ticked off a whole bunch of photographers. This technology is now widely available and relatively inexpensive today. Many DJs bring video projectors and show the pictures almost instantly on a screen.

Budget Video

Before we had a full-fledged video company, we would carry a consumer-grade video camera to weddings. We'd record the titles (John and Jamie's Wedding Reception) prior to the affair, then have an assistant shoot the key events at the wedding reception in order as they happened. At the end of the reception, we'd enclose the tape in a nice video case and give it to the bride and groom as a gift. They had a wedding video the same day! We stopped doing this when we created our video company because we obviously wanted to make some extra bucks, but it's a great idea for someone just starting out.

Recording the Introductions and Toasts

One of our DJs did some work as a recording engineer, and he came up with a cool idea. He would use a cassette recorder to record the best man's toast. At the end of the wedding during the last slow song, he'd replay the toast over the song. He'd then hand the cassette to the bride and groom as a keepsake. Of course they loved this, and it became standard procedure.

 NOTE: Beware that it's technically illegal to record the music behind the introductions, or any music used for dances. Technically, you would need to secure "synchronization rights" to legally record and distribute the music. It's a ridiculously tedious and expensive project to get the rights to use these songs in a recording. You've been warned.

Of course you could sell these ideas as add-ons if your DJ service is already established. But if you're new in the business, you'll generate all kinds of noise by giving these away. You too can invent new cool things to add to your package by simply opening your eyes and watching unrelated businesses and their promotions. Use your imagination!

Contracts and Forms

I've included some sample forms for you to review only for your use in familiarizing yourself with the terms and items in these forms. You'll definitely want to build your own custom forms that specify the way you do business.

Wedding Information Sheet

[Your logo here]

Please take a few moments to complete the following questions. We will need this information to help us program your wedding so that we may work in conjunction with the hall, the photographer and your videographer.

Listed below are the events that take place at a "traditional" wedding. Let us know which of these events you want at your reception, then fill in the appropriate person or requested song for the event. If you have any questions, feel free to call 555-555-5555. Thanks for choosing [Your name here]!

Your Name: _____

Date of Wedding: _____

Time of Reception: _____

Location of Reception: _____

Your Phone: _____

Please complete the following as you would like your guests announced. Please spell difficult names phonetically.

Grandparents: _____

Parents of the Bride: _____

Parents of the Groom: _____

Bridesmaids and Ushers (in the order they will be introduced):

_____

_____

_____

Please check the events you want at your reception, and then list the appropriate song or person.

Flower Girl: _____

Ring Bearer: _____

Maid/Matron of Honor: _____

Best Man: _____

Bride and Groom as you would like to be announced: _____

__Bride and Groom Dance (song) _____

__Dance Before Dinner   __ Dance After Dinner

__Toast to the Bride and Groom (name) _____

__Benediction/Blessing (name) _____

__Father and Daughter Dance (song) _____

__Mother and Groom Dance (song) _____

__Parents and Bridal Party Dance (song) _____

__Bouquet and Garter Ceremony _____

__Cake Cutting Ceremony (song) _____

   __Messy (going to smash it all over my partner's face)   __Not Messy

If you have requests for music for a special event (birthday, anniversary, someone who could not attend for some reason, etc.), please let us know. Also, please indicate the songs that you do and do not want played at your reception. You may return our song list, or you may write your selections on a separate page.

Equipment Checklist

__Entire regular mobile music library

__Specially requested songs

__CD player or turntable

__Backup CD player or turntable

__CD power cables

__RCA connection cables for CD players

__Mini-jack to RCA adapters for portable CD players

__Wired microphone

__Wireless microphone

__Microphone cables

__Headphone

CHAPTER 3

___Mixer

___Mixer power cable

___RCA to 1/2" or XLR cables from the mixer your amplifiers

___Amplifier(s)

___Amplifier power cable

___Backup amplifier(s)

___Speakon, 1/2" cables, or XLR cables from the amplifier to your speakers

___Speakers and bass cabinets

___Speaker stands and mounting hardware

___Power surge protector

___Extension cords

___Tables if required

___Mixer power cable

___Extra adapters and cables

___Duct tape to secure cables to the floor

___Tools, fuses, emergency backup kit

___Formal attire

___Personal grooming effects

Sample Contract

Once again, I reiterate, please do not copy this contract word for word, because it may not be valid in your state or region, and it may not apply to your particular situation.

(YOUR LOGO HERE)

DJ PERFORMANCE CONTRACT

This AGREEMENT is made effective this [Day of month] day of [Month], [Year] by and between [Customer's full and legal name], located at [Customer's home address if an individual, business headquarters if a business] (hereinafter referred to as the "Purchaser") and [Your company and your address here] (hereinafter referred to as the "Entertainer").

In consideration of the terms and conditions as specified in this agreement, the Purchaser and the Entertainer agree as follows:

The place of performance is located at [The name of the hall or physical location of the party] (hereinafter referred to as the "Venue").

The date of the Performance shall be [The day and date of the affair] and the time of the Performance shall be from [The actual time of the gig]. This Performance shall have a duration of [How many] hours.

Purchaser agrees to pay the Entertainer a fee of [How much you've agreed to charge written out in words] DOLLARS ($xxxxx.xx) for the Performance. An initial deposit in the amount of [Required deposit] is due upon execution of this contract in [Whatever means of payment you accept, cash, money order, credit cards, etc.]. The remaining payment must be made in full prior to Performance in cash, money order or cashier's check. In the event of non-payment prior to the Performance, the Purchaser agrees this Agreement shall be cancelled immediately with no performance required and any previous payments shall be immediately forfeited to the Entertainer. In the event of non-payment after the Performance, Purchaser further agrees to remit any uncollected balance including a ten dollar per statement fee plus reasonable collection or attorney fees. Purchaser shall be charged $30 for each returned check plus a $10 service charge for each collection notice. Past-due balances will incur interest at the rate of 2% for each month in which the balance is outstanding.

The entertainment to be provided by the Entertainer is described as the playback of musical recordings through sound equipment with occasional "DJ" narration (hereinafter referred to as the "Performance"), and includes any additional props or games as specified in this Agreement. The Purchaser reserves the right to control the manner, means and details of the performance of services by Entertainer via a written event planner or music request list prior to the event. Without a planner or request list, Entertainer shall attempt to play Purchaser's and Purchaser's guests' music requests but shall not be held responsible if certain selections are unavailable. Entertainer reserves the right to censor music requests that may be considered offensive or inappropriate for the event. Entertainer reserves the right to choose the sequence of songs played for the good of the majority and the flow of the event.

This agreement to perform shall be excused by detention of personnel by sickness, accidents, riots, strikes, epidemics, acts of God, or any other legitimate condition beyond Entertainer's control. If such circumstances arise, all reasonable efforts will be made to find comparable replacement entertainment at the agreed upon fees. Should Entertainer be unable to procure a qualified replacement, Purchaser shall receive a credit or full refund of all prepaid fees. Purchaser agrees that in all such circumstances, Entertainer's liability shall be exclusively limited to refunding the fees paid and Entertainer shall not be liable for indirect or consequential damages arising from any breach of contract.

Purchaser agrees to provide a secure parking space in a reasonably close proximity to Venue's loading area for Entertainer's vehicles for a period commencing two (2) hours prior to the performance and continuing for one (1) hour following the performance.

Purchaser and/or Venue shall provide adequate security for the Entertainer and their property before, during and after the Performance.

Sound and Lighting. The Entertainer shall furnish all sound equipment, microphones, lighting and power strips necessary for the Performance. Purchaser agrees to provide two six-foot (6') long tables for the Entertainer's equipment, and access to at least two three-prong grounded 110 Volt/20 AMP wall plugs. The Entertainer agrees to provide all personnel required to assist the setup for and conduct of the Performance and takedown after the Performance.

This agreement cannot be canceled except by mutual written consent of both the Purchaser and Entertainer. If cancellation is initiated by the Purchaser in writing and agreed to by Entertainer in writing, Purchaser will be required to pay any unpaid costs already incurred by Entertainer, but not more than the total fee agreed upon.

Purchaser agrees to defend, indemnify, assume liability for and hold Entertainer harmless from any and all claims, demands, damages, losses, suits, proceedings, penalties, expenses or other liabilities including attorney fees and court costs, arising out of or resulting from the performance of this contract, regardless of the basis (except for gross negligence on the part of Entertainer)

Purchaser may not transfer this contract to another party without the prior written consent and approval of Entertainer.

Both Purchaser and Entertainer are legally able and have full legal capacity to execute this Agreement on the day and year first above written.

AGREED TO AND ACCEPTED:

BY: "ENTERTAINER"

[Your full name and company name]

_____

(authorized signature)

_____

(printed name)

BY: "PURCHASER"

[Customer's full name or company name]

_____

(authorized signature)

_____

(printed name)

MOBILE AND CLUB DJ EQUIPMENT

If you're brand new in the business, you're probably all excited and ready to run to your local DJ store and purchase thousands of dollars of equipment. Fight that impulse with all your power! You've got several important decisions to make first.

Are you planning on pursuing mobile jobs or club gigs, or both? Will you spin vinyl, CDs, MP3s, or a mixture of all? Sliders or knobs on your mixer? Would you prefer a spherical stylus on a straight tone arm, or an elliptical stylus on a curved tone arm for your turntables? High impedance or low impedance microphones? All these questions will need to be answered accurately, or you're in for some expensive mistakes and a whole lot of eBay transactions selling stuff for half of what you paid for it.

If you haven't been hanging out with other DJs and getting a true sense of what equipment and formats you're digging, do not go out and buy equipment right away. Do you have any DJ friends with equipment you can work on? Can you get a job with a local DJ company that has its own equipment? Do you have a home system or a good boom-box you can patch into? Many new DJs who make rash purchasing decisions can't figure out why they can't get in the groove and end up deciding that the DJ thing isn't what they really want to do. You may luck out and find one of those people who'll be eager to sell you his barely used equipment, maybe even the same exact stuff you're looking for, at a fraction of its original cost.

As you're going through the learning process, you'll eventually discover which turntables, CD players, mixers, and related accessories will work best for you. It's a very personal decision. Usually, another DJ will be your biggest influence in all these decisions. Most people tend to stick to the machines they learned on for the first few years, and maybe later start to experiment with other equipment. I'm a technology wizard by nature, and I fought CDs when they first appeared on the scene because my roots were firmly engrained in spinning vinyl. It took a while, but I realized how much smarter CDs were, and I made the transition.

If you can, try to experiment with as many brands or types of equipment as possible before you make your big purchase. Most DJ stores will let you mess with the equipment in the store, but that's usually not the right situation and never enough time to make an accurate evaluation of your needs and wants.

Your sound is a direct reflection of you. The overall sound in a bar, club or banquet hall actually can affect your credibility. If your levels are right where they're supposed to be, if your voice sounds strong and understandable, and if your words make sense, people will perceive you to be a leader. But if your music is distorted and people can't understand a word you're saying, they'll think you're mildly insane.

If it's too quiet, you'll lose valuable energy and look like a wuss. You've got to constantly monitor the sound levels not only on the dance floor, but all over the entire room. Many clubs are wired in "zones" so you can control different areas right from your DJ booth.

To make things even more complicated, your levels will change as the night progresses. As more people fill the room, their bodies will start to suck up all the sound waves. You've got to recognize this and adjust your levels accordingly. Eventually, you'll get to know your room and you'll automatically know where the levels should be during the night. If you're not sure if it's too loud, take a brief survey. Ask four or five different people from unrelated groups how they perceive the sound levels, and gauge from there. Try to avoid asking miserable looking older folks, because music simply being *on* is usually too loud for them.

Introduction to Sound

As a typical young DJ, I thought I knew everything about everything. I initially ignored basic sound principles because I was too cool to study "science." Besides, I thought all that was important was that I somehow managed to get sound to come out of my speakers. After a few fried amplifiers, a bunch of blown speakers, and a lot of wasted hard-earned dollars, I finally realized I needed to get schooled in the science of sound. Bobby Domenico at Pat's Music, a DJ store in Philadelphia, took the time to sit me down and explain how it all works.

The first step to understanding your equipment needs is first understanding the basics of sound. If you plan to take this business seriously, you'll want to produce the best sound you can. By knowing the science involved, you'll avoid problems that cause equipment failures, which can be very embarrassing and ruin your reputation. I ignored these principles my first few years as a DJ. Later in my career, after learning about all this sound stuff, I made a few bucks personally designing and installing a few small nightclub sound systems. This section has taken years of experience (mistakes) to gather, and should be a big help to even experienced DJs.

The second step is deciphering all the terminology that sound equipment manufacturers and retailers may throw at you when you're going to buy your equipment. If you can "talk the talk," you stand a much better chance at not getting ripped off by some greedy schmuck at a wannabe DJ store.

First off, sound, by definition, is a fluctuation in air pressure perceived by the human ear. The fluctuation is caused by anything that disturbs the equilibrium of still air, which is what we perceive as "silence." Sounds can be produced by moving air past your vocal cords, strumming a tuned guitar string, or by striking a blunt object with, well, another blunt object.

When you speak, your vocal cords vibrate creating waves that travel through the air. When you whistle, your lips vibrate. Musical instruments have strings that vibrate. When you are sick or yell a lot, your vocal cords may become swollen to the point of where they have difficulty vibrating. When this occurs, you have laryngitis and you lose your normal voice. Basically, it helps to think of the world and everyone in it as a bunch of great big vibrators (snicker). A sound occurrence produces vibrations of a certain frequency, which produces the specific "tone" of what we then hear. The level or pressure of air fluctuation (its "volume") and its frequency (its tone) is what makes a "sound wave," also known as "acoustic energy." Lots of different types of acoustic energy occurring at the same time originating from different sources creates what we call "noise."

Sound waves are inherently slow compared to other things we perceive. Sound's speed limit is approximately 766 miles per hour at room temperature, also known as "the speed of sound." Light and electricity are capable of traveling about 186,300 miles per *second*, also known as "light speed," which Einstein theorizes is the fastest speed possible. Seven hundred miles per hour seems pretty darn fast until you consider the physics of sound waves. Sound is actually vibrating air molecules bumping into each other, and anything else they happen to run into, until they finally bump into your eardrum. This process is relatively fast, but does takes some time. Depending on the orientation of the source of the sound and the physics of the room, it's often hard to tell which direction sounds are coming from. They're usually coming at you (and going away from you) from several directions at once. This is why in a very large hall you can often see someone's mouth moving before the sound actually reaches you.

Many inexperienced DJs will simply raise the volume to over compensate for these and other inefficiencies, which often overdrives the equipment and leads to equipment failure. If you understand the basics of sound reinforcement, you can often purchase less equipment, and make it last much longer.

Not all sound waves can be heard by people. "Hertz" (Hz) is the scientific term for the rate of vibrations, otherwise known as "cycles per second." A "cycle" is the measure of change between a certain sound's high and low pressure energy, kind of like an ocean wave cresting and falling. Hertz can be used to numerate a wide scale of sound vibrations that start at 0 Hz (silence) and ranges all the way through ultrasound, which is the same ultrasound you hear about in the medical imaging field. Normal human hearing perceives a range somewhere between 20 Hz all the way up to 20,000 Hz (also written as 20 kHz, or 20 *kilo*hertz). Most people cannot hear vibrations slower than 20 HZ or faster than 20 kHz, but dogs and certain other animals can hear vibrations that are faster than this. A dog whistle produces vibrations well above 20,000 Hertz. Many professional DJs and musicians have subjected their ears to unusually high sound pressure levels over several years, which causes hearing loss. Someone with hearing loss may not be able to hear the average human spectrum between 20 Hz and 20 kHz.

When Bell Labs developed today's telephone, they determined that telephone frequencies needed to be somewhere between 300 Hz and 3,000 Hz so that people could understand each other. If DJ sound systems sounded like telephones, this whole DJ thing would have never got off the ground and live music would still dominate the world. In order for voice and music to sound natural, a sound system's frequency response should be at least low enough to reproduce low bass frequencies of about 60-80 Hz and continue well above 15,000 Hz. There are also additional bonus tones known as "harmonics," which are more subtle additional tones created by musical instruments and the human voice. Harmonics are much higher in the Hertz scale. Without these harmonics, things just wouldn't sound natural.

To explain this concept in terms a DJ needs to know, here are how most sounds we hear fall into the Hertz scale. These are only estimates of the "meat" of these sounds roughly analyzed using digital sampling software on my computer.

* Barry White's sexy low crooning is about 80-90 Hz
* Mariah Carey's weird shriek may hit about 2,000 Hz
* Harmonics in a human singing voice can exceed 20,000 Hz
* Pianos range from about 30 Hz through around 4,000 Hz
* Synthesizers can artificially produce sounds from less than 20 Hz to more than 20,000 Hz
* A guitar ranges from about 80 Hz to more than 10,000 Hz

* A bass guitar ranges from about 40 Hz to 300 Hz

* A cymbal crash is about 2,000 Hz through about 14,000 Hz

* A real dog whistle is over 20,000 Hz, and not audible by humans

Another important quality of sound is "Dynamic Range," which is basically the difference between the quietest sound someone can hear and the loudest sound a sound system can produce. Dynamic range is measured in sound pressure units called "decibels" (dB SPL). A sound of zero dB SPL is the quietest sound that can be heard by the average human ear. A sound of around 125 dB SPL is the loudest sound that can be heard without producing pain.

Note this: prolonged exposure to any sound above about 90 dB SPL can cause hearing loss! Normal conversation is about 50-65 dB while a club or a concert can be as high as 120 dB. A jet airplane up close can range as high as 140 dB, well over the average human pain threshold, which is why those airport dudes wear those funny looking yellow headphones to protect their ears. To put things into perspective, there's a complex mathematical logarithmic formula that shows that with every 6 dB increase in sound pressure levels, we perceive that sound as being twice as loud. Our ears only perceive something being twice as loud when it's 4 times more powerful (a 400 watt amp is twice as loud as a 100 watt amp). This logarithmic relation between what is happening and what we hear means many of our calculations could have many digits in the result.

Thirdly, there's a concept known as the "Signal-to-Noise Ratio." This is a measure of the strength of a recorded signal relative to any audible background noise. Think about having a conversation in a crowded room. Your voice is overshadowed by the rest of the noise in the room, which is an example of a low signal (your voice) to noise (the crowd) ratio. Now if the entire crowd shuts up to listen to what you have to say, you'd have a high signal to noise ratio. In sound equipment, the signal-to-noise ratio is a comparison of the desired signal and the unwanted noise (usually a hiss or hum sound) that is generated by the recording or playing equipment. This measure is also expressed in decibels (dB). Here's a comparison of signal-to-noise ratios of some basic sound equipment:

* Cassette tape deck with no Dolby noise reduction: about 50 dB

* Cassette tape deck with Dolby B noise reduction: about 65 dB

* MiniDisc or CD player: about 85-90 dB if an analog output is used; 95-100 dB if a digital output is used; 105+ dB in Super Audio CD players.

The important thing to remember is that higher is better—a higher signal to noise decibel value results in a cleaner sound.

A sound you want your audience to hear can be heard better if you "amplify" the sound, by electronically increasing its volume so that it's louder than the noise that's competing with it. When amplifying sound, we first convert it to an analog electric signal, which moves somewhere near the speed of light. The amplified electric signal is then fed to speakers, which are usually located closer to the listening audience so there's less of a perceived delay. The speakers reproduce the amplified sound at a much higher volume than the surrounding noise, and voila, you've got a party.

You got all that? It's really just the tip of the iceberg when it comes to sound, but it's just about enough to get you through. If you want to know more, and you should know more, you can chat with a professional sound engineer, or pick up a book on the topic.

The Basic Equipment

Sound systems consist of five basic groups of equipment.

1. At least two music playing sources. Since DJs must keep a continuous flow of music, they use at least two music sources. These sources can be any equipment that plays pre-recorded music. Today, one can choose from CD players, turntables, MiniDisc players, cassette tape players, DAT decks, computers, digital DJ systems, or stand-alone MP3 players. Any combination of these will do for playing straight music, but performance DJ setups are more picky. You can mix from one turntable to a CD player. You can even mix from a computer to a cassette player. Using the second player allows you to mix in another song before the initial song has ended, allowing for a continuous program without spaces between the music. Most mobile and club DJs use two CD players, two turntables or a combination of both to play their music. Many mobile jocks are now utilizing new technology such as MiniDisc and MP3 players, which we'll discuss later.

2. Mixers, also known as "preamplifiers." Your music sources output a really weak electronic signal that must be amplified and converted into a controllable line-level signal. Mixers control the individual volumes of each music source and let you determine the output level of each channel.

3. Amplifiers. The preamplified line-level signal is then electronically amplified so that its resulting volume is strong enough to significantly overpower the room noise. The amplified signal is sent over wires to remotely placed speakers that produce the sound we hear.

4. Speakers. Paper, plastic, or urethane cones are attached to a mounted coil of wire that is vibrated by a magnet that produces an electronic vibration based on the signal that comes directly from the amplifier. The coil moves the cone, the cone moves the air molecules touching it, and those vibrating air molecules are sent all over the room hopefully ending up in your eardrum.

5. Other stuff. Microphones, headphones, booth monitors, cables, connectors, and other stuff that make your DJ job possible, easier, and/or more fun.

Let's take a brief look at each component as they'd appear in a typical mobile or club DJ setup.

Turntables

Fortunately for all you "vinyl junkies" in DJ land, record players or "turntables" are still being mass-produced and more popular than ever. New professional turntables can easily run you from $800-$1,500 a pair. There are less expensive options; you can often find this equipment for sale used in classified advertisements or on an Internet auction site. I sold a bunch of my old equipment on eBay for much less than I bought it for.

As a matter of fact, vinyl is still so cool that a company called Vestax, well known for its popular mixers, manufactures a pretty amazing unit that records audio from any source, CDs, MP3 players, microphones, computers, or whatever else you can plug into it directly on to Vestax vinyl blank records. Imagine having the ability to press your own vinyl—how cool would that be! Vestax's VRX-2000 unit has a small cutting head that actually cuts the grooves into the vinyl blanks. These recordable records will hold up to 14 minutes of audio on each side. The stylus cutter is replaceable, and has an average lifespan of 200-300 minutes of recorded audio. At about $375 per cutter, this can get kind of pricey if you decide to make a lot of records. Oh, and the unit itself is in the neighborhood of $9,000.

Professional turntables differ from consumer versions in several ways. Pro turntables have a "pitch" (speed) control, which allows you to physically change the speed of the record with a sliding control. This allows you to speed up or slow down your incoming record so that you can more easily "mix" the two records for a smooth transition between songs. Most pro turntables will allow you to speed up or slow down a record by 8% or more. Pro tables are much more durable than consumer tables, and this is very important if you're going to be throwing them in the back of your car and slamming through potholes on your way to gigs.

Most pro turntables have a colored strobe light on them with little metal nubs on the platter. These are used to show that your turntable platter is rotating faster or slower than exactly 33 1/3 or 45 revolutions per minute (RPM).

Pro turntables usually have a mechanism known as "quartz lock," which helps make the speed constant when locked in the zero-pitch change position. I've heard of some DJs having the quartz lock removed for more control while mixing, but I never found this necessary.

Belt Drive vs. Direct Drive

Turntables come in two flavors—direct drive and belt drive. Belt drive turntables use something that looks like a giant rubber band that connects the motor to the platter to spin the platter. Due to the inherent stretch factor of that rubber belt, belt drives are typically less stable when it comes to trying to maintain a constant tempo, which could be a bummer if you're planning to beatmix. Other issues with belt drives is their sluggish startup, slow response to pitch adjustments, and lack of torque (a measure of the physical force delivered to rotate the platter), which pretty much kills their scratching potential. My first turntables were belt drives with a pitch control. They were meant for home stereo applications, but I didn't have enough money for real DJ turntables at the time. They skipped all the time, and the shaky unreliable belt drive tempo adjustments made my beatmixing a complete nightmare. If you're in a stable environment on a concrete platform with an earthquake resistant DJ booth, and you won't ever beatmix or scratch, you may be able to use belt drive turntables. Their main advantage is their cost—you can get belt drives for less than $100 each.

There are no belts in direct-drive turntables. Instead, these turntables utilize a complex magnetic mechanism that connects the motor directly to the platter. This allows direct drives to start and stop a whole lot quicker than belt drives, and pitch adjustments are virtually instantaneous. Plus, their added torque helps them get up to playing speed much quicker than belt drive. Direct drive turntables tend to keep their speed much more constant. Virtually all pro DJs use direct drive turntables. Trust me, you want direct drives if you can afford them, no matter what kind of DJ you plan to be. They'll cost anywhere from $200 to $1,000 each, cartridges not included.

Technics 1200s

Ask any pro DJ, and he or she will tell you the undisputed king of all turntables is the Technics "1200" (Figure 4.1). In 1969, Technics (a division of Panasonic, which is a division of Japanese electronics conglomerate Matsushita) produced the world's first direct drive turntable, the SP-10. Ten years and several engineering refinements later, Technics made history with the first SL-1200, and then the SL-1200 MK2, the industry legend. To this day, more than three million Technics 1200s have been sold, and are still the smartest and best made turntables in the entire world. There have been a few minor changes here and there over the past few years, but the 1200 still looks virtually identical to the way it looked when it was first produced. It was made so well that there are several 10-, 15-, and even 20-year-old 1200s still in service!

My personal 1200 MK2s are over 15 years old and they work perfectly even after thousands of club and mobile gigs. I've personally used several 1200s that have run 5-7 nights a week for over 10 years with not even one major problem. Those tables saw cigarettes, fog, dust, smoke, water, spills, chills, and other abuse that would have rendered virtually any other non-alien mechanical component dead and buried. Heck, even the Maytag repairman envies the 1200! Sure, some parts wear out with heavy use, but Technics sells a wide range of user replaceable parts. They're incredibly durable, and very easy to use. The Technics 1200 (shown in Figure 4.1) is nothing less than the perfect electronic component. Even though I gave away most of my vinyl, I'll probably never sell my set.

Technics SL 1200 MKII. Photo courtesy of Matsushita Electric Corporation of America.

Technics 1200s have some pretty cool features that other turntable manufactures have borrowed over the years. They've got massive "torque," meaning they'll get up to speed incredibly fast, and easily let you drag a record with a slip mat on top of the platter that's spinning at full speed with no noticeable changes in tempo or pitch. They've got a really cool "strobe" effect that visually shows the relative speed of the platter, including when it's locked in the zero pitch change setting. There's a small pop-up light that's just bright enough to show your stylus and the record grooves in really dark DJ booth or party situations. There are four shock-absorbing legs and a rubber base to help isolate bass feedback and skipping caused by unstable floors. There's a neato cueing lever that DJs aren't ever allowed to use (because it's not "cool" for DJs to use it). And the curved tone arm assembly is completely adjustable to accommodate a very wide range of DJ styles, cartridges, and styli. They just feel good; heavy and solid.

A set of two 1200s will cost you anywhere from $400 - $800 used, and from $800 - $2,000 new. There are four or five models of the 1200 available today, each with slightly different features, but all still with the same basic look, their original tone arm, and direct drive motor. Cartridge, stylus, and a travel case are all not included.

I learned on 1200s, so it's very difficult for me to be objective about other turntables. Most other 1200 users will agree. If you're new, you should approach your turntable choice with an open mind, and go try a bunch of different brands to see which is best for you. Stanton makes some pretty chic turntables that are barking at the heels of the 1200, including its STR8-150 with a straight tone arm, and some scratch DJs are lovin' it. Numark, Gemini, and several other companies produce some less expensive belt and direct drive turntables. Feel it out for yourself and go with what feels right for your art, not your pocketbook.

Turntable Cartridges and How They Work

To add even more costs to these already pricey machines, you'll need professional cartridges and styluses to complete them. To fully understand the function of cartridges and styli, let's take a brief look at how record players work.

A record groove can have high frequency analog musical signals pressed in the vinyl that are hundreds of times smaller than the diameter of a piece of your hair. The "stylus," also known as "the needle," is the jewel-tipped virtually microscopic head of a cartridge that physically comes into contact with those tiny grooves. The stylus vibrates as it rubs against the tiny variations in those grooves producing the sound that was recorded into those grooves. If you're in a quiet room with your amplifier off, you can actually hear a tinny sound coming from the stylus and cartridge as it progresses across the record. The cartridge electromagnetically captures that signal and shoots it over wires to your preamp.

Back in the heyday of pressing records in the 1960s, the major record labels agreed on an industry standard known as "The Recording Industry Association of America (RIAA) Curve." Using this equalization curve improved the signal-to-noise ratio of records by boosting the high frequencies cut on the record while greatly extending the play-back time by reducing the low frequencies (the lows take up wider groove spaces, dramatically decreasing the amount of music you could fit on a record). Another benefit of removing lows with the RIAA Curve is that low frequencies caused distortion and occasionally made needles skip off some records. All the record companies agreed to basically shave off the same exact levels of bass frequencies less than 1 kHz so that all vinyl records are consistently cut with reduced bass levels and increased treble levels. The RIAA inverse curve reverses the process, replacing the bass that was removed and producing an accurate sound without all the inherent issues. This process requires a different electronic input known as the "phono" inputs of mixers, preamps and amplifiers. This is why you can't plug a turntable into a CD line-level input—the bass frequencies won't get replaced and it'll sound nasty. Since CDs don't suffer from analog issues, there is no RIAA Curve applied to them.

Scratching a record across the grooves with a hard jewel (not the good kind of scratching, which follows the grooves of the record) will permanently damage the record by cutting into the pre-pressed grooves causing skips and nasty "pop" type sounds. Don't worry—it takes a significant amount of force to slice into those hard grooves. A brief slide across a record isn't good for the record, but chances are it won't produce a noticeable scratch in most cases.

An important term to know when evaluating your cartridge purchasing decision is something called "tracking force." Tracking force is a measurement of the actual weight that keeps the stylus in place in the record's groove. The amount of tracking force is directly proportionate to record wear—the heavier the force, the more it'll eventually tear up the tiny nubs on the walls of the grooves in the record that ultimately produce the sound. Consequently, the lower the tracking force, the lower the record wear, but then you sacrifice "trackability" and introduce a propensity to skip.

Finally, there's the "spherical" vs. "elliptical" battle, which basically describes the shape of the stylus. A spherical stylus is more rounded, kind of like the bottom of a sphere, and has a better chance of staying in the groove while scratching. For that benefit, you'll sacrifice the aural accuracy of an elliptical stylus, which is much more narrow and pointy so it's more able to pick up the more subtle nubby information in the grooves of the record. Typically, most scratchers go spherical, and beatmixers and audiophiles choose elliptical.

You've got to decide what kind of DJ you want to be before you can make an educated decision on which cartridges to purchase for your turntables, unless you're bleeding money and want to purchase one of each. In that case, send me a check too.

For scratching DJs, one of the most popular cartridge and needle packages is Shure's $75 M44-7 (see Figure 4.2). The M44-7 was designed specifically for scratching and weighs in at 1.5 to 3 grams of tracking force using its spherical shaped stylus. Although the M44-7 cartridge will wear out your records the quickest, most scratchers love it because of its resistance to skipping out of the groove and ruining a perfectly good baby scratch. Shure also makes the $60 SC35C, another all-purpose DJ cartridge with a whopping 4 to 5 grams of tracking force! Stanton's $40 505 SK II is also a very good and well known spherical stylus for DJs with a wide range of 2 to 5 grams of tracking force. It's important to realize that most scratching needles do not produce the full range of audible audio frequencies. Some of the higher treble frequencies are sacrificed due to the non-skip mechanics of these needles and cartridges.

Shure's M44-7 cartridge mounted to a Technics headshell. Image courtesy of Shure Inc.

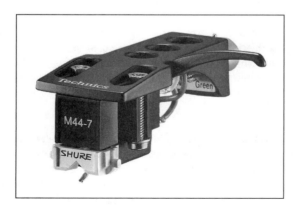

For mobile DJs and non-scratching club DJs, Stanton's $60 full-range 680 EL II seems to be the king of cartridges. My original 680 ELs have taken abuse from rampant dust bunnies to beer spatters, and ten years later, they still sound sweet! Their elliptical stylus with 2 to 5 grams of tracking force isn't specifically optimized for scratching, but rather for better frequency response when playing normally. Shure's $65 M44-G is another great an all-purpose cartridge with 0.75 to 1.5 grams of tracking force.

Ortofon makes pricey alternative all-in-one sleek looking cartridge assemblies. Their $170 Concord Nightclub S with its fluorescent yellow tip and spherical stylus is used by many club DJs. The Concord Nightclub E version is essentially the same unit, except an elliptical stylus is used for a more full frequency response. Ortofon fans feel the design of this cartridge avoids skipping while helping to preserve the life of their records. Another bonus is that its stylus is easily visible while in the record groove, so you'll always know exactly where you are in the song (important for scratching) and how soon you have until the break. Shure has released a competing design in this family called the "Shure Whitelabel" cartridge (Figure 4.3) that runs about $175.

Shure's Whitelabel cartridge.
Image courtesy of Shure Inc.

Finally, some DJs insist on only purchasing cartridges in "matched pairs." Many cartridges are sold in sets of two. The theory is that if they're produced together and sold together, chances are they'll perform in a similar manner. I'd guess that with modern production techniques, even if there were a difference in production, the response from that difference would be so small it wouldn't be noticeable.

Tone Arms

Professional turntables have adjustable tone arms, which is the rounded metal tube that connects the cartridge to the turntable itself. The industry standard Technics 1200 series tone arms are bent in kind of an "S" shape, which forces the cartridge and ultimately the stylus to follow the curvature of a record. This was engineered for minimum tracking errors (most tracking errors will occur in the beginning and at the end of a record due to their extreme positions), the highest and most accurate fidelity, and reduced record wear.

Several turntables engineered specifically for scratching DJs are on the market. Stanton's STR8-150 turntable (Figure 4.3) has a straight tone arm that's more skip resistant than curved tone arms. Numark sells a turntable (TT-X1) with a standard straight tone arm and an optional curved tone arm. The problem with straight tone arms is record damage due to extreme tracking errors in the beginning and at the end of a record. The straight tone never gets itself angled perfectly, and the tone arm forces the usually spherical stylus to rub the inner and outer grooves with a weird angle. Since scratchers typically use the center areas of the record, this usually isn't an issue.

Stanton's STR8-150 Straight Arm Turntable. Image courtesy of Stanton Magnetics.

One of the most frequent questions I've ever received from DJs is "How do I adjust the 1200 tone arm so it doesn't skip as much?" The Technics tone arm can be adjusted in the following manner:

1. Install the cartridge and stylus you've decided to use.

2. Release the tone arm from its locking arm clamp. Push the cue lever down if it is in the up position.

3. Adjust the horizontal balance. First, set the anti-skate dial to "0." Then turn the balance weight (the round part at the back of the tone arm) so that the arm floats horizontally evenly above the record without falling forward or backward. It will simply float evenly once you have it adjusted. Important: try not to let your stylus touch or bounce around on your platter or you may ruin your fancy new stylus.

4. Once the tonearm is floating, turn the black dial on the back of the weight to the "0" setting. You won't want to turn the whole weight, just the black dial with the numbers on it which will move independently from the whole weight.

5. Turn the whole weight (along with the dial) to adjust the stylus pressure to the cartridge manufacturer's recommended setting.

6. Adjust your "anti skate" dial to the same number as your stylus pressure. If your stylus pressure is over 3 grams, just leave it on the max setting of "3."

7. Place a record on your turntable, and with the power off, place the stylus somewhere in the beginning of a record. Use a record you don't care about, because it's likely that you'll knock your needle across it while trying to make this adjustment! Adjust your tone arm height by releasing the arm lock, and then rotating the hard-to-turn big black rubber dial until the tone arm appears parallel to the record. Re-lock the arm lock.

Slipmats

Slipmats are cloth-like mats that replace the big thick rubber mat that comes with your turntables. This allows the record to slip more easily when maneuvering it while preparing for a mix.

For years, the Technics 1200 came with a big, heavy, thick rubber mat that's terrific for audiophiles who don't mix or scratch, but typically terrible for performance DJ applications. We used to buy green or grey felt and cut it ourselves to make our own slipmats back in the day. For even more slipperiness for scratching applications, we'd cut the plastic sleeve from 12" singles into a circle, poke a hole in it, and place it underneath the felt. Most newer turntables come with pretty cool slipmats with your turntable's logo on it.

You can jazz up your rig with hundreds of wildly designed slipmats that'll run you about $20 each. You can even get local artists to do a custom graffiti-type design with your DJ name on it. Thud Rumble makes a sweet product called the "Butter Rug" for $20, which is a custom slick slipmat created by DJ Q-Bert specifically for scratching.

Hooking Up Your Turntable

Although typical turntable connections look simple enough and use the identical "RCA" type connectors that most other audio components use, there is a difference in the voltage produced by a turntable connection that's different from that of a CD player, and this will drive you crazy if you don't understand it. As previously discussed, if you were paying attention, vinyl records are pressed with the bass sucked out of them to avoid skipping and feedback, and your mixer or amplifier somehow knows how to replace it. The turntable is connected to the "phono" input in most mixers, and there should be a switch somewhere near the slider or knob that you'll need to switch from "line" to "phono" so your mixer will properly convert the signal.

The Technics 1200 and most other analog turntables have a thin wire with a "U" shaped connection on the end of it that's called a "ground" connector (see Figure 4.5). This must be hooked up to the ground connection terminal of your mixer. Almost any pro DJ mixer has a ground terminal. Without the ground connection, you'll often hear an annoying hum or a buzz through your speakers.

"Digital turntables" are simply analog turntables with a digital out connection that's useful for connections to computers, special effect generators, or digital recording equipment. The Stanton STR8-150 is considered to be a digital turntable. Most digital turntables are self-grounding, meaning you don't need to hook up a ground wire to your mixer.

Ground connection wire.

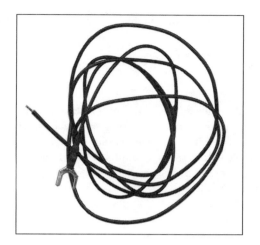

CD Players

Once the arch nemesis of turntablists, professional CD players are beginning to share a peaceful coexistence with their older vinyl-based cousins. And now there are table top CD players that are once again attempting to replace turntables. Except this time, they actually look, feel, perform, and sound like turntables! The argument has been that in addition to alleviating the manual touch element that makes working with vinyl so cool, CDs simply cannot duplicate the rich tones and luscious harmonics captured in a brand new vinyl pressing. A few years ago, you might have shrugged your shoulders and thought these were valid points. But today, this is a pretty weak argument. Technology is finally filling in the missing pieces.

There are scores of professional DJ CD players on the market in various sizes, shapes, and complexities. The most popular CD players since the early 1990s have been the Denon dual CD decks, beginning with their DN 2000 F. This was the first CD deck I had ever seen that had a pitch controller on it, as well as two individual CD players built in. The 2000 was the final push I needed to begin the switch from vinyl to CDs. Since I was doing both mobile and club gigs, I was forced repurchase my entire music library on CD.

All professional CD players, like professional turntables, have a pitch control for effective beatmixing. To simulate dragging your finger on a turntable platter to temporarily slow it down or twisting the center nub to speed it up a bit, most pro CD decks offer a control called a "pitch bender" that essentially does the same thing electronically.

CD players are virtually perfect in holding time without drifting, and no ground wires are ever necessary. They're also much more compact and lighter than turntables, and you never have to replace belts, needles, or worn out records. Many newer models have special effects built in, such as vinyl emulation, looping and sampling effects that can enhance your performance.

Better models have "anti-shock" memory or buffers, which will keep a song playing where normal CD players would jump and skip. Some decks will actually let you prerecord 30 seconds or more from a CD so you can actually eject the disc and pop another one in while the song is still playing.

There are four types of CD decks; dual CD players, single table top decks with scratching capabilities, portable CD units, rack mount single radio type units, and Super Audio CD (SACD) units. We'll explore the first two types since these are the most popular with DJs.

The Dual CD Deck

The dual CD player is probably the single greatest invention ever for the mobile DJ. Two individual CD decks are combined side by side in one compact unit that's easily mountable in any transportable rack or case. The only disadvantage is that if this unit fails for some reason, you'll lose both decks at the same time. If you were using single units, you'd still have one operational unit. I once lost a turntable at a club gig. The cantilever, the tubular unit that holds the stylus in place, broke off, and I hadn't yet realized the importance of carrying a spare. Fortunately, I had a cassette deck that I used to record my mixes. The tape from the prior night was still in the player. I hooked up the cassette deck and managed to mix back and forth from the still functioning turntable and the tape deck, and got through the night without a major incident. If all I had was a dual CD player, I wouldn't have had the option of a single CD deck to work with, and I would have been reduced to my cassettes. Fortunately, CD player failures are rare.

In the mid to late 1990s, the now discontinued Denon DN 2000F MKII CD player was the industry standard. Complete with two individual CD decks all in one unit, shock protection, a countdown display option, and pitch control, Denon's DN 2000F gave a DJ everything he or she needed to perform at just about any bar, club or private party. Today, there's more fragmentation. Numark, Pioneer, Stanton and Denon all have some pretty decent products and now seem to share the market.

Although a dual CD deck may look difficult to use, it's actually relatively easy and very intuitive. The two sets of identical controllers for each of the two decks double the number of buttons, so your eyes will tend to go wacky trying to find the right buttons for a short while. Similar to a regular CD player, you've got play, pause, and track advance controls as well as a display of track and elapsed time. Since there are two separate CD players, you'll need to connect the output from each player to two separate channels on your mixer. This will allow you to play two CDs simultaneously, which lets you fade one song into a new song, and also beatmix two songs together. The players are connected to your mixer via a standard RCA stereo connector which is accepted by any DJ mixer. Some newer CD players also have a coax-digital out for connection to other digitally compatible units.

Dual CD decks typically come in two separate parts. The first is a remote control unit that's usually mounted somewhere near the mixer so it's convenient for you to control. The second part is the actual dual CD player unit, which can be mounted somewhere out of the way. The two units are connected via a proprietary remote cable that comes with the unit.

Denon Dual CD Decks

I've used Denon decks for well over ten years, and I've always been impressed by their reliability and versatility. While some other CD players wouldn't play CD-Rs when they first appeared on the DJ scene, my Denon 2000F unit never met a disc it didn't like. One unit outlived me at a certain nightclub - over six years with at least 40 hours a week of constant use. It held up to smoke, dust, and an occasional beer and still performed like a champ. Denon's current workhorse dual CD deck is their DN-D4000 (Figure 4.6). This deck supports CD-R and MP3 playback, which is a must these days. It also lets you loop, set cue and stutter points, and also has up to 100 seconds of shock proof memory. What's really cool is that this deck is software upgradeable! Simply burn the upgrades to a CD and use the CD to install the upgrades. If you want to move up to their phattest dual deck, check out their feature-laden DN-D9000. This wild unit does everything the D4000 does, but also lets you scratch, sample, splice loops, count BPMs automatically, filter, transform, delay, flange, and other amazing things that are guaranteed to make your head spin as fast as the CD does.

Denon DN-D4000. Image courtesy Denon Electronics.

Numark Dual CD Decks

Other dual decks include Numark's $700 CDN88, which features automatic beat mixing and remarkably cool digital effects including reverse play, flange, phase, echo, and live scratching. I did a demo with this unit that blew some hardcore vinyl minds. Or, step up to their intensely cool sci-fi looking CDN90 that'll set you back about $900, which also features a bunch of cool digital effects including real time scratching.

Numark CDN-90. Image courtesy Numark DJ Products.

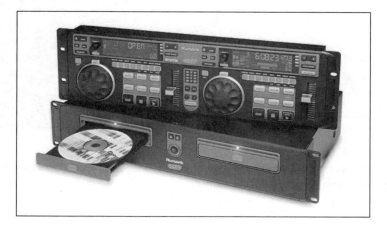

Other Dual CD Decks

Pioneer makes the $900 CMX3000 unit that also includes scratching, seamless looping, a visible BPM counter, and a cool wave display. Lower priced dual decks by American DJ, American Audio, Gemini, Stanton, and Tascam will also get the job done in most situations. I've heard reports from some DJs that some of the lower priced decks have some issues reading certain CD-Rs. If you use CD-Rs, and at some point you probably will, I recommend bringing your own burned discs to the store when you try these units. No matter what, definitely try before you buy to see what feels right for you.

Tabletop CD Players

Now here's where CD players finally have a chance at killing vinyl for good. Four important units are on the market that are as close to old fashioned vinyl turntables as CD decks as you can get—so far.

The Technics SL-DZ1200

Technics, the legendary vinyl turntable maker, has finally come out with a CD player that's looks and feels so similar to their 1200 turntables, it's frightening! The $1,200 SL-DZ1200 is a wicked piece of digital mastery that acts amazingly similar to my old 1200s. It begins with its 8" platter, which is 4" smaller than a 12" record, to which I easily acclimated. There's a thin piece of silver vinyl-ish material complete with simulated record grooves that acts as the slipmat, and it is incredibly responsive. What's wild is that the platter actually spins using the same high-torque motor found in the 1200 turntables, and the strobe hits the platter to show the relative speed of the CD, just like the 1200 turntable.

Technics SL-DZ 1200.

The SL-DZ1200 has a number of wicked effects and adjustments, including eight vinyl sound simulators, eight dynamic scratching effects, and an instant reverse setting for some really sweet effects. It also has a free-wheel setting that allows you to move the platter just like you'd move vinyl in scratching situations, which I found to be incredibly responsive considering there is no real physical contact between the wheel and the CD. The digital turntable has several banks available for saving loops and cue points, and you can actually export these to a Smart Media (SD) card for use later.

It also reads music effortlessly from CD-Rs and SD memory cards, and decodes MP3 and AAC files instantly, and counts the BPM of each song automatically, and pretty accurately. It's selectable "Pitch Lock" setting allowed me to play MP3s up to 16% faster or slower with no perceivable change in the key of the song (the unit allows up to +/- 50% with pitch lock when you play regular CDs or CD-Rs). I played with the scratching function with a CD-R with 150 tracks on it, and this unit responded in "real time" with absolutely no delay whatsoever.

Best of all, I couldn't get the darn thing to skip no matter what I did to it! I moved it. I slightly bumped it. I turned it vertically and upside down while a song was playing. I moved the platter in all kinds of quick and weird ways. The DZ1200 took a lickin' and kept on stickin'. This is a huge plus for mobile DJs, and for folks new at the scratching game.

The only issue I could see with this unit is that it's not a vinyl turntable. Braking had a remarkably weird digital sound, no matter how I tweaked the digital brake adjustment on the back of the turntable. For me, that's no big deal. But for vinyl purists, they'll probably find many faults with the DZ1200.

At $1,200 each, it's a pricey choice because remember, you'll at least need two. I found the price comically coincidental—it's like one dollar for each of the 1200 whatevers. But if you too are rooted in the original 1200s but you're thinking of going digital, definitely get your hands on one of these units and check it out. You too will be amazed.

The Numark CDX

Next up is Numark's answer to Technics SL-DZ1200, their equally sick CDX (Figure 4.9). This killer digital turntable actually has a full 12" platter with a real vinyl disc on top for the real feel. You can even put your own record on it. It's got multiple scratch modes and some really cool effects; including a "key lock" which allows you to speed a record up or down a full 100% range without changing the key of the song; 48 seconds of built in anti-shock read-ahead memory for skippy situations; and an exciting and unique feature they call a "Beatkeeper," which supposedly is able to make perfect seamless loops using digital quantization (a method of counting beats automatically, then digitally trimming the excess sample away so the beats line up in a perfect even count). Despite Numark's offer to visit their offices and sample the unit, I didn't have a chance to get my hands on one by the time this book was published. This unit will be wildly popular by the time you read this.

Numark CDX. Image courtesy Numark DJ Products.

The Pioneer CDJ-1000 MK2

After pioneering this category a few years ago with the CDJ-1000, the first scratchable stand alone table top CD player, Pioneer made it even better with their CDJ-1000 MK2 Digital Turntable (Figure 4.10). This unit features a 7" "touch wheel" controller that's not a vinyl record. This also has a scratch feature when in its vinyl mode, and its Master Tempo feature allows you to change the speed of the song without affecting the pitch. It has a more than adequate 16 seconds of shock-proof memory. I've played with these at a few DJ shows, but I couldn't get a true feel for them in the limited time I was there. I did witness some of Pioneer's DJs doing some pretty amazing stuff with these units.

Pioneer CDJ-1000 MK2. Photo courtesy of Pioneer Pro DJ.

The Denon DN-5000

Finally, Denon's DN-S5000 (Figure 4.11) is another digital vinyl component that has some fairly wack features. It's got a clear top that allows you to place your own custom graphics underneath it that can resemble your own personalized slipmat; or you could place a 7" 45 RPM vinyl record on top for a vinyl feel. I saw a demo at a DJ convention in Orlando where a DJ displayed this unit's "Alpha Track" functionality. He actually ejected the CD, and this deck kept playing the song while he inserted another disc, which he then proceeded to mix with the original song! The secret is a 35-second read-ahead memory function that allows two simultaneous audio streams to be played from the same unit. Remember that problem with my broken turntable? If I had one of these units, I could have DJd the whole night seamlessly with one deck. You'll need to drop about $900 for each S5000. There's another version with a few less tricks called the S3000, which runs about $800.

Denon DN-5000. Image courtesy of Denon Pro Electronics.

More Table Tops

American Audio, American DJ, Denon, Gemini and Numark make some lower priced units that sacrifice some of the features listed above. I do recommend giving them all a spin at your local DJ store. You may find that you might not need all these features, especially if you're planning on becoming a wedding DJ.

The Skippies

In my early days, I used to DJ at a hotel where many wedding receptions were held. After the weddings, the group of drunken fools would all spill into the club getting rowdy and infusing all kinds of energy into the room. Sometimes these people were a bit too rowdy, which caused some problems for the bouncers and also for my DJ booth.

My DJ booth was on the same level as the dance floor, raised only a few inches. When some idiot would jump up and down in one of those drunken stupor mosh-like dances, my CD players would freak out and start to skip. Of course, these idiots figured this out and exacerbated the problem by getting more people to jump even harder which made a mess of my show.

If you're not in a secure situation with solid, stable floors and you're subject to what I used to call "The Skippies," there are a few things you can do.

* Get a dual CD player with "shock memory." These CD players use some pretty cool technology that stores 10 or more seconds of music in their memory so that if they are bumped or knocked, the music will not jump or skip. Most newer CD decks have this built in.

* If you're still using turntables, suspend them from the ceiling. Many clubs in the 80s used chains attached to the ceiling to create a suspended virtually shock-proof platform.

❋ Figure out which songs make people jump around and play them on a cassette player or a solid state MP3 device, like an iPod. Cassettes sound like crap, but they never skip. Big jumpy songs include House of Pain's "Jump Around," "I Wanna Be Sedated" by The Ramones, "It's The End of The World As We Know It" by REM, "Tubthumping" by Chumbawamba, and virtually any heavy rock song with a nasty guitar or hip-hop song with a slammin' beat.

❋ Thick, insulated foam pads under your CD decks or turntables will often prevent skippies, although these too sometimes may fail. You need special acoustic dampening foam that's at least two inches thick. This can make things wobbly, so be careful.

❋ If your owner/manager is too cheap to recognize the value of a continuous uninterrupted music program, pour a large beer over his or her head, and then invoke the "last chance solution." Physically lift your CD player off the platform and hold it in the air while the song plays. This will give it an air cushion and avoids the skippies. It'll also make you look insane, which can be kinda cool in some situations.

❋ Too much bass can cause a vibration also, so either use one of these anti-skippy methods, or turn the bass down a bit in your equalizer.

Microphones

Microphones (often referred to as "mics") are an important tool for mobile and club DJs. This powerful tool gives you the ability to completely control the crowd's attention, since your voice will be the only voice amplified hundreds of times louder than anyone else in the entire room or arena. Microphones are fairly simple electronic devices. Again, rather than bore you with the official engineering descriptions (that I don't completely understand, either), I'll describe what you need to know in layman's terms.

Microphones pick up sounds in the form of frequency vibrations caused by a change in air pressure when a sound occurs within a microphone's proximity. All of these sounds are converted into electrical voltage by a thin plastic sheet called a "diaphragm," which is connected to a wire surrounded by a magnet (known as a "voice coil"). The moving coil interacting with the magnet converts the vibrations into a tiny electronic signal that contains the information that will reproduce the frequencies of the sounds it picks up. The resulting electronic signal travels through a microphone cord and is ultimately fed to a mixer (or preamplifier) for processing and amplification.

Mics are sort of the opposite of speakers or headphones, which produce sound rather than gather it. In fact, if you plug your 1/4" headset's plug into a matching microphone jack and speak through it, you'll actually hear your voice come over the system! It'll sound pretty nasty because headphones aren't built to capture sounds, but it illustrates my point. I used to do this to simulate a low quality bullhorn-type sound or a telephone call as a special effect during my DJ shows at nightclubs.

Types of Mics

Most wired DJ and band microphones are known as "dynamic" mics. They're pretty rugged and hard to mess up, even with super high sound pressure levels, smoke, dust, fog, humidity, temperature extremes, and other things most DJs subject their microphones to. All you have to do is simply plug it in to just about any mixer you're ready to speak to your peeps.

"Condenser" microphones are a little more complicated in terms of their electronics, and a lot more expensive. Their diaphragms are usually made of gold or gold plated metal, and require a separate power source known as "phantom power," which is a small 48-volt charge usually supplied from the mixer to the microphone via the microphone cable. Their response is much more sensitive and accurate than most dynamic mics, which is why condenser mics are used primarily in studios. They're not a practical choice for DJs because they're much more fragile and not suited to the dust, smoke, dampness, and general pounding that most DJs will give them.

For me as a new DJ, the most confusing classification of microphones was the difference between "low impedance" and "high impedance" mics. Technically, "impedance" is the measure of the opposition of the flow of a current in a circuit, measured in Ohms. From a layman's standpoint, it's not really all that confusing once you know what's up. High impedance (sometimes called "Hi-Z") mics typically have a stronger signal and don't require as much amplification. The main difference between these two types of mics is the cable length you intend to run between your microphone and the mixer. Low impedance (also known as "Low-Z") mics can support a virtually unlimited cable run, while high impedance mics encounter more electrical resistance and start to freak out after cable runs of fifteen or more feet. Most professional mics are low impedance mics, which usually have a "XLR" or "Cannon" round three-prong connector and are much more reliable.

All microphones have directional characteristics. The two main types of DJ mics are "omnidirectional" and "unidirectional" or "cardioid." Omnidirectional microphones will pick up sound equally from all directions around the head of a microphone. Bands often use omnidirectional mics to capture complimentary sounds from instruments around the stage. Unidirectional or cardiod mics are most sensitive to sounds coming from one specific direction, usually the flattened head of the mic. You have to speak directly towards the diaphragm of a directional mic or it won't clearly pick up your voice. For most DJ applications, cardioid or unidirectional mics work fine because all you'll need your audience to hear is your voice. Some DJs prefer an omnidirectional mic simply because you don't have to look at it and position it before you talk into it for it to work. It's important to know that omnidirectional mics are more likely to pick up and reproduce speaker sounds, which can cause some ugly feedback.

Finally, there's the issue of "frequency response." Most mics are rated in a range of the lowest frequency they can reproduce, meaning the bass side of your voice, to the highest frequency they can handle, meaning the treble side of your voice or the inherent harmonics that make your voice sound natural. Typically, you'll find most pro mics are rated somewhere between 50 Hz to 18 kHz, and any range in between those numbers is fine in most cases. Remember, most voices and their harmonics only have a range between 80 Hz and 4 kHz.

My favorite DJ mic is the old original Shure SM-57 dynamic unidirectional low impedance mic, typically used by bands for micing various instruments. I also used several Shure SM-58s (see Figure 4.12) throughout my career, the most popular live band microphone in the world. But for some reason I felt the 57 made my voice sound deeper. This is a result of "proximity effect," meaning that the closer the capsule is to your voice, the more low frequencies the mic picks up. Since the 57 has a flat head, most folks practically eat the mic while they're speaking, resulting in more bass.

Shure SM57 and SM58
Microphones.

Wireless Mics

Wireless microphones have gotten so much better and affordable, and are a must for today's successful DJs. There are many advantages to wireless microphones, such as easy maneuverability and no wires to trip over. You can choose a typical handheld microphone that features your favorite mic head as its pickup. You might want a wireless headset like Madonna and Britney Spears wear in concert. Or you might want to look like a news reporter with a wireless lavalier microphone, but then you'd look like a complete dork, so please don't do that. There are a myriad of hardware choices available in an even wider range of prices.

"Diversity" is an option in better wireless systems. With a diversity receiver, the receiver will actually have two separate receivers so that it may automatically pick up and amplify its choice of a cleaner signal. Non-diversity systems have only one antenna and receiver, and may be subject to "dropouts" in the signal when the signal is temporarily blocked or affected by interference. Diversity systems dramatically reduce dropouts.

Wireless microphones are available in different frequency bands called Very High Frequency (VHF) and Ultra High Frequency (UHF). In the United States, signals allowed to broadcast on these frequencies are tightly controlled by the Federal Communications Commission (FCC).

Lower end wireless microphones are Low band VHF (around 49 MHz), which are usually kids' toys. They're susceptible to interference from cordless telephones and other toys. Television channels use the VHF frequencies between 54-88 MHz, and radio stations kick in from 88 MHz to 108 MHz, otherwise known as "the FM dial." Low band VHF microphones should be avoided if possible because they could cause nasty problems in a professional DJ situation. High band VHF is a better choice for wireless DJ microphones since there's less competing traffic than on low band VHF. This band is becoming congested; so coordinating your frequency with other nearby users is important (unless you want someone else's toast to the bride and groom coming across *your* speakers). The highest frequency band is the UHF band, which has very low interference. Many systems can be operated at the same time without interfering with each other. These are the systems that you see the big stars use in concert, so you'd be correct if you guessed that these cost more.

Shure, Samson, Sennheiser and Audio Technica all make popular high quality wireless mics.

 TIP: Always leave the microphone's volume down on your mixer unless you're using it. You never know when some drunken fool may pick up your wireless mic and start yelling profanities over it. Or, some other knucklehead DJ in the same building may have the same microphone that's on the same channel as yours. If he or she is a practical joker (like I was), there could be big fun had at your expense.

Using a Microphone

Mics are engineered to capture sound from a certain, specified distance from the source of the sound. You'll notice that your voice will sound deeper with more bass response if you speak straight on with about an inch between your lips and the top of the mic. The farther away you move from the top of the mic, the tinnier your voice will sound! That's the result of the "proximity effect" as discussed previously. Alternatively, if you talk too closely to the top of your mic (known as "swallowing the mic"), you'll often get a distorted sound, not to mention your words being garbled because you're speaking with something in your lips preventing proper speech. The best way to figure out what sounds right is to use your microphone and listen to yourself either live, or better, recorded on tape or CD, and determine where your best microphone placement should be.

A microphone picking up sounds from the main speakers causes "feedback," that really annoying and sometimes painful high pitched "WHEEEE!" sound you've probably heard somewhere. Feedback is caused by your microphone capturing the sound coming out of your speakers and then sending it through your system again with the microphone capturing the resulting new sound and repeating the process infinitely. Very quickly, this process turns into a loop effect that causes a very annoying note that's incredibly bad for your speakers (and bad for business). Some feedback can be eliminated by proper equalization. Sometimes you'll just need to move out of the path of your speakers. If this doesn't eliminate it, you'll need to lower your microphone volume on your mixer. The person using the mic will then need to simply talk louder, or get closer to the microphone. There are electronic units known as "feedback destroyers" or "feedback eliminators" that bands use that can eliminate this problem.

There is a level of mic utilization that's perfect for every situation, but it changes constantly. This is something you'll have to learn to read for yourself, and it only comes with experience. The only thing worse than a DJ who overuses a microphone is a DJ who underutilizes its power.

Mixers

Your audio mixer, sometimes referred to as a "preamplifier" or "preamp" in the live music business, is the key component in any DJ setup. Think of this as the "brain" of your system, because it takes all the audio inputs from your CD players, microphone, turntables, DVD players, Karaoke players and controls the volume of each while changing their signals into something that your amplifier will be able to understand. Since microphones, turntables, and CD players all produce a different voltage or signal, it's your mixer's job to convert those signals into a basic "line-level" signal that your amplifier will be looking for in order to convert it to the power that will ultimately feed your speakers.

DJ mixers allow you to connect as few as two music sources and as many as ten. Most scratch or mix DJs only need two channels, one for each turntable (or CD player). These two-channel mixers, known as "battle style mixers," are usually the same length as a typical turntable, and fit neatly between them allowing easy access to all the controls.

Pro mobile and club DJs need more inputs for mics, DVD players, samplers, special effects. Most non-battle mixers have at least four individual channels. Most professional mixers will allow you to assign each source to an individual "knob," "fader" or "slider," which are all different names for individual volume controls. And, you've got the ability to cue (monitor) what's playing on every channel before your audience hears it. All professional mixers have a cue input with its own volume, sometimes called a PFL (pre-fader listen), where you can plug in a set of $\frac{1}{2}$" headphones in order to hear what your next song sounds like without playing it over the loudspeakers. This enables DJs to prepare their next mix and also to make sure the next song up is what you want it to be.

"Sliders or knobs" is the question of the day. If you ask scratchers, it's definitely sliders. If you ask house, trance, or techno beatmixers, it's probably knobs. Basically, it comes down to your preference. Knobs allow more of a fine-tuned individual volume control, which helps when blending and controlling multiple sources. Knobs were the choice of professionals when Urei and Bozak mixers ruled the DJ scene in the early 1980s before scratching got big, and they're making a bit of a comeback today. Sliders allow super quick volume bursts needed for scratching. Sliders took over as the most popular mixers in the mid to late 80s.

Battle Style Mixers

Mixers have some a long way since I learned how to baby scratch on a Urei 1620 knob-only mixer! Most of today's hottest scratches would be impossible to do with a knob-based mixer.

All battle-style mixers have a "crossfader." This control allows you to fade the music between two inputs. You can do this manually by raising or lowering the individual volume controls for each source, but many DJs prefer the fader method when beatmixing or scratching.

Older mixers used something called a "potentiometer," which is an electronic thing that increases or decreases the signal between the two channels. The signal had to physically pass through this potentiometer causing resistance depending on how much you move the crossfader. When the metal parts of the crossfader began to wear out, you'd experience a phenomenon called "bleeding," where you could hear the other channel's sound bleed through even when the crossfader was moved entirely to the other side. When it got worn really badly, you'd begin to hear bleeding along with nasty crackling sounds when you moved the crossfader.

Today, most DJ mixers use "VCA" (Voltage Controlled Amplifier) crossfaders. This is a technology borrowed from expensive sound boards. VCA faders don't actually pass sounds, they only control the volume of the individual channels so they usually won't bleed or wear out. There is also an "optical" fader, but they're affected by smoke and dust which are found in most bars, clubs, and yes, bedrooms.

Rane mixers took the VCA thing one step forward. Their popular TTM 56 battle-style mixer (shown in Figure 4.13) features magnetic "non-contact" crossfaders and channel faders, which they claim are "the fastest, most accurate, and long lasting on the planet." Rane's design uses non-contact magnetic position sensor technology similar to that used in aerospace and industrial applications. The TTM 56 crossfader boasts no travel noise and no bleed - ever. Plus, unlike normal or optical crossfaders, this bad boy is impervious to smoke, moisture, temperature and aging. The mechanical life of the magnetic fader is supposed to exceeds 10 million scratches or mixes. Those wacko engineers at Rane actually produced a video of their crossfader submerged in a cup of soda, still working!

Rane TTM 56. Image courtesy Rane Electronics.

Today's battle-style mixers feature several adjustable settings for their crossfaders, so you only have to move it as little as a fraction of an inch, sometimes as little as just a couple millimeters, to get full volume on each of the channels. Is it because DJs are getting lazy? No, some special scratching effects require lightning quick fades that would be almost impossible if the crossfader had to be moved all the way to the other side and back. Most battle-style mixers have a setting for "crossfader curves" which indicate how far you'll have to push a crossfader to achieve maximum signal on either side.

Most mixers also have built in three-band equalizers. Some DJs use the EQ to remove bass or treble during mixes or scratches for an additional special effect. There's nothing more weird than stealing the bass and watching your dance floor waive their hands in the air in an almost trance like state.

Some higher end mixers include assignable on-board special effects, such as flanges, echo, reverb, chorus, phase, and other sweet stuff that can make your mixes sound a little cooler than usual. Remember not to use special effects in excess, or they won't be special.

For even more detailed and interesting information about crossfaders, check out Rane's article "History of the DJ Crossfader" at http://www.rane.com/note146.html.

Popular battle-style DJ mixers are made by Rane, Stanton, Vestax, Numark, and Gemini among others, and range in price from $50 (for lower end mixers with non-VCA faders) all the way up to $1,300.

Multi-channel DJ Mixers

In the mid 1980s through today, one of the most popular nightclub DJ mixers was the discontinued Urei 1620, a rotary knob based mixer. Like the Technics 1200 turntable it often accompanies, the Urei laughs at dust, smoke, spilled drinks, and even humidity! I've left one powered on for seven years straight without a hiccup, and it's probably still on today.

The main selling point for this mixer wasn't its durability or the rotary knobs, it was the tremendous amount of assignable inputs this thing had. There were two separate turntable inputs on channels 1 and 2. Then there were four additional channels, each with six assignable inputs! The 1620 allowed ten different sound sources plus a microphone. Many mobile and club DJs, including myself, found uses for every last one of them. You could assign a channel for your DVD player, your MP3 player, a digital sampler, a keyboard, a VCR, two turntables and a microphone, your dual CD player, and still have room for an iPod. Some house, techno and trance DJs use three CD players or turntables to mix dub and club versions for their own unique on the fly edits, so the additional inputs were necessary.

Rane answered the call for an up-to-date high quality knob-based DJ mixer with their MP 2016A (see Figure 4.14). To answer every Urei user's wish list, Rane added an optional accessory called the XP 2016A to accommodate the needs of various DJ mixing styles. The XP 2016A adds dedicated high performance 3-band EQ controls for each of the six input buses plus an assignable active crossfader with a full-range contour control. It plugs directly into the MP 2016A.

Rane MP 2016/XP 2016. Image courtesy Rane Electronics.

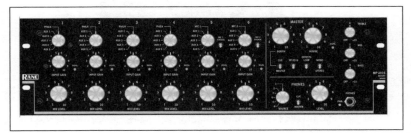

Allen and Heath makes another great rotary knob mixer called the Xone V6 that's reportedly one of the best mixers ever created. If you're a true audiophile who'd rather buy a mixer than an automobile, the $4,800 you'll pay for this unit, along with the optional crossfader unit that runs another $1,700, won't kill you. American Audio and Pioneer also produce rotary multi-channel mixers. It's important to note that the "pots" (short for potentiometers) on rotary mixers tend to be a little more expensive to manufacture than sliders, so expect to pay quite a bit more for your mixer if you too dig rotary controls.

If you're going the slider control route rather than the rotary know way, you've got hundreds of mixers to choose from. Sliders, as found on battle-style mixers, are arranged in vertical rows with one assigned per channel. A typical DJ mixer will have about four sliders with three sliders to control the volume of music either from turntables or CD players, plus one or two sliders or knobs for your microphones. You'll also have a master volume slider along with an assignable crossfader. Numark's $200 DM1200 is an affordable but very capable mixer that's perfect for most mobile DJs that includes all these options plus a six-band stereo equalizer and some other cool stuff. Numark, Rane, Gemini, American DJ, American Audio, Pioneer, Technics, Behringer, and others make several quality slider-based mixers complete with lots of channels, crossfaders, onboard EQs, effects, and all kinds of other options.

Hooking Up Your Mixer

Most professional mobile DJ mixers have several inputs for the various types of components you'll need to hook up. Note that some of the smaller mixers used primarily for scratching only have two inputs, and that may not enough for a typical mobile DJ setup. To demonstrate, we'll use the Rane MP 2016A, my all-time favorite mixer, which is widely used in nightclubs all over the world. The connections are similar to most professional DJ mixers used today.

The back of the mixer is where the magic begins. You've got XLR connectors, RCA connectors, and ½" connectors on this bad boy, which makes it a perfect mixer to learn from. From the front of the mixer, you can see that each of the six channels is numbered 1 through 6. The corresponding inputs for those channels are also numbered on the back, although you'll only see 1 through 4 on your first look.

I used channels 1 through 4 for my primary components. The really cool part of this mixer is that it has a six-way assignable input selection switch, so you can customize your channels and place them wherever you want them! Channels 5 and 6 can be switched to "microphone" or to any of the auxiliary inputs (labeled 1 through 5). Initially, you might think that this is more inputs than you'll ever need. But as you grow, your rig will also grow to add new components. For instance, one of my typical setups was arranged using channels 1 through 4 for my main components.

> Main input 1: RCA cable from turntable # 1
>
> Main input 2: RCA cable from turntable # 2
>
> Main input 3: RCA cable from dual CD player, deck 1
>
> Main input 4: RCA cable from dual CD player, deck 2

I then hooked up my other less-used components as follows:

> Aux input 1: RCA cable from third CD player (used for sound effects and DJ Drops)
>
> Aux input 2: RCA cable from DVD player (used to route sound from the DVD player through the system)
>
> Aux input 3: RCA cable from PC connection (⅛" stereo mini-jack converted to RCA cable used to play MP3 files from the computer)
>
> Aux input 4: RCA cable from VCR connection (used to play sound from live TV broadcasts)
>
> Aux input 5: RCA cable from cassette tape connection (used to play sound from cassettes when strippers, singers or other fools came in with a tape that needed to be played)

I used channel 5 to switch among my auxiliary inputs, since those were used less frequently. For example, if I wanted to play an MP3 file from my laptop, I'd go to channel 5, switch the Input Selector switch to "3", and my MP3 connection would now be assigned to channel 5. Since I was always wild on the mic, I reserved channel 6 for the microphone. You can switch these however you want them—see what works best for you!

Rane MP2016 mixer inputs.
Image courtesy Rane
Electronics.

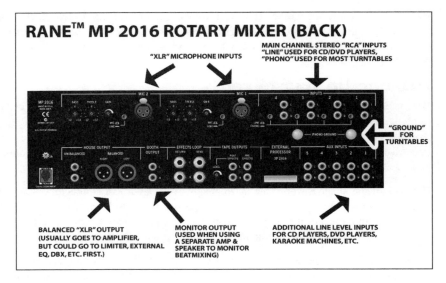

Amplifiers

I needed to understand the basics of amplification to help me do my job better, so I called in the specialists for help. QSC Audio's Paul Kenline, their Senior Technical Trainer, was kind enough to help me work through a painfully basic description of how amplifiers work. I've used QSC's amplifiers for years, mainly because their products are incredibly reliable, and their folks have always been superb in their customer service.

If the mixer is the brain of your system, then your amplifier (known as an "amp") could be known as the "heart." This is the unit that takes the low voltage signal from your mixer complete with all the sounds you've decided to pump out to your crowd, and converts it into raw power that's sent through wires to your speakers so people can actually hear what you want them to hear. Amplifiers can cause embarrassing and expensive problems if you don't know how to operate them correctly.

This unit amplifies the signal coming from your mixer into a signal that is powerful enough to power a speaker system so that your audience can easily hear it. Amplifiers have circuitry that collects and converts the lower voltage electricity signal produced by your mixer into a much higher powered master sound signal. The amp then releases that powerful electrical signal through wires connected to your speakers at about the speed of light.

Amplifiers are rated by manufacturers in terms of their output in "watts per channel." The higher the rated output, the louder the sound they can produce. Amplifiers are sometimes rated at their maximum watts per channel, also known as "peak power," which can be very misleading since it's way higher than the recommended power an amp produces. An amplifier has a reserve power system used for lightning quick bursts of bass or treble when needed. The important thing to look for in amplifiers is "continuous RMS," which is the normal watts-per-channel power rating. RMS stands for "Root Mean Square," in case you find yourself faced with that question on trivia night.

The other important factor in evaluating amplifiers is watts per channel at a certain number of "Ohms." An Ohm is a unit of electronic measurement used to describe the "impedance" that a particular piece of equipment or cable may have. This factor evaluates how much power your amplifier will produce with different quantities of speakers hooked up. Amplifiers that run into less impedance than they can handle may overheat and fail. You've got to read the amplifier specs carefully. Usually, most two-speaker stereo DJ setups use plain old 8 ohm speakers. If you use two speakers per channel, your impedance decreases to 4 Ohms. If you use four speakers per channel, your impedance decreases further to 2 Ohms, and so on. To be safe when you start running multiple sets of speakers, you'll need to check the owners manual for your amplifier and speakers to make sure you've got compatible systems.

Many DJs wonder if they should have the level controls on their amplifier turned all the way up. It depends on the system and how much gain your mixer is providing prior to reaching the amplifier. I've been told that the level controls do not limit the power available from the amplifier—an amplifier can still reach full rated output power if the level from your mixer is high enough to drive it. You should set your mixer's individual channel sliders and master gain to reach "o dB" (usually the end of the green lights on mixers with output LED lights) on the mixer output monitor, then adjust the amplifier level controls to the desired sound level.

Choosing Your Weapon

A good way to choose an amplifier is to choose one that's about double your speaker's continuous power rating, or about equal to its peak power rating within a few percent. This builds in a little "headroom" which will allow you to run your program with peaks that approach your amp's "clipping point," but the average power level will usually be safely below the loudspeaker's continuous power rating, as long as you avoid clipping the amplifier for an extended length of time.

Clipping is caused by an electrical signal that's "too hot" or too strong for an amplifier to handle. You'll usually notice this when you raise your faders too high, resulting in a blinking or solid red light, called "red-lining." Red-lining a mixer results in pushing an electrical signal that will make an amp exceed its output voltage. The amplifier has no way to fix the signal, so it kind of chops off the part of the signal that exceeds the amp's output voltage resulting in a nasty sound known as "distortion." The distorted signal can be much more powerful than your amplifier's rated power, which may be too powerful for your speakers. This could cause permanent and expensive damage to your speakers. Clipping usually happens when an inexperienced DJ thinks the sound isn't loud enough, so he or she keeps pushing the mixer levels higher in an effort to get higher volume. Clipping is easily avoided by using a more powerful amplifier.

For most mobile gigs of 150 people or less, you'll usually be fine with an amplifier that produces anywhere from 300-800 watts per channel, depending on how much cash you want to spend and the types of parties you'd like to DJ. If you're looking to do traditional non hip-hop weddings, a lower power amplifier may be fine. If you're looking to do proms and club-type gigs, you'll probably need the higher power to produce the bass your customers will want to hear.

My DJ crew always used QSC amplifiers for our mobile gigs and for any club installations we've done. Their reliability, power, great support policies, and fair price made it an easy choice for us over the years. QSC's RMX 4050HD (see Figure 4.16) has more power (800 watts per channel RMS at 8 ohms) and connections than most DJs need for mobile and club applications. The RMX 4050HD features balanced ½",

XLR and barrier strip inputs (used for background music systems in stores and restaurants, but not for DJ applications). Its output options include binding posts (also known as "Banana Plugs"), and Neutrik Speakon outputs. It has front-mounted gain controls, plus signal and clip LED indicators to monitor performance. A really nice feature the RMX 4050HD has is separate circuit breakers, one for each channel. I've had incidents in which one side was overdriven for one reason or another, and the whole amp shut down causing this very unpleasant and embarrassing silence. With this feature, one side will still run so you may not have to lose your entire sound all at once.

QSC RMX 4050HD Amplifier.
Image courtesy QSC Audio.

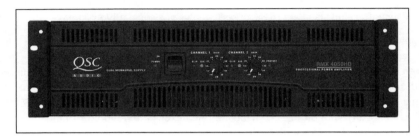

Power—there is no substitute! Get as much power in your amplifiers as you can afford, and match your speakers to that power. Speakers can be damaged because you have too much power, or in some cases, when you don't have enough power. Just because you have an amp that's 800 watts per channel amplifier doesn't mean you have use all 800 watts all the time.

Hooking Up Your Amplifier

Your professional mixer will have either an XLR or balanced TRS ½" output which will be "male." As you can see from the RMX 4050HD in Figure 4.17, both the XLR and TRS ½" inputs are "female", meaning you'll need XLR or TRS ½" patch cables that are female on one end and male on the other. Simply insert one end from the "left" output of your mixer to one of the corresponding inputs on your amplifier, then connect the right output to the other amplifier input. Most DJs use "Channel 1" as their left side, and "Channel 2" as their right side. In most nightclubs and permanent installations, sound systems are often run in mono, so the left/right split is irrelevant.

Once your mixer is connected to your amplifier, you'll then need to connect it to your speakers, effectively completing your sound producing circuit. Depending on the inputs of the speakers you've chosen, you'll need to decide which connection to use to connect them to your amplifier. Most newer DJ speakers use the "Speakon" connection, which is a special more secure foolproof twist-on connector that's "male" on both ends. Other speakers will utilize the "binding post" or "dual banana plug" connection. With the binding post or dual banana connection, make sure you've matched the positive connection (usually noted as "+") on the amplifier to the positive connection (+) on the speaker, and follow by connecting the negative connections (denoted as "—"). Usually, the positive wire will be either red or white, and the negative is usually black, but that's not always the case depending on who wired the connection. The color doesn't necessarily matter, as long as you're certain that the positives are connected by the same exact color, and the negatives are connected by the same exact color.

QSC RMX 4050HD amp
connections.

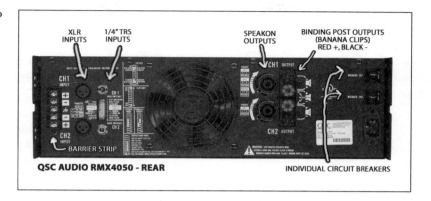

Speakers

The first part of a DJ setup is the component that actually produces the sound, either a CD player, and MP3 player, your microphone, a DVD player, or a turntable. That signal is processed through the mixer, then through the amplifier, and finally to the last part of this electronic series, the speakers.

The short non-technical explanation of a loudspeaker, usually known as just "speaker," goes something like this. An amplifier provides an electronic charge that's transferred over speaker wires to the speaker. The electric charge interacts with a large magnet that vibrates a coil attached to a speaker's very thin "cone" or "diaphragm," causing the physical movement of the cone, which produces vibrations with the same frequencies as the sound that's coming out of your mixer. The vibration causes fluctuations in the air, and these fluctuations ultimately produce sounds that are hopefully very similar to the music a DJ plays.

Speaker cones are built to handle a certain range of frequencies. When an amplifier attempts to push and pull the thin speaker cone with frequencies that are below or exceed the normal range of frequencies, the cone could tear or crack. If you run more power through the speaker than it can handle for an extended length of time, the magnet and other internal components could actually catch fire. I've actually done this to a speaker, unknowingly of course! These failures are known as "blowing" speakers. Blown speakers are usually not covered under warrantees, so you've got to be really careful not to make expensive errors.

Speakers are usually run in pairs of two or more. Most mobile DJs run two speakers, since they run their system in stereo. One speaker will broadcast the left channel and the other will broadcast the right channel. Bigger multi-speakers systems, such as those used in most nightclubs, bars, and concerts, typically run their systems in mono rather than stereo, with the left and right channels mixed together so more power can be directed where it's needed without worrying about signal separation.

Like amplifiers, all speaker systems are rated for a maximum "watts per channel" they're capable of handling in "peak" or "continuous RMS" modes. The "peak" rating means the peak power produced only once in a while, like when the song you're playing or knucklehead yelling into you microphone produces a very loud, above normal sound. The "continuous RMS" rating is the typical volume that's produced by your amplifier under normal party conditions. Most of the time, you won't exceed the continuous RMS watts per channel rating, but it does happen, which is why your speakers should exceed the continuous RMS power of your amplifier. Anything over your speaker's maximum peak rating for any length of time, even a second or two, could permanently damage your speakers. If you're not sure, ask your music store person about compressors and limiters, which can actually step in and electronically curb potentially damaging signals before they get to your speakers.

I've had really good luck with JBL, EV, Bose, and Community DJ speakers. There's a wide variety of "powered" speakers on the market today. These are speakers with small but powerful amplifiers built into them. This can save you space if you have a small vehicle and need to move these around frequently, but obviously adds to the cost of the speakers.

When you're purchasing speakers, you should listen to them individually. For example, I was recently helping someone purchase new powered speakers at a local music store. Most DJ oriented stores are very liberal about hooking things up and letting you try things out before you decide on a purchase. He narrowed his decision down to two pair of speakers made by leading manufacturers. The woofer size was the main difference in the two speakers. They both sound pretty incredible with most pre-recorded music. But, there was an interesting difference when he pulled out one of his hip-hop discs and played it on both systems. The smaller but slightly more powerful speakers seemed to provide a little more "punch" (bass response) with the hip-hop music. However, the bigger speakers seemed to have more of a "full-range" sound, which is important when playing rock music with various instruments and vocal harmonies. Since my friend uses Karaoke in some of his shows where many of his customers sing rock songs, he opted for the larger speakers, and purchased a separate "sub" unit (also known as a "sub-woofer," a separate speaker used to provide lower bass tones only) to provide more punch when he was kicking out a hip-hop set.

JBL Eon15 G2 Powered Speaker.
Photo courtesy JBL
Professional.

It's easier than you think to kill your speakers! Try not to do the following things and your speakers will last longer:

❋ Don't overdrive them with too much power. Note the highest recommended wattage permitted in the literature or usually printed on the back of the speakers.

❋ Don't over-equalize! Use equalizers to cut frequencies, not to enhance them. Most CDs are professionally produced and pre-equalized by dudes who make six-figure incomes, so don't screw with them.

❋ If you're overdriving your amplifier and it is clipping, you're probably tossing too much power or dynamic frequencies at them that they can't handle, which can produce clipping and harmonic distortion that could ruin your speakers.

❋ In my youthful carefree days, I used to make a loud popping sound by blowing into a microphone that sounded like a cool explosion. I later learned that this is one of the worst things you can do to a microphone and a speaker! Avoid those "turn-off thumps" and the pops associated with plugging in, unplugging or dropping microphones. These noises produce bass levels that are very low, usually well below the physical limits speakers are meant to handle, and can permanently damage your equipment.

Headphones

When beatmixing, scratching, or simply cueing up your next song, you'll need to preview it before it goes over your sound system. You can't use any consumer headset though because they won't be loud or clear enough for mixing. Look for a headset that has a closed back to eliminate sounds you don't need to hear. Also, look for good bass response and a wide dynamic range. One of the more popular headsets today is the Sennheiser HD280 Pro series, which I use for my studio work. There are several specially made DJ headphones with neat stuff like built in microphones, cordless receivers and even swiveling earpieces. Try a couple sets to see what works best for you. Personally, I dig headsets that I can hold between my shoulder and my ear and drop into my hand as soon as my mix is over. I still use an old Radio Shack headset that I cut in half and rewired for my personal use (shown in Figure 4.19).

Radio Shack split, Sennheiser HD280 Pro.

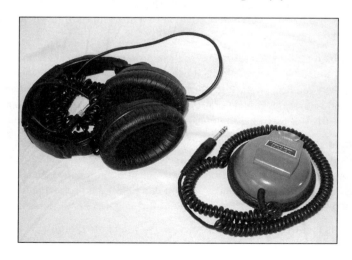

Equalizers

Equalizers ("EQ") are used mostly by bands in live and recorded performances to tame harsh and unwanted frequencies from voices and live instruments. EQs can come in the simplest form, a two-band EQ which is seen frequently as "bass" (low frequencies) and "treble" (high frequencies) controls on most consumer electronics. Most DJ mixer based EQs add a "mid" (middle frequencies) setting to the bass and treble. Professional EQs used in band settings and permanent installations can have 40 or more bands of EQ ranging from 20 Hz all the way through 20 kHz, with one separate set of controls for the left and another for the right side.

Most new DJs seem to use equalizers as a happy decoration. For some reason, all new DJs arrange the EQ in a "smile" formation, with the bass and treble frequencies boosted way up and the middle frequencies turned way down. Sound guys recognize this smile as inherently evil because "it's laughing at you for being a dummy."

"Smile Formation."

The truth is you rarely need to equalize anything. The CDs or records you purchased have been equalized by some engineer making six figures who would have a heart attack if he could see you smiley-facing his already perfect mix!

Some DJs will use an EQ for special effects. You can drop the bass at a certain point during a song that can make a song sound like you're playing it over your mobile phone; it'll make people wonder what's going on. And when you bring it back to normal, just at the right time, they'll be thinking how cool you are. Some DJs will reduce the bass on one song during beatmixing to avoid a sometimes "muddy," muffled sound. And some DJs will use the EQ to enhance or trim noise and feedback from vocals.

If you walk into a nightclub, you'll typically find the EQ has a wire mesh cover over it. This is there for a reason. An experienced sound engineer most likely ran pink and white noise generators and used special engineer sensors and equipment to set the correct equalization for the room. Don't ever unscrew the cover and mess with the settings; chances are you don't have the professional knowledge to set the EQ correctly. Incorrect settings could cause damage to the amplifiers and speakers.

The bottom line is that DJs should use EQs very sparsely, and for special effects only.

Hooking Everything Up

In this section, we'll show you the basic components of a typical mobile DJ setup and how they're connected to each other. Your first couple times setting things up will almost always be unsuccessful, so we'll provide you with the information we never had in an effort to help you understand the connections.

The Cables

There are a bunch of different cables used to connect DJ equipment components. We thought that since these cables can get confusing for new DJs, a brief description of these cables and their connectors might be a good introduction to the DJ setup. Thanks to the folks at djcables.com for their help with this section.

The most common connector cable is known as the "RCA" patch cable (see Figure 4.21), invented years ago by the RCA company as an industry standard for audio cables. The male part of this cable has a long rod in the center surrounded by thin, curved metal to create a simple audio connection. They're usually paired for stereo usage, with one side used for left signals and the other for the right signals. Although most people use the Red cable for the right channel and the White or Black cable for the left channel, the cables are identically made and completely interchangeable.

The RCA cable is also widely used for video connections known as "composite" video. The video connector is usually yellow, but again, it's the same exact cable as the audio connectors and entirely interchangeable.

RCA Cables.

Another common audio cable is known as the "quarter-inch" or ½" cable (shown in Figure 4.22). These cables are sometimes referred to as "patch cords." They're widely used in live music/band situations, but can be used as either microphone cables for "Hi-Z" or wireless microphone connections. They're sometimes used as speaker cables in some DJ systems, but it's a bad idea to use a ½" instrument cables for speaker connections. While there are speaker cords with ½" connections, the important thing to look at is the wire. Speaker wires are two separate wires running side by side through an insulator. Instrument cables, on the other hand, are coaxial, meaning one wire runs inside the other wire. This can cause unwanted capacitance in the cable, which is negligible at line levels, but becomes a major force when dealing with the amplified currents sent to a speaker.. The ½" connector is also the typical connector for most DJ headphones. These cables can be monaural or stereo (two black bands near the tip of the plug). Stereo connections are typically used for high-end headphones.

½-inch Patch Cord.

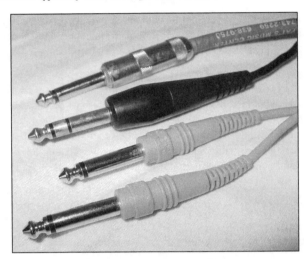

There's another closely related cable known as the "stereo minijack" or ⅛" connector (see Figure 4.23) that's typically used to connect the output from laptop computers or iPods via a RCA conversion cable. Connections using minijacks are usually the lowest quality of any DJ cable, and should only be used as a last resort when no other connection option is available.

Minijack.

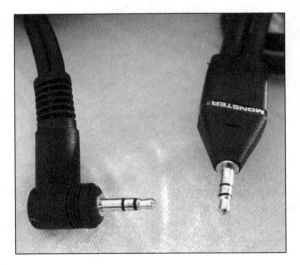

Many professional "Lo-Z" microphones and mixer to amplifier connections are made with balanced "XLR" cables and connectors (see Figure 4.24). These connections offer a shielded three-way positive, negative, and ground connection that often alleviates hums and noise that other cables may introduce in some long cable run situations.

XLR Cables.

A newer entry into the cable game is the Neutrik Speakon connector (see Figure 4.25). This is a pretty cool interlocking cable used for many speaker systems. Older ½" connectors were easily pulled out of speakers, but these connectors twist in and lock making those mishaps less frequent.

Neutrik Speakon
Connector.

Finally, there's the "binding post" connection, or as I thought they were called for years, the "banana plug" connection (Figure 4.26). They got this name because they kind of look like a banana that's about to peel itself apart. These come in groups of two called a "dual binding post" connector, with one side that carries the positive signal and the other carrying the negative signal. These are used primarily for amplifier to speaker connections when the Speakon connection is not available.

Binding Post Connection
("Banana Plug").

Wire Considerations

There's another effect in the sound business called "power dissipation." This involves the loss of power from your amplifier to your speakers due to leakage through your speaker wires.

Tiny electrons that carry the signal and power to your amplifiers don't actually pass through the wires from your amplifiers; they actually travel along the outside of the wires. During their trip, electrons try to find the path of least resistance, which is often somewhere else but on the surface of a thin wire. A bunch of electrons go joyriding with their buddies and get lost in space, effectively decreasing power to your speakers.

For the least amount of power loss, you should use the heaviest gauge (thickest) wire that's practical. Typically, the shorter the run, the smaller gauge you can use with minimum power loss. The longer the run, the heavier gauge you'll need to contain the power. You'll also want to consider the power of the amplifier you're using — the more powerful the amp, the heavier the gauge. Gauge measurements work in reverse. The lower the gauge number, the higher the thickness of the cable. I use 12-gauge wire all the time simply because I couldn't comprehend this whole concept and wanted to play it safe. I tried expensive cables to see if there was an audible difference, but I couldn't determine one.

Hum or Buzz

Anytime you use cables, you're laying out metal wires. Metal wires, like antennas, attract all kinds of electronic noise known as "Radio Frequency Noise" (RF). And since DJs can run hundreds of feet of wire in some cases, your wires will pick up all kinds of nonsense. Lighting dimmers and ballasts, radio transmissions, and all kinds of other random signals can create interference that could produce noise, usually an annoying hum, hiss or even a radio transmission, that will be amplified by your speakers for all to enjoy. Once we did a gig about 200 feet away from a 50,000-watt radio station antenna. Every once in a while, the news station would come over our speakers. Some local residents even admitted that they've heard the radio station in their dental fillings!

"Balanced" cables help fix the noise issue. There's an extra conductor in a balanced connection wire. While an "unbalanced" connection only has two conductors, a balanced connection uses three. The signal is simultaneously sent over two conductors, only one is flipped 180 degrees out of phase. Typical noise enters the line as usual, but when the signal is flipped once again back to its normal position, the noise cancels itself out, and you've got a nice clean connection.

Typical balanced connectors include the three-pronged XLR or 1/4" TRS connectors. Balanced wires cost a bit more, but are important for DJs who depend on clean sound.

Once in a while, you'll hear a pesky audio hum that will drive you nuts while you're trying to find it. Sound engineers refer to this as a "60 Hertz hum," which is usually a result of having a "ground loop" in the audio system. This is where there are two or more ground references in the system, and current is flowing from one ground point to another, which is bad. Some audio components need their own separate ground reference. If an amplifier gets its ground from the AC power cord, and your mixer also receives its ground from the AC power cord, the audio cable that connects the mixer to the amplifier sees a second ground from the mixer, effectively forming a ground loop. If your amplifier or mixer doesn't have a "ground lift" setting on it, you'll need to find an alternate power circuit for one of the units to eliminate the hum.

Sometimes you'll get an annoying buzz over your system. Your turntable grounds not being attached to the grounding post on your mixer can cause this. Another cause of system buzz is having a sensitive component too close to a power transformer. Amplifiers have large power transformers and can induce a magnetic field into other equipment. You can sometimes kill a buzz by simply moving your amplifier.

Ground loops, buzz, and all kinds of other nasty noises are sometimes hard to find. You may have to try a bunch of different approaches before arriving at the fix. That's why you should always get to your gig nice and early.

Crossovers

A crossover is an electronic device that is used to separate an audio signal into two or more bands of frequencies above and below a certain frequency, called the "crossover point." Crossovers can be active or passive. A passive crossover is built into most pro speaker cabinets in order to separate bands of frequencies from the full range speaker signal produced by the amplifier. An active crossover is a separate electronic component that's used with larger sound systems that have many amplifiers and many speakers. It separates the audio signals into bands of high, mid and low and fed to specially designed speakers built to handle only those frequencies. These systems are very common in larger nightclubs.

Packages or Starter Kits

There are quite a few DJ starter kits on the market. In the old days, you were limited to a couple nasty belt drive turntables and a mixer. Today, you can get two leading direct drive turntables and a pretty decent battle mixer or an all-in-one dual CD player plus mixer unit for under $500. Some come with tiny little desktop speakers that are pretty much useless. Obviously, if you want to use the same gear as the few highly paid pros use, you'll easily spend four times that much. Packages and starter kits are a good way to spend less money as you're experimenting with the DJ thing. The downside is that you'll usually outgrow them quickly and end up spending the big bucks for the pro-level stuff sooner than later. And it's often to be difficult to do all the cool tricks pro DJs do with less professional equipment.

Used Equipment

Sometimes it makes more sense to hunt around and hook yourself up with a second hand set of real equipment. You can usually get the same stuff the professionals are using at less than half the price. Just like with anything else that's used, you're got to be careful. Always ask for pictures of the real equipment that's for sale, and don't accept the product's marketing photos. Don't buy stuff that's too beat up. If you have a chance, go to try the actual equipment before you make a decision.

When looking at turntables, don't necessarily make a judgment based on their overall appearance. I've had Technics turntables that were 10 years old that looked nasty but worked perfectly. You'll simply want to inspect the turntable to see that it actually produces sound, and that it keeps its pitch or speed locked at the 0% setting.

While searching for CD players, try them out to ensure they play and don't skip. Bring your own CDs to try out, especially if you use recordable CDs. Some CD players, mostly older ones, won't recognize some brands of CD-Rs and CD-RWs because of differences in their reflectivity. Test the pitch control to make sure it speeds up and slows down. Check the drive doors to make sure they're lined up correctly and open and close easily.

When shopping for used mixers, it's much more important to actually try it out while actually playing music. On some older non-VCA and optical fader mixers, dirt collects under the volume knobs or sliders over time and can make strange crackling sounds when you adjust them, and this is bad. Try the crossfader to make sure it works without crackling. Many pro mixers offer replacement crossfaders. Finally, look at the inputs on the back of or on the bottom of the mixer. If wires have been tightly tugging on the inputs over time, they can become loose and eventually fail to work, which can cause an entire side of your system to fail.

Since microphones and headsets get in close contact with your body, I personally would rather buy these new. Many DJs tend to "swallow" microphones by putting their lips all over them, which is kind of sick. And headphones can accumulate all kinds of sweat over time. You're usually better off purchasing these more personal items new.

Maintenance Anyone Can Do

There are a bunch of things you can do to keep your equipment functioning reliably. This will ultimately help you by producing less equipment failures in the middle of that busy night when it can be most embarrassing, even when you are ready for it.

Believe it or not, one of a DJ's worst enemies is dust. Those little balls of fuzz can come back to bite you when you least expect it. Not only do they clog your nose and make you sneeze, they get caught in the cooling fans of your lights and amplifiers, which can cause overheating and thermal shutdowns. And dust can get on the laser pickups of your CD players and on the needles of your turntables, which causes tracking errors and skipping. You've got to keep your equipment as clean as possible to avoid potential problems. If you're a club DJ, I recommend using an air cleaner in your DJ booth to keep the dust away from your equipment. Buy a CD cleaner for about $20 and use it in your CD players once a week. Pull the dust bunnies off the cooling fan covers on your amplifiers and any lighting fixtures you have access to.

Cigar and cigarette smoke is another of your enemies. We all know what it does to our lungs. Imagine the same thing happening to your CDs and the laser pickups of your CD players. Smoke leaves a nasty film on these things, which can eventually impede a laser from correctly reading a CD. Your CD cleaner can take care of your laser pickup. If you keep your CDs in protective sleeves, they should be fine too.

Do this maintenance routinely and keep a list with dates on it where everyone can see it. A little prevention will avoid a potentially embarrassing situation.

Emergency Kits and Backup

It seems Murphy's Law applies to this job more than any other one in my experience, probably because you're stuck directly in front of hundreds or thousands of people where any wrong move will be noticed.

If you're prepared, you'll not only save face, but you can save an entire night. Luckily, most equipment failures in come from blown fuses or bad wires. With a little professional training, you can fix these situations in minutes.

Whatever you do, NEVER open a piece of equipment! There's nothing you can do if a piece of equipment crashes beyond a blown fuse. Leave these repairs to a qualified professional. Any emergency repairs that you will be able to make will be related to the wires that connect the components together, or the fuses inside these components. Fortunately, this is where most problems occur.

Since these components are often very different from the ones you may have in your home, it's best to get a lesson on how these are all wired together from your local sound people before you try any repairs on your own. Do not guess; if you're not sure what you're doing, don't do it. You could seriously hurt yourself or blow up the entire system. Get to know your sound equipment. Make a list of all the different types of equipment and connections that you can see. This will help you to put together your emergency backup kit.

Get yourself a cheap toolbox. In that toolbox, you'll want a set of basic tools including flathead and Philips screwdrivers, an adjustable wrench, electrical tape, pliers, a wire stripper and a wire cutter. Toss in a flashlight and some batteries because the stuff you'll need to get to is probably in a dark area. Get yourself a bunch of fuses at your local Radio Shack. You'll probably need to do a once over on your club's amplifiers, mixer, and lights and dimmer packs to see what type and rating the fuses are. Check the manuals if it's not obvious, but don't guess because the wrong fuse can fry a component.

Never, ever remove or replace a fuse while a component is plugged in. These components are usually live even when turned off and can give you a very bad shock. I once saw a DJ get tossed back a few feet once while trying this. He's all right, but he was lucky. I've seen fuses blow on amplifiers, mixers and lights during a show. My fuse kit always came in handy.

You should also pick up all kinds of adapters too. Stereo RCA to mono RCA and $\frac{1}{2}$" plugs, balanced XLR to $\frac{1}{2}$" plugs, "Y" cords of all types, 6' runs of RCA and XLR and $\frac{1}{2}$" cords, female-to-female RCA and $\frac{1}{2}$" connectors for long runs, banana plugs, and a roll of shielded audio and speaker wire. Sometimes you may have a bad wire that's causing all your trouble. I've run into situations where someone stole a mixer from a club before the DJ's shift. I managed to rewire the system so we had a VCR with a 6-hour premixed tape running directly through the system until we were able to get a replacement a few hours later. The replacement mixer was incompatible with our existing wiring, so these adapters and connectors allowed me to temporarily wire it up and save the night.

Pick up a cheap set of headphones, too, in case yours dies or disappears. If you're playing or mixing dance music, you'll be in a world of hurt without your headphones. Someone once stole my headset that I left at a club. Since I was still using records, I was at least able to visually see where the breaks were, and I could put my ear close to the needle to hear the beats.

An extra cheap microphone isn't such a bad idea either. Make sure that their outputs plug properly fit into your mixer, or you have the proper adapter or connector. The wrong size plug won't do you any good in a pinch. I've encountered situations where a DJ forgot a microphone, so I instructed him to plug his $\frac{1}{2}$" headset into the mic jack and speak through that. This sounds kind of like a megaphone. You can do this as a special effect.

Draw a diagram of your system. It doesn't have to be neat. In this diagram, show how each unit is connected to the other units, and with what kind of wires. Label each of the wires with a hand written tag or with colored tape so you'll know what goes where. This will help you to thoroughly understand how your system works, and how to troubleshoot it. I happened to be in a club once where their DJ quit in the beginning of the night, and pulled all the wires out of the sound system to make it difficult for a replacement. I helped to rewire the system without a diagram, but it took us a while to figure out what went where. A diagram sure would have helped.

Hopefully, you'll never need to use any of this stuff. But it'll give you peace of mind just to know you've got it all just in case you need to make that emergency repair to save the day.

5

ALL ABOUT THE MUSIC

While radio DJs get their music playlists handed to them with zero tolerance for variation, club and mobile DJs must spend countless hours going through piles of music looking for current hot songs (usually decided by the radio stations) while trying to predict the next big hit. Once you do find those songs, you then have to listen to them over and over again to learn them inside and out. You need to know which versions work for you, how each of them begin, where they kick in, where they drop out, where the breaks are, and how to avoid the stupid elongated crap that some remixers add to a song that can completely kill a dance floor.

As a mobile or club DJ who's primary responsibility is to make people dance, your music decision is always based on the response of your audience. So let's look at who influences your audience.

Here in the States, it seems a few purely money-motivated radio company and television network executives determine what's going to be hot. I've always imagined four or five pot-bellied billionaires sitting on a golf course going through a pile of music they all hate in an effort to decide what they think should be the next big hit. They then do a secret handshake and create a marketing conspiracy so they'll all make even more money and effectively kill any notion of free will. This has to be the way these decisions are made because there's no rational explanation why people like Eminem, Puff Daddy, or Britney Spears become superstars.

Fortunately, Europe and other parts of the world are still fairly open-minded when it comes to music. Some of their influence spills over to the States and creates what record executives darkly refer to as "The Underground." Most worthwhile DJ dance music begins in the Underground, then gets sucked into the marketing vacuum where it gets commercialized and played to death. This cycle begins and ends hundreds of times a year. Your challenge is to stay on top of it. That in itself is a full-time job.

It's much easier to maintain your music library as a mobile DJ. Since weddings and other private parties have a wider assortment of ages and music tastes, your music selection must be varied with respect to era and genre. These people want to hear what they know, and you've only got a few hours to cover it all. In most cases, mobile DJs can get away with a collection of proven hits without taking chances on new music.

Some older mobile jocks I know rarely purchase new music. These guys are pompous individuals who consistently play the same exact music at each affair regardless of their audience's requests or tastes. This is not recommended, for several reasons. First, anyone who becomes too complacent with any job risks obsolescence. Eventually, you'll develop a bad customer service reputation. Secondly, doing the same exact thing over and over causes burnout. When this job begins to seem like a job, you become a liability. You'll become short tempered and may risk ruining some bride's wedding reception with an attitude problem. At best you will get a bad reputation that'll kill your business. At worst, you could get your butt kicked and equipment smashed in the parking lot after the wedding by an angry groom and five of his best friends from his college football team.

On the other hand, nightclub and bar DJs must delve into the new music bins at record stores and on the internet. Nightclubs and bars have a younger and more hip audience that demand a mixture of recurrent (older) dance hits, the latest dance hits, and an infusion of new music. But there are several variations that will drive you crazy. Typically, big city nightclub audiences enjoy music they've never heard before, while smaller suburban and hotel bars won't respond to music they don't know. Throw in the exception to every rule, and you've got a puzzle you'll need to solve yourself in each situation.

It's All About Your Audience

Are you playing for swing dancers or snotty 16-year-old punks? Do you have roots in hip-hop but your crowd is begging for dance rock? Is some guy in a cowboy hat sucking down a Pabst Blue Ribbon giving you an evil eye because you're playing Eminem? Does the girl with the pierced eyelids truly appreciate the Mozart you're bustin out? (Can she even see?) This might seem far-fetched but you'll run into similar situations at many mobile parties. The key to success as a mobile or club DJ is timing combined with effective and relevant music programming. You've got to know your audience and what they'll respond to. Hopefully, you'll have a clue before you get tossed into the situation, but you'll often walk in blind. Even the best prepared mobile DJs with all of their forms and music lists submitted before the affair can run into unexpected surprises that find them unprepared.

I had that experience at a wedding reception. I wasn't aware that the bride's mother had filled out the song request sheet in advance because the bride assured me that she and her fiancé worked on it together. Obviously, mom's tastes were a little different than her daughter's. I was prepared for this big elegant affair with lots of disco and traditional dance rock. The bride and groom had recently come back from an early honeymoon cruise to the islands where all they danced to was reggae, and naturally, they wanted major reggae at their wedding reception. The problem was that no one told me this, so I was short on reggae that day. Fortunately, I brought my cell phone and arranged to have someone bring my reggae collection to the affair.

I constantly had to remind myself that I was buying this music specifically for DJ use. I didn't necessarily like the songs I bought, but I knew that a majority of my mobile and club customers would respond to it. Unless you're becoming a DJ as a hobby and just making mix CDs or tapes for your friends, it's important to remember that you're usually not playing for yourself. You'll need to open your mind play a lot of music you'll probably hate.

Most situations a beginner DJ will face involve familiar music rather than non-familiar music. Mobile DJs and mainstream club DJs are limited to playing music everyone already knows. Big city club audiences tend to be trendier, always looking for the next big thing. So big city club DJs can get away with breaking new records no one has ever heard. Fortunately, this is a good thing for new DJs. You'll have the luxury of time to learn the classics you'll need to learn before you'll get a job at the big city club. By that time, you'll have a large knowledge of music, and a better sense of which new or non-familiar records will generate a positive response.

Another thing about big city clubs that should be mentioned is the level of artificial and illegal substance usage as it relates to music tastes. People who are drug-induced couldn't care less what they're dancing to, as long as it's fast. Techno and trance sets in this environment can range up to 160 beats per minute, well over what a sober and traditional crowd would dance to. Unfortunately, recreational drug usage seems to be popular in big club situations. You don't have to judge this behavior, but you should know about it so you can program accordingly.

Club Mixes, Remixes, and Radio Versions

Depending on where you're working, you'll need the most appropriate version of a dance song. For instance, if you're working in a big city cutting-edge dance club, you'll need the hottest energy-packed remix that's available. You may have to purchase an imported mix that'll run you a few extra dollars. On the other hand, if you're working a private party, a smaller bar or a corporate club, you'll need something more along the lines of the popular radio version, or your customers may yell at you.

Club versions often include longer introductions and breaks that make a DJ's job easier by allowing pre-determined points where the mix will start or end. Be careful with certain club versions and remixes. Many times these remixes are done by a producer who's not familiar with the dynamics of dance floors rather than a working DJ. The producer types often change the song so it's virtually unrecognizable rendering it useless in most mainstream clubs, bars, and mobile parties. I imagine some of the non-DJ friendly remixes may be intended to be listening rather than dancing. While they may be great for car stereos, they can be disastrous on a dance floor.

Does The Music Matter?

The music in a bar or club can help set the mood for the entire night. In most small to medium sized clubs, music that seems too similar blends in to itself and gets lost, causing the room to become stale. But if the DJ throws an effective change-up in there somewhere, people take notice. A DJ has the power to turn a somber room into a massive party with nothing more than his or her music mix.

A private affair typically demands a fairly standard program of well known rock, disco, oldies, and current dance music. The timing of your selections is the key to mobile DJ programming success. Playing the right well known party song at the right time can make a party legendary. Playing the right songs too early or too late, or playing the wrong songs can create a lame atmosphere leading to a poor reputation for your business.

Anyone can say they're a DJ and play records or CDs. But what most people fail to understand is in order to be an effective DJ, you've got to be a smart music programmer. To achieve this, you've got to be a very aware person. In clubs and bars, you've got to consider the desired clientele the owners and managers are looking for. Hopefully they've already discussed and agreed on this, because many times there is massive confusion. You've got to know what kinds of music (genre, artists, and songs) their target clientele would desire. You've got to have a keen eye to determine which songs are working for that audience. You should always be watching the crowd looking for hints, such as people lip singing, tapping their hands on their chairs or the bar, swaying their feet to the beat of the music, humping their friends, etc. At mobile affairs, you've got to have impeccable timing. You've got to know exactly when to play what. You've got to learn how to recognize blood-alcohol levels so you'll know when you can change gears and take chances to create a frenzy of excitement. And you've got to have the confidence to try something different and ride it out even if it doesn't work, so you can figure out just how far you can push the limit on any given night.

Dance music fans are extremely fickle. I remember the first time I played Crystal Waters' "100% True Love," one of my most requested dance songs of all time. It cleared the dance floor. I let the song play out and announced that I would never play that song in that club again. Two weeks later, people were begging me for it. If a song is hot this week, it may be cold next week for no apparent reason. If a record is tearing up clubs and charts all over the world, but that same record hasn't made its MTV debut in America, you may lose your dance floor when you play that record. It makes no sense! This is the most frustrating aspect of being a mainstream club DJ. As you gain more experience, you'll learn to gauge your record buying by your budget. If you're short on cash, don't take as many chances and wait for the record to prove itself. If you're working in the hottest progressive club in your area, you'll have to keep up on the music no matter what. Hopefully you're making enough money to support your habit.

Being a DJ can be a very stressful job, especially when you've got some drunken fool yelling at you because you didn't play that Led Zepplin song in your dance club. But it can be so rewarding when you're pushing that edge; hearing people scream when you spin a certain song that no one expected you to play. You're king of the world for that brief moment. And then that drunk sprays you in the face again, effectively grounding you in reality.

As I got bored with the same old club thing night after night, I devised several experiments to see if the music really mattered. I love to mess with people and see if I can predict their reaction. One of my favorite tests was where I displayed a glowing personality but purposely played a monotonous house music mix for three straight hours. At one point, I mixed out of a house song and started tapping a house beat on the microphone with my finger to see what people would do. They kept dancing! As my friend managed to collect his dropped jaw, I managed to mix another house song one-handed while still tapping. No one left the dance floor. It was freaky.

Personality does go a long way, but the room was stale after a few hours. The dance floor was fairly consistent, but I could tell they were waiting for something else. The bar was sluggish and there were people just standing around blankly staring at things. So I shifted gears and threw on some "fun" music (i.e., classic disco, fun songs, etc.), and the place went nuts. The bar started moving, and the dance floor regained its energy. Personality alone wasn't enough to carry me through the night. In this case, the music did matter.

And I've done tests where I've said as little as possible during the night, but played the most killer music sets of my life. The mixes were flawless and the programming was perfect. The music took on its own persona and become the voice of the room. But there was something missing. Again, there were parts of the room that were stale and bored.

I learned that great nights need a well-balanced combination of the right music for your audience, and a personality that guides them through the night. The music definitely does matter, but the human element is still important. Unless you're working in an all house-music club in the basement of some factory in New York City, you'll need a good combination of music programming and personality to get things going, especially in the mobile DJ trade.

Building a Collection from Scratch

Regardless of your choice of the bar or mobile DJ profession, you've got to start somewhere. Mobile DJs have to spend more cash up front, and club DJs spend more money keeping their libraries current.

If you're becoming a mobile DJ, get ready to open your wallet widely. Due to the diversity of these affairs, you're going to need a wide variety of music from all different eras. The advantage is that mobile DJs don't have to take chances on unproven songs because all you'll usually play is well known hits.

GOOD COMPILATION CDS

The Source Presents Hip Hop Hits series. A series produced by The Source magazine that's a good starter collection of all the big names in Hip Hop including Jay Z, Eminem, Nas, Missy Elliott, Ludacris, and more. All these discs have at least three or four mainstream hits you can use.

Now That's What I Call Music series. It began in Europe back in the late 1990s as a comprehensive top-40 compilation series that wasn't available here in the states. Well, now it is! Lots of great hits by big names that you'll find useful at mobile events, and some lesser known filler songs just for laughs.

Totally Hits series. It's similar to the Now That's What I Call Music series that may fill in some of the holes in your popular music collection.

Time Life's Rock N' Roll Era, 1954-1961. Knock out about 90% of all the dance rock oldies you'll ever need with this series I wish I had so I wouldn't have had to buy hundreds of 45 RPM vinyl singles! Includes "16 Candles", "Johnny B Goode", "The Lion Sleeps Tonight", "Rock Around The Clock", and scores more.

Time Life's Classic Rhythm and Blues Collection, 1955-1969. A compilation series with huge R&B hits from the likes of James Brown, The Temptations, The Four Tops, Ben E. King, The Supremes, and many more.

Rasta Jamz, single CD. Finally, a reggae CD with more than two hit songs! Razor and Tie music hits gold with huge hits like "Boombastic", "Murder She Wrote", "Action", "Hotstepper", "Informer", "Move It", and "Sweat". Fun songs that most reggae fanatics and wannabes will all love. Ya, mon.

Pulse, two disc set. Most of the big 90s house and techno dance jams your 30+ crowd will scream for. Available at musicspace.com.

Fired Up, two disc set, as seen on TV. Late 90s and early 2000 well known house, trance, and techno jams that'll bring you into the current decade and make even the most irrelevant DJ seem halfway phat. Also at musicspace.com.

Non-Stop Hip Hop, yet another musicspace.com double disc. Fill in the holes with this killer hip-hop compilation from the 90s. I saw at least 14 smash hits that are guaranteed to pack most mobile or small bar dance floors.

Monster Booty, single disc. I liked the name of this collection, and then I saw eleven solid booty call jams that no DJ should be without. Where else? Musicspace.com.

If you're just starting out in the club and bar business, remember that your main goal should be to get as much popular dance music as you can get. Bar DJs needn't worry about picking up The Chicken Dance or Johnny Mathis' Greatest Hits—but you'll need proven dance hits that will work at your club or bar, and those hits can change weekly.

You can save thousands of dollars while building your collection by purchasing compilation CDs from almost any record store or online retailer. Since many CDs only have one song you'll need, it makes more sense to purchase a CD that has that one song along with at least one or two others you'll need for the same price. Compilation CDs contain several hits by various artists, and are usually arranged by genre or year. Occasionally, movie soundtracks can have multiple songs you can use. Try to get dance music compilation CDs that aren't already pre-mixed. The problem with pre-mixed discs is that you'll have a hard time using these mixes since someone's already mixing on the breaks. Plus, many people own the mixed CDs, so they'll know if you're trying to get over and pretend you're doing it yourself.

Another economical way to build your collection is to search your local used CD or record store. You can find compilations and full CDs here in great shape for the fraction of the price of new ones. Make sure you check the CDs and records for any surface scratches or warping. Most used music stores will let you listen to the CDs or records before you buy them. Take them up on their offer.

I do recommend dropping a substantial amount of money at your local specialty DJ store so they'll get to know you and like you. Their advice and special favors (like saving copies of a limited release for their favorite customers) can help in a pinch.

There is a basic group of dance songs you'll definitely need to get started listed later in this chapter. Another great source for figuring out what's what is *Mobile Beat* Magazine's annual Top 200 list. They survey mobile DJs all over the country to see what their most requested songs are. My personal top 200 has never matched the order of theirs, but it's a great place to start regardless. You can subscribe to their magazine or review their latest lists at www.mobilebeat.com.

CDs vs. Vinyl vs. MP3

For many years there's been a secret battle brewing between CD DJs and vinyl DJs. When CDs emerged as the dominant consumer format in the early 90s, many DJs shunned them. DJs were used to the physical feel and control of the vinyl record, a feel that couldn't be duplicated or replaced with the hardware available at that time. And there were no DJ CD players that offered a pitch control, so beatmixing was impossible unless you were mixing from a CD to a turntable. There was also a huge cost involved in replacing perfectly good vinyl with CDs. Since there was no trade-in option, DJs had to repurchase their entire music libraries. It took me two full years to complete my conversion.

The battle lines used to be drawn specifically by the DJ's year of origin, but that's no longer the case. Now that vinyl production has been ramped up to pre-CD days, the battle is more fierce than ever. And there's a new competitor, the "Digital DJ" who uses a compressed computer file rather than vinyl or CDs. It's a bigger mess than ever.

The driving forces behind your format decision are generally your idols and what they use; and the equipment that's available where and when you'll be learning to DJ.

The Advantages of Vinyl

My favorite part of working with vinyl was the visual bonus. You can actually see where the breaks are because the grooves look wider apart where there's only bass and drums. With a CD, you have to know the song by heart to know when the break is coming. You can cue up drop-ins easily on vinyl. It's much quicker to physically plop the needle down on the area of the record than it is to fast-search with a CD player. Sometimes this quickness factor comes in handy. Backspins (spinning the record backwards for a special transition effect), scratching, and power-downs (turning the power off so the song gradually slows to a stop), aren't readily available on CD players or with digital DJ systems. Some new DJ CD player products do include similar effects that are pretty darn close to the real thing, but the performance just doesn't look as cool with vinyl substitutes. The famous look of two or three turntables with vinyl spinning can add entertainment to some shows. Some people are just mesmerized by the whole vinyl process.

Many DJs simply prefer the perceived control and feel of a vinyl record. The ability to physically see and control a song with your hand rather than with a remote control appeals to a lot of people. Pushing a record to make it faster and slowing it with your fingers offers a physical control that can't easily be duplicated digitally.

Audio enthusiasts insist that vinyl reproduces music with much more accuracy than any digital means ever will. That's just dang foolish, especially with innovations like Super Audio CDs and variable bitrate lossless compression, but whatever. The question is where you draw the line of aural perception, meaning how many normal humans using non-audiophile equipment can tell the difference and actually hear a more accurate reproduction. I've tried to tell the difference several times, but I just can't do it. It's like Coke and Pepsi—you'll get a caffeine and sugar boost with both, but which one gets you higher? For arguments' sake, score a point for the vinyl people.

Finally, carrying heavy wood or plastic crates of vinyl for long periods of time is great cardiovascular exercise. I remember the days of climbing three flights of stairs six times carrying six heavy crates of vinyl during my early days at Club Atlantis, as the evil manager sat in front of the elevator and smiled. My back doesn't miss those days.

The Advantages of CDs

Vinyl cueing must be done manually over and over again, and you've got to physically hold it or you'll lose your place. And once you let it go to do something else, you've got to cue it up again. There's nothing like cueing a CD up to the exact millisecond of the beat where you want to bring a song in, then having it wait for you indefinitely at that same exact point without ever worrying about it drifting. Go grab a drink, chat with your friends, have a nap, and it'll still be cued up waiting for you at the same exact spot. It's perfect.

CD players hold perfect time. Even the best turntables have a small degree of speed shifting. Better CD players allow you to sample and loop segments of a song over and over again, which can give you some pretty neat control over a mix. Plus, the loop will be consistently perfect (if you programmed it correctly). You can loop with vinyl too, but you'll need two copies of the same record and a third turntable to mix out.

Many record labels are releasing multiple mixes on CDs, including "bonus" mixes that may not be offered on vinyl. Although all forms of recording music have space limitations, vinyl has a limitation in terms of the amount of time you can physically record on a 12" disc without losing volume and sound quality.

Finally, I could fit 152 CDs into my Case Logic CD book and bring my whole night's playlist with me in one hand with a big old Dunkin Donuts coffee in the other. My record crates at home took up the length of the entire basement wall, while my entire CD collection fit comfortably in a single cabinet. My wife and mother in law did a dance of joy the day I dumped all my vinyl behind Pat's Music in Bensalem, PA. To this day, no one has a clue where those 2,000+ records went!

The Advantages of Digital

I had the pleasure of working with the creator of the DJ RAK digital DJ system, Todd Sun. His system is amazing! He controlled lights, sound, and was able to pack over 20,000 CD-quality songs in a system that would completely and easily fit in the back seat of a Mini Cooper. He didn't have to worry about lost, stolen, or scratched CDs, since perfect digital copies were available for immediate usage. And no more fuddling around looking in CD books or record crates for a song; all he had to do was type in the first few letters of the song title or artist and the song instantly came up ready to play. For the smallest, lightest and most efficient DJ system, digital is the way to go. More scoop on the digital thing can be found in Chapter 9, "The Digital Domain."

Full CDs vs. CD Singles

You've got to make a decision on what format you want your music collection. Like most things in life, there are perceived advantages and disadvantages to each format. If you're just starting out, you probably should pick up the full CDs. You'll get more music for your money. As long as you're not saddled with a one hit wonder, chances are the full CDs have multiple singles on them, so you can save both money and space by purchasing the entire CD. Full CDs stay in stores much longer than the singles, so it can be easier to find rare songs. The downside to getting CD versions is the mixes may not be the popular club versions of the songs you want. As you become more aware of the music you'll need, you'll figure out the best solution for your situation.

Cocktail Music

Wedding and private party DJs spend a lot of time playing filler music while guests are arriving or stuffing their faces. In most cases, these are rare times when you don't want people to dance, so it's time to dig out some special listening music. I've always had success with a nice mix of smooth jazz and classy traditional music. What you don't want to do is put people to sleep! If you've decided to pursue mobile DJ affairs, here are a few discs you might want to pick up. Club DJs should never need this type of music.

* Greatest Hits of All, George Benson. "Turn Your Love Around" sounds impressive on pro DJ systems no matter where you're playing. Also includes the very classy "This Masquerade" and one of my favorite songs, "I Just Wanna Hang Around You."

* The Best of Earl Klugh, Earl Klugh. "Midnight in San Juan" is the perfect opening song for any affair anywhere. "Kissin' on the Beach" is a good choice to liven things up if the room appears to be stale. Klugh's classy guitar could class up a greasy garage.

* The Best of Al Jarreau, Al Jarreau. Smoother than a chocolate bar on a hot summer day. It's one of the few discs you could pop your player and walk away for a half hour without feeling guilty. "We're In This Love Together" and "Moonlighting" are two very memorable songs that are guaranteed to get smiles and thumbs up from your clients.

❋ Ultimate Kenny G, Kenny G. Sure, it's overplayed, but you'd better have this disc! "Silhouette," "Forever In Love," and "The Wedding Song" are standards that will be expected from most normal people. Grandma and grandpa will appreciate the break from beats. There's nothing like a little good sax to get the blood flowing.

❋ The Best of Anita Baker, Anita Baker. "Sweet Love" and "Caught Up in The Rapture" are very popular smooth grooves for a loose mood.

❋ The Best of Sade, Sade. The definition of smooth jazz! "Smooth Operator" was the first cocktail hour song I ever played as a professional DJ, and I played it at every wedding I ever did. Other great hits include Sade's "No Ordinary Love," "Your Love Is King," "The Sweetest Taboo," and just about every other track on this CD.

❋ Collection, Larry Carlton. Check out "Sleepwalker" and you'll know why Carlton is a classic. Some guy gave me a $50 tip for playing that song!

❋ Michael Buble, Michael Buble. Our era's Frank Sinatra. Seventeen completely useable classic wedding standards.

❋ The Look of Love, Diana Krall. I don't get it, but this chick is insanely popular in this genre. Get it because someone will ask for it eventually, and you'll look great for having it.

❋ When Harry Met Sally (Soundtrack), Harry Connick Jr. Two charming must have songs that'll win over the older crowd, including "It Had to Be You" and "Let's Call The Whole Thing Off." Warning: the volume on this CD is all over the place! The music is excessively low in places, and Harry's butter voice kicks in massively by surprise, so be ready for it.

❋ Clear Horizon: The Best of Basia, Basia. For a while, I swore every wedding band in the world performed her hit "New Day for You." Seventeen powerful and engaging songs perfect for chewing to the beat.

Slow Jams

If you're doing mobile DJ work, you'll definitely need some bump and grind material. Many smaller bars and mainstream clubs like to hear a few slow jams once in a while to break things up. Slow songs have a way of pulling people who don't usually dance on a dance floor, and it's a great way for guys to break the ice and meet a woman for the first time. Remember to keep in mind that you want happy slow jams to keep your crowd happy.

Here are my top 40 must-have slow jams, based solely on audience response. Feel free to add new hits and your personal favorites to the list. You can never have too many slow songs in your collection because you never know what someone will request.

❋ Anne Murray—"Can I Have This Dance"

❋ Atlantic Starr—"Always

❋ Ben E. King—"Stand By Me"

❋ Bette Midler—"Wind Beneath My Wings"

❋ Billy Joel—"Just The Way You Are"

❋ Boyz II Men—"On Bended Knee"

❀ Bryan Adams—"Everything I Do, I Do It For You"

❀ Celine Dion—"Because You Loved Me"

❀ Climax Blues Band—"I Love You"

❀ Commodores—"Three Times A Lady"

❀ Elvis Presley—"Can't Help Falling In Love"

❀ Eric Clapton—"Wonderful Tonight"

❀ Etta James—"At Last"

❀ Faith Hill—"Breathe"

❀ Flamingos—"I Only Have Eyes For You"

❀ Four Tops—"I Believe In You And Me"

❀ Hall and Oates—"You've Lost That Lovin' Feeling" (original by the Righteous Brothers)

❀ Heatwave (or Luther Vandross)—"Always and Forever"

❀ Honeydrippers—"Sea Of Love" (original by Phil Phillips)

❀ Jackson 5—"I'll Be There"

❀ Joe Cocker—"You Are So Beautiful"

❀ Joshua Kadison—"Beautiful In My Eyes"

❀ Journey—"Faithfully"

❀ KC & JoJo—"All My Life"

❀ Kenny Rogers—"Through The Years"

❀ Larry Graham—"One In A Million"

❀ Lionel Richie/Diana Ross—"Endless Love"

❀ Lonestar—"Amazed"

❀ Louis Armstrong—"What A Wonderful World"

❀ Luther Vandross—"Here and Now"

❀ Mel Carter—"Hold Me, Thrill Me, Kiss Me"

❀ Michael Bolton—"When A Man Loves A Woman" (original by Percy Sledge)

❀ Nat King Cole—"Unforgettable"

❀ Olivia Newton John—"I Honestly Love You"

❀ Patsy Cline—"Crazy"

❀ Righteous Brothers—"Unchained Melody"

❀ Shania Twain—"From This Moment"

❀ Van Morrison (or Rod Stewart)—"Have I Told You Lately"

❀ Vanessa Williams—"Save The Best for Last"

❀ Whitney Houston—"I Will Always Love You"

House and Techno Music

House music started somewhere in Chicago in the 1980s. House is identified by an easily recognizable bass drum that beats about once for every beat per minute. It's that fast "thump, thump, thump" that you hear in most clubs. This music is usually very melodic with some chick belting out vocals about love. House and techno songs typically range from 116 through about 140 beats per minute. House music was the most popular club music during the late 80s and early 90s, before being booted by the hip-hop movement. House is still popular because it's easily recognized and its tempo is easy to dance to.

Techno, also formerly known as "Rave," is an offshoot of house that incorporates a more mechanical or digital sound with wild synthesizers filling in the melody. Techno is a little faster than traditional house, beginning at about 124 BPM and going all the way up to 160 BPM. Techno is basically dead today and has been replaced by the trance movement.

Here are my top house and techno records for mobile DJs. These are not the hottest house and techno songs out today, so you'll have to do your homework to find more current house hits. Do realize that since most wedding and private party guests tend to be a little older, many folks will know and respond to these songs and generate referral business because you played the music they really wanted to hear.

House

- 2 In A Room—"Wiggle It"
- Amber—"One More Night"
- Amber—"Sexual"
- Bizarre Inc—"I'm Gonna Get You Baby"
- Black Box—"Everybody Everybody"
- Black Box—"Strike It Up"
- Blackout All Stars—"I Like It Like That" (X-Mix remix)
- CeCe Peniston—"Finally"
- Crystal Waters—"100% True Love"
- Funky Green Dogs—"Fired Up"
- Haddaway—"What Is Love"
- Livin Joy—"Dreamer"
- Marky Mark—"Good Vibrations"
- Maximillion—"Fatboy"
- Reel to Real—"I Like To Move It"
- Robin S—"Show Me Love"
- Rupaul—"Supermodel"
- Snap—"Rhythm Is A Dancer"
- Technotronic—"Move This"
- Technotronic—"Pump Up The Jam"

Techno

- ❋ 2 Unlimited—"Get Ready For This"
- ❋ 2 Unlimited—"Twilight Zone"
- ❋ AB Logic—"The Hitman"
- ❋ Apotheosis—"O Fortuna" (hard to find)
- ❋ Culture Beat—"Mr. Vain"
- ❋ Faithless—"Insomnia"
- ❋ Lords of Acid—"Take Control"
- ❋ Real McCoy—"Another Night"
- ❋ Real McCoy—"Runaway"
- ❋ The Movement—"Jump"

Trance/Progressive House

Over the past few years, techno and house have evolved into a new genre known as "trance" featuring a more melodic but repetitive and often psychedelic, addictive, soothing, and sometimes monotonous electronic beat. Trance is a hybrid of new-age, techno and house music that surfaced in the late 1990s in Europe. Most trance songs have few, if any, words, which are usually sampled and repeated rather than continuously sung. Most hard-core trance fans won't settle for anything less than their favorite hard-core trance music.

Progressive house is similar to trance, only that it's got more vocals along the lines of a house song. It's not as "harsh" as techno music, meaning the chords and beats are more subtle and melodic. Techno, progressive house and trance are often confused.

For most of your purposes, the following popular trance songs should get you through a trance request situation and help you understand what trance is. The typical club-goer or party person will probably refer to this music as "techno." The more popular songs are easily findable on most mainstream trance mixes, compilations and collections, such as the Trance Party series, available at any large music retailer. To get a feel for some more underground trance mixes, check out mix CDs by DJ Tiesto.

- ❋ Alice Deejay—"Better Off Alone"
- ❋ ATB—"9 PM (Til I Come) "
- ❋ Azzido Da Bass—"Dooms Night"
- ❋ BT—"Dreaming"
- ❋ Chicane—"Saltwater "
- ❋ Darude—"Sandstorm"
- ❋ Dirty Vegas—"Days Go By"
- ❋ DJ Sammy—"Heaven"
- ❋ Ian Van Dahl—"Castles in the Sky"
- ❋ Iio—"Rapture"

❋ Kernkraft 400—"Zombie Nation"

❋ Paul van Dyk—"For an Angel"

❋ PPK—"Resurrection"

❋ Robert Miles—"Children"

❋ Sash—"Encore une Fois"

Freestyle or Club Music

This music is hard to explain in terms of its beat——you've just got to hear it. Some people call this music "freestyle," and others call it "club." This genre was huge in New York, Philly, Miami, and Texas probably due to its close relation to Latin music rhythms. The freestyle heyday was in the late 1980s and early 1990s while I was spinning at Club Atlantis just outside of Philly. I'd do hour sets of this music and people couldn't get enough! It's surprisingly still popular in some areas, like New York City. DJ Bad Boy Joe spins freestyle mixes for WKTU in NYC, and he's got a few killer freestyle mix CDs in his "Best of Freestyle Megamix" series you can pick up at any big music retailer to really get the flavor of freestyle. Many of your customers will appreciate this music and request it at clubs, bars and private parties, so you should have a few of the classics in your collection. Here are my top freestyle records:

❋ Afrika Bambatta—"Planet Rock"

❋ Corina—"Temptation"

❋ Coro—"Where Are You Tonight"

❋ Cover Girls—"Show Me"

❋ Cynthia & Johnny O—"Dreamboy & Dreamgirl"

❋ Debbie Deb—"When I Hear Music"

❋ George LaMond—"Without You"

❋ Information Society—"Running"

❋ Johnny O—"Fantasy Girl"

❋ Judy Torres—"No Reason To Cry"

❋ Lil' Suzy—"Take Me in Your Arms"

❋ Lissette Melendez—"Together Forever "

❋ Nayobe—"Please Don't Go"

❋ Nice and Wild—"Diamond Girl"

❋ Noel—"Silent Morning"

❋ Stevie B—"Party Your Body"

❋ Stevie B—"Spring Love"

❋ Suave—"Crying Over You"

❋ TKA—"Louder Than Love"

❋ TKA—"Maria"

Disco

This should technically be called "Oldies" in today's time, but this music was so big, it's got a genre all to itself! I'm not really sure exactly when it started or where the cutoff point was, but neither does anyone else. Some folks say disco evolved into house at some point. But everyone knows what disco is, and you absolutely have to have a strong disco collection if you're a mobile DJ. Here's my all-time top-25 most requested disco song list.

* Abba—"Dancin' Queen"
* Anita Ward—"Ring My Bell"
* Bee Gees—"Stayin Alive"
* Bee Gees—"You Should be Dancin'"
* Donna Summer—"Bad Girls"
* Donna Summer—"Heaven Knows"
* Donna Summer—"Last Dance"
* Evelyn Champagne King—"Shame"
* Gloria Gaynor—"I Will Survive"
* Hues Corporation—"Rock The Boat"
* KC and the Sunshine Band—"Get Down Tonight"
* KC and the Sunshine Band—"That's The Way I Like It"
* Kelly Marie—"Feels Like I'm In Love"
* Kool and the Gang—"Celebration"
* Lime—"Babe We're Gonna Love Tonight"
* Lipps Inc.—"Funkytown"
* Michael Jackson—"Don't Stop Til You Get Enough"
* Miquel Brown—"So Many Men, So Little Time"
* Rick James—"Superfreak"
* Sister Sledge—"We Are Family"
* SOS Band—"Take Your Time"
* Sylvester—"Do Ya Wanna Funk"
* Village People—"Macho Man"
* Village People—"YMCA"
* Weather Girls—"It's Raining Men"

Hip Hop and Rap

Believe it or not, hip-hop has been around since the mid 1970s, with the 1979 Sugar Hill Gang hit "Rappers Delight," firmly entrenching it as part of mainstream music. Thanks to MTV and your local Top-40 radio stations, hip-hop is now THE mainstream. By definition, you really can't call yourself a club that plays

Top-40 without playing any hip-hop. Just one look at current music charts or a ride to any suburban mall will tell you that people of various colors and income levels have firmly embraced hip-hop as today's mainstream music and culture.

Hip-hop, often called "Rap Music," is loosely defined as a collection of slower tempo music with urban-inspired lyrics, which are either rapped or sung over very heavy bass lines. There are several different types of hip-hop including old school, hardcore, gangsta rap, east coast rap, west coast rap, and other fragmented forms that seem to be created daily in the back of a Cadillac with the boomin' system. Billboard Magazine wraps hip-hop and R&B into one single chart, and so do most DJs.

Nothing has caused more controversy in the DJ field than the emergence of hip-hop music. The main issue is that many narrow-minded people immediately associate hip-hop music with trouble. Due to inherent social prejudice by certain groups, many DJs face the constant struggle of working the "right" hip-hop music into their playlists. Here's how I solved this dilemma.

Back in the early 1990s, I was DJing at three separate large suburban clubs. My playlists were mostly comprised of house, techno, freestyle, 80s top-40 dance, modern rock, and a lot of recurrent disco music. In all three clubs, managers made it insanely clear that I was to try and avoid playing any type of "rap" music, because this was surely the "kiss of death" according to these club owners. While always clearly explaining to me that their decision was not racially motivated (most of these clubs had a nice mix of white, black, Asian and Hispanic people already), these owners and managers thought that rap music would bring the wrong type of customers to their clubs. They cited stories of fighting, weapons, and generally bad behavior as portrayed in the lyrics and videos of many rap songs.

As rap music began to morph into the hip-hop fold, and the genre began to solidify its roots in American pop culture, I had no choice but to slowly infuse this music into my playlists. The requests for hip-hop were overwhelming, and the response on the dance floor was always phenomenal. When challenged by managers, I would bring out a copy of my latest Billboard Magazine Top-40 charts and show them that this music was indeed considered "mainstream pop." Sometimes they agreed, sometimes they didn't. As I gained more and more experience with these challenges, I began to develop my own sub-groupings of hip-hop, and played them as short sets in between the disco, rock and house songs that management was used to. This worked perfectly!

My hip-hop classifications are as follows.

"Whitebread" Hip-Hop

Most of these are popular crossover hip-hop songs that have remained hot over the years. The magic of this category is that many managers don't consider these songs to be hip-hop! You'll hear these songs in suburban clubs regularly. Some may now qualify as "oldies!" This category includes songs like "It Takes Two" by Rob Base, "Ice Ice Baby" by Vanilla Ice, "White Lines" by Grandmaster Melle Mel, and "Rapper's Delight" by The Sugar Hill Gang, and virtually anything by Will Smith. For some reason, Will's music never qualifies as hip-hop in the manager's eyes. I don't get it, but I never complained because he had some of the hottest stuff out there. True hip-hop fanatics and youngins' will consider Whitebread Hip-Hop as lame.

No or Low-Rap Hip-Hop

These songs have the traditional hip-hop beat and feel, but most of the lyrics are sung and not rapped. These are usually stories about sex and love, with lyrics (but not concepts) most English speaking people can actually understand. This category includes songs like "Return of the Mack" by Mark Morrison, "Rock Wit U" by Ashanti, and almost anything by Beyonce, Nelly, and TLC. These songs are very popular and safe just about anywhere. And even youngins' will feel your flava.

Fast Rap

Although these songs are all rap, these songs always slipped under the "Rap Detector" probably because they were faster than traditional hip-hop beats. These songs are wildly popular among all crowds. For examples of fast rap songs, check out "The Thong Song" by Sisqo, "Da Dip" by Freak Nasty, "C'mon Ride The Train" by The Quad City DJs, "The Cha Cha Slide" by Casper, or almost anything by OutKast.

Possible Trouble

These songs are the hottest songs anywhere. Everyone requests these, but I always get the evil eye from my suburban club owners when I play them. This is the stuff you hear on your local dance stations and all over MTV, like Missy Elliott, Lil Kim, AZ, Chingy, DMX, and Eminem. In most mainstream clubs, you can get away with playing maybe one or two of these an hour without being branded as a hip-hop club. This should keep your crowd happy.

You can classify most hip-hop into one of the above categories. If you're working the mainstream club or bar scene, make a list for your managers and go over it with them. Watch how the crowd responds to each of these subcategories. And make sure your request sheets are written down so you can show your managers what people are asking for. If you're doing mobile parties, simply play whatever the person who's paying you wants!

Here's a list of my most-requested hip-hop and rap songs over the years. I've included some old-school classics that will never die. But hip-hop changes more frequently than most people change their underwear, so these songs may be irrelevant by the time you read this. Just turn on your local top-40 radio station or MTV to catch the latest jams.

* 50 Cent—"In Da Club" (Clean radio version!)
* Big Pun—"Still Not A Playa"
* Busta Rhymes—"Put Your Hands Where My Eyes Can See"
* CC Music Factory—"Gonna Make You Sweat"
* DMX—"Party Up (In Here) "
* DJ Kool—"Let Me Clear My Throat"
* Fabolous—"Young'n (Holla Back)"
* Grandmaster Melle Mel—"White Lines"
* House of Pain—"Jump Around"
* Ja Rule/Ashanti—"Mesmerize"
* Missy Elliott—"Work It"
* Montell Jordan—"This Is How We Do It"
* Mya—"Ghetto Supastar"
* Naughty By Nature—"Hip Hop Hooray"
* Naughty By Nature—"OPP"

❋ Newcleus—"Jam On It"

❋ Nelly—"Hot in Herre

❋ Notorious BIG—"Mo Money Mo Problems"

❋ Rob Base and DJ EZ Rock—"It Takes Two"

❋ Rob Base and DJ EZ Rock—"Joy and Pain"

❋ Salt n Peppa—"Let's Talk About Sex"

❋ Sean Paul—"Get Busy"

❋ Sugarhill Gang—"Rappers' Delight"

❋ Vanilla Ice—"Ice Ice Baby"

❋ Will Smith—"Getting Jiggy With It"

Alternative or Modern Rock

Back in the late 1970s, rock music took a strange twist in an effort to become different. It started with Punk Rock, then evolved into a genre all its own, sometimes called "Post Modern." I built a sold-out Tuesday night at the legendary M-Street Nightclub in Voorhees, New Jersey in the early 1990s with this music. Anyone who knows anything about the club business will tell you it's darn near impossible to get anyone to go out on Tuesday nights! Modern Rock finally peaked sometime around 1994 before fading into oblivion and yielding the stage to Alternative Rock where everything began to sound like Pearl Jam. This music still has a very strong following. Beware, much of this genre is limited to listening music. Its enthusiasts are very opinionated, and aren't afraid to share exactly what's on their mind. If you're playing the wrong alternative or modern rock songs, they'll yell at you.

Here are my top-20 most requested alternative dance rock songs.

❋ Adam Ant—"Goody Two Shoes"

❋ Alice In Chains—"Man In A Box"

❋ Billy Idol—"Dancing With Myself"

❋ Deee-Lite—"Groove Is In The Heart"

❋ Depeche Mode—"Personal Jesus"

❋ Erasure—"A Little Respect"

❋ Gary Numan—"Cars"

❋ Men Without Hats—"Safety Dance"

❋ Modern English—"Melt With You"

❋ Morrissey—"Suedehead"

❋ New Order—"Bizarre Love Triangle"

❋ R.E.M.—"End of the World"

❋ Rage Against The Machine—"Killing In The Name"

❋ Soft Cell—"Tainted Love"

❋ Talk Talk—"It's My Life"

❋ The B-52s—"Rock Lobster"

* The Cure—"Just Like Heaven"
* The Ramones—"I Wanna Be Sedated"
* Violent Femmes—"Add It Up"
* Violent Femmes—"Blister In The Sun"

Dance Rock

Many tattooed, mullet-headed, pickup-truck driving men will approach you and ask you to "Play some Rock N' Roll, man!" So you've got to have something for them too, especially at mobile DJ gigs. The important thing to consider is that you can't dance to many rock songs! So here's a few danceable rock n' roll songs that I've used over the past years to keep those drunk rock n' rollers happy. There are hundreds more, but these are guaranteed to cover your butt in a tight spot.

* AC/DC—"Shook Me All Night Long"
* Aerosmith—"Walk This Way"
* Billy Idol—"Mony Mony"
* Billy Joel—"Only The Good Die Young"
* Lynryd Skynrd—"Sweet Home Alabama"
* Meatloaf—"Paradise By The Dashboard Light"
* Neil Diamond—"Sweet Caroline"
* Rolling Stones—"Honky Tonk Woman"
* Rolling Stones—"Satisfaction"
* Rolling Stones—"Start Me Up"
* Sly and the Family Stone—"Dance to the Music"
* Steve Miller—"Jungle Love"
* The Beatles—"I Saw Her Standing There"
* The McCoys—"Hang On Sloopy"
* The Romantics—"What I Like About You"
* Three Dog Night—"Joy To The World"
* U2—"I Will Follow"
* Van Halen—"Dance The Night Away"
* Van Morrison—"Brown Eyed Girl"
* ZZ Top—"Sharp Dressed Man"

Oldies

When the world was new and things were simple, the term "oldies" was easy to define. It encompassed the era of the 1950s and 1960s music, which includes rock n' roll oldies and Motown. But now, most folks consider "Disco" and even Old School Hip Hop oldies. And some radio stations have redefined the term to include anything that's over 10 years old, so technically you can have oldies from the mid-1990s!

Yikes! Just make sure you ask your clients what they mean by "oldies" so you won't disappoint them. Occasionally, a popular movie will come out that features an old song in a new way that'll generate a strong buzz and lots of requests.

Here are my most requested "oldies" songs from the 50s and 60s.

* Beach Boys—"Barbara Ann"
* Bill Haley and The Comets—"Rock Around the Clock"
* Chubby Checker—"The Twist"
* Chuck Berry—"Johnny B. Goode"
* Diana Ross and the Supremes—"Stop In The Name of Love"
* Dion—"Runaround Sue"
* Elvis Presley—"Jailhouse Rock"
* Martha Reeves and the Vandellas—"Dancin' In The Street"
* Martha Reeves and the Vandellas—"Heatwave"
* McCoys—"Hang On Sloopy"
* Otis Day and the Knights—"Shout"
* Roy Orbison—"Pretty Woman"
* Smokey Robinson—"Tears Of A Clown"
* Surfaris—"Wipeout"
* Tempations—"Ain't Too Proud To Beg"
* Tempations—"Get Ready"
* The Beatles—"I Saw Her Standing There"
* The Beatles—"Twist and Shout"
* The Champs—"Tequila"
* The Contours—"Do You Love Me"

Top Country

I know next to nothing about Country music. But I always managed to fake it well enough to get by. The country genre is very popular and it's not going away anytime soon. As a matter of fact, hits by Shania Twain, Faith Hill, Tim McGraw, and other country artists are crossing over to the top-40 charts. And country songs have a much longer shelf life, since its fans aren't as fickle as the pop crowd. Here are twenty classics that'll save you if you're as lost in the woods as I am.

* Alabama—"Mountain Music"
* Alan Jackson—"Don't Rock the Jukebox"
* Anne Murray—"Could I Have This Dance"
* Billy Ray Cyrus—"Achy Breaky Heart"
* Brooks & Dunn—"Boot Scootin' Boogie"
* Charlie Daniels Band—"The Devil Went Down To Georgia"

- ❋ Faith Hill—"Breathe"
- ❋ Garth Brooks—"Friends in Low Places"
- ❋ Garth Brooks—"The Dance"
- ❋ Joe Rednex—"Cotton Eyed Joe"
- ❋ John Denver—"Thank God I'm a Country Boy"
- ❋ John Michael Montgomery—"I Swear"
- ❋ Johnny Cash—"Ring of Fire"
- ❋ Leann Rimes—"How Do I Live"
- ❋ Lee Greenwood—"God Bless the USA"
- ❋ Lonestar—"Amazed"
- ❋ Patsy Cline—"Crazy"
- ❋ Soggy Bottom Boys—"I Am a Man of Constant Sorrow"
  (from O Brother Where Art Thou soundtrack)
- ❋ Tammy Wynette—"Stand by Your Man"
- ❋ Willie Nelson—"Always on My Mind"

Latin Music Explosion

About 10% of all Americans, over 30 million people, are of Hispanic heritage, and that number is growing faster than any other group in the United States. With numbers like these, Latin Americans and their taste in music are definitely a segment you cannot afford to ignore. The 1980s and 1990s gave us twenty years of partnerless dancing, and people seem to be ready to hook up and get close again. Latin dancing is sexy. It's entertaining. And it sure looks like a whole lot of fun.

As Latin music becomes even more and more popular, more and more people will start to request this music from club and wedding DJs. Before you reach into your collection and play a set of what you think Latin music is, read the following information. We may save you some embarrassment. Most Latin-American customers will laugh at you (or worse, yell at you) if they specifically ask for Latin music and you play any one of the following songs. While shopping some clubs on a consulting gig in a certain southern state, we asked some DJs for "Latin Music" to see which songs they had, and this is what some of them came up with:

Not Latin Music:

- ❋ Any Santana
- ❋ Any J-Lo
- ❋ Most Los Lobos
- ❋ Any old freestyle or club music by George Lamond, SaFire or India
- ❋ "La Isla Bonita" by Madonna
- ❋ "To All The Girls I've Loved Before" by Willie Nelson and Julio Iglesias
- ❋ "La Macarena" by Los Del Rio
- ❋ "Dangerous on the Dance Floor" by Musto and Bones

- "Livin La Vida Loca" by Ricky Martin
- "Maria" by TKA
- "Tequila" by the Champs
- "Hot Hot Hot" by Buster Poindexter
- "Tarantella" by Chuck Mangione
- "Kokomo" by the Beach Boys

Real Latin artists include Marc Anthony, most Ricky Martin, some Enrique Iglesias, Celia Cruz, Frankie Ruiz, Tito Rojas, Frankie Negron, Manny Manuel, most newer Gloria Estefan and Jon Secada, and so many more. It's all about the beat. Did you know the "The Macarena" was actually a modified rumba beat? And Miami Sound Machine's "Conga" is a mambo? Latin music has been all around us for years in a subtle manner. Until now in the U.S., it hasn't pronounced itself as "Latin music." Record companies have always disguised it as something else as an effort to fit in to the fickle American mainstream.

Just like Rock n' Roll has subcategories such as Grunge, Metal, Alternative, Punk, Classic, Gothic, Light and more, Latin music too has broken off into several subcategories. Here are a few of them for you to digest:

- Mariachi
- Cumbias
- Tangos
- Boleros
- Cha Chas
- Bossa Nova
- Bachatas
- Samba
- Mambos
- Rumbas
- Flamenco
- Quebraditas

All these sub-genres have unique origins, and they tend to appeal to the descendants of the countries that spawned the sub-genres. Brazilians who have migrated to America prefer sambas, while Cuban Americans tend to prefer mambos. Mexican Americans dig Tex Mex and quebraditas while Columbian Americans groove to cumbias. Puerto Ricans dance to salsa, merengue and bachatas.

Geographically in the US, there are individual areas where some types of Latin music are more popular than others. New York and Miami are known for their salsa influence. Philadelphia pulls more of a merengue and bachata crowd. The West Coast tends to prefer Tex Mex and quebraditas because most of their Hispanic heritage hails from Mexico. In the Northeastern United States, there are two main categories of Latin music that account for about 95% of the Latin music DJs play at parties, nightclubs or weddings: Salsa and Merengue.

So you've got a daunting task in front of you. Don't worry, it will all start to make sense soon. If you can master the genres that apply to your geographic area, you'll be ready for almost anything.

CHAPTER 5

Salsa

Unfortunately, if you some DJs what Salsa is, they'll reply "isn't it that stuff that Mexican restaurants give you with nacho chips?" Salsa was the hottest segment of Latin music from our nightclub experience in the Philadelphia area. Today's hot salsa artists include artists like Marc Anthony and India. Salsa music is rich in layered horns, trombones, keyboards and various types of pronounced Latin percussion. It has an unmistakable beat that you must hear to understand. The smooth rhythms and melodic flow of this music seem to be a prelude to making love on the dance floor.

Here's a list some great Salsa songs compiled by one of Philadelphia's leading Latin DJs, DJ Jose Miguel. I tried to get him to limit his list to "the top ten songs that he guaranteed would pack any Latin dance floor," but he found it impossible to do so. Jose Miguel notes that although these are all great songs, some may be classified as Mambos rather than Salsa songs. But you can Salsa to a Mambo, and playing Mambos will score you some major points with your older customers.

* Adolescent's Orquesta—"Arrepentida"
* Celia Cruz—"La Vida Es Un Carnival"
* Charlie Cruz—"Bombon de Azucar"
* El Gran Combo—"Me Libre"
* El Gran Combo—"Que Me Lo Den en Bida"
* Frankie Negron—"Una Gota de Lluvia"
* Frankie Ruiz—"Mirandote"
* George Lamond—"Que Te Vas"
* Gilberto Santa Rosa—"Que Se lo Lleve el Rio"
* Gloria Estefan—"Mi Tierra"
* Hector Lavoe—"El Cantante"
* India—"Ese Hombre"
* Kevin Ceballo—"Como Fue Capaz "
* Luis Damon—"Se Nos Acabo el Amor"
* Marc Anthony—"Nadie Como Ella"
* Marc Anthony & Jennifer Lopez—"No Me Ames"
* Marc Anthony y India—"Vivir lo Nuestro"
* Oscar D'Leon—"Deja Que te Quiera"
* Pedro Congo y Su Orquestra—"Donde Estas"
* Puerto Rican Power—"Tu Carinito"
* Tito Nieves—"Mas"
* Victor Manuelle—"Volveras"
* Willie Colon—"Todo Tiene Su Final"
* Willie Rosario featuring Gilberto Santa Rosa—"El Apartamento"
* Willie Rosario featuring Tony Vega—"Juntos de Nuevo"

Keep in mind that Salsa dancers get all crazy if you end a song early, before its natural end. They seem to prefer a space between songs so they can finish their dance routines completely. Forget beatmixing your Salsa sets—just enjoy the music.

Merengue

Merengue is gaining steam in today's clubs with artists such as Elvis Crespo becoming mainstream. Traditional merengue songs are usually in the neighborhood of about 130-160 beats per minute. People are MOVING when dancing merengue! Today's merengue has a big-band sound that's reminiscent of salsa music, using heavy saxophones and horns. It's got a very fast thumping 1-2-3-4 bass drum beat that you just can't miss.

DJ Jose Miguel says this is a dance that is much easier to learn than a salsa, probably helping to increase its popularity. Here's a list some great Merengue songs compiled by various Latin DJs:

* Angie Martinez—"Live at Jimmy's"
* Elvis Crespo—"Suavemente"
* Fulanito—"Guallando"
* Fulantio—"El Padrino"
* Grupo Mania—"Linda Eh"
* Grupo Mania—"Me Miras y Te Miro"
* Los Sabrosos del Merengue—"Chiquilla Bonita"
* Manny Manuel—"En Las Nubes"
* Oro Solido—"La Merena"
* Wilfredo Vargas—"El Africano"

Other Popular Latin Dance Music

Boleros are the slower, romantic Latin songs similar to our top-40 ballads. These songs have been rich in guitar and melodies since the 1950s. Popular bolero artists include Luis Miguel, Julio Iglesias, and Jose Feliciano. Boleros are much more popular at weddings, as slow songs are in American weddings.

The Cumbia (pronounced "COOM-bee-yah") comes from Columbia. It is reminiscent of the Lambada type dancing that was popular in the late 1980s. It's a little slower than salsa and the movements are smooth and rhythmic. The basic step goes from side to side, like a combination of a Lambada and a slow merengue. Cumbias range from 100-120 beats per minute.

The Bachata (pronounced "bah-CHA-tah") is danced almost the same way a merengue is danced, except the bachata is a two-step dance while the merengue is a one step side to side. It's hard to tell the difference between the beats of a bachata and a merengue song. The distinguising feature of a bachata is the presence of a certain guitar sound. Bachatas can be fast like merengues, ranging from 130-160 beats per minute.

The Rumba started in Cuba in the 19th century. The Rumba came to the US around 1930 as a mix of the original rumba and other Cuban dances popular at that time. The music emphasizes the movement of the bodies rather than the feet, especially the hips. Rumbas are a little more moderately paced, usually from 110 to about 130 beats per minute.

CHAPTER 5

The Cha Cha was big in the 1950s with artists like Perez Prado, Bény More, Tito Puentes, and Tito Rodriguez on the charts. These are still huge at weddings! The cha-cha inherited sounds from the Cuban rumba and mambo, but differentiates itself by incorporating a double beat on the three count. Cha Chas run anywhere from about 90 to 120 beats per minute.

Mambo was salsa's predecessor. The Mambo dance originated in Cuba, and is attributed to Perez Prado who introduced it at nightclub in Havana somewhere around the early 1940s. Popular Mambo songs include "Guantnamera," "Cuban Pete," "Mambo #8," and "Ran Kan Kan." Many of these songs can be found on the Mambo Kings soundtrack. At the time of this writing, Lou Bega's "Mambo No. 5" is screaming up the charts all over the world. A remix of a former classic mambo song, this one's even got its own line dance. Due to the popularity of mambos in the 1940s and 1950s, you'll find yourself being asked for mambos at weddings by baby boomers and their parents. Mambos range widely from 110 all the way to 150 beats per minute. Jose Miguel says that the mambo is one of the most difficult dances to learn. One of the other great contributions of the mambo is that it led to the development of the Cha-Cha.

Helped in part by the efforts of artists such as Linda Ronstadt, the Mariachi movement in the United States is still strong and growing. You're most likely to hear Mariachi music at weddings, social functions, and at Mexican restaurants. Mariachi is the national sound of the Mexican cowboy. The music has native roots drawn from Spanish, French, German and African influences. You can hear bits of polka, waltzes and other styles in some of the songs. Mariachi groups feature stringed instruments distinct to the music.

The Quebradita (pronounced "Kay-bra-DEET-ah") is a high energy heavy-duty Spanish rock n' roll sound with that Mexican type yelling that's become popular in movies portraying Mexico in the 1960s. This explains its popularity with teenagers, because you need a whole bunch of energy to dance to these. The tempo is way high——anywhere from 150-200 beats per minute. It's usually done with couples dancing together with a lot of stomping. Quebraditas were formed by mixing the traditional cumbia and mixing break dancing and moves from the some American fifties dances. It's not uncommon to see very quick and dangerous movements, including flipping the female partner in the air! Quebraditas are very popular in the southern and southwestern parts of the United States.

The Tex-Mex Sound hails from the same areas as quebraditas. The music resembles a pop-rock sound with a bit of influence from waltzes and polkas. It's more of a rhythmic type dance than the quebraditas. People usually dance in groups similar to country line dances. Selena and Los Lobos were instrumental in bringing this type of music to American mainstream audiences.

Tangos came from Argentina in about the 1930s. It's basically a ballroom dance that takes years of practice to learn. Chances are that older people who want to show off may ask you to play a tango at a wedding. One of the most famous tangoes is called "La Cumparsita."

Samba is a musical form that has its origins in Brazil. It's influenced by rhythms brought over to that country by West African slaves as well as the native rhythms of South American Indians and the Portuguese. "The Lambada" and "Ritmo de la Noche" are two of the more famous sambas. Tempos vary widely, anywhere from 120-180 beats per minute.

Latin House is mostly remixes of bolero and merengue songs turned into American house or club music. In the second half of the eighties, many artists released house records both in English and Spanish. "Break 4 Love" by Raze is a good example of this, with both versions appearing on the extended 12" single. In the early 1990s, some dude brought us some killer white label Latin house tracks from Italy called

"Sueño Latino" by Sueño Latino and "Hazme Soñar" by Morenas. These two songs tore up the dance floor all over Philly and New Jersey. At about the same time, a remix of Barry Manilow's "Copacabana" came out and became an instant club classic. The late 1990s saw hits by New York's Proyecto Uno, who combined house and merengue in their songs.

Maintaining Your Library

There's a reason that you won't usually find a nightclub jock schlepping around a consumer music store. Most of the time, they just don't have the songs and remixes working DJs need. You need to find a record store that specializes in supplying DJs with music. You'll then need to establish a relationship with them so they'll be able to recommend new music that'll work for your situation. When you get to know the guys at the record store, you may be able to get first crack at new shipments as soon as they come in. This can be key when the radio stations are playing that pre-release single that everyone at the club has been requesting—you'll be the first on the block to have it.

Pat's Records in Philadelphia has a great system for screening new music. First of all, they have a turntable and a CD player hooked up to a DJ sound system that customers can use to hear the music in its true environment before they buy it. You're lucky if a retail music store has a set of headphones and a few songs to listen to. Secondly, nearly every working DJ in Philly goes there to get their music and equipment, so there was always an active information exchange. That exchange caused me to drop at least $200 a week!

When evaluating new music, listen to as much of the song as you can. Look for really weird twists in mixes that could destroy your dance floor, like an over extended beatless chant or some strange shift in the song that's not made for dancing. Genius in the studio doesn't always translate to genius on the dance floor.

I know a DJ who used to buy music based on a slick looking sleeve or cover. He especially liked covers with pretty women. Big mistake. He spent countless dollars on worthless music! Some of the best music comes with the least flashy and ugliest cover. Some of the hottest European house, trance, and techno songs are printed on "white label" vinyl, with nothing more than a plain, blank, white label. The artist and title aren't even listed on a white label.

There is a huge underground digital file trading system that makes music more readily available than ever. It's important to note that most of these copies are illegal and can get you into trouble if you're found with them. I've always thought that since club DJs are promoting this music, the least the record companies could do is give them promotional copies at the same time the radio stations get them. But unfortunately, we live in a silly and confusing world. Just try to do the right thing; purchase your music legally and keep yourself out of trouble.

Record Pools and Promotional Services

If you're lucky enough to get a job at an "influential" club or bar, you may be able to get into a record pool. Record pools are agencies that distribute records and CDs before they're released in exchange for your feedback in an effort to gauge how hard they should push the record, or if they should scrap it.

I was in a pool called "Philly Metro" for several years with other well known Philadelphia area DJs including Josh Wink before he became a best selling DJ and producer. Among the bad points of record pools is that you get a lot of nonsense you'll never play live, but you're supposed to take time to listen to each and every record and evaluate it. Technically, you're supposed to actually try all of them at your club or bar, but some of them sucked so bad it just wasn't a realistic expectation.

Your record pool agreement specifically states that these records are for promotional use only, and the record company owns them, indicating that you may actually have to give them back someday. So I kept everything. At one point, I had an entire room filled with vinyl garbage I couldn't play anywhere! I tried to give it back to the pool manager, but he didn't want it either. The garbage men didn't want it. The folks at the rifle range didn't even want it. Some DJs create funky looking ashtrays and bowls by sliding unwanted records into an oven for a few minutes! I don't recommend this because it could cause a fire and dangerous fumes.

Promotional services are similar to record pools, except that the music is typically better and useable, and your feedback is optional. And instead of weekly dues, you'll pay a monthly service fee. You're supposed to get singles before they're released like radio stations do, but it rarely seemed to work that way. Many of the promotional CD services segment their music by type, which creates a monthly series of really cool compilations for about $15-$20 per disc. Back issues are usually available also if you're building your collection. And you don't have to be a big-shot superstar DJ to get these. Just prove that you're a working DJ, sign an agreement that promises you won't make copies or do anything else illegal, and you're in. These are a great way to affordably keep up with new music.

Promotional services usually mark their CDs with the song's BPM, length of intro (for a talkover or mix in), and type of ending (cold or fade out).

Unfortunately, promotional services can only distribute songs they've been "serviced" with, meaning that record labels only send them the songs they feel need a little extra push to create additional sales. Some songs by bigger named artists like Madonna and the like are usually omitted from these promotional services because the labels feel these songs are strong enough to sell well on their own. For the most part, these services do include about 90-95% of everything you'll need.

ERG Music (www.ergmusic.com) produces the popular Nu Music Traxx series that's been around since 1990. ERG produces nine different series of monthly hit compilation formats programmed by real radio folks. Their big bi-monthly Nu Music Traxx series spans rock, pop, adult contemporary, country, hip-hop, house, urban and dance. Their CDs feature sometimes hard to find radio edits of songs that strip the nasty words away so you can play the latest hip hop jams with kids in the room. ERG's other series include dance, urban, rock, country, Latin, import, and Contemporary Christian.

Promo Only (www.promoonly.com) has been around since the early 1990s providing CD-based music. They've got 15 different series available, including their own basic Mainstream Radio series with songs from various formats.

RPM's Top Hits USA series (www.tophitsusa.com) has been around since the 1970s providing music for radio stations and working DJs. Top Hits' Top 40, Country and Adult Contemporary series issue new discs weekly, so you get a lot more music with this service. Obviously, it costs a bit more than the monthly or bi-monthly service. They've got seven other bi-monthly series to choose from.

If you're a remix fan, look into X-Mix (www.xmix.com) and Ultimix (www.ultimix.com). These folks specialize in creating extremely DJ friendly mixes of current hits featuring extended mixable intros, breaks, and outtros. Better remixes retain the basic essence of the song while making it even better.

There are several other promotional services and remix services on the market.

Legal Music Download Websites

The future of music is here. With a cheap CD burner, a fast Internet connection, and about a buck a track, you may never have to visit a record store again!

After the RIAA successfully sued the original Napster and Kazaa file-trading folks and a bunch of their users, several smart people realized there was actually a market for downloadable music. The problem was that no one knew how to control it so users wouldn't be able to steal music without paying for it. The solution? DRM, or Digital Rights Management. In order to appease the billions of lawyers who work for the record labels and the RIAA, Microsoft and online music delivery services created a method that controls a built-in music license that DRM enabled software can read. With this licensing scheme, DRM can limit the amount of times you copy a song or burn it to a CD, or even deny you the right to play it altogether. DRM is like a lock and key to a music file. The music file is locked until the content owner of the song lets you unlock it.

The DRM scheme has some inherent flaws that don't affect the music's quality or stability, but it generally works pretty well. For instance, theoretically, if you had downloaded a bunch of tracks to your portable computer, then didn't connect that computer to the Internet for an extended period of time, the DRM scheme could potentially render the license for your tracks useless. Boy, would that suck if you went on a weekend mobile job with nothing more than a laptop! But the DRM scheme will get better over time, and I'm sure they'll work out all the silly bugs.

As far as sound quality goes, I downloaded a bunch of the same songs from various services. I couldn't tell the difference between the digital downloads or the subsequent CDs I burned on my Sony stereo hooked up to my external Edirol sound card. I use the Sony to gauge what the music will sound like on a typical stereo system.

I'm a huge Van Halen fan, so I decided to put the boys to the test on all the big music download sites. Using the multi-platinum Best of Van Halen Volume 1, I searched each of the services to see if there was any difference in the quality of the tracks and how easy it would be to burn a CD. For the dance music genre, I did a search on all of the services for Madonna, but came up with only a few of her newer songs and no classic hits on any of the services. You won't be able to find everything, but you'll be surprised how much you will find.

Napster

After being the first bad boy of the music industry, Napster has cleaned up its act and is now a legitimate pay service with hundreds of thousands of music selections. Roxio, the producer of Easy CD Creator, a leading CD burning software title, acquired Napster and incorporated its burning software right into the Napster interface. After a reasonably short download, Napster installed without a hitch. I created an account, signed up for the premium service, and within minutes, had more than a half million songs at my fingertips.

I found Napster's intuitive interface easy to use. Genres were clearly indicated and easy to surf. Search functions found just about everything I was looking for. Napster features two sets of charts, their own brand, and Billboard Music charts dating back to 1955.

If you don't sign up for their premium service that charges a monthly fee, you will only see tracks that are available for purchase either individually or as part of an album. This gives you access to most, but not all, of their catalog. Premium service members have access to all the tracks that are available to Napster members and additional tracks that are on their service (for listening) but not available for purchase. Premium members can also "stream" unlimited full-length CD quality tracks while you're connected to the internet. You can also download an unlimited number of CD quality tracks to up to three of your computers without having to purchase them. Napster will let you listen to those unpurchased downloads on your computers as often as you like, but only as long as your premium service membership remains active.

Napster downloads use the WMA (Windows Media Audio) format, which are encoded with Windows' DRM. I was able to play my unpurchased downloads with my Winamp software, but I had to do some sneaky conversions to get files that my digital DJ software could use.

Finally, Napster failed the Van Halen test. Tracks 10-17 were not available for purchase, although they were available for streaming. And track 11 ("When It's Love") was completely missing from action.

iTunes

Originally built for the Apple platform and its portable iPod player, iTunes carried its Mac-looking interface over the the Windows environment. The program makes you think you're actually working on a Mac computer! The iTunes installation was also easy and flawless. The interface is intuitive, and its small fonts and images allow this program to cram a whole lot more on to a single screen.

iTunes uses a file encoding scheme called AAC that has its own version of DRM. To get these files to play on Windows, you'll need to use the iTunes software or burn them to CD and then rip them back to MP3. I was able to locate a non-Apple plug-in that allowed me to play AAC files with the Winamp software.

You can purchase thousands of individual songs or albums from the iTunes Music Store, and download those tunes directly to your computer's hard disk. There's no signup or monthly fee, but you'll have to provide a credit card if you want to purchase music.

I dig iTunes, and I've spend a good amount of cash there. But I have two issues with this service. First, you can't stream more than 30 seconds of anything. Sometimes 30 seconds ain't enough, especially for DJs who need to hear the intro, break, and outtro of a song. And secondly, you've got to buy a song to play it on your computer because there was no monthly subscription option at the time of publication. With Napster, I downloaded about two hundred songs for under ten bucks, and I can play them as long as I continue to pay the monthly fee. iTunes is a good service for people who know exactly what they're looking for.

But although iTunes fared better than Napster, since it allowed me to purchase every Van Halen song except track 11 which was completely missing from the list, it also failed my Van Halen test. This CD was listed as a "partial album."

Rhapsody

Real Audio got together with listen.com and created a neat software based service called Rhapsody. Rhapsody is an on-demand streaming service, which means there are no music download options available. You've got to be connected to the internet with a high speed connection to do anything with this service. It's got a cool and easy to use interface with its own integrated music player, plenty of search options, and a ton of popular music. The streaming music was crisp and clean. You can burn your own CDs for small fee per track if you're subscribed to their "All Access" subscription plan at about ten bucks per month.

Rhapsody passed the Van Halen test. I could stream and/or purchase all 17 tracks, including the elusive track 11.

Wal-Mart

Wal-Mart doesn't have a fancy software interface like the other big three services, but what did you expect? It's Wal-Mart! The king of discount retailers created a web-based digital music merchandising system that competes on price. Similar to iTunes, there are no subscription or streaming options. You'll get a 30 second preview, and that's it. Wal-Mart features hundreds of thousands of songs to choose from that you can download to your computer and play forever using the latest Windows Media Player to read the DRM enhanced WMA files.

Wal-Mart also passed the Van Halen test. I could purchase and download all 17 tracks, then burn them to a disc.

Master Programming

The most important part of all of the DJ disciplines isn't your mixing or scratching skills, it's your selection of music, also known as programming. You are the program director. You're the one who's in charge of ultimately creating the mood and controlling the energy in a room with little more than your electronic toys and the music you choose to play on them. You'll bring them up and let them down at your whim. You'll have them scream when you want them to, and cry when they should cry. The DJ is the entertainer, the booth is your stage, and everyone else is your puppet.

It used to be much simpler to program music in the 80s. There were fewer categories of music, so it was easier to determine what type of music you should be playing. Later in the 80s, music started fragmenting into rap, hip-hop, alternative rock, modern rock, house, Latin house, freestyle, jungle, acid, techno, trance and all kinds of other weird stuff that music executives have a difficult time categorizing. Latin music is crossing over to mainstream now. Ricky Martin, Enrique Iglesias, and Marc Anthony combine English and Spanish lyrics (known as "Spanglish") with traditional Latin rhythms. And it seems country music will live forever in a world of its own. It's much tougher now to find the lines and predict exactly what your audience will appreciate.

The only thing that will guide you through this fragmented mess is keeping your finger on the pulse of current trends. You'll succeed by playing music that your audience will recognize and enjoy.

Dance Music vs. Listening Music

In the pre-hip-hop days, I'd guess that only five to ten percent of all commercially released music could be classified as "dance music." Today, with hip-hop dominating the top-40 charts, the percentage of danceable songs is much greater. The rest of the music is classified as "listening music," and with few exceptions, it's virtually worthless to DJs. A club or mobile DJ's job is to get people rockin' on the dance floor, and a number one listening music hit won't help a DJ do this.

I've tried to explain this to hapless customers looking to hear their favorite light rock song in the middle of a hot dance megamix, and found it only leaves me with a headache and an unhappy customer. To save time and grief, I learned to tell a little white lie, which I'll detail in the Handling Requests section later in this chapter.

Sad Music vs Happy Music

Since DJs provide entertainment at bars, clubs, parties, and other generally happy events, it's your job to keep the mood upbeat. Sad songs should be reserved for DJs who perform at funerals. And since the funeral DJ business is pretty dead these days, feel free to bury these songs in your library.

Most average folks identify a song solely by its title and artist. They don't analyze the words of sad songs, so you'll often find yourself shaking your head as a bride and groom choose "My Heart Will Go On," a song by Celine Dion from the Titanic soundtrack that's really about losing a dead partner. So don't lose too much sleep over isolating sad songs from your library. Just be aware that some alert people may look at you funny when you bust out one of these sad hits with a smile on your face.

Reading a Room

As you gain more experience and evolve into a seasoned DJ, you'll be able to walk into a room and figure out what type of music your audience might like simply from evaluating the age of your clientele and the way the customers are dressed. It doesn't always work that way, but more often than not, your analysis will give you a better place to start than a blind guess.

There are several body language indicators that will let you know if you're on the right track with your music programming. Watch the customers closely and they'll tell you a story without even opening their mouth. You should learn to view a large cross section of the room as you progress through your nightly show. Facial expressions can tell you so much about how your music mix. If some chick is scrunching her face, chances are you're barking up the wrong tree, or she's just a miserable person. You can also determine if you're on track by watching people tapping their feet, fingers, or moving their lips to the words of the song.

Rotating the Dance Floor

In order for bars to maximize profitability, they've got to sell a lot of drinks. It seems that not many DJs understand the business side of a bar or club. Although it's very important, most DJs tend to be overly concerned with managing a dance floor. Even at weddings and other private affairs, you've usually got a wide range of ages and ethnicities who'd all like their type of music to be played. If you want to build your business on referrals, you'd better break things up and play something for everyone.

In clubs, you can watch the bars, watch the room, and watch the dance floor. Know when the bar is sluggish, and know you can do something about it. This is a perfect opportunity to throw one of those curve balls. Take a chance by playing a ballad, showing short funny video clip, initiating a promotion, or just playing a really weird song that you'd never expect to hear in a club. The dance floor will probably clear, and people will probably stare at you for an instant. But all the sudden the bar and the dance floor will both be busy again!

I call this the "incremental drink" program. Customers are buying another drink that they may have skipped had I not changed the programming so drastically, because they're not quite sure what to do at that instant. It's a sneaky way to increase the bottom line while giving people something to talk about. So don't be afraid to break it up a little; just have something planned for that dead space before you initiate this. Make sure you tell your manager that you plan to do this, so that he gives you the credit for the increased sales. This will be important during your next salary negotiation.

Developing Effective Music Programming

Here's how to figure out the right music programming formula specifically for your bar or club. Get a pencil and answer these questions:

* Define the club or bar's target market. If you're not sure, ask your manager. If he's not sure, you're in trouble.

* What types of music is that target market into? Top 40? Disco? Hip-hop? Trance? Oldies? A combination of two or three of them?

* Which artists perform that music? Who's hot now, and who's got classic songs that still make people go wild?

* Which of those songs are danceable? And which of those songs are recurrent and still popular?

* What other songs (not necessarily in the above categories) consistently fill your dance floor (better known as "floorpackers")?

* What are the top current dance songs in your overall area (from observing good DJs at other clubs and checking your local radio airplay charts)?

* What "fun" songs are very popular, but aren't songs you wouldn't usually program? Fun songs include songs that people will sing or dance along to, such as "I Will Survive," "YMCA," or even the "Electric Slide."

Effective programming is simply taking the music that fits into the categories listed above and determining the estimated current popularity of each song. Although most experienced DJs will preach that you should never plan a set in advance, it's entirely acceptable when you're a new DJ. A good rule of thumb is to arrange your music into 3-5 song sets, with the number of songs in each set based on the length of the songs.

In a nightclub or bar situation, you'll want to mix your sets up, so each set of the same type of music never immediately precedes or follows another. Play the less popular songs, often referred to as "fillers," early in the evening while we're all warming up. As you progress through the night, you'll tease your crowd by tossing in one of your hot songs here and there to start the excitement. During the prime time hours of the night, you'll want to play a set of the top dance songs in your area. Your prime time hours will be the most crowded hours of the night, and it's imported to have that room slammin'.

In a wedding or mobile DJ situation, you probably won't have time for fillers because the dinner hour and the events you'll have to MC suck up a disproportionate amount of the party time. You'll still play sets, but your sets will be varied by genre rather than pure energy.

Sample Floorpackers

I spent years developing a list of can't miss songs that were virtually guaranteed to get people running to the dance floor in almost any mobile DJ or mainstream nightclub and bar situation. I called that list my "Floorpackers." These are the songs that I used to energize a stale and boring room. Most of them are considered old and fairly lame, but they're still insanely popular. Your list may vary depending on your location, so feel free to adjust your own personal list as necessary. Here is my list of the top floorpacking songs in the Philadelphia area.

- ❋ "Brick House", Commodores
- ❋ "Bust A Move", Young MC
- ❋ "Da Butt", EU
- ❋ "Dancin' Queen", ABBA
- ❋ "Don't Stop Til You Get Enough", Michael Jackson
- ❋ "Electric Boogie", Marcia Griffiths
- ❋ "Everybody Everybody", Black Box
- ❋ "Getting' Jiggy With It", Will Smith
- ❋ "Gonna Make You Sweat", C&C Music Factory
- ❋ "I Will Survive", Gloria Gaynor
- ❋ "It Takes Two", Rob Base and DJ EZ Rock
- ❋ "Love Shack", B-52s
- ❋ "Macarena", Los Del Rio
- ❋ "Oh What A Night", Frankie Valli and the Four Seasons
- ❋ "Rappers' Delight", Sugar Hill Gang
- ❋ "Stayin' Alive", The Bee Gees
- ❋ "Superfreak", Rick James
- ❋ "That's The Way I Like It", KC and the Sunshine Band
- ❋ "This Is How We Do It", Montell Jordan

Sample "Fun" Songs

Somewhere during the prime time hours of your gig, you may want to dig out a few "fun" songs to create a total frenzy. Again, this depends on the feel of your room at that time. An experienced DJ will know exactly when this should work, and even then it'll fail once in a while.

Here's a list of my top "fun songs" songs that I played at clubs and mobile DJ parties. These are the songs that I pulled out in the middle of a night when I felt the room needed a kick in the butt. Some of them are not even close to dance songs, but they're so strong that people will try to dance to them. These are the songs that get people singing on the bars and going nuts.

* "Bad Girls", Donna Summer (yet another chick song)
* "Bad To The Bone", George Thorogood (a male song!)
* "Brown Eyed Girl", Van Morrison (big sing-along song)
* "Can't Touch This", MC Hammer
* "Centerfold", J. Geils Band (hottie song)
* "Come On Eileen", Dexy's Midnight Runners
* "Dancin' Queen", ABBA (see above)
* "Electric Boogie", Marcia Griffiths (same as above—no rhythm required)
* "Get Down Tonight", KC and the Sunshine Band
* "Girl You Know It's True", Milli Vanilli
* "Hot Hot Hot", Arrow (starts conga lines)
* "I Saw Her Standing There", The Beatles
* "I Think I Love You", Partridge Family
* "I Wanna Be Sedated", The Ramones (slam dancing)
* "I Want You Back", The Jacksons
* "I Will Survive", Gloria Gaynor (angry chick theme song)
* "I'm A Believer", The Monkees
* "Ice Ice Baby", Vanilla Ice
* "It's Rainin' Men", The Weather Girls (chicks dig this)
* "Jessie's Girl", Rick Springfield
* "Jump In The Line", Harry Belafonte (from Beetlejuice)
* "Macarena", Los Del Rio (even white people can do this)
* "Macho Man", The Village People (another male song!)
* "Margaritaville", Jimmy Buffet (total sing-along frenzy)
* "Mony Mony", Billy Idol (caution—some people will yell "get laid, get f-ed")
* "Rappers' Delight", Sugar Hill Gang (rap old people can understand)
* "Safety Dance", Men Without Hats
* "September", Earth Wind and Fire
* "Shout", Otis Day (From Animal House)
* "So Many Men", Miguel Brown (chicks also dig this)
* "Stayin' Alive", Bee Gees (bust out the polyester)
* "Sweet Caroline", Neil Diamond (BIG sing-a-long!)
* "Sweet Home Alabama", Lynryd Skynrd (still don't get why it works, but it works!)

* "The Theme to The Banana Splits" cartoon
* "The Theme to The Jeffersons" TV show
* "The Twist", Chubby Checker
* "Walk This Way", Run DMC with Aerosmith
* "What I Like About You", The Romantics
* "YMCA", Village People (people spell the letters with their arms)
* "You Shook Me All Night Long", AC/DC
* "You're The One That I Want", John Travolta and Olivia Newton John (from Grease)
* "You've Lost That Lovin' Feeling", Hall and Oates (from Top Gun, another big sing-a-long)

Handling Requests

Requests are important part of your job. They're a direct reflection of your company or club's customer service policy. There are only two ways you can handle requests—the right way, and the wrong way. Since we've already established that you are in charge of your room, you ultimately make the call whether or not the requested songs fit within your format, and when those songs should be played.

The wrong thing to do is to play a requested song immediately. This gives the customer the impression that you are not in control of the room. It also opens the door to allowing that one customer to attempt to control your music. I recommend waiting at least a few songs before playing a request for someone you don't know. Obviously, if they're actually sliding you large cash tips, you'll have to exercise your own judgment. Even if they tipped me, I would still make them wait at least one song so it looks like you're serious about your job. That'll make them want to tip you even more.

My response to listening music requests, no matter what they were, became something like this. "Wow, I love that song too! But you know what, I think I left it in my girlfriend's car. Hey, I've got some other great songs coming up soon. What's you're name? Can I send one out to you?" This sneaky subject change usually does the trick, and everyone wins. But you always run the risk of an overachiever who offers to run to her car and grab her personal disc from her CD player, if she hasn't already done this. In this case, I invoked Plan B, and explained that my CDs are special DJ only CDs that are licensed especially for radio, nightclub, and mobile DJ play, and that I risk legal prosecution if I violate my agreement and play a non-licensed CD. Usually, she'll be so befuddled with your confusing explanation that she'll smile and walk away.

If the requested song absolutely doesn't fit into your format, politely inform the customer that it doesn't fit. Some people will continue to ask you why you won't play it anyway, because "everyone wants to hear it." Wow, that jackass must have formally polled everyone in the club! I've learned to avoid this situation in most cases by writing the request down and always adding the following statement: "I'll see what I can do for you." This usually ends the begging right there. Try it yourself.

It's also good to get the name of the person who requested the song. This makes the requestor feel special when you announce it, and further helps your goal to be seen a person in a position of power. Dedications are cool too. Sometimes I would dedicate the entire night to a hot chick. They got a big kick out of it, and it greatly helped my social life, if you know what I mean.

Drunk people can incredibly funny when you know how to deal with them. My friends and I used to keep a request book in our DJ booth to track what people were asking for over time as an aid to help my newer DJs learn what was popular. But the back cover of this book was reserved for all the incredibly stupid things people will say to you in an effort to get you to play their song next! I've included a sample of some of the better lines so you'll know what you're up against. Once you recognize these lines as B.S., you'll be much more prepared to make better programming decisions. I've included things I've said under my breath in case you need to blow off some stream too, so have fun!

* Can you play something we can dance to? (In some countries, people dance to beating sticks together. What's your f-ing problem?)

* Why don't you play some real music? (Sorry, haven't you heard? Tonight is "fake music night." Please come back some other time.)

* Can you please play something with a beat? (Can you turn up your hearing aid?)

* I need you to play a song, but I don't know what it's called or who does it. (Well, that's a start. Thanks for the hint. Next, please!)

* Can you please play this song next? I'll be your best friend... (Honey, with friends like you, I don't need enemies.)

* Shut this off—nobody likes this song. (Full dance floor... maybe nobody likes *you*, buddy!)

* You have to play it—it's the only song my friend knows how to dance to. (Have your friend call Arthur Murray in the morning.)

* Hook me up and I'll make it worth your while... (Flashes cash, never returns. If he pays first, well, that's different!)

* Play this song and everybody will dance. Everybody told me they want to hear it. (Can I see that in writing, then I'll see what I can do for you.)

* Can you play [this song] next 'cause we have to leave soon. (Sure, we'll play your song now so you can leave and not purchase any more drinks from the bar, decreasing tonight's revenue and making me look like a schmuck. Go buy another drink and I'll get to it when I get to it.)

* Yo cuz, what songs you got? (Yo cuz, how much cash you got?)

* You know the song... it's really hot! It goes "Bum bum boom boom bum bum boom..." (Oh sure, no f-ing problem. I'll get right on that, Sparky, right after we play "boom boom hiss hiss boom boom.")

Strange Requests and Other Issues

While working primarily in a hotel-based nightclub, I was faced with the issue of entertaining not only our regular outside clientele, but also the hotel's guests and customers who were considered their number one priority. Many of the hotel guests are what we call "amateurs," people who don't get out too often and can't really comprehend the dynamics of a nightclub. These are the people who will demand to hear listening music like The Beatles, Jimmy Buffett, and maybe even some Grateful Dead. Since my management team had identified these guests as their target market, I had no choice but to try and satisfy their requests even though it would upset the outside clientele who are really the people paying our bills.

I needed an impossible solution that was amicable to everyone. So I invented one through creative programming I called "The Midnight Moldy Oldie." Every night at midnight, I gave myself free reign to play those unusual requests, plus the songs I wanted to experiment with for future "fun" sets. I now had 15-20 minutes each night to squeeze in all the lame song requests of the evening. Our regular people hit the bar because they now expected to hear cheesy music for a short while. Amateurs run to the dance floor in disbelief and enjoy the songs. Everyone's happy.

Here are some of the best moldy oldies to play in a bar or club of almost any mainstream format. It's all high-powered super popular stuff that makes people say "Wow, I love this song!" Some of these songs are also in the "floorpacker" category. The only criteria I used to choose Midnight Moldy Oldies was that the song must be at least 10 years old.

* "ABC", The Jacksons
* "Atomic Dog", George Clinton
* "Bad Girls", Donna Summer
* "Brick House", Commodores
* "Bust A Move", Young MC
* "Can't Touch This", MC Hammer
* "Come On Eileen", Dexy's Midnight Runners
* "Get Down Tonight", KC and the Sunshine Band
* "Girl You Know It's True", Milli Vanilli
* "I Saw Her Standing There", The Beatles
* "I Wanna Be Sedated", The Ramones
* "I Want You Back", The Jacksons
* "Ice Ice Baby", Vanilla Ice
* "Jessie's Girl", Rick Springfield
* "Mony Mony", Billy Idol
* "Safety Dance", Men Without Hats
* "September", Earth Wind and Fire
* "Stayin' Alive", Bee Gees
* "Tainted Love", Soft Cell
* "The Twist", Chubby Checker
* "Walk This Way", Run DMC with Aerosmith
* "Wanna Be Startin Something", Michael Jackson
* "What I Like About You", Romantics
* "You Shook Me All Night Long", AC/DC
* "You Should Be Dancin'", Bee Gees

Remember, your moldy oldies don't have to be all that old. You should substitute these songs with your strange requests, or any songs you'd like to try. Be creative and have some fun!

Breaking New Music

All the way up until the late 1970s, before the few big major labels and record companies decided to completely monopolize the music industry, radio and club DJs were responsible for breaking and testing new music. I still support this and think we need to start controlling this again.

Unlike radio DJs, club DJs are in the best position to break new music. We're the only ones who can immediately witness and evaluate the people's response to a new song. Work as many new songs into your program as you can, and watch how they do. You can then say that your customers heard it in your show first.

6

PERFORMANCE DJS

This chapter pertains to the art and culture of being a DJ. There is essentially a fourth type of DJ that's much different than radio, club, or mobile DJ, which I call the "Performance DJ." This is the fastest growing segment of the DJ industry, often called "The Bedroom DJ" category. Makeshift studios in bedrooms, garages, basements, and anywhere else DJs can find solace are the locations of choice for thousands of DJs working hard to hone their skills in search of creating the elusive new hit remix. The category is expanding into places you wouldn't normally think you'd find a DJ, like in shopping malls, retail stores, carnivals, youth and recreation centers, gyms, professional sporting events, and other great places where a performance DJ can show his or her "skillz." This category often overlaps into the mobile and club arenas.

Scratching, beatmixing, editing, and remixing are all forms of art, each worthy of their own genre in music. In the old days, people used to downplay a DJ performance, citing that we were simply playing other people's music. Fortunately, DJs have gained widespread recognition of being musicians in their own right. It's the essence of recreation that spawns all new music and mixes that can be indistinguishable from their original cuts—and often more popular. Scratching and mixing have evolved into something called "turntablism." This is where DJs combine scratching, beats from multiple songs, and samples into a creation that sounds entirely like a new song. It's kind of cool if the DJ is really good at it, and it will usually sound terrible if the DJ is inexperienced.

There are a few unwritten rules that seem to apply especially to the scratch DJ category. For the first time ever, they're written in black and white. If your goal is to be a Skratcher, immediately copy the following section, enlarge it, and post it prominently near your turntables:

* All scratch DJs must shave their heads. For some reason, almost every time you see a scratch DJ featured in a video, advertisement, or magazine article, they've got next to no hair on their heads! I originally thought that the friction generated by scratching somehow removed hair follicles, but I've been told by leading biologists that this is not physically possible. I'm probably shaving my head as you read this.

* All Scratch DJs may not use legible handwriting or standard typefaces in any of their correspondence. Instead, they are required to use virtually illegible graffiti-esque printing. And computer printers, pens, and pencils are not permitted——all documentation must be completed with thick Sharpie pens or spray paint.

* All For some reason, all scratch DJ'z hate the letter "s." From this point forward, all scratch DJ'z must substitute the letter "z" for the letter "s" (and it must always be preceded with an apostrophe, no matter what) for pluralization and possessive circumstance'z.

In the real world of being a *professional* working disc jockey, sampling, scratching and remixing skills aren't as important as you might think, although mass media would have you think otherwise. My guess is that one percent or less of all DJs are actually getting paid to be a performance DJ. To most of them, pay doesn't matter, because they sheer enjoyment of this art is payment enough. But if you're looking to turn your scratching skills into a full-time job, know that it is a long shot unless you've got undying dedication and a whole lot of time. It's equivalent to someone buying a guitar and dreaming they'll be the next Eddie Van Halen. It can be done, but not without sacrifice.

Beatmixing, on the other hand, is important in the mobile and nightclub fields to promote the continuity of your dance floor during music sets. But *flawless* beatmixing skills are also not necessarily needed for success. Ironically, there are several big name DJs who aren't proficient beatmixers. I've heard some awful train-wreck mixes in New York and Miami that would make an earthquake seem tame. Most of the big name guys use their meticulously perfect music programming to get them by.

Although Karaoke jocks, often called KJs, are growing in numbers and share the same music, some equipment, and even many of the same disciplines as DJs, they're not really DJs, *per se*. A mobile or club DJ's job is to concentrate on music mixing and programming in an effort to make people dance. A KJ's primary concern is to facilitate his or her audience singing and performing songs. Karaoke hosts are really MCs and board operators. Some KJs perform DJ duties between Karaoke sets. Karaoke is an important topic, but it's beyond the scope of this book.

Performance DJs are fun to watch and even more fun to be, but these skills are difficult to learn. If you're young and free, please proceed to bust out a funky mix. But if you're juggling a wife, kids, a job, and a mortgage, you probably will not have the time required to master these skills.

The Basics of Beatmixing

"Beatmatching" is the process of matching the tempo or speed of the drumbeats in the currently playing song along with the tempo of the drumbeats of the new song you'd like to play, or "beatmix," with the current song. You'll let the two songs play simultaneously for a few seconds, then fade out of the old song and into the new one for a pretty cool sometimes seamless effect called "beatmixing" or "blending" that's great for keeping people on a dance floor.

Not all songs will beatmix well. If the speed of your currently playing song has a much faster or slower tempo than the next song you'd like to beatmix, it simply won't sound right no matter how much tempo correction you might introduce. This is why you can almost never beatmix a hip hop song with a trance song; hip hop songs have a much slower tempo than most trance songs.

Important considerations include beatmixing in time so that your "downbeats" match perfectly on their one-counts. Beatmixing is usually performed within an even set of eight downbeats; and almost never over someone singing.

For songs you desire to beatmix with each other, you should always try to abide by the Ye Olde Chuck Fresh "Four Percent Rule" (see Figure 6.1). This rule states that you should never attempt to mix songs with a tempo that is more than four percent faster or more than four percent slower than your current song. For example, if your current song is 100 BPM ("Beats Per Minute," a measure of the tempo of a song), you shouldn't try to beatmix a song that's either more than 104 BPM or less than 96 BPM. If your current song is 130 BPM, you shouldn't try to beatmix a song that's less than about 124 BPM or higher than about 136 BPM. As you can see, the higher your BPM, the wider your range; and subsequently, the lower your BPM, the less your range. Any more or less than four percent will usually cause a noticeable change in the "pitch" of a song, meaning the singer's voice or synthesizer parts will sound like they're artificially higher or lower than someone who has heard the song before would recognize. There are now ways to adjust a song's tempo without altering the pitch with hardware and software solutions, but in most situations due to constant song repetition on the radio and in the clubs, most people are used to a song's real tempo and will notice a difference. A blatant tempo or pitch difference will often freak people out, causing them to look at you thinking there's something wrong.

Chuck Fresh's "Four Percent Rule."

Chuck Fresh's "FOUR PERCENT RULE"

Current BPM	+4%	-4%	+/- range
80	83	77	6
81	84	78	6
82	85	79	7
83	86	80	7
84	87	81	7
85	88	82	7
86	89	83	7
87	90	84	7
88	92	84	7
89	93	85	7
90	94	86	7
91	95	87	7
92	96	88	7
93	97	89	7
94	98	90	8
95	99	91	8
96	100	92	8
97	101	93	8
98	102	94	8
99	103	95	8
100	104	96	8
101	105	97	8
102	106	98	8
103	107	99	8
104	108	100	8
105	109	101	8
106	110	102	8
107	111	103	9
108	112	104	9
109	113	105	9
110	114	106	9
111	115	107	9
112	116	108	9
113	118	108	9
114	119	109	9
115	120	110	9
116	121	111	9
117	122	112	9
118	123	113	9
119	124	114	10
120	125	115	10
121	126	116	10
122	127	117	10
123	128	118	10
124	129	119	10
125	130	120	10
126	131	121	10
127	132	122	10
128	133	123	10
129	134	124	10
130	135	125	10
131	136	126	10
132	137	127	11
133	138	128	11
134	139	129	11
135	140	130	11
136	141	131	11
137	142	132	11
138	144	132	11
139	145	133	11
140	146	134	11

CHAPTER 6

There are three exceptions to the Four Percent Rule. First, if you're beatmixing using a CD player, digital turntable, or digital DJ software with "Time Stretching," you can get away with up to a 16% tempo gain or reduction with some songs. Time stretching is a complex mathematical algorithm that implies changing the tempo of a song without changing the key of the singer or music, or adding audible artifacts (weird garbled digital noise). This allows a DJ to speed up or slow down a song without it being as obvious. Secondly, you can use the pitch control (*without* time stretching) to change the speed and the pitch or key of the music if you're into beatmixing while key matching. Some DJs prefer a seamless mix that seems like one long continuous song that never changes. This can get monotonous in some situations, but it's popular in trance type environments where monotony is the rule anyway. Finally, some scratch DJs will increase or decrease tempos up to 100% (always without time stretching) to achieve a unique type of scratch sound. This allows for some devilish effects with voices and other sounds.

Time-Stretching has been used for a few years in studios and in professional DJ gear. Hardware devices use Digital Signal Processor chips (DSP) which usually sound pretty good. This process is also called "Master Tempo" by Pioneer, "Key Lock" by Numark, "Time Compression," "Time Expansion," "Time Scaling," and "Tempo Change." Don't be confused—they're all basically the same thing, although each manufacturer may use a slightly different algorithm, which will result in a slightly different processed sound. This opens the unlimited possibilities with beat matching. Songs that were once too far off in BPM range can now be mixed. This doesn't mean that over-pitched songs won't sound weird. Obviously, if you played a 100 BPM song at +10%, or 110 BPM without time stretching, people would notice a difference because the key of the voice and instrumentation would sound very different. With time stretching, you can often achieve large beat gains or losses with less people noticing. The evil side of time stretching is that depending on the EQ and instrumentation of a particular song, the time stretching process may introduce artificial digital artifacts that may sound strangely distorted. In a nightclub setting, your guests may not notice these artifacts. But you and other DJs will notice, and believe me, it'll freak you out. Try a few different units with the same exact songs and listen for yourself.

Although beatmixing may be relatively easy to master in a bedroom, it's much more difficult in the real world. In your bedroom, no one messes with you so you can concentrate on the mix. In the real world, you'll have real world distractions to deal with, usually mostly while you're trying to beatmix. People will rudely ask for requests even while your headphone is up to your ear and you're obviously busy mixing. Some folks will tap your arm, wave their hands in front of your face, or yell loudly to try to get your attention. But rude people aren't the only distraction. In a real club, most DJ booths are out in the open, so you'll have various echoes emanating from all over the room messing up your monitoring with a fractional second delay that's just enough to throw off your mix. You'll think you're hearing the first downbeat of an eight count, but it may be a few milliseconds late. It might not seem like a lot, but even milliseconds will mess up a potentially great mix. And there are always the occasional skipping and other potential hazards and equipment failures you might have to deal with, all while your main goal is to mix that perfect mix.

The hardest thing to get used to is actively listening to two different songs at once. Set up a computer, CD, or tape recorder and record your mixes. Listen to them when you're done practicing—you'll know what sounds good and what doesn't. And when they don't sound good, you'll have to figure out what went wrong so you won't make that same mistake again.

Once you get the hang of it, you'll learn how to handle the distractions, and you'll be surprised how easy the actual mixing techniques are. You'll instantly begin to recognize a song's beats per minute, and then you'll automatically think of another song that has a similar beat and count.

Always be prepared to get another song on before the one that's playing ends, even if you have to slam it out of phase and in an awkward position. Just like on the radio, nothing sounds worse than unplanned dead air.

Basic Dance Music Theory

If you have training in music, you're probably familiar with measures and counts. If you're musically challenged, I've provided the quickest lesson in music theory ever taught because I'm officially putting you on a "need to know basis."

Basically, all music is divided into segments called "measures." Most dance music is written in a "4/4" measure, meaning there are four quarter notes that comprise a measure. Basically, that means a part of a dance song should neatly fall into a multiple of four counts of four before changing into a chorus or some other part of the song. To simplify this even more, all you need to know is that 99% of popular dance music is consistent with an "eight count," which is nothing more than two 4/4 measures back to back. Every hip hop, house, trance, techno or virtually any other dance song has an easily recognizable "downbeat," a "thump" or heavy bass drum beat that begins an eight count (illustrated in Figure 6.2). To hear this for yourself, play any dance music song. Darude's "Sandstorm" is a great example—it's chock full of downbeats. Count from 1 to 8 beginning with the first downbeat after the big synthesizer intro. You'll notice that most songs will change melodies, add or drop cymbal crashes and extra bass drum thumps, instruments, or the vocals will start or stop right around an even multiple of an eight count. Many house, trance and techno songs have drum rolls that swell up and finally end after a certain number of eight counts. The best way to begin to recognize these eight counts is to listen repeatedly, and count aloud as you're picking up the downbeats.

The "Eight Count."

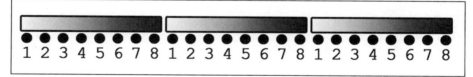

Some songs may not match the eight count exactly with their downbeats (like Sonique's "Feels So Good"). Other songs may throw you off with a cymbal or high hat sound that leads into the actual downbeat in an unexpected place. Once you've reoriented your counting around the downbeat, you can still count along and visualize how it keeps in perfect time with your eight count as you count aloud.

The eight counts combine to form evenly divisible multiple segments of 16, 32, 64, 128, or more downbeats, where different elements of the song tend to kick in. In Figure 6.3, you'll see the bass drum begins the song, followed by cymbals at the beginning of the third eight count. At the sixth eight count, the synthesizer begins to play. Obviously, these counts have been simplified for illustration. Real dance music songs can be this simple or much more complex. The eight-count rule still applies no matter the complexity of the song.

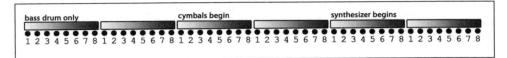

Multiple eight count segments forming a typical dance song

There's a whole other thing called song "keys" or "pitch," which describes the actual musical note a song is based on. Most songs remain consistent within a certain musical key, maybe changing to a complimentary key during a chorus or a break. Some DJs go nuts trying to match keys as well as tempo, but it's incredibly hard to learn, and usually not worth the payoff. Most audiences won't appreciate your additional effort.

Beats Per Minute

After you've mastered the eight count thing, the second thing you must do is identify the "beats" or bass drum hits in a song. The easiest way to do this is to count these beats, beginning on the first downbeat, for 15 seconds. Then multiply your result by four to get the amount of bass drum hits in a minute. This will be your "Beats Per Minute." You don't have to be exact; what you're really looking for is a ballpark estimate of the song's BPM in order to compare the current song with others in the four percent BPM range that you could mix into it. The pitch or speed control on the turntable will make up the differences. Some mixers and digital DJ software counters have a BPM built in that will count the exact BPM down to a tenth of a beat.

 SECRET: Newer DJs typically use a permanent marker or stickers to label their CDs or records with its BPM, and that's completely cool. As I hit my stride as a professional DJ, another more experienced but less friendly DJ saw my marked up record sleeves and made disparaging comments about me being a "newbie" because I had the BPMs written on my record sleeves. I asked him what his problem was. He replied, "Real DJs don't need to write BPMs on their record sleeves—we can *feel* the BPMs." He was right. I hadn't noticed that I could listen to a song for a few seconds and immediately identify several songs that would mix with the record. From that moment on, I never measured BPMs or wrote them on my record sleeves again. If you are new and still need to measure BPMs, you can save yourself from being the brunt of a joke by writing your BPMs in pencil somewhere less conspicuous.

Basic Beatmixing

Beatmixing is manually adjusting the speed of the beats of each song so they're the same speed ("beatmatching"), then correctly lining up the beginning of the eight counts 1 by 1, and running both songs together for a few eight counts during a song's break before bringing in the new song at full volume while simultaneously reducing the volume of your current song.

After choosing your next song, you will "cue up" that song so that you can hear it in your headphones only using your mixer's "cue" or "PFL" setting. While listening to the new song in your headphones, you will locate the first downbeat of the song, and set this as your "cue point." You'll use your turntable, CD player or computer's controls to fine tune that cue point so that when you press "play," the new song will start exactly where you want it to, right at the first downbeat of the new song. You'll then listen to your monitor speaker and wait for the first downbeat of an eight count in the song you're currently playing. You'll then press the "play" button at the exact moment when the one counts of both songs occur. On the deck with the upcoming song, you will adjust your turntable or CD player's "pitch" controller to match the speed or tempo of the downbeats of the upcoming song so they match the tempo of the downbeats of the currently playing song, so that they're running together perfectly. This process is known as "beatmatching."

The hardest part of beatmixing is learning how to immediately recognize where the first beat of the eight counts are so that when you blend your mix, the songs will be in proper phase. Figure 6.4 shows this graphically. You'll be amazed how quickly you'll begin to recognize how the eight counts virtually scream at you to notice them.

Eight count segments from two different songs lined up correctly.

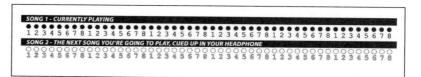

While listening to the current song playing over the speakers, you'll cue up the first downbeat of an eight count of the new song in your headphones. The volume on your mixer for the new song will be set to zero so your audience won't be able to hear you preparing for your mix. Without turning the volume up on the new or incoming song, simply use your headset to listen to the new song. If you have a DJ booth monitor speaker, turn it up so you can avoid the room delay echo that can throw off your mix. Synchronize your ears to the eight count of the song that is already playing. Figure out where the first downbeat is within the eight count. On the first downbeat of an eight count of the current song, release the new song on the beat you've got it paused on. With a CD player, all you'll have to do is press the "play" button. With a turntable, you'll need to give the record a slight forward push to allow it to catch up with the platter slipping underneath it. While running the songs together, you'll be able to adjust the speed of the incoming song so that it matches the song that's playing with the CD or record player's pitch control. Once you feel comfortable with the speed match, back the new song up to the original first downbeat you originally started with. You may want to repeat this a few times until you're comfortable with the flow of the mix, and comfortable with the timing of your release or button pressing.

If you're using vinyl, you'll need to physically grab and hold the side of the record as soon as you hear the first downbeat, carefully trying not to skip the needle out of the groove and lose your place. Most DJs will push the record forward and backward to fine tune where the first beat is actually located, then pull back the beat about an eighth of a rotation and hold the record with their hands while the platter spins underneath it until they're ready to begin the actual mix.

If you're using CDs or a digital DJ system, you can press the pause or cue button to set your exact cue point. Most professional CD players have a "jog wheel" or some other means of fine tuning the exact spot, so you can cue up your song to instantly begin exactly where the first downbeat starts.

When I was new, and even in certain situations later on with tricky mixes or new songs, I would rehearse my mixes in my headphone before going live. Again, you'll need to wait for the first downbeat in an eight count to come around, then start running the songs together. You'll make some manual pitch adjustments with the pitch slider to make sure they're running together.

If your mix isn't lined up correctly, your mix won't sound right (see Figure 6.5). You'll hear something resembling what my mentor DJ Richie Huber would call "a freight train pummeling through a china shop." It's an awful sound that will usually kill a dance floor and make you feel like a fool. And it doesn't matter how long you've been DJing, something always happens and you too will spin a train wreck mix once in while. Make sure there's always adequate room to hide in your DJ booth.

Eight counts lined up incorrectly, leading to a bad mix.

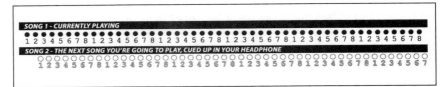

Eventually, when you've lined everything up completely, you'll notice the two songs are running together in perfect time. Again, your audience will not be able to hear your practice mix. You are now ready for the real mix.

Occasionally, running two dance songs together at the same volume can sound kind of muddy because of the way the two bass drums interact with each other. Some of the bass frequencies may phase together effectively canceling some of the signal out. In this case, you'll want to bring down the bass of the old song or new song during the blend. If you take it out of the new song, be sure to kick it back in as soon as the mix has been completed.

The Right Place at the Right Time

Most extended, remix, dance, and/or DJ mix versions of dance songs dedicate a small section of the song specifically so that DJs have a place to mix in and out of them. These areas of dance songs are known as a song's "break." Normally during a break, the vocals and instrumentation purposely drop out to give you a chance to more easily beatmix another song into it.

You'll need to listen to a song quite a few times to recognize when to expect the break to begin. With a CD, there's usually no advance warning, so the only way to know is to virtually memorize a song. As a DJ, this is relatively easy since you'll be playing most of the same songs over and over and over again. You usually won't want to mix out of or into a song when someone is singing. In most cases, it sounds very unprofessional.

With a vinyl record, you can actually see the grooves widen up a bit during the break (see Figure 6.6). With some digital DJ systems, you can visually see upcoming breaks (see Figure 6.7). This is perhaps the only real advantage vinyl and digital DJ systems have in common.

Most dance versions usually have a DJ friendly "intro" too, so you can smoothly beatmix the beginning of your new song in over the break of the song that's playing. You'll need to carefully listen to the intro too.

A visible vinyl break.

A visible digital DJ break in Native Instrument's TRAKTOR DJ Studio.

Some all-instrumental intros are ridiculously long and boring, so you might want to skip most of it and begin your mix well into the song. Some intros might seem too long, but it may be very important to play them because of their instant recognizability or "hook."

Of course, due to the inherent creative nature of the DJ business, there are exceptions to every rule. As you progress and get better at beatmixing, you'll begin to think or alternative ways in which you can mix songs. You might want to overlay dub tracks, drop the beats and substitute an *A capella* track for a neat effect, or completely create your own remixes or edits on the fly. But for now, as a new beatmixer, try to follow the rules and restrain your creative juices until you've got the technique perfected.

You Can Do It In The Mix

So you're ready to roll. You're nervously anticipating the break in the song you're already playing. You've re-cued your incoming song with the first downbeat of the eight count ready to roll. And here comes the break, right after this... five, six, seven, eight, and... BOOM! There went the first downbeat of the break's eight count, you missed it! No problem, sit tight and wait for another eight count to pass so you're ready to mix on the first downbeat of the third eight count in the break. Here it comes, five, six, seven, eight... and you release your new song's downbeat perfectly on the current song's downbeat! Your palms sweat as you're slowly raising the volume of the incoming song on the mixer. They're still beating together in harmony, and you've got a successful overlay going. You begin to lower the volume of the current song. And just as the singer begins to wail on the new song, you've brought the volume all the way up and cut the volume of the old song off. A perfect-blend beatmix!

In reality, your first few mixes won't be perfect. The sheer terror of having to do four things at once—listen to song A on the monitor, listen to song B in the headset, start the new song, fade the volume of song A, and raise the volume of song B—can raise some serious stress in the hearts of new DJs.

Once again, it seems tough at first, but this too will become natural. I remember the day it happened to me. I was working at a bar called Polo Bay late on a Friday night. This club had a giant one-way mirror behind the dance floor that enabled the DJ to see out, but no one could see in. Girls would routinely stand in front of this mirror and adjust all kinds of clothing and body parts, but I digress. Anyway, I was doing something else (probably watching some girl "adjustments") and at the last moment, I noticed my break was coming in seconds! I rather calmly ran to the second turntable and quickly grabbed a record with a similar tempo, threw it on, found the first downbeat, raised the volume and began to beatmix immediately. The mix was perfect! From that point, I realized something was different. I could now beatmix *naturally* rather than *mechanically*. I got chills for a second, and proceeded to build several sets that completely rocked the house. My manager came up to the DJ booth at one point to see who was DJing because she couldn't believe it was me.

Your goal should be to start the incoming song exactly when the first downbeat of the break comes in the playing song (see Figure 6.8). The volume should be raised slightly just before you begin your mix. You'll then use your pitch control to adjust the speed of the incoming song so that its beats match the beats of the song that's playing. Even if you think you've lined them up perfectly in your headphone, turntables and even songs themselves can drift slightly, changing the tempo. Once you've got the beats perfectly lined up, bring the volume of the incoming song up, and let the two ride together for an eight count or two. Completely mix out of the old song just before the first downbeat of an eight count in the incoming song when you're ready.

A perfect mix!

If the mix starts to fall apart, you can "ride it" using the pitch control or pitch bend while trying to get the beats back in synch. Or, you have the option if backing off the mix and returning to the old song for a second chance. If you wait too long, you'll have a mix that sounds kind of like an unpleasant herd of stampeding horses. You usually get another chance to mix during a second break that typically occurs around the end of most dance tracks. Line it up and get it right this time!

Slamming

"Slamming," also known as "cutting," is a less smooth alternative to traditional beatmixing. Slamming uses the same exact eight count techniques, except there is no riding beats together. When you "slam" two songs together, you're merely bringing the incoming song in on its first downbeat of an eight count, and at the same time, immediately cutting the song that's playing just before it has a chance to reach it's corresponding downbeat. I use the slamming technique for songs that are really difficult to mix due to an alternative measure (not a straight eight count, like many guitar rock songs); strange introductions that don't make dance music sense (the introduction to "Buffalo Stance" by Neneh Cherry, or "Givin' It Up" by The Goodmen); and for those songs that simply don't fit into my Four Percent Rule, including when I'm changing sets from trance to hip-hop or vice versa.

Slamming.

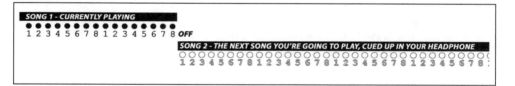

Slamming is not as smooth as beat mixing, but knowing how to slam well can come in really handy when you don't have enough time to properly beatmix. It's also a good method when you can't find a spot in the song to mix smoothly.

Slamming can also be a lazy DJ's crutch, since you don't have to line up the tempos identically as with beatmixing. But it can also be a really cool effect, especially with hip-hop songs with very recognizable introductions.

Sample Slamming

"Sample Slamming" is also based on the eight count technique. The difference with Sample Slamming is that you'll sample or scratch using a phrase or some kind of sound effect from the new song in a repetitive motion that flows with the tempo of the current song, and then, perfectly in time, slam into the next song at the end of an eight count. The most famous sample slam song of all time is the beginning of "It Takes Two" by Rob Base and DJ EZ Rock, where the intro leads into the classic "HIT IT" sample that sounds great when scratched. The effect would sound something like, HIT, HIT, zigga zigga (baby scratch noise), HIT HIT, zigga zigga, HIT, HIT HIT HIT, HIT IT! The massive bass beat kicks in just after the "hit it." Many DJs use this technique on mix CDs. This method is also helpful for songs that are really difficult to mix, or if there's a change in tempo greater than 4%.

Beatmixing No-Nos

There a few beatmixing rules that won't make sense at first. You'll probably break all of them, but you won't realize why you shouldn't break them until you hear someone else break them.

❀ Do not mix over lyrics. It sounds terrible, and it's kind of rude! One DJ explains this to being similar to one of those old time Vaudeville hooks you see on cartoons, where somebody yanks someone off stage with a big hook while they're in the middle of a performance.

❀ Try not to slow currently playing songs down. Songs tend to lose a tremendous amount of energy and sound almost lethargic when slowed down even a tiny bit, and people usually notice this.

❀ If you've got a song that has a piano or synthesizer solo during the break, do not adjust the pitch or your audience will notice that you're doing it! Pitch changes are easily heard with these types of higher frequency instruments. Try not to mix musical parts of a song. Wait for a part of the break that is bass and drums only, because it'll sound better. You'll usually know it's a bad mix by listening closely. It'll just sound wrong.

❀ Abide by the Chuck Fresh Four Percent Rule. Do not pitch/speed records up (or down) by more than 4%. Some newer CD players will let you speed a record up to twice its normal speed! It's fine to temporarily exceed 4% if you're playing catch up, but gradually bring it back down once you've managed to match the beats.

❀ Do not ride out really bad mixes. Quickly complete the mix, slam the song, or cancel the mix attempt immediately. You've only got a few seconds to fix a problem mix. In my experience, if it's going bad, chances are you may not be able to pull it together in time. If your mix is in trouble, cut your losses. Wait for the next break and try your mix again.

❀ Do not bring in a new song at a lower volume. You should always bring your next song in at the same volume, or slightly higher. A lower volume will greatly diminish the energy of the song. It's pure psychological nonsense, but it's true! Remember to adjust your levels by ear after the song is already playing and established. You'll usually need to bring the volume down a bit on the current song just after you've completed your mix.

❀ Do not try to mix everything! I know a pretty bad DJ who refuses to play any songs that don't mix together. He still tries to beatmix fast rock songs with house music. If he were an excellent music programmer, I could live with this. But his selection stinks because he bases his music program purely on beats per minute. He'll actually play crappy songs just because they mix well! Don't sacrifice your program for the mix. When you're changing up music styles or about to do a major tempo change, slam the new song, fade it in, play a DJ Drop, or do a talk-up.

❀ Never apologize for a bad mix because it'll make you look weak. If you botch a mix slightly, chances are most people won't even notice. If you cause a complete train wreck, calmly walk away from the DJ booth and go stretch your legs for a minute or two. Nobody's perfect; even seasoned pros make mistakes once in a while. I can't count the times I lifted the wrong needle off a record while it was playing.

Advanced DJ Performance Mix Tricks

Here are a few tricks of the trade you can use rather than simply beat mixing every song together. You should add a few tricks to your show once in a while to keep it exciting and unpredictable. You'll get everyone's attention when you do these things, which will help you become even more popular. This is what will differentiate your style from everyone else.

Power Downs

If you're using turntables, you can end a song by turning off the power (see Figure 6.10) on the turntable for a cool way to break up your sets. As the outgoing song slows to a halt, you should have an announcement, a promotion, or another hot song cued up ready to start. This will get everyone's attention, because they'll think you screwed up. But you'll be ready to recover and people will think that's intensely cool. You can now do this on many CD players and with some digital DJ systems.

Using the Power Switch for a Powerdown.

The Brake

On most turntables, hitting the stop button (shown in Figure 6.11) while a song is playing will stop a song very abruptly, resulting in a sound that kind of sounds like slamming on the brakes in a car and the wheels screeching briefly. Again, you should have another hot song cued up ready to start immediately. Some newer CD players and some digital DJ systems offer this effect.

The On-Off switch on a turntable, used for fast braking.

Backspins

You'll wait for an eight count in a break. On the end of the eight count, grab the record and spin the record backwards quickly. Before the record has a chance to stop and start forward again, you can let the new song rip right on the first downbeat and immediately fade out the old song. Or, when you get really good, you'll eventually be able to backspin directly to the beginning of the phrase or eight count that you just played! Many DJs will use tape or markers to physically mark the inner label of their records with the beginning of their favorite backspin segments. Like power downs, you can now perform backspins on some CD players and with some digital DJ systems.

Looping

If you've got a mixer, CD player, or digital DJ software with a built-in sampler, or if you have two copies of the same song, you can loop a part of the song. This entails finding a popular part of the song, usually a hook or chorus, and playing that same exact part two to four times in a row continuously. Be careful not to loop too long, or it will become monotonous.

Phasing

Phasing is a cool phenomenon that occurs when two identical stereo sounds are played within a millisecond of each other. When you get it right, the bass drops out almost completely and it sounds kind of like the song is being played in a wind tunnel. You'll need two copies of the same exact mix of a song to do this. Play one of your copies in your normal program, then cue the other copy in your headphone at the same exact place. While they're both simultaneously playing, adjust the speed of the second copy so that it very slightly varies from the song that's playing. While leaving the volume of the song that's playing as it is, bring the volume of the second copy of the song up with your mixer. Use your pitch control to move the second set of beats either a tiny bit faster or slower than the original song. You should begin to hear the weird effect. It'll drift in and out because the speed slightly varies, so it's up to you to constantly adjust the pitch control to keep it in phase. Be careful not to ride it too long, or you may lose the phase and your beats will start to lose sync emitting a nasty double beat sound. Phasing works best on faster tempo house type songs with a consistent bass beat.

Dropouts

Dropouts (see Figure 6.12) occur when you bring the volume of a playing song down for one beat. You add a real quick moment of silence usually on the eight count of a song during an instrumental part or break, which gives you a neat variation. Be careful not to do this while playing part of the song where vocals would be abruptly cut off, or it'll sound terrible.

Dropouts.

Treble Kicks

Sound engineers have a love-hate relationship with Treble Kicks. People have told me that this is one of the worst things an inexperienced DJ can do to a sound system because they always go too far with it.

Sound engineers dig this because they can sell you replacement tweeters when you blow yours up. This happens when you use the treble controls on your mixer during a dance song to quickly emphasize cymbals or high hat sounds to the beat of the music. You quickly raise and lower the treble when the cymbals crash or the high hats are hit. Don't forget to put the treble back to where it was when you're done with this trick, or your music will sound too tinny.

The Bounce

If your club or bar is wired in stereo or in mono with the left and right channels going to different sets of speakers, you can bounce parts of your song from left to right using the left-right balance control on your mixer if you have one. This sounds pretty sweet with instrumental fast paced parts of dance songs. For an even cooler trick, another form of bouncing is actually swapping beats from one song to another! Try to alternate beats as shown in Figure 6.13. The spaces are obviously where you use a crossfader to completely cut off the volume to one side while raising the other side very quickly. If you have a slow crossfade option, you'll want to turn it off for this trick.

The
Bounce.

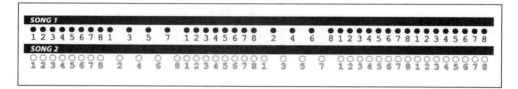

Hits

Some songs have big orchestra or bass drum hits, and you can emphasize these by quickly raising and then immediately lowering the volume during that bass hit. This sometimes sounds like an explosion and gets everyone's attention. Warning: going overboard with this trick can blow your speakers, so please use it with care. Spin responsibly.

Beat Juggling

Now here's where things get really tricky. What you're doing here is a combination of other beatmixing tricks that will ultimately create loops or perhaps all new beat patterns from the same or different songs. First, you'll need two copies of the same song, or you can use edits, beats or mixes of different songs you know very well cued on separate decks at about the same BPM. You'll start running the beats on the first deck while setting your cue point on the second deck. Then through a quick process of backspins, loops, and fast crossfades, you'll essentially "juggle" the beats by quickly going back and forth between the two decks while constantly re-cueing the other deck as the current deck is playing. This can sound really cool when you get good enough to bust out a funky groove varying between two to eight beats per side while banging back and forth exactly where you want it. Advanced beat jugglers can perform live remixes by alternating bass drums and cymbals between the two sides, or even adding manual in-time pauses that sound like they belong in the song. Some DJs use three CD players or turntables, so they have a main deck for a backbeat, and then they can use two decks for special effects like beat juggling.

There are so many more tricks that you'll pick up by listening to other DJs, or by inventing them yourself! Just be careful not to overuse any of the tricks, or you run the risk of being predictable, which is one of the greatest DJ sins. Practice these tricks before you go live with them.

Scratching

Scratching, sometimes known as "hand sampling" or "cutting it up," might seem like a relatively recent phenomenon in the DJ business, but it has actually been around for over thirty years. This takes a lot of practice, because it's pure physical contact between your hands and a record. Your fingers and wrists need to be quick and well coordinated. You'll need to have the record in one hand, the headset between your head and shoulder, and the fader or volume control in the other hand, and you'll need to be able to control everything naturally and instantaneously.

When I was DJing at a club in central New Jersey, some guy would come in every Friday night and ask me, "Hey, man, you want me to show you how to cut it up, man?" I thanked him and kindly declined his offer for months. I was amazed at how persistent this fool was, as he asked me the same exact question for at least three months straight. Finally, after wearing me down to the point of exhaustion, I reluctantly gave him his big break. He ran to his car and brought two crates of records into my already crowded DJ booth. There was a twinkle in his eyes as he prepared for his set and cued his first record. I couldn't wait to see what kind of magic this young DJ was concocting. All the sudden, he completely cut off the song that was playing in the middle of a vocal verse. The packed dance floor froze in shock. He then proceeded to play some kind of generic hip hop beats as he cued up a second record. He then started to scratch. "Hey, hey, h, h, h, hey!" The dance floor was still frozen. "Hey, we want some (expletive deleted)!" His set continued for about three minutes, all with a completely empty dance floor. People were sitting at the bar with a confused look on their faces. Some folks headed for the door. After his third or fourth record, he got upset that no one was dancing, and turned his record off abruptly, and yelled some more expletives at the crowd. He packed up his records and never came back to the club.

Scratching is not a necessary skill to be successful DJ business. Many people will find scratching extremely annoying, especially at wedding receptions and mainstream nightclubs. Most scratching is done in bedrooms and at small parties.

Preparing to Scratch

When preparing to scratch, the turntable platter has to be very easy to slip. Most well worn slip mats will do the trick. If not, you can trim down a piece of thick paper or wax paper underneath the slipmat to help it slip better.

Another typical problem scratchers who use vinyl face is a hole that's too tight or too loose—it's got to be just right. Depending on the record manufacturing process, the hole that fits over the metal spindle in the center of the platter may be too large, which may cause your records to quiver and subsequently cause tracking errors and skipping. An easy way to fix this is by using a small piece of tape inside the hole to tighten things up. If it's too tight, you'll have problems moving the record back and forth. You can make that hole a little bigger with a piece of rolled up sandpaper to keep the sides perfectly round. In a pinch, I've used other things including ballpoint pens and nail files. Be careful not to make the hole too large. If you're using CDs or MP3s, you obviously won't have this problem.

With turntables, your tone arm and cartridge will probably have to be weighted down slightly more than with traditional beatmixing. Depending on the type of cartridge and stylus you've decided to use, you'll need to adjust the tone arm weight according to the manufacturer's recommendations. Other DJs I know would tape a dime to the headshell. There are all kinds of specialty scratching cartridges and styluses on the market today. Back in the day, I used a plain old Stanton 680 EL and it worked fine most of the time. Know that you will go through records and needles much more quickly when scratching.

Finally, you'll need to choose your weapons, meaning your battle and break beats records. These records are manufactured especially for DJs with compilations of sound effects, noises, samples, and raw beats that work well when performing various types of scratching. You can choose plain old hip hop records, but then you'll have to find cool places to scratch on your own. Battle and break beats compilations have already done this for you. DJ QBert, one of the best scratchers in the world, has two great records that are perfect to get you started. His "Toasted Marshmellow Feet Breaks" is a classic with lots of good scratching material. And QBert's "Scratchy Seal——Sealed Breaks" is considered an "unskippable" record. It's not that it won't skip, but when it does, it simply bounces into another similar beat for a virtually seamless skip.

The key to scratching is getting comfortable handling records, and learning how to do so without making the needle jump out of the groove. Some people grab the record by the side, some put their whole hands directly in the middle of the grooves, and yet others use the clean middle part of the record without grooves. It's all up to you—whatever makes you comfortable. Your personal technique will depend on how tall you are and where the turntable is in reference to your height. In many clubs, you won't have the option to raise or lower the turntables, so you'll have to work around this with your personal technique.

And I hope you ate your Wheaties, because it's time to lift up those heavy turntables and flip them ninety degrees so the tone arm mechanism is positioned further away from you, so that they're in "battle position.". The whole "battle" thing may sound kind of angry, but its roots stem from sponsored mixing competitions that used to be referred to as "mixing battles." When scratching took over in the eighties, the "mixing" somehow disappeared and we were left with "DJ Battles." A battle is usually a very friendly competition between two or more DJs to determine the most dope scratcher.

Scratching Techniques

Basically, scratching is finding an interesting noise, like a voice, synth, sound effect, or even a drumbeat on a record, where you physically move the record back and forth over that noise to the beat of a song playing on another deck.

First, you'll find a scratch spot. You'll need to listen to the record thoroughly and experiment with different sounds. Grab the record (or digital controller pad on a scratchable CD player) with your hand as the platter spins beneath it and move it back and forth over that spot with a rhythmic beat. The record will make different types of noises depending on the length of your movement over that spot, the speed at which you're moving the music, and the level of your crossfader. An important element of scratching is volume control. Using the fader, you can enhance scratching effects by raising and lowering the volume of the scratch motion. Depending on the particular type of scratch you're doing, you may want to play an entire forward motion, just a quick piece of the forward motion, or some other combination of back and forth motions. Most DJs use the crossfader control for scratching rather than the individual volume controls.

There are tons of popular scratches with new variations being invented every day, some of which might even bear your name someday. It's virtually impossible to show you how to scratch in a book, but I've attempted to explain some of the basic scratches to help get you started. You'll need to see the motions and hear the results to truly understand it. Get a video and watch the masters in action if scratching is what you have your heart set on. DJ QBert's scratch video is pretty darn informative and funny. More scoop on that at www.djqbert.com.

Baby Scratch

The simplest and original scratch is a quick rhythmic back and forth scratch now widely known as the "Baby Scratch." You simply leave the crossfader full on and move the record back and forth over the same sweet spot to the beat of the music. It's similar to producing a special effect on a synthesizer, and can sound pretty cool if it's done correctly. You can alter the sound by changing the speed or the length of the scratch.

Scribble Scratch

Scribbles are basically Baby Scratches on crack. You move the record back and forth with the fader fully up in very small and fast rhythmic movements. For a sweet twist, you can bring the fader up and down during your Scribble, of course, always following the beat.

Forward/Backward Scratch ("Cutting")

After you've got the feel for the Baby Scratch, it's time to try Forward and Backward Scratches. Forward Scratches are where you find your scratching sound in your headphone, cueing it up by pulling it back a bit, then letting it rip with the fader up. The twist is that you'll slam the fader down while you pull the record backwards (a backspin, remember?) to re-cue the forward scratch. This is done very quickly at different lengths as you see fit to make it sound interesting, and always to the rhythm of the beat. Backwards Scratches are the exact opposite.

Tear Scratch

Tear Scratches sound like you're physically tearing the record! You'll either push or pull your record in a larger forward or backward motion, pause briefly, then continue the motion, again to the beat of the song. Tears can be done all forwards, all backwards, or a combination of both. There is no crossfader used in a Tear.

Chirp Scratch

This is a popular and relatively simple back and forth scratch that sounds like a bird chirping. You'll fade the sound out with your crossfader as you push the record forward, and then fade the sound back in when you pull the record back. This sounds pretty cool when done at varied speeds.

Transformer Scratch

Here's where things get kind of complicated, and we find out who can walk and chew gum. Transformer Scratches are where you move the record forwards and/or backwards with one hand, while quickly moving the fader to raise and lower the volume in a rhythmic motion with the other. Some DJ mixers have a transformer switch that kills the sound when used, which some DJs prefer rather than using the fader. I've heard this called a "Crab Scratch," because you'll cup your hand over the crossfader like a crab with your thumb kind of stiff and the rest of your fingers a little more loose. You'll push the crossfader with one finger at a time as your thumb pushes it back to achieve an insanely cool broken up effect. Some DJs compare this to being able to snap all your fingers simultaneously. The resulting effect sounds like a perfectly timed stutter. It's a killer sounding effect and even cooler to watch when someone's really good at it. This is probably the most difficult scratch to perfect, and probably the leading cause of used turntable sales by frustrated DJs.

Flare Scratch

The Flare Scratch is kind of similar to a Transform Scratch. The difference is the timing. Flares are done by playing a forward scratch with a quick mute (by slamming the crossfader to the other deck then back) in the middle of it that divides it in half, then finishes off with a single reverse scratch. There's a big subset of various types of Flare Scratches identified by DJs by something called "clicks." A click is where you slam the crossfader to the opposite deck, effectively killing the sound and making a loud "click" noise as the metal bar in the crossfader hits the side of the mixer. You can have "Two Click Orbits," "Three Click Transforms," and all kinds of other craziness these bald guys who hate the letter "s" are creating daily.

There are a ton of other scratching tricks that you can learn from watching hip-hop masters in action. There are also videos available that you can buy to really learn the intricacies of scratching. DJ QBert's "Complete Do It Yourself" scratching videos (Thud Rumble Video) are the best in the business. This fun DVD actually shows over two scratches each with four selectable angles you can choose so you can visualize QBert's methods different ways, which makes various scratches easier to understand. And if you're not careful like I wasn't, you may learn how to fix your plumbing using rubber from your car's tire (featured in the bonus footage on the DVD).

The Art of Remixing and Edits

First things first. Believe it or not, it's technically illegal to remix or edit someone else's song without the permission of the copyright owner. But almost every performance DJ does it—it's the nature of the art. What's even more stupid is that for well over two decades now, many "legal" extended dance mixes and DJ records include "*A capella*" (the words with no music behind them) and instrumental "bonus versions" of the songs on the record or CD. If they didn't want you to remix the record, then why would they include those tracks? Do they honest expect anyone in their right mind to play a three-minute long *A capella* song with no beats? Copyright laws are getting to be almost ridiculous, and there's not a whole lot you can do about it. As long as you're using your remixes solely for your own personal enjoyment and *not* duplicating them and/or freely giving them away, or selling them on your own "remix CD," or placing them on a website so your friends can hear them, you probably won't be arrested and sued. Thanks to the Napster fiasco, the RIAA is fiercer than ever in prosecuting whatever they consider to be copyright violations this week. Be safe, and don't take any silly chances.

The first step to becoming a producer is learning how to listen to songs and figure out ways to make them even cooler. In some cases, you might thing a longer intro would sound better. A little more energy during the chorus build might help a certain song sound better. Or perhaps a longer break is needed so DJs can mix out easier. DJs have a feel for what works on dance floors, which is why many pro DJs eventually become dance music producers.

Remixing

Remixing is defined as taking the original tracks of a song, and then manipulating and rearranging them. Essentially, you're recreating the song from scratch, and making it your own special sound.

CHAPTER 6

Remixing can be done live or with a digital studio. Obviously, studio remixes can be much more complex since you have the luxury of time and virtually unlimited layers of tracks. Multitrack software like Steinberg's Cubase, Cakewalk, or Sony's Vegas are popular tools for remixing.

The tough part of remixing is getting your hands on the original tracks. Many promotional extended and remix versions will have instrumental or *A capella* versions. Unfortunately, if you're not a professional working DJ with verifiable employment at a club, it can be very difficult to get your hands on the individual tracks you'll need to remix. Although many tracks are widely available via file sharing networks on the internet, your only legal option is to contact the record labels directly to get your hands on individual tracks to reassemble them. This process can take some time. And by the time you get permission, and that's only *if* you get permission, the creative spark has probably passed and you'll be on to something new.

You'll digitize and arrange your loops, voices, and other interesting elements you'd like to include in your own personal remix, and then it's time to create magic.

Basically, most remixing is done by taking vocal tracks from one song and placing them over the beats of an entirely different song. In some cases, you may be lucky enough to have an alternative instrumental version of the same song, but typically, that's not the case. Many DJs will use loops (constantly repeating segments of 4, 8, 16, or some other even multiple or four) they sampled from another song, or ready-made loops from a royalty-free loop production company (which you'll usually have to purchase). If an *A capella* version is not available, you can sometimes use an equalizer to remove as much of the unwanted bass, drum, or synth tracks as you can from the original song mix. It's common to have a little of the unwanted sounds bleed into your mix, but don't worry. The fierce replacement beats will cover most of those up.

In your multitrack software program, you'll be busy cutting and pasting and adjusting everything so it's perfectly lined up. When it finally sounds ready, you'll then "master" the final stereo mixdown, which will add equalization and normalization so that your remix can sound just like it came from a major record label.

Live remixing, sometimes called "hotmixing," involves reassembling a song in a live setting, with no stopping to perfect the mix, because you are either performing in front of people or recording your mix. The pressure is on! This is much more difficult than studio remixing, but it's also a much bigger rush. I used to do live remixing using *A capella*s and instrumental tracks when performing at a club.

Mashing or "mash-ups" is a phenomenon that's big in Europe. Basically, a mash is a remix that combines two entirely different songs into one. One of the best I've ever heard is a mash-up of Justin Timberlake's "Rock Your Body" with 50 Cents' "In Da Club," renamed "Rock Da Club." Typically, the new titles combine the original titles. Mash-ups can also be a humorous play on words, involving creatively reassembling songs based on nothing more than their titles. The funniest I've heard is Eminem's "My Name Is" mashed with the TV theme from the kid's show Bob The Builder, called "My Name Is Bob." Mashing is also referred to as "bootlegging" in some parts of Europe.

Edits

Edits are rearranging a song with existing parts, and are usually done in a studio. Once in a while, record labels release painfully bad remixes of popular songs. Sometimes DJs decide to take matters into their own hands by creating their own extended edits of the popular radio versions. Since most DJs aren't lucky enough to have access to the individual tracks that remixers use, it's virtually impossible to do a remix. So the only solution is often creating an edit.

Typically using a home computer, DJs "rip" the radio version on CD to a digital file, then proceeded to edit the song by adding an extended looped intro, moving the end to the beginning, extending breaks, and other cool stuff that just works better in a dance environment. Again, it's important to remember that changing a song without the permission of the copyright holder is technically illegal! Chances are you won't get in big trouble as long as you never sell or give away copies of your remixes or edits.

Some DJs will create edits on the fly while mixing live using two or more copies of the same song. I think this is technically illegal also, but it's usually overlooked (unless you're recording it). I used to do most of my edits live.

If you're interested in trying to obtain permission to do a real remix or edit, good luck. Record labels are notoriously reluctant to issue permission to non big name DJs. Here's a copy of a letter I e-mailed to Maverick Records to request permission to create a legal edit of "Ray of Light" by Madonna. I'm probably still waiting for a response.

> *Greetings.*
>
> *I am requesting permission to create an edit of Madonna's "Ray of Light" to be played in by myself while performing as a DJ in the state of Florida.*
>
> *I wish to use your existing radio edit that I purchased legally several years ago and recreate a longer introduction and break using existing elements of the song. If permission is granted, I will only make one (1) copy to a CD for my personal use only, and I shall never loan, give, sell, publish on the Internet, and/or allow anyone to copy my edit, ever.*
>
> *Please forward information about how I could go about creating this edit legally.*
>
> *Also, I would like information on how to obtain the master tracks to "Ray of Light" so that I could create my own remix of this song. I may utilize certain sound effects and other royalty-free beats to accentuate certain parts of the song. I understand I would also require your permission to create this remix, and I am hereby requesting permission to do so.*
>
> *Thank you for your consideration and your prompt response.*
>
> *Regards,*
>
> *DJ Chuck Fresh*

Producing Electronic Music

The easiest way to become a big name worldwide DJ is to create a hit song like Moby, Paul Van Dyke, DJ Rap, and scores of others already have. The final kind of Performance DJ is the Producer DJ. He or she is an electronica wizard, a person who creates wild psychedelic house and trance tracks by arranging loops, sounds, and special effects in the studio with special multitrack software using multiple records, keyboards, and digital effects. Unfortunately, you'll usually need some talent to do this. Hopefully this section can help you find the talent that's hidden somewhere in your soul.

Dance Music Structure

The first thing you'll need to know is basic dance music structure. Let's look at a popular dance song as an example, because it's generally better to emulate something successful rather than something that sucks. "Sandstorm" by Darude was a huge worldwide hit a few years ago, and it's a pretty basic stucture. For simplicity's sake, we'll analyze the radio edit.

* Synth intro for 32 beats (4 eight counts, or 8 measures)

* Synth intro with building percussion for 32 beats (4 eight counts, or 8 measures)

* The "meat of the song," with a prominent downbeat for 64 beats (8 eight counts, or 16 measures)

* 144 beat instrumental break with building synth (18 eight counts or 36 measures, which is slightly weird because most songs are multiples of 4 eight counts or 8 measures)

* 128 "meat" repeat, crash end

The basic radio edit of "Sandstorm" is fairly DJ friendly, probably because Darude is also a DJ. So if you adopt something similar to this basic formula, you'd write songs with a nice and DJ friendly eight-count intro (which would actually be 16 "measures"). A longer intro gives a DJ an ample chance to mix into the song without having to rush things. The "meat" of the beat in most trance and techno jams is usually a repetitive series of vocals and/or synthesizer "hooks," which are the more catchy parts of a song that you'll find yourself humming in the car or whistling in the bathroom. You'll then treat your fellow DJs with a break that's adequately long enough for even amateur DJs to successfully mix. Then it's back into the repetitive catchy meat beat again for a short while, ending up with a crash ending that's perfect for slamming, or yet another DJ friendly beat at the end.

The beauty of making music is you've got a few rules to follow, but after that, you've got virtually unlimited freedom to do whatever you want. And it's lots of fun.

Synthesizers

Today's digital keyboards, often known as "synths" because of their abilities to synthesize and reproduce several different types of sounds, come loaded with hundreds of original and sampled sounds that are usually cool enough to produce killer house, trance, or hip hop tracks. Most synths offer optional add-on sound modules or "expansion packs" with even more sampled sounds, usually dance music kits with lots of cool drum sounds. And cooler synths offer built in samplers, so you can actually record sounds yourself, legally, of course, and use them in your compositions. People sample songs, vocal tracks, instruments, and all kinds of other things including tools and household items while looking for the next big sound.

Most newer synths have built in "sequencers." A sequencer is a hardware or software based program that allows you to separate your song parts into individual sequences of a number of eight counts, which you can then arrange in any order you want. You can create an eight count intro with some basic synth notes, and save it as sequence 01. You can then copy that same sequence 01 to sequence 02, so you won't have to start from scratch. Then, on sequence 02, you may want to add some cymbals or a bass drum beat. When you're done with that, you'll then copy sequence 02 to create sequence 03, and so on (see Figure 6.14). When you've got several sequences saved, you'll then tell the sequencer which sequences to play, and in which order. For instance, you might program your sequencer to play your sequences as follows:

Sequencing.

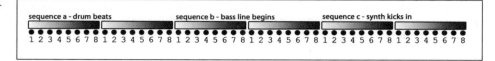

sequence a - drum beats | sequence b - bass line begins | sequence c - synth kicks in

1 2 3 4 5 6 7 8 1 2 3 4 5 6 7 8 1 2 3 4 5 6 7 8 1 2 3 4 5 6 7 8 1 2 3 4 5 6 7 8 1 2 3 4 5 6 7 8

A sequencer allows people who can't play a single note (including myself) a way to actually create some pretty cool music. I wrote over 200 songs with an inexpensive old Ensoniq keyboard (a discontinued model), some of which I played during my gigs. I've tried Korg's Triton and Karma's keyboards and Yamaha's Motif workstation, and they're both incredibly powerful dance music making machines that are light years ahead of the equipment I was using back in the day. There are hundreds of other more advanced programmable hardware and software solutions, but an all-in-one sequencer/synthesizer is a great place to start.

Some things you'll want to look for in a synth are heavy duty "polyphony," the synth's ability to play several notes and sounds at once. Older keyboards had 16-note polyphony, which would cause certain notes or sounds to disappear during complex parts of the song. Most new synths feature 62-note polyphony, which is usually more than enough for even the most complex passages. Look for the ability to save your own samples, either through a computer connection or a compact disc drive. Some artists like to create their own sounds by tweaking the waveforms of the built in sounds. Many DJs create their own signature sounds that can't be found anywhere else in this manner. A "quantizer" helps to automatically line up beats that aren't perfectly recorded on the counts. You'll need your beats to be perfectly lined up or you can't make seamless loops. Finally, make sure you've got the ability to use expansion boards, so your synth can grow with you.

Music Making Software

An even easier way to create killer tracks is to use loop-based software, such as Ableton's Live or Sony's Acid. Basically, all you need to do is import a bunch of readily available royalty-free drum, bass, synth and sound effect loops into the software, layer them all on separate tracks, drag and drop them exactly where you want them to come in, then simply export your mixed tracks to a CD or MP3 file. It's easy! See the Digital Domain chapter for more information on several software products and how to use them.

The Flow of Your Show

No matter which type of performance DJ you're longing to be, the applicable techniques take many hours, days, weeks, months, and sometimes years of practice. But once they become natural to you, you will no longer have to waste brain cells mechanically thinking about eight counts, beats per minute, or how to correctly time a transformer scratch. And then you can begin to concentrate on making your music programming more compelling.

In most mainstream bars and smaller clubs, your shift will usually be 4 to 5 hours. In big city clubs, several DJs will split the night with a headliner, so you're lucky if you get to play more than two hours. A 4-5 hour shift in a smaller bar or club will really help develop your programming ability, and it's the only training ground I recommend. It's difficult to hype up a crowd and bring them down and back up again in a two hour shift, especially when your shift is early at night while warming up for the big guys.

CHAPTER 6

With a normal 4-5 hour shift, you've got the opportunity to see how the entire night flows. You can watch people come and go, and see how their attitude changes depending on the level of artificial stimulants. The experience is invaluable.

A music "set" is a group of similar songs with a similar style and tempo range known as "beats per minute" (BPM), a measurement of the amount of times a downbeat occurs within the span of a minute. A set will usually start at a certain BPM, and in most mainstream bars and clubs, it will gradually increase throughout the set. Your sets can be anywhere from 2-50 songs depending on your crowd's tastes and the depth and your knowledge of your music library. In a typical mass-market nightclub or bar, most of my sets were 5-10 songs long, ranging from 84-118 BPM for a "hip-hop" or rap music set; and ranging from 114-150 BPM for a house/techno/trance set. I found that, among other reasons, longer sets would tend to bore the crowd or wear the crowd out, and the dance floor would subsequently thin out as dancers took a break.

The last thing you'll want to do as you blow through a night is keep a constant level of energy. Even constant high energy loses its appeal after a while. People enjoy it better when you take them for a ride with your music. Strive to mix it up, not just with your energy, but with the types of music you play. You should try to build energy throughout your sets, saving your highest energy songs for the perfect times during your sets. Sometimes you'll need to start with a really hot song to get people going, then play some other popular songs, and then play another really hot song two to three songs later. Think of a rollercoaster going up and down. The riders are enjoying the highlights of the coaster, the loops and drops, and always nervously anticipating the next one. As you progress and gain experience DJing parties, you'll learn which songs are just hot, and which songs are *really* hot, and you'll be better prepared to create killer music sets.

7

THE MC

A Master of Ceremonies (MC) is a person who has been chosen to lead a group of people in some sort of event, celebration, or awards ceremony. This person needs to be an enthusiastic speaker with a likeable personality. All MCs need to guide a party or event from beginning to end. An MC at a wedding reception is the leader of the entire event—he or she says what gets done and when. One thing all successful DJs have in common is that they're both great DJs and effective MCs.

An MC has an important job. You've got to be on your toes, since everything you do affects the entire room. If a bartender or waitress spills a drink or screws up an order, it only affects a few people. But if you, as an MC, mispronounce the groom's last name, or your record or CD skips, everyone in the room will notice. Stuff happens. It helps tremendously if you've encountered that stuff before and you're prepared to handle it with a twist of humor. Experienced MCs can actually make an unfortunate event look like it was part of the show! Making mistakes and learning from the different situations that occur at parties, nightclubs or bars will help you to develop a quick wit that will help you too make the most of it.

What Makes a *Great* MC?

A successful MC is the host with the most! A great MC can lead a crowd of any age, size, or ethnicity, and appear to have them all eating out of his or her hands. It takes several different skills and a lot of practice to pull this off. Don't worry—these are skills that can be learned with little effort. Let's take a look at the three main components that all great MCs have in common.

One Part Comedian

You should strive to be an entertaining speaker who recognizes in the importance of humor in everyday life. Humor is the best medicine for daily stress, and most folks appreciate a good laugh. If you can tickle someone's funny bone, they'll trust you, follow you, and recommend you to others.

A great MC is part comedian. You've got to understand and deliver mostly clean, always clever, and hopefully relevant comedy (relevant to today's trends, the current situation, and/or your clientele). It's not the type of comedy where you'll have the opportunity to tell jokes, but more hitting the crowd with cute and well-timed one-liners that are often unexpected and relevant. For example, you'll often see a pretty girl who's had too much to drink take over a dance floor with a sensual dance that's well beyond the "R" movie rating. If it's cool with your boss, you'd let her finish her dance, then announce something like, "Let's give it up for Nasty Nina, and her nasty moves! Make sure to see her new release at the Adult Cinema on Chestnut Street, downtown." Thanks to your quick wit, she lives the rest of her natural life with her permanent new nickname, Nasty Nina. The crowd chuckles, and you look like a professional funny guy.

Most of what you say should be in an almost silly style that's friendly and light-hearted, but cool enough to demand respect. Some of your material may be so ridiculously silly that it's obviously meant to be funny. For example, in some of my bar accounts, I would announce that all drinks were free after 2 AM with a completely straight face and a serious tone. People would cheer until they realized that since my bar closed at 2 AM, I obviously meant your drinks were free somewhere else, like at home. This is often called "dry humor," and it works best in a nightclub or bar situation.

It's best to be known as a nice guy, so always try to play on important people's misfortunes in a positive manner. If someone trips while walking on stage to accept an award, and the entire audience is watching, a good MC will take the attention away from the hapless tripper. Depending on the situation, I'd quickly divert attention to something else that I deemed to be interesting; or I'd somehow make the whole thing look like it was my fault. I've dropped a microphone stand on a stage to cover for a boss's trip. The resulting sound was so loud and obnoxious that the audience immediately forgot about my boss's stumble as they jumped in shock. I picked up the microphone stand and said "Darn termites!" My boss got a few seconds to regain his composure, I got a quick chuckle, and then I resumed my program with no one feeling silly.

Eventually, you'll run into a situation with some obnoxious fool who's going to try to steal your show, commonly known as a "heckler." Remember that no matter how loud he or she is, you're the one with the microphone, and that gives you a level of authority. Sometimes you can ignore him and he'll usually go away. Sometimes you can smile and mention you agree with him, and he may be embarrassed and go away. But once in a while, you'll run into a relentless heckler that will force you to engage him to retain the respect of your audience. In this case, first notify the manager and security staff and explain what's going on. If they decide that this person is over the line, they may decide to remove him from the room, which is their prerogative. This is the easiest solution, because everyone will laugh at him as he's being escorted from the room. If he's allowed to stay, you've got a free ticket to give him the tongue lashing of his life in front of all his stupid friends.

In responding to a relentless heckler, you have artistic license to borrow a few lines from established comedians' material. A relevant line from a popular movie is always a huge hit. Humor targeted towards business people or family audiences is the safest. Adult-oriented humor tends to be more effective in getting a rise out of people, but must be used very carefully in family audiences. Just remember to keep it light and humorous! This is one of the things that you may have to practice or get ready for. I hung out at comedy clubs and watched the masters handle hecklers. I got some really good tips from them, which I later unleashed on these poor fools. Classic quick and witty one liners from the likes of comedians like Rodney Dangerfield are easy to remember and virtually harmless. Here are a few I've created or used over the years.

- ❉ *I see you've set aside this special time to humiliate yourself in public.* This is a light hearted and fun way to address the situation. He'll usually come back with something stupid, and may have to hit him one more time.

- ❉ *Ah, to be young and silly again.* Short and sweet, and not too offensive to anyone.

- ❉ *He's so bright his mother calls him son.* Another harmless pun safe for any audience.

- ❉ *Wait—there was a joke there somewhere. Could you repeat that?* Any time you force a heckler to repeat himself, you've killed him. It's never as funny the second time around, and he'll feel like a fool repeating it.

* *I'm not sure what your problem is, but there's probably a powerful medication for it.* This works best with older audiences who can identify with lots of doctors and tons of prescription drugs.

* *Listen. I'd love to stay and chat with you, sir, but I refuse to have a battle of wits with an unarmed opponent.* You have to be careful with this one because it's kind of challenging your heckler to come back at you. Always have another comeback in reserve!

* *I've always wondered how long someone can live without a brain. How old are you?* A nice way to call someone an idiot without it appearing that you've done so.

* *Yeah, I remember the first time I had a beer.* Steve Martin's classic. One of the more pleasant ways of implying that someone is acting childish.

There are several more nasty comebacks, but they're not usually applicable to a DJ or MC situation.

Whatever you do, don't take hecklers personally. A heckler is looking to attract attention to himself. You've got to remain in control of your show, and you've got to firmly establish that it is *your* show and not the heckler's. If the heckler was obviously drunk or just plain stupid, depending where I was, I'd walk over and give him (or her, but usually a him) a microphone (not my microphone, but a cheap one I didn't care about). The guests would be shocked, so there would be an eerie dead silence. Since it was my show and I operated the controls, I would turn his volume down a bit so that his little tirade wasn't nearly as loud as mine, which would naturally steal a little more of his thunder. In my experience, this always allowed the heckler to bury himself. He'd say a few stupid things, complain about the music or whatever, and utter some choice profanities. He'd then realize he had nothing else to say above the continued silence, and usually put the microphone down and walk away in less than a minute. I would then calmly shake his hand, thank him for this interlude, collect my cheap microphone, spray it with Lysol (so that the audience could see this), use a quick one-liner to show how silly he was, and then continue with my show uninterrupted because no one else would dare mess with me after witnessing his embarrassment. Obviously, you shouldn't try this at a wedding reception or at a party with children attending. I've only done this at bars and adult parties.

Comedians rarely apologize and never back down, unless they've said really something stupid, wrong, or hurtful. Just think about what you're going to say before you say it.

One Part Politician

It's human nature; people are like sheep. They're begging to be led. Very few people can handle the responsibility of being accountable when something goes wrong. The rewards are big for people who can handle the pressure.

Real leaders are supposed to be fair and unbiased. Although we know that's a naive notion, you should at least try to *appear* to be fair and unbiased. If you're judging a bikini contest, your chubby girlfriend should obviously not win without giving all the contestants a fair shake.

In a wedding or private party mobile DJ situation, you're going to need negotiation skills so you can help coordinate the affair before a war of self interests dominates and ultimately ruins the entire day. The photographer, the caterer, the videographer and your bridal party will all need to be in cahoots so the affair will stay close to schedule. The DJ is the host of the entire event, and it's typically your job to tell your guests when to dance, when to participate, what they should do, and how they should do it.

For some reason beyond my limited male knowledge, women consider photography to be a very important part of their wedding day. I've seen occasions where the photographer has consumed the entire day, leaving no time for dancing or enjoying the moment. To me, this destroys the wedding experience and turns it into a vanity modeling session. The groom hates it, and many brides regret it later. A wedding photographer is the only wedding professional that makes money after the wedding, so he'll try to monopolize the entire wedding day so he'll have something to sell later. Some wedding photographers can be very rude, making it very difficult for you as a DJ. Remember that your bride is the ultimate boss, and not the photographer. You've got a job to do, and your customer expects you to do as you promised, so don't allow a photographer to push you around. In the event that he does try, be polite, tell him you agree with him, but you'll need to check with the bride first.

You'll need to develop an almost psychic ability to know what's going to happen next in a particular situation. For example, if your bride is a chain smoker, you'll need to calculate when she'll be back in the room from a smoke before you call her up for the garter ceremony. If the scheduled meal is running late, which is very typical, your entire schedule will need to be adjusted so you can fit everything in. You may not have enough time to play all the songs the bride requested. Or you may have to rush other traditional events. Either way, you'll need to think about how you want to handle the situation, then negotiate your proposed solution with your bride.

Finally, you'll be expected to present yourself as the host of the party, which means you'll need to speak clearly, professionally and with authority. You don't have to take public speaking courses, but it could help.

Ninety Eight Parts Entertainer

The most important element of a great MC's bag of tricks is expert crowd motivation. You've got to get your audience to take a step away from the norm. You might have to lead them in a lame line dance. You could juggle compact discs to get people's attention. Sometimes you'll be required to run into the crowd like a crazed lunatic and give everyone high fives. Occasionally, you'll even pull an eighty-year-old grandma off her chair and jitterbug with her. You might have to wear a stupid looking hat and act out a silly song. A great MC will do whatever it takes to get the party going.

Props, Confetti

People dig props because it makes them feel like they're part of the show. Inflatable guitars, saxophones and microphones along with the right rock song like AC/DC's *You Shook Me All Night Long* or Sly and the Family Stone's *Dance to the Music* will almost always get people involved in an "air band." Large foam hands are great for waving in the air and attracting attention. Sunglasses work well in a number of ways. First, they look cool. Secondly, when the room appears a bit darker, inhibitions fade away. There's a direct correlation between the level of visible light and inhibitions.

Confetti simply screams "party!" Kabuki brand shooters feature all-in-one setups that are affordable, easy to use, and easy to clean.

Costumes and Skits

Costumes aren't just for Halloween! The right costume can liven up an entire party. Kokopeli Dan, a very popular DJ here in Florida, loves to dress up as rock stars, cartoon characters, or even dead celebrities simply as an added visual effect. Skits incorporate several people wearing costumes involved in a coordinated and rehearsed entertaining event. When you incorporate costumes and skits into your act, you've effectively branched out into the live entertainment field, and you can demand even more money from your customers.

Group Dances

Group dances and line dances are huge attractions at almost any mobile DJ party, and are still surprisingly effective crowd motivators at many mainstream bars and clubs. Strap on your wireless microphone and jump out on the dance floor to lead your customers in any of the following group dances.

- ❀ "New York, New York"
- ❀ "Shout"
- ❀ "The Alley Cat"
- ❀ "The Bunny Hop"
- ❀ "The Cha Cha Slide"
- ❀ "The Chicken Dance"
- ❀ "The Electric Slide"
- ❀ "The Hokey Pokey"
- ❀ "Macarena"
- ❀ "YMCA"

Sing-a-long

Sing-a-longs aren't necessarily great dance songs, but can be even more powerful at whooping up a crowd. Some of the most popular sing-a-long songs include the following.

- ❀ "Margaritaville"
- ❀ "You've Lost That Loving Feeling"
- ❀ "Paradise by the Dashboard Light"
- ❀ "Old Time Rock n' Roll"
- ❀ "Achy Breaky Heart"

Lead by Example

One of your most difficult tasks will be getting people involved in your games, contests, or dancing. Sometimes it seems impossible to get people going for whatever reason. Maybe the room feels lame. Maybe everyone in the room had a bad day. So how can you spark up some excitement? Do it yourself first!

Announce the event, promotion or contest you plan to run. To get things moving, get your butt out of the DJ booth and get everyone's attention. Push your ego aside for a moment, and show these people exactly what you want them to do. If you're running a wet underwear contest, drop your drawers and have someone pour water on your ass. If you're having a sexiest kiss contest, get out there and suck face with some chick or guy (with his or her advance permission, of course). If you're having a baby bottle sucking contest, fill one up with beer (preferably non-alcoholic) and bottoms up! You are the leader, the entertainer, the star. This is your show, and you are the host. Play the part, and you'll have everyone eating out of your hand. That's what it's all about.

Recognizing the Line

The Bill of Rights of the United States Constitution guarantees the right of free speech. In other countries, your mileage may vary. But in our contemporary American society where everyone's so quick to launch a frivolous lawsuit, you've got to be careful with what you say in public. The envelope of humor and satire will cover most of what you say. You've got a right to say what's on your mind, as long as it's true and doesn't permanently damage anyone's reputation.

If you're not careful, you run the upsetting the wrong person who could make all kinds of trouble for you. I've witnessed situations where DJs bad mouthed their managers or certain VIP customers and were immediately fired. If you do make things up and say something false or unfounded that permanently damages someone's or some company's reputation, you could be held personally liable, and that would suck. As discussed in the Radio chapter, "slander" is publicly saying something that cannot be proven in an effort to injure another's reputation. And remember, saying that someone else said it first won't fly in a court of law.

Recognize the line of what you can say and what you shouldn't say, and don't cross it. You can get pretty outrageous and still be within your boundaries. If you're not sure, don't say it. It's better to be safe than sorry.

MC Tools

You've got to use your voice to take control of your room. People are counting on you to lead them, so you've got to sound authoritative. Simply believe that you are the man, and you'll be the man (or woman). It's really all in your head and totally up to you.

You've got your audience captive in your room. Unlike the TV, the radio, or the Internet, they can't change the channel or switch to something else. The people in the room are forced to watch what you do and listen to what you have to say. For the short while that you've got them in your room, you are the king! Use this to your advantage.

Voice

You can sound authoritative even if you don't have a deep voice. Half of it is your attitude, and the other half is how you project your voice. It's good to use a tape recorder here so that you can actually hear the difference in your delivery. Take a deep breath. Say something normally. Take another breath, and now reach back from where your voice normally originates. You can make your voice sound deeper and more professional by forcing your voice to originate directly from your diaphragm. When you do this, you're physically changing the shape of your vocal cords by constricting them and only allowing the lower tones to come out. This takes weeks of practice, but you'll find it well worth the work.

I once told a mystery DJ to practice his speaking at home. Every time he said something, all that came out was word barf. His delivery was lame and he would always miss key points. If you're not a natural born speaker, suck it up and use a tape recorder to practice at home. Listen to yourself objectively. Evaluate your performance and perfect it.

If you've got an inherently wimpy voice, don't be afraid to use some effects just like wimpy voiced radio people do. I had a wimpy voiced DJ that worked for me—he was funny as all hell but he sounded like a freakin' 10-year-old. I hooked up a voice effects processor between the microphone and the mixer, which added a lower pitch to his voice. Shocked the hell out of people who came up to the DJ booth and heard his real wimpy voice, but it sounded great over the sound system. There's a company called Alesis that makes a processor called Midiverb that works pretty well for just over $200.

When you're speaking to the public, always speak clearly and loudly. There's nothing worse than someone who gets on the microphone and mumbles or speaks too quietly. Use your microphone as a weapon to beat people over the head with what you've got to say! Say it loud and proud. Turn the music down or even off if you need to get your important point across.

While you have the captive attention of your audience, you've got the perfect opportunity to promote upcoming events so that these people will return to your club or use your services again. Let the people know why they need to come back again and again, and why your company or club is better than your competition! It helps to write down what you're going to promote and read it rather than make it up as you go. Promoting yourself or your bar or club is a terrific way to gain respect from management, and also gives you something to say throughout the night.

Image

I can't count how many sloppy DJs I've seen. Unfortunately, most managers, bar patrons, and people in general are very judgmental. Like it or not, you'll probably be evaluated within seconds of meeting someone based solely on the way you look and present yourself. If you think you're going to earn big bucks with greasy hair and a Beavis and Butthead t-shirt, you'd better prepare for a career in the fast food business instead. Think about it... you're attempting to project presence, star quality. I'm sure you've seen well-dressed people that walk into a room and just looked a step above everyone else. You can do it too—all you've got to do is invest a few bucks into some nice, fashionable clothing. Splurge and pick up some nice collared shirts and a sweet sport coat or two. Go to a hair stylist and do something cool with your hair. You should consistently be one of the best-groomed and best-dressed people in your room. It's part of your overall package.

Working Directly with Management and Owners

If you're serious about a career in this business, you'll need to start a direct, professional relationship between you and your managers and owners. If you're not doing this already, simply ask them to start a weekly or bi-weekly meeting to discuss changing trends in the music industry and promotions for the upcoming month. Keep the meetings as short as possible, and try to have them at the manager's convenience. And make sure you don't let these meetings pass. Remind your managers that this meeting is very important to the overall operations of the club and bar. This will show them that you're absolutely serious about their business and your job.

Becoming a Promotions Coordinator

As you begin to invent and arrange promotions and prizes, you will begin to become your club's Promotions Coordinator. Ask your manager if you can officially have this title, and begin to have all promotional inquiries sent directly to you. Put this on your business cards and on your resume!

Working with Local Purveyors

Your beer distributors and liquor promotions people are in your club or bar all the time. If you don't know them personally, ask the manager to set up a meeting between you and those people. They do promotions for a living, so they're the perfect source for some new promotions and especially prizes.

Cooperative Promotions

Most clubs have stores or a strip mall somewhere in their vicinity. You'll probably run into people that work and shop at these places in your bar. If you think about it, there's probably something that these stores or businesses can offer for prizes in exchange for you advertising them and mentioning their name in your bar! Contact the managers or owners of these businesses, and give them a detailed, well thought out proposal showing them what you want to do and why you think it would be a good idea. If your room is big enough, you can host concerts or events in conjunction with your local radio station in exchange for advertising. This gets your name and your bar's name all over the radio, which doesn't hurt while building your popularity! You can watch and learn from other cooperative arrangements in unrelated businesses for ideas.

Presence

Madonna appears somewhere and thousands of people are in awe. Will Smith walks on stage and everyone cheers. Some hot babe or buff dude walks into the room and everyone stops to stare. These people haven't said or done a thing yet, but people are taken aback just from their mere being. Presence is the power of being perceived as a leader, or being recognized as someone different or special. You, as a successful DJ, must emanate presence. Presence comes from being confident and comfortable with your job as an entertainer of the masses. Some people have it naturally; some people earn it over years with hard work and sacrifice.

If you weren't naturally gifted, hope is not necessarily lost. You can project a "quasi-presence." It's almost like acting; being someone who you're really not. It takes a little rehearsal work, but almost anyone can do it. All you have to do is pick a celebrity who you admire, preferably an entertainer of some sort. Study them and read about them. Get to know his or her personality as well as you can. Then find the parts of their persona that you admire the most and emulate them. Pretend you're the rock star, the actor, the superhero. Don't do a stupid and obvious imitation of the celebrity; just borrow the strong parts that make these people admirable.

Being confident is really being a good actor, because we're all basically made of the same stuff. Will Smith is nothing more than blood and bone with an attitude, but he had an opportunity to rise. Well, you, too, now have an opportunity to become a star. Be confident, you have been chosen to be the star of tonight's show! Take your confidence and presence with you to your gig.

Much of dealing with unavoidable problem situations, like a skipping song or a clipped amplifier, comes with experience. Unfortunately, I wasn't prepared to deal with these situations the first time they happened to me. I usually thought about what happened later that night, and figured out how I should have handled it. How could I put a spin on these mistakes to make them look like they were part of my show?

Simple. When a CD or record skipped, I always had the next song cued up. While the song was still skipping, I would announce that this was the new Puff Daddy remix. I'd then roll my next song, and everyone would laugh about it. If an amplifier clipped or overheated, which happened a lot when I worked those cheap cheesy clubs for that DJ service, I'd turn up the lights and make it look like I turned the music down to put on a contest or a drink special. After the first time that happened, I had a meeting with my manager and cleared an emergency drink special or contest in case of such a situation. This way my manager was aware that his equipment sucks and also that I'm not an idiot.

Another thing you shouldn't do is stop and correct yourself after saying something you realize is inaccurate. Unless it's something material, such as a date of a promotion, the price of a drink special, or something that everyone else would obviously know, just let it disappear. More people will realize you screwed up if you stop and correct yourself. If the mistake is too obvious or material, follow it up with something else that is obviously a stretch of the truth as soon as you can. This makes it look like you were joking around! Then follow it up with the correct information. To totally turn a mistake around to make it look like it was part of your show is true power.

Just knowing these easy remedies for the above situations has already given you a big edge in the DJ industry! Practice these, and think about strange things that have happened or could happen to you while being a club or bar DJ. What could you do to make the incident look like it's part of your show? As you gain more and more experience, you'll learn even more of these secrets. Eventually, you'll automatically know exactly how and when to cover your ass.

Material

To be perceived as charming, you'll need charming material. Relevant comments, relevant music, and relevant contests and activities are all a must for any interactive DJs repertoire. Where do you get this material? From popular movies, TV shows, radio promotions, and your own ingenuity. Watch what people do to get excited and think, "How can I fit that into my shows?"

Making a Name for Yourself

Bars and clubs spend a small fortune on advertising and promotions, but don't get all they should get from it. In most cases, clubs are missing the most important opportunity of all. I've always stressed that in a club, the person with his or her finger of the pulse of the customer is the DJ. So why not have the DJ write and perform the advertising?

One of my pet peeves over the years is the really lousy job local radio stations do when producing club and bar radio commercials. It's like they consider DJs to be second-class and don't take us seriously. Most radio jocks play their assigned playlists, take their commercial breaks, and really have no clue what's going on in the real world. Radio sales people and production people are even worse. And guess who's writing your club's commercials? Did you wonder why many of them all sound alike?

Face it, this business is show business. You are tonight's scheduled performer. People are counting on you to show them a good time. There are a number of reasons that clubs should promote the DJ's name in all of their advertising, mainly to create a miniature celebrity. It's giving chicks one more reason to choose your club over hanging at the mall, going to the movies, or patronizing your competition. They have a need to tell their friends that they met "DJ _____," who they've all heard on the radio. It makes them cool. And we all know where the girls go, the guys will follow.

Eventually your name will become as prominent as the radio DJs that your local radio station sends to your club for special promotions. Your managers usually pay these people $100/hour for a minimum of two hours. That's a whole shift for most club jocks! Have your manager put that money back into the advertising budget and get some more people through that front door.

Tell your manager that you want a crack at your club's next radio spot. You can probably write advertising that sounds different and better. Go to the station and perform it yourself. It will sound better and work better than the cookie cutter crap they're doing. Promoting the DJ on-air really works. It's strange, but I still have people come up to me and say they listen to me on a radio station I'm not even on all the time.

If you're running a mobile DJ outfit, make sure you use your name in all your advertising. You have the power to make your name a household word. Remember, if you position yourself as a celebrity, people will gladly pay more to hire you personally for their next private affair.

Value Added

Seems they'll let any nut with a few records or CDs become a DJ today. And with all this competition, it's getting harder to keep a well paying DJ job, not to mention to get one. So what are we real DJs to do?

You need to take your superior experience, draw from it, and create an edge for yourself. It's self-marketing in its simplest form. Working for companies with their eyes fixated on their bottom lines, I've learned to look for that one extra reason they should keep the real Chuck Fresh at my high hourly rate rather than hour rather than some other boring schmuck who'll charge a fifth of what I wan.

It'll take some thinking on your part. A good starting point is your resume. What have you done with your life so far? What kind of training do you have? What are you good at that could give you an edge? It doesn't necessarily have to be DJ related. Figure this out, then ask yourself the toughest question: how can you translate that talent to something useful in a bar or club?

I've had all kinds of strange jobs in my short life, from washing dishes to fixing computers to singing in a band to producing television commercials. I've taken at least one small piece from each of those jobs and incorporated it into my DJ responsibilities. I've helped bus tables at the end of busy nights. I've rewired sound systems at no charge. I've brought in a ladder and changed bulbs and cleaned intelligent lights. I've created monthly calendars and newsletters on my home computer at no extra charge to my clients. I've written and produced radio commercials for my clients. I've performed live music on off-nights and filled in for late bands. And in addition to leaping tall buildings in a single bound, I've produced in-house promotional video and audio shorts in my spare time. Managers *love* this type of spontaneous help.

Still have no idea what you could value-add to your DJ services? My biggest hit ever was my CLUB TV system. I carried a Sony Mavica digital camera and a laptop computer to the club one night, took some pictures, and had them on our TV monitors intertwined with promotional slides within minutes. The manager was so impressed that I got a free trip to Hawaii! Since many of you full-time DJs will be working 4- or 5-hour days, take some of that leisure time and add something extra to your service. A small investment can add thousands of dollars in future business.

Promoting New Talent

The artist who approaches you with her brand new song just might be the next Mariah Carey—you never know! And wouldn't that be cool if they got famous and remembered you played their song when they were nobody, so they feel they owe you a favor.

When new artists approach you about playing their music, don't instantly blow them off. Be polite, and check their songs out first. If you can't hear it at the club, promise them that you'll take it home and call them the next day to tell them when you're going to feature their song. If they ask you why, tell them that your club has a policy of fully previewing all new music to make sure that if fits within your club's format. Tell them that you need to make sure that the song doesn't skip, and you need to ensure that the song doesn't play for a minute and then break into some vile spoken words that could get your club sued. I've personally done that to one of my DJs as a joke on an off night, under controlled circumstances of course. Pretty damn funny. Ask them to audition for a live show at your club if their music fits your format. If they do become a big star, they'll remember you as the cool person that featured their song way back when. That person may be inclined to throw you a favor a year or two down the line by making a special no-charge return performance in the middle of their world tour. How cool would that make you look?

If the song totally sucks, politely tell them that this music doesn't fit within your strict music format, and thank them for thinking of you. Wish them tons of luck with their CD.

Spotting New Trends

To stay fresh, you've got to be aware of what's going on, because your customers will be on top of it. In your role as an entertainer, you are held responsible for keeping on top of and incorporating popular current entertainment trends that are relevant to your show. Watch the news, read magazines. Stay on top of things or you'll be history! Inventing new promotions Use your head. Take chances. Try anything that you can think of. Make things up that make no sense, because they're often the most fun. A good source of promotions is college and frat parties because they do all kinds of crazy things that normal people wouldn't think of. Your wackiest idea could be the next national smash!

Group Dynamics

In my early days as a DJ, I often missed something very important. The entertainment business is a very dynamic business. Just like a TV show, you've got to stay exciting, or you're in trouble. Even if you say or do something once or twice a shift that gets a crowd hootin' and hollerin', you've made a difference that a jukebox or a computer can't do. You've let people know that you are there to entertain them. You've shown them your presence. You've established yourself as a leader. And that's the beginning of a successful career.

I visited a strip of nightclubs along the Riverwalk in San Antonio. One club had a DJ tucked away from everyone. I looked around the room and saw about 20 people kind of staring blankly into space. No one was dancing until the completely polluted bunch of idiots I happened to be with eventually managed to fall on to the dance floor and make fools of themselves. Earlier that night, we were all at a bar with "dueling pianos." This same Tuesday night, there were about 200+ people singing, screaming, and standing on their chairs totally involved in the action.

DJs sometimes think they can be successful by just playing music and keeping a dance floor. If you think your DJ can just look pretty and play good music, your days are numbered. DJs, bands and other entertainers need to get people involved in the show, either directly through some of the promotions described in this book, or indirectly through clever things we're learning to do behind the scenes. Lowering the volume during the hooks in a song so people sing along works well. Mentioning people's names on the microphone is excellent. Dueling pianos once a month is total audience involvement and is a great idea if it can work in your type of venue.

There are hundreds of sneaky things you can do to create excitement and energy without saying a single word or spending any money. In this section, check out some of the tricks we've used to create energy.

Lights, or Lack Thereof

In one of my clubs, a frequent occurrence was the accidental raising of the lights in the bar. Everyone looked around to see if something's wrong. What this had actually done is created an event in the room. It's stirred things up and created energy. If people were starting to get bored and were thinking of leaving, this little infusion of energy might be enough to keep them there to buy another drink. And if many people buy more drinks, your club's bottom line increases. And the more money the bar makes because of you, the more you can ask for.

Silence

Never underestimate the power of silence. People have been in your bar for a few hours and they've grown accustomed to the loud music coming from your jukebox or your DJ. Suddenly remove that music, you've got their attention. You've created an event, and that is energy. Now you've got their attention, you can utilize that instant to promote an upcoming event, tonight's drink special, or any other message that's important enough to increase sales.

Strangeness

Sometimes when the room is a little slow and needs a little shaking, one of my managers would come in and start playing with the DJ equipment. His favorite toy seemed to be the pitch control on my Denon CD player, which slows down or speeds up the song by moving the pitch slider. Songs sound very strange when they're continuously sped up or slowed down by up to 8%. But people notice this. Sure, they looked at him like they wanted to kick his butt, and if he kept messing with the song they probably would have, but he got their attention. He didn't even realize that he created energy!

Unexpected Downshift

In most dance club settings, there's a constant beat of music for hours at a time. This is a sometimes annoying skill known as "beat mixing" music, or blending one song into another so it seems like there was no change between songs. Like anything, constant repetition causes a monotonous tone in the room which sucks all the energy out. Most DJs can't comprehend this concept and are always overly concerned about keeping a constant dance floor. I remember the one night in 1989 when this became apparent to me. I changed my entire approach to this DJ thing. During an audition for a nightclub, I stopped a song in its tracks and played "The Jeffersons" TV theme. The assistant manager ran up and screamed at me like

I was a total idiot. I yelled back "HELL WITH THE DANCE FLOOR; THEY'LL COME BACK WHEN I'M GOOD AND F*ING READY FOR THEM TO COME BACK." People were so energized that they started singing and dancing on chairs. Against his decision, I got the job. I hear he's working at the local Best Buy now.

Getting a Little Free Help

While you're doing all these big promotions, you'll probably need some help coordinating everything. Every bar and club I've ever worked has regulars that hang out every night. It's a fairly safe assumption that most of these people have no life, and your club comprises their entire social life. The nicest thing you could possibly do for them is to include them in your show!

Enlist their help in exchange for you mentioning their name as part of your team and teaching them the DJ or promotions business. You probably won't have to pay these people for their help since they'll be elated that you're paying special attention to them. These people already know the room and how it works, so they're probably the most qualified helpers you can find. I've even eventually hired some of these people as DJs as their skills progressed.

Contests and Promotions

To make a lot of noise and get recognized as a leading DJ, you'll need some really cool ass promotions. Leave the lame stuff like the Limbo or Closest Birthday contests for weaker DJs. You're gonna want to do stuff that raises the hair on the back of your next, like Baby Bottle Beer Sucking or Shocking Roulette. This stuff gets people's attention! Borrow what you can, and even invent some. A great source for some wild stuff is one of my other books called "Wild Party Contests." Much of this stuff can be adapted for private parties and/or radio shows.

Of course you'll need to tailor your contests specifically to your client and their audience. If you've got kids in the room, you obviously don't want to do the Wild Vibrator Races contest. There are plenty of things you can do to get people involved.

Kids' Games

For the kiddies under 12, there are a bunch of contests that will keep them busy and hopefully away from your expensive equipment. A few of these are:

Coke and Pepsi

Practically anyone who's been to a mitzvah has seen or played the game "Coke and Pepsi", so they'll often expect to play it. You'll set up two lines of an equal amount of people on each side of the dance floor. You'll label one side "Coke", and the other side "Pepsi". You'll play some fun music in the background—I actually made a remix of Coke and Pepsi jingles from old TV commercials. When you call "Coke" or "Pepsi", that side must run to the other side and sits on the knee of their partner. The last person to successfully sit on someone else's knee is "out", and is removed from play. The object is to find the fastest couple through elimination and award them a prize. In his book "DJ Games", Marc Pears suggests mixing things up by using other names and other things to do, like saying "Doctor Pepper" or "Seven Up", and assigning various tasks with those names. For instance, you would explain that if you call

"ROOT BEER" both sides would have to run to the middle and give a "high 5" to their partner and quickly return to their spot, with the last couple to return being disqualified. Or, perhaps saying "Seven Up" means both sides must exchange places, again, with the last straggler disqualified. It's a silly but fun game that kids seem to enjoy.

Huggy Bear

"Huggy Bear" is another silly elimination game. All players are invited to the dance floor. You'll play a song and tell everyone to dance. Most people won't really dance, they'll all kind of stand in a position because they know exactly what they're supposed to do. You'll then stop the music and say a random number like "Five!", and your contestants must get into groups of that number. Whoever is not in a group with five people is "out". You keep doing this, obviously with numbers that work for the amount of contestants you have left. Obviously, you can't call "TEN!" if you've only got nine people left.

The Balloon Relay

Blow up some small balloons. Get three or four groups of two or more to play. Line up the couples at one end of the dance floor. Directly across from each couple, place one of the balloons on the floor. Once you say go, the contestants run one at a time to sit on the balloon until it pops. The first group to pop all their balloons wins.

Mummy Wrap

Divide kids into pairs, with one the Mummy and the other the Mummy Wrapper. Give each wrapper a roll of toilet paper or crepe paper streamer. On the word "Go!" have the wrappers race to see who can wrap up their mummy first. The game is tricky because the faster they try to wrap, the more the tissue will tear, causing them to keep restarting!

Teen Games

Teenagers are a little more difficult because they're in that weird "cool" stage and it's hard to get them involved in anything. Boys are much worse than girls. The following few games seem to get teens to crawl out of their shells and get into the action.

Basketball Shoot

Every party should have a regulation basketball hoop somewhere in your arsenal. It takes up the least amount of physical space of all the popular professional sports, and it just opens your gig up to so many cool things you can do. If you don't have the space or ceiling clearance for a regulation hoop, you can adjust the games and prizes to fit a shorter, adjustable hoop, or even a cheap, smaller kid-sized hoop.

These promotions are based on a combination of skill and luck. Hand out numbered tickets to each guest who wants to be involved. Once an hour, call out a random ticket number. The person with that ticket gets to take one shot for a big prize. Chances are the person you selected probably won't make the shot, but you never know, so be ready! Make sure the person who actually got the ticket is the person who takes the shot by writing their first name on the back of the ticket and the receipt ticket. Do this to avoid "pass-along"; where the person with the ticket passes it along to the budding college star player who happens to be sitting next to him or her.

Prizes for this promotion should be fairly generous to create a big buzz.

Here are just a few of the things you can do with that hoop. Alternate them throughout the night for a better variety! Feel free to mix them up or come up with your own based on these:

* Slam dunk for big bucks.

  Choose a contestant from the numbered tickets. Tell this person that if he or she can slam dunk a regulation ball in a regulation hoop, he or she will win some obscene dollar amount. Since you've got to be at least 6 feet tall with an amazing vertical jump to slam, chances are very slim that you'll randomly choose someone will actually be able to do this, but you never know! Coax them on anyway for the chance at the big dollar amount. If you've got an adjustable hoop, you can bring it down a foot for really short people or women if you'd like for some extra excitement to get your crowd going. Be ready to pay if you have to.

* Air Hamilton.

  Your contestant must make one basket from a spot you've pre-designated in the room to win a ten dollar bill. Don't make the shot too tough; you'll want someone to win because winning creates excitement.

* Three points for a prize.

  Measure out a regulation three point radius (about 19 feet from the center of the basket) and mark it off with masking tape. If you're faking it in a smaller room with a toy basket, wing it. In a bar or club situation, if the person with the chosen raffle ticket makes the three pointer, he or she gets to buy up to X-amount of people beers or well drinks on the house. Have some specially printed drink tickets available for the shot maker to give out to the people he or she chooses if the three-pointer was successful. In a party situation, you can offer some other free gift, such as a gift certificate or something, to the shooter — or all your guests. It makes the shooter a hero, and gets the whole room cheering together collectively.

* Reverse basket.

  Here's an unexpected twist; the person with the correct numbered ticket must make a reverse basket using a small helium-filled balloon! Have the person stand directly underneath the basket and release a balloon that will obviously fit through the hoop. If the balloon goes through or gets stuck in the hoop, he or she gets a nice prize. It's pretty tough to do, especially if you've got a strong ventilation system blowing around in your room.

* Half court challenge.

  Here's your home run, if there was such a thing in basketball! You'll need a big room with a pretty high ceiling to pull this off effectively. Find a spot in the room that's about at regulation half-court distance (about 43 feet from the backboard), and randomly choose a contestant from the numbered tickets. This person gets one chance to sink a basket from that point in the room. If he or she makes the shot, they win a big prize. Half court shots are nearly impossible for non-basketball types, but as we've seen on TV, they can happen.

If he or she makes the shot, you can supplement this promotion with the "betcha can't do it again clause"—if he or she chooses to do this, it's a double or nothing situation. This is when things really get interesting—your crowd will go absolutely nuts. Offer a pretty big prize like a portable TV or CD player or something, and be ready to double it in the rare instance where you may have to. You can also scale this down for smaller rooms using toy basketball hoops, but try not to make it too easy.

❋ Backwards basket.

When I was eight years old, I didn't have the arm strength to make a traditional basket. So I figured out that if I turned my butt to the basket and launched the ball over my head like a catapult, I could actually make a basket! Choose a spot in your room and demonstrate if you have to. Warning #1: the ball could end up flying anywhere, so make sure there's nothing breakable in its path. Warning #2: this type of basket is pretty easy to do, so don't give away the house!

❋ Minimum number of free throws (consecutive or timed).

There are two ways to do this. You can choose a minimum number of consecutive baskets your contestant must make from the free-throw line. Obviously, if they miss the first one, the game is over. Depending on how generous you're feeling, a good number to start with is three.

Or you can choose to let your contestant keep shooting to make as many shots as he or she can make in 30 seconds. If they meet your minimum number of baskets, they win a prize.

Or, you can choose as many people as you like, and have them each shoot for 30 seconds one at a time, and the person who makes the most baskets in that time wins.

Have people on either side of the basket return the ball to the contestant as quickly as possible for the fairest chance to win. In a nightclub or bar situation, this contest is a good spot for you to give out a bunch of small prizes to add more pressure on the contestant.

❋ Select free throw.

This contest allows the person with the selected numbered ticket to pass it on to anyone they choose to. If they make a basket with the free throw, both the person who had the ticket and the person selected to make the shot both win a prize. To make this more difficult, combine it with number seven above.

❋ Bounce basket.

Selected contestant must make a basket by bouncing the basketball off the floor first. Contestants are limited to one bounce only.

❋ Sit down basket.

Selected contestant must make a basket while sitting in a chair at a point you've pre-selected. It's difficult to do, since you don't get the benefit of using your back and legs! We used to call this "Wheelchair Basketball" until we were yelled at by some oversensitive knuckleheads. People who are actually using wheelchairs love this variation, and are pretty darn good at it!

All these variations are possible, and some are downright easy! If you're feeling really generous, you could give your contestant up to three tries to make a shot. And if you're the gambling type, you could offer a "double or nothing" shot if someone makes their first attempt. Just make sure you're not going to give away the house for a difficult shot, or you just might find yourself homeless. Your cost: Applicable prizes, plus a kid-sized hoop for about $40-$75, or a full-sized hoop for about $250 and up.

Music Trivia

Mix up your questions on current hot artists. Jot down little known facts about current artists on TV, in magazines or newspapers, or on the Internet. Make your trivia questions fun, like, "How many pounds did J-Lo lose on her Atkins diet?"

Baby Bottle Sucking

This is one of the oldest Spring Break promos anywhere, but we're still amazed at the number of people who have never heard of this. It's a nice medium impact promotion where you can involve a whole bunch of people all at once. The whole thing takes less than three minutes, but gets the crowd energized. And this contest is very inexpensive to run, and you can do it anywhere. We've even pulled this contest off in bars without entertainment.

You'll need about a dozen cheap plastic baby bottles that you can get at any discount store, enough non-alcoholic beer to fill them all, a pair of scissors, and some towels. Fill a bunch of baby bottles up with the non-alcoholic beer. We've seen this done with real beer (not mentioning any names here) only to later find that it was a direct violation of that state's liquor control laws (whoops)! You should enlarge all of the holes of the nipples with a pair of scissors so that this contest will not take forever. Line up your contestants together. The first to completely finish the entire bottle without spilling wins the prize. Keep the towels close in case there's a mess. Have someone designated as a judge in case there's a close call.

Your cost: about $30 for empty baby bottles and some beer. Good prizes for this contest include cash, gift certificates, or a large baby bottle! Let your contestants keep the baby bottles too. It's very amusing to see that most of your contestants will use the baby bottle for their beer the rest of your party. Makes for some good pictures.

Inflatable Games

There are many cool games you can rent like the Flypaper Game, Human Bowling, Sumo Wrestling and others that will keep your teen customers busy.

Games for All Ages

Here are some tried-and-true contests that everyone knows, and almost anyone can do.

Limbo Contest

Get a long bamboo pole at your local hardware superstore or gardening supply center. It should be bamboo to represent the islandy character of this game. You could use a long wooden dowl or even a broomstick in a pinch, but get yourself some bamboo for authenticity.

Yell out to your crowd that you're about to have a Limbo Contest. Have folks line up on the far side of the dance floor. Enlist one or two people to help hold the Limbo stick. The correct way to hold a limbo stick is to simply let it rest on that spot of flesh located right between your thumb and fore finger. You don't want to handle the stick tightly because you want someone to eventually win.

You'll then announce you're going to begin. At first, the limbo stick will be very high, tall enough for most people to walk under. Remember who the first person is. When that person comes around for the second round, you and your trusty partners will lower the bar roughly six inches. Eventually, you'll work your way down to less than 12" off the floor, and only boneless snake people (and small children) can pass under.

The only rules are that you can't touch the bar at anytime. If you nick it, scrape it, whatever... you're supposed to be disqualified.

Hula Hoop Contest

Toss out two to four hula hoops to anyone who wants to participate in your hula hoop contest! Men, women and kids all love to hula hoop for money. Here's how it works.

All contestants must stay within their box drawn on the floor until the music stops. When the music starts all contestants must start to hula and cannot touch the hoop with their hands again until the music stops. When a hula hoop touches the floor the contest is over for that participant, but they must remain in the box until the music stops and not disturb the remaining contestants.

The difficulty factor could increase from Double Hula Hooping, to Double Hula Hooping on one foot, to hopping on one foot while Double Hula Hooping, if necessary, to determine a winner. Additional difficulty factors may be added if three medalists cannot be determined.

Twist Contest

The Twist is more like a fun group participation event than a contest. But some folks will still ask for it, so be ready. Find up to four contestants who would like to play. Have groups, couples come to the dance floor, and give them a minute or two to freshen up. Have your couples get on the dance floor one at a time. Play Chubby Checker's "The Twist" song, and give each couple about a minute to do their routine. Whoever you or your audience decides to be the best couple is wins the contest. Optionally, for a quicker contest, just have all the couples dance at once, and hand select your favorite couple as the winner.

Horse Racing

We saw this promotion for the first time on a Royal Caribbean cruise ship. It was a great contest because it involved six people all at once, and the whole crowd cheered for their favorite contestant. All you need is three dice, six horses (they used a flat, painted, plywood horse head on a stick that was held up and moved by volunteers), and some kind of equally spaced markings on the floor (can be chalk or masking tape) with ten evenly marked spaces with a finish line at the end.

The game was played by having the host shake up the three small dice in a cage. You'll have three sides of the dice facing up, and each of those numbers will correspond to one of the horses. For instance, the dice may land on one, three, and six. This result means that horses #1, #3 and #6 all may advance one space on the marked spaces on the floor, getting closer to the finish line with each space advanced. If two or three dice had the same roll, that particular horse would move two or three spaces closer to the finish line.

The key to the success of this contest is a strong host. On the ship, the MC gave each of the six horses a funny name, such as "the famous Chinese horse named "Ah So," or the Mexican champion horse named "Taco," or the All-American favorite, "Pork and Beans, the horse you never want to follow."

Variations include large, oversized foam dice actually rolled by spectators would be an exciting enhancement to this game. We also thought some kind of horse head costume worn by each contestant would cause some heavy hootin' and hollerin'.

Your cost: A couple thin sheets of plywood cut to look like a horse head that's glued or screwed to a 2x4 or some other stick, some paint and your artistic talent, some large dice and some decent prizes shouldn't run more than $50-$100.

Thumb Wrestling Championships

So mud wrestling, arm wrestling and sumo wrestling might be a little much for your crowd. Here's something you can get the average Joe to do! You can even put men against women in this contest. The object is to find the ultimate thumb wrestler in your room.

Start with two, four or eight groups of two contestants to keep things simple. Just like most of us did when we were kids, have your contestants interlock their right hands with their thumbs exposed and ready to go, as shown in the illustration. They touch thumbs to the opposite sides of the other person's hand three times, then come out wrestling! The object is to manage to hold the other person's thumb down for a count of three, using only your thumb. The only rule is that they must all keep their hands flat on the table. Separate each semifinal by about 20-30 minutes to build up the excitement of your final competition.

At the finals, stop the music and incite all kinds of fanfare. Mention that you have a really cool prize for the official thumb wrestling champion. If you've got the budget or a hot looking lady available, have her act as a model (or ring girl!) to present the winner with a printed winner banner and a small trophy. Silly over-indulgence in ceremony is what makes this contest really fun.

Your cost: If you're throwing a big event, you can order hundreds of the Thumb Wrestling rings with your own logo on them! Add your prizes, maybe even a model for your "ring girl," and a small engraved trophy would be a sweet add-on.

More Quick Fun for All Occasions

These contests are used as quick hits to raise the level of excitement without bringing everyone down for an extended period of time.

* Closest birthday

  Person or people with a birthday today wins. If there are no current birthdays, the closest to today's date wins. Birthdays are one of the big reasons some people come to a party, so it's always good to make a big fuss about them. Prepare to issue multiple prizes!

* Shortest man

  If early in the night, this works better if you have a measuring tape and measure them individually out of the spotlight rather than stopping everything to measure them together. If late at night, do it in front of everyone! Better prizes given to the less fortunate. Mini-Me's come out of the woodwork!

❀ Shortest woman

Similar to the shortest man contest, but not as brutal.

❀ Tallest woman

Men dig this. We've always wondered why tall women always wear 3" heels making them ridiculously tall... anyway, line up your volunteers and measure your contestants without shoes.

❀ Baldest man

Men hate this. We've even counted the number of hairs left on people's head. This is hilarious!

❀ Biggest ears

Everyone with big ears hates this, but it's a very funny game. Use a ruler to measure from the top of the ear to the bottom of the earlobe, or the total width of the ear. Award a nice prize to encourage participation. We usually offered $20.00.

❀ Pointiest nose

What you're looking for here is the most pronounced angle of a nose. Many noses are close to a 90-degree right angle, but there are folks with strange out of the ordinary slants that warrant a prize. We actually measured angles with a professional contractor's protractor/anglefinder.

❀ Funkiest Nail Designs

Chicks totally dig people making a fuss over their nails. They've got all kinds of funky stuff on them like rings, rhinestones, jewels, and all kinds of crap. Award a prize for the funkiest design, like a free manicure. A good variation is the funkiest toenail design.

❀ Longest Nails

Measure up those nails and award a prize for the longest one. Hopefully, a woman will win this. But we've seen men come darn close.

❀ Coolest Belly Ring

These are everywhere now! They've got danglers, hoops, chains, blinkers, and all kinds of other cool stuff. Entice people to show their midriff and allow the audience to judge the winner.

❀ Roots

Find the woman in the room with the most prominent hair roots of a different color showing, and award her some valuable hair products.

Good Prizes

Don't skimp on prizes! If you want your dog to do a trick, you've got to condition him to think that there's some kind of benefit for doing that trick. Pavlov hit it right on the nose, because people are the same exact way. Prize values should increase as does the difficulty or level of embarrassment of the contest or promotion. A better prize almost always guarantees a better level of participation, which is something that a DJ will appreciate immensely. I'm still amazed at what drunk nightclub patrons will do for a stupid t-shirt. Here are a few nice prizes that will encourage group participation:

* CASH!
  It's an investment. This is the most effective prize, and the one people talk about the most.

* A nice collared shirt or a jacket with your company or club's logo embroidered on it. It's free advertising!

* Dinner for two at a local restaurant.
  If you've got a local restaurant you deal with or a restaurant in the facility in which you're working, you could work out a trade for promotional mentions.

* A $50-$100 gift certificate to a local fashion clothing store (great for men and women).

* A complete makeover, nail design, hair appointment, or tanning coupons.

* How about $25-$50 gift certificates to a music store?
  Everyone likes music!

* A limousine ride to and from a restaurant or from a bar on a future visit (offnights only). This is a neat prize that you can usually get for free for mentioning the limo company.

* A promotional trip for two to an island.
  There are companies on the Internet that specialize in these bare-bones trips. Be careful and read the fine print.

Drinking on the Job?

Here's a topic sure to stir up all kinds of controversy. Many club managers in hotel clubs or chains totally forbid the DJ from drinking. However, I've seen those same managers hand deliver beers to members of a band performing at the same club! What's up with this double standard? I approached a particular manager on this situation, but he was speechless. He could not explain it.

This was the thing that initially sparked my curiosity about the differences between the level of respect that bands, comedians and DJs get. One of the clubs I worked allowed the DJ a strict three-drink house tab every night. They made it clear that if a DJ ever got intoxicated beyond the point of being able to perform, he would be fired immediately. This made me feel like they respected me as an entertainer, and it increased my respect for that management team.

I absolutely do not recommend drinking on the job because it slows your reflexes, and you need to be quick on your feet. But some DJs I know feel they need a drink or two to get a slight buzz on so that they're at the same level as the customers they're trying to entertain. It eliminates their inhibitions and allows them to fully express themselves, so that they can be crazy and totally lead a crowd.

It's much better to be up front about this situation so you don't have to risk your job by sneaking around. Avoid having the waitress or bartender sneak you drinks for several reasons. They all talk behind the bar, so there are no secrets there. If someone gets pissed at you for some reason, you may end up getting yourself and the person who served you fired. Also remember that you'll probably have to drive home at the end of the shift, and drunk driving is plain stupid. You could end up in jail or worse. If you do have permission to have a drink or two on the job, be responsible about it. Do it early in the night and stop long before your shift is over.

8

DJ RESOURCES

In this quickly changing business, you'll quickly learn that information is king. You'll need to know as much as you can not only to stay on top of current music, techniques, and trends; but also to create and maintain a successful business.

The Internet is an amazingly instant and powerful channel that can help you tremendously as a relevant DJ. There are hundreds if not thousands of websites dedicated to DJ art and the DJ business where you can find anything from how to disassemble a turntable to a video with your hero proudly displaying today's hottest scratch. You can almost instantly find out which songs are ranking high on your local radio station's playlist, and what songs your competing mobile DJ companies are playing to make their crowds go wild. And you can find a rare record or CD that you'd probably have no way of finding before the net. I remember finding Colonel Abrams' "Trapped" 12" single on eBay for a friend of mine. "Trapped" was a fairly popular club song in the late 1980s that I had since given away. I looked for this record for about a year and finally found it being sold by a small record store in California. Had it not been for the Internet, I probably would have given up.

DJ Magazines routinely cover new innovations and important trends in our industry. You can learn marketing techniques, the latest dance steps, and make equipment purchasing decisions based on preliminary reviews in these magazines.

DJ Associations are also a useful resource for education and business tasks. Monthly newsletters review important extraneous factors that could affect the DJ business.

The DJ industry is finally showing signs of maturity as evidenced by the growing attendance at trade shows and increased membership in professional DJ associations. It's an exciting time to be a DJ!

DJ Websites

Although there is no "official" DJ website or repository, yet, you can get a strong sense of what you're looking for by simply comparing the information among several unrelated websites. Beware that many individual DJ websites and forums seem to be very opinionated and not objective.

Before I recommend any DJ websites, perhaps the most important website should be mentioned first. You'd probably never guess that it's eBay, the world's largest Internet auction website. If you're looking for equipment, music, lights, games, how-to information, or anything else pertaining to the DJ industry, a great place to start is eBay.

Scanning the listings gives you an idea of what things are worth. In addition to finding used products, many dealers supplement their incomes by selling new products on eBay. Many listings also include personal reflections about certain pieces of equipment. Some sellers will actually list their honest reasons for getting rid of old equipment, what they upgraded to, and why. Remember that since people are trying to sell things, they may be slightly bending the truth a bit, but it still makes some interesting reading. If you're in the market for equipment, check out the eBay listings first.

Pro DJ Web Sites

Here's a list of a few DJ websites of interest. Bookmark these sites in your web browser and sit back in a comfy chair for hours of tantalizing reading.

prodj.com

Prodj.com is one of the first real professional DJ websites. Run by a well-known industry insider, Ryan Burger, there are gobs of useful information mainly for mobile private party DJs. They've got a popular forum, which is a central repository of comments from a handful of DJs who actually have time to comment on things. Of course, Burger has to pay his bills too, so there are tons of links to books, games, and other useful things.

thedjlist.com

This European website attempts to rank the world's nightclub DJs based on its visitors' votes. Profiles including biographies, discographies, and appearances are listed and updated frequently. The fun part is that you can actually list yourself along with a profile and get ranked among the world's best DJs. A friend of mine listed me just for kicks, and I was ranked somewhere towards the bottom of the list last time I looked. Vote for Chuck Fresh and I promise, a digital turntable in every garage!

mobilebeat.com

Home of *Mobile Beat* Magazine and their Top 200 music lists. They've got DJ forums, trade show schedules, some archived articles, and lots of ads.

djzone.net

A website with DJ industry news, DJ games, and general business tips.

djresource.com

My own self-serving website with forums, tips, tricks, and equipment reviews. This is where I'll post the official addendums to this book.

DJ Magazines

And there are several magazines that provide helpful tips for the business-oriented DJ.

Mobile Beat Magazine

Mobile Beat Magazine focuses primarily on the interests of mobile DJs. Their typical audience is probably wedding and party disc jockeys and karaoke hosts. Each issue has reviews of new equipment and music along with marketing tips.

Mobile Beat offers columns such as Play Something We Can Dance To, Crowd Pleasers, Music News, Club View, Tech Talk, Reality Check, Sing-Along Essentials, and Nightmares/Historic Affairs. Their annual *Mobile Beat* Top 200 Song Survey is immensely popular throughout the industry. Special features such as *Mobile Beat*'s Truck, Van and Trailer issue and Best Business card competition are fun reading.

Mobile Beat is available at book stores, pro sound dealers, and by subscription. Visit www.mobilebeat.com to subscribe or for more information.

DJ Times Magazine

DJ Times is more of a well-rounded publication, featuring nightclub DJs, remix DJs, as well as mobile DJs. This magazine usually features an interview with a big-name DJ or producer in each issue. *DJ Times* spends more time on the studio thing, offering reviews of software-based production systems. This magazine realizes the way to become a big-name DJ is to create and release a hit dance song.

DJ Times is widely available at major bookstores, or click over to www.djtimes.com for subscription information.

DJ Mag

England's *DJ Mag* features interviews with the world's top touring DJs as well as their slant on new equipment and DJ innovations. The magazine is rooted in dance music; mostly house, techno, and trance.

This magazine is a bit more difficult to find here in the States, but most larger bookstores in major markets do carry it. More scoop and article excerpts are available on their website at www.djmag.com.

Nightclub and Bar Magazine

NC & B used to have a really nice section for DJs a few years ago, but they've dumped it for whatever reason. This magazine primarily features beverage and management tips for nightclub and bar owners, which may be important to you if you think you've got a future in owning or operating a nightclub or bar.

I've never seen this magazine on a newsstand, but subscriptions are available at www.nightclub.com.

DJ Conventions

Each year, there are at least two giant DJ conventions sponsored by the leading DJ magazines, *DJ Times* and *Mobile Beat*. These are great places to meet other DJs from all over the world and pick their brains about what's working and not working for them. Most conventions offer educational seminars hosted by industry leading DJs as part of their full program. Topics include crowd motivation, games, marketing, operations, equipment, and more. Expect to drop a few hundred bucks between admittance fees and travel expenses.

DJ expos are a neat way to learn about the new trends evolving in the business, ways to make your shows better, and ways to make your life easier. They're basically an educational vacation.

The main part of most business expos is the exhibit floor. In the larger shows, traditionally hosted by one of the DJ magazines, everybody who is anybody in the business has a booth on the exhibit floor. This provides you with a terrific opportunity to see, touch, try and ask questions about all the new cool toys and equipment you've been hearing about. It's hard to make a decision on a piece of equipment until you actually use it, and these shows afford you the opportunity to do so. I hear that the last day of these expos is the day to make some killer purchases, since many vendors would rather sell the equipment at cost rather than pack it up and ship it home. Keep your eyes open.

Expos also have different types of educational "forums." You can learn everything from how to energize your next Bar Mitzvah to advanced scratching to the legal aspects of the DJ contract. Some DJ expos will even teach you new group dances that you can use at your next gig. Field experts are hired to spill their guts to help you better your business. These forums can be extremely helpful to new DJs.

Lastly, these shows get all kinds of DJs from all over the country together, which provides an opportunity for making new friends and networking. You can trade ideas with someone across the country without having to worry about giving away the shop to a local competitor. There are usually all kinds of parties and special events associated with the expo that will provide many opportunities to meet new people. DJ conventions typically offer nightly events showcasing local area nightclubs, which always provide very interesting entertainment. Drunk DJs can be complete idiots, but they're always fun to watch from afar. There are mixing contests, games, and lots of other fun.

Expos are a pretty good idea for the most part. You'll get to learn stuff, network, and get a bunch of free stuff to take home with you. You can also mess around with all kinds of cool equipment, and if you break it, you won't usually have to pay for it. Don't plan to go to more than one or two a year, or the information will become repetitive. Try to space them out. Go somewhere you've never been!

DJ Times magazine and its publisher, Testa Communications, produces one of the more popular conventions annually in Atlantic City, New Jersey. Over four thousand people converge in AC every August to experience the latest and greatest stuff in the DJ industry. See www.djtimes.com for dates and information.

Mobile Beat Magazine holds a convention in Las Vegas in February and in Orlando during the summer months. Three days filled with seminars, exhibits, parties, contests and giveaways are guaranteed to wear you out and force you to take a vacation. See www.mobilebeat.com for more information and upcoming show dates.

The National Association of Music Merchants throws the world's largest trade-only music products show. It's one heck of a party that's attended by over seventy thousand people every January in Anaheim, California; and a summer session held in Nashville. Since this is a mass-market retail show, you'll mingle with the biggest players in the music industry, and enjoy concerts by big-name recording artists. More information is available on the show at www.namm.com.

Every March, thousands of music industry professionals from all over the globe gather in Miami Beach for one of dance music's most anticipated events of the year, the Winter Music Conference. You'll meet international artists, DJs and industry professionals while strolling on South Beach. Every aspect of the industry is represented including the top technological innovators, artists, DJs, producers, radio and video programmers, retailers, distributors, audio manufacturers and many more. Learn the scoop at www.wmcon.com.

Finally, *Nightclub and Bar* Magazine has an annual show that's more geared towards nightclub and bar owners and operators. Several music and lighting companies do attend this show in Las Vegas every March, so there are quite a few things for DJs to play with. Propaganda and more available at www.nightclub.com.

DJ Associations

As with most other businesses, there are organizations that try to capitalize on the benefits of pulling a bunch of people together for a common purpose. Theoretically, that purpose is to better the industry through education and developing common industry standards. Industry standards are important because they help to protect your DJ business. Well known standards give customers certain expectations about what a DJ is supposed to provide, and consumers feel better about dropping a few hundred bucks on something that they can easily understand. For instance, it's an industry standard that most wedding DJs will introduce a bridal party and follow a traditional program of certain events during a wedding reception. A new DJ may not realize this, or worse, choose to ignore it, and this makes all DJs look bad. With so many wannabe DJs running around making up their own rules and making mistakes as they go along, a lack of industry standards confuses people, and it's bad for the industry at large.

Communication is another important responsibility of DJ associations. Contrary to the belief of some DJs, no one person or company knows everything. If all DJs share ideas among each other, we will all benefit in the long run. The Internet has fostered open communication among DJs that simply didn't exist a few years ago, and the benefits are already evident. Reputable DJ associations will offer to mail or at least e-mail their members a newsletter featuring industry trends, current events, and litigation they find relevant to their membership. The costs for this type of communication should be covered in your annual dues.

Professional associations are supposed to do public relations blitzes and industry advertising to better the image of the industry. Better associations will have a web-based searchable database with their members listed as recommended DJs. Proper public relations skills include being the "voice of the industry." Any time a journalist has a question about something pertaining to the DJ industry they should automatically pick up the telephone and call their contact at the DJ association. This will only happen if your DJ association has done their homework and properly introduced themselves to journalists at large.

It's no easy task, but it's a necessity for a reputable DJ association. Industry advertisements include bridal magazines or other national consumer-based magazines that say things along the lines of "all DJs are terrific—and DJs who are part of our association are even more terrific."

Associations also fight for your rights and try to lobby against local, state or national legislation that would make our business harder to do or less profitable. The digital DJ revolution is the latest battle. Hopefully, your DJ association is doing its job fighting this battle for you. Professional associations will often offer to act as a mediator should you and your client have some kind of disagreement over your contract or complaint about your performance. Consumers will often think since it's your association, they won't be objective, so they'll pass. But it's nice to have the offer available.

Finally, groups of large numbers are more easily able to purchase things at a discounted price. You can get better deals on music, equipment, web hosting, car rentals, and other fun stuff with a professional membership card or code. They can help you get started in the nutty process of accepting credit cards. They've got people who have set up DJ accounts before, so the process tends to go smoothly, and at better discount rates.

Better deals on health, dental, equipment, and liability insurances are available at better rates to groups of large numbers as opposed to individual policies. This is the main reason most DJs join associations. Many commercial insurance agencies are reluctant to write policies for DJ, probably because their underwriters don't understand the industry and its inherent risks. Make sure your insurance policy provides coverage for computers, computer peripherals, and trailers, if you use these things. Some less stellar banquet halls are now requiring DJs to carry their own million dollar liability insurance policy with the hall named as a beneficiary, possibly to earn a small discount on their own rates.

There are a bunch of different DJ associations you can choose from. Before you shell out those hundred or so bucks, make sure your money is going to good use. Consider the following items.

* Can you actually speak with a warm body when you really need something, or do you continually get an answering machine? Test them by leaving a message at a strange hour and timing how long it takes them to get back to you.

* Make sure they send you a copy of their by-laws or their charter to get a good idea about what that particular organization is trying to promote. Ask for their "charter" or "organizational statement."

* Ask them for a comprehensive written list of member benefits. Compare them to other associations and choose which one gives you the best benefits for your personal needs. Most DJ associations offer discounts to their members. But are these meaningful discounts you can use, or are they a silly list of crap just written to make the list seem longer? Read them all thoroughly and evaluate carefully.

* Ask for several personal references that you can actually contact. You should actually contact a few of them to ask what their experience has been. Remember that they'll probably only give you references that they think will favor them, so keep this in mind when questioning them about their experiences.

* Ask for samples or copies of industry advertisements. Make sure they're putting your hard earned money to good use.

In most cases, it's fairly easy to join an association. All you need in most cases is a copy of your business contract and about a hundred or so bucks. DJ associations may require you or your DJ company to have one or more of the following:

❋ **You must have a written contract for all events.** This makes sense, since in many states any transaction over a certain dollar amount must have a formal, written contract signed by both the entertainer and the client.

❋ **You must have real business card or some kind of real stationery.** Associations believe that you take your business more seriously if you've invested time, money, and effort in printing expenses.

❋ **You must carry backup equipment.** Any professional DJ should have some kind of reliable backup equipment or plan, because things can and will go wrong. The last thing an association wants is non-reputable fools damaging its reputation.

❋ **You must have a written cancellation policy available on your contract.** Things happen during the planning process on your customer's end. Some couples break up before a wedding. Whether you offer a 100% cancellation guarantee or no refunds at all, reputable businesses make their intentions clear before asking their clients to execute any contract.

❋ **You must pay annual dues.** This is a must for almost all professional associations. Professional associations require rent, telephone lines, staffing, advertising, printing expenses, and other things that cost money and time. You'll want a real, full-time association that's there when you need them, and not just at their convenience. Typically, professional associations charge about $100 a year in dues. Fortunately, professional association dues are tax deductible in most cases.

❋ **You must have insurance.** This requirement has always puzzled me. What does your personal liability have to do with communication, networking, and your reliability? Some DJ associations use this as a qualifier, like the stationery thing, to prove you're a real DJ. Other DJ associations use this as a tactic to sell you insurance, which may or may not be a profit center for the association. Don't sweat it. If you don't have insurance, the association will probably happily take your annual dues anyway.

❋ **You must offer a pre-event consultation.** It makes good business sense to have a pre-event consultation between you and your customer so you're both on the same page regarding expectations. Definitely incorporate this into your routine if you haven't already. But it's a silly qualifying requirement, and it's impossible to prove. Simply nod and try not to smirk as the association tears your annual dues check from your grubby little hands.

❋ **Two or three client references.** Just what your client wants - to be bothered during dinner by some knucklehead sitting behind a desk calling to verify that you're actually the DJ who performed satisfactorily at their wedding reception. Like if you sucked, you wouldn't list your mother, second cousin, and co-worker to cover for you. If I were running a DJ association, I wouldn't think this qualifier was effective or necessary.

CHAPTER 8

❊ List of professional equipment including make and model numbers. Time to break out your copy of the Pro Sound and Stage Lighting catalog (get it free at www.pssl.com—great stuff!) and rattle off some names like Shure, Technics, Rane, QSC, and Community. They don't require serial numbers, although that would be smart and actually helpful in the event of theft. I suppose some associations may actually refuse dues paying members for using home stereo equipment. What the brand and model of your equipment has to do with someone wanting to be involved in an association is beyond me.

At the time of print, these were the more popular DJ associations. New geographically local associations appear to open all the time, so keep your eyes and ears open for an association that's right for you. Visit their websites or call their representatives for more information on their policies.

The American Disc Jockey Association ("ADJA") is another popular DJ association based in California, with localized "chapters" all over the United States. They've got two levels of membership, the "standard" and "apprentice" levels, created to differentiate the level of compliance with their requirements. Surf over to www.adja.org or buzz them at 1-888-723-5776.

Global Mobile Entertainers Association, Inc. is a full-time national 24-7 DJ and KJ association run by well-known industry pioneer Art Bradlee from New Jersey. Visit their website at www.globalmobile.org or call 1-877-DJ-ASSOC.

The National Association of Mobile Entertainers ("NAME") is a full-time national DJ and KJ association headquartered in Pennsylvania. Learn more about NAME at www.djkj.com, or call 1-800-434-8274.

The United States Online Disc Jockey Association (USODJA), a dues-less, national, non-profit trade web-based association for professional disc jockeys, karaoke jockeys and entertainment companies headquartered in Michigan. Check them out at www.usodja.org.

THE DIGITAL DOMAIN

Every few decades, the music industry shakes things up with a new trend or a new format. The last big change was the introduction of the CD format in the 1980s. This time, things were a bit different. The music industry was caught with its pants down as compressed digital music exploded out of control. It seemed the consumer finally had taken control of the music industry.

But the music industry's powerful lobbyists and attorneys wouldn't go down easily, and the war begun. It appeared to be a wide open battle at many points with this judge issuing an injunction and that judge removing it. In the end of the seesaw battle, the RIAA prevailed. Thousands of lawsuits were subsequently filed against music traders, some as young as 12 years old. Thousands of dollars of fines were collected. And then the music industry realized there was money to be made in this new format, as long as they could figure out a way to control the distribution.

The industry is far from emerging from the legal turmoil. Once the digital cat got out of the proverbial bag, everyone knew it would be virtually impossible to get it back in there. Legal digital encoders and decoders are widely available and inexpensive enough for almost anyone to get. Although copying and redistributing copywritten music is technically illegal, human nature ensures that this movement will remain strong.

Remember that DJs are not exempt from copyright laws! Copying your friend's CDs for your professional use is a big illegal no-no. You still will have to head down to the local music store and purchase legal copies of the latest hits. The RIAA (Recording Industry Association of America) says that when disc jockeys compile a CD or cassette of tracks from a number of unrelated albums to use in their work, each song must be properly licensed and authorized regardless of who makes the CD. The law is relatively simple: duplicating copyrighted sound recordings without the authorization of the sound recording copyright owner is a violation of federal copyright law. This includes copying all or some of a sound recording to analog or digital tape, CD-R, mini-disc or a computer's hard drive. Violators could be civilly liable for statutory damages of up to $100,000 per infringed sound recording, in addition to costs and the copyright owner's attorney fees. There are criminal liabilities too which could include up to five years imprisonment and/or a fine of up to $250,000.

Most of the RIAA's enforcement efforts focus on the manufacture and distribution of illegal DJ compilations throughout the DJ community, including compilations that allege to be authorized but really aren't. The RIAA also addresses flagrant copyright infringement by DJs who create and manufacture multi-disk compilations of top hits without obtaining appropriate licenses from the copyright holders.

If you're making compilations of songs from CDs that you legally purchased, chances are the RIAA won't target you. But you never know! Keep an ear open for new legal developments in this area to make sure you're on the right side of the law.

Today you have to be careful where you buy CDs. The RIAA confiscates thousands of illegal CD-Rs each year, and won't reimburse you for your media. The equipment required to manufacture illegal CD-Rs is portable and inexpensive. CD-Rs used to be easy to spot; they were typically gold on one side with a greenish tint on the non-graphic or "read-only" side. Now printable silver CD-Rs are available along with consumer CD printers, making it more difficult to spot phonies. The RIAA states that you can determine if a CD is counterfeit or pirated by checking these seven points:

* The packaging has blurry graphics, weak or bad color.
* The package or disc has misspelled words.
* The price is way below retail value.
* You're buying it at a flea market, from a street vendor, or in a concert parking lot.
* The record label is missing or it's a company you've never heard of.
* It has cheaply made insert cards, often without liner notes or multiple folds.
* The sound quality is poor.

Going Digital

To get started with digital music, you'll need a pretty decent computer with at least an 800-megahertz processor and at least 256 MB RAM. You'll also need at least one sound card. It can be external or internal, separate or included with your computer's motherboard. Storage is more affordable than ever, so the more gigabytes of hard disk space you've got, the better. You'll have to download some software to convert and play the digital music files. And if you want to convert your existing CDs to digital files, you'll obviously need a CD-ROM drive. And you'll probably want a pair of speakers so you can actually hear your music.

If you plan to download legal music from the Internet, you'll need a fast broadband Internet connection or a lot of patience, since digital audio files are relatively large and can take a while to download over a dial up connection.

Ripping and Encoding

The first thing you have to do in order to use digital music is to convert your existing music from your CDs or records into a digitally compressed format. You'll first need to decide on a codec that will best suit your needs, and then stick with it so all your files are consistent. Mixing different codecs will usually get you confused or into trouble somewhere down the road when you run into a cool new software program that may not support a particular codec, rendering a large part of your digital music collection useless.

The process of converting your CDs into the digital format of your choice is known as "digital audio extraction," or the more popular term of "ripping your CDs." Software programs that rip CDs, known as "rippers," digitally copy music from audio CDs on to your hard drive. But rippers only know how to save music files as huge uncompressed files, which can use up to 10 megabytes of storage per minute of music. The uncompressed files must then be converted into MP3 files in a process called "encoding." Newer rippers will also encode your CD files directly to MP3, skipping the separate encoding step altogether. You can avoid the multi-step process with a piece of software called "MusicMatch Jukebox" (musicmatch.com). If you're hooked up to the internet, MusicMatch will even look up the names and titles of your songs on your CD via the CDDB database, then automatically fill them in before you've ripped and encoded a single thing. Digital enthusiasts prefer a program called Exact Audio Copy (EAC) to rip their CDs along with a plugin called "Lame" to convert those ripped files to the MP3 format. Lame won't work on its own; it needs a host program to tell it what to do.

The speed of your ripping process depends on a number of things including your processor speed, the amount of your computer's memory, the maximum speed of your CD drive, and the software you're using. Most newer rippers and encoders contain a special program that will automatically analyze the highest reading speed your particular CD player. Some rippers also have error detection capabilities, which can actually detect read errors and force the software to try to correct them.

The quality of your encoding depends on the level of obsessive compulsiveness of the lead programmer of your encoding program or plugin. Gizmo Labs' founder Jörgen Hedberg tells me that digital compression programs involve a series of complex mathematical algorithms, and some audio encoding programmers don't bother to verify that the algorithms are programmed correctly. This results in a nasty, noisy digital music file that reflects poorly on digital compression as a whole. Don't worry, most of the bigger name properly licensed companies that produce encoding software do verify their compression algorithms.

Burning

Now that you have an incredibly basic idea about what ripping and encoding are, it's time to define "burning" so you'll have all the important terminology of the digital music revolution.

Almost all new computer systems come with a CD burner standard. "Burning" is the process of taking your compressed or uncompressed digital music files and writing them to a recordable CD, known as a CD-R. It's called "burning" because the laser actually burns little pits into the chemical layers of a CD to write the digital binary information (simply a huge series of zeroes and ones) that later will be read by your CD player and translated into music. Now that CD writers are available for as little as forty dollars and blank compact discs are less than a dollar each, many professional DJs have burned some or all of their music collection to CD-Rs.

There are specially formatted CD-Rs known as "music CD-Rs" which cost slightly more than plain old CD-R discs. Certain standalone consumer based standalone CD recorders will only let you use the special CD-R discs. The music industry is paid a higher royalty for music CD-Rs because they're sure you'll be burning copyrighted music on them. Most DJs use plain old CD-Rs burned directly from a computer.

Digital Storage

Anyone who's anyone who knows anything in the DJ business will tell you to always have a backup plan. This is especially important to DJs getting involved in the digital domain. Digital storage has become very reliable, but it's far from perfect. CDs, hard drives, and solid state memory devices can be fickle and fail for a number of reasons including power surges or accidental drops, usually at the worst possible time. Most digital DJs I know, including myself, carry two separate formats to paid gigs. Our digital DJ systems are our primary systems and a backup plain old dual CD player with a bunch of compilation CDs is always close by, just in case.

Recordable CDs

CD-Rs are often the most popular choice for storing digital music files because they're cheap, portable, and remarkably reliable. There are many CD compatible formats, including CD audio format we're all familiar with, and the data CD format that stores only files. With traditional CD audio discs, you can store up to 80 minutes of music including the breaks between songs, which works out to roughly 18-20 songs depending on the length of the songs. If you choose to burn your discs as data discs, you can store up to 700 megabytes per disc, which works out to about 150 CD-quality songs. I've had some experiences where I had "read errors" on some of my older (and cheaper) CD-Rs, rendering those particular CD-Rs and all their data useless. CD-R reliability depends on a number of things, including:

* The quality of the manufacturing of the disc.
* The materials and workmanship used to build the disc, including the color and type of dye used in the protected layers of the disc.
* Whether or not you've scratched your disc.
* Whether or not you've left it sit in summer heat.

CD drives are limited to the maximum capacity of the discs they read, which is only 650 or 700 megabytes of information. CDs take longer to "spin up" to their maximum read speed and have slower access rates than hard drives. CDs can get scratched and skip, and could shatter if handled incorrectly. And due to their conveniently small size, CDs can easily be lost or stolen.

Recordable DVD

Recordable DVD discs can't be played in audio CD players, but they can store large amounts of data, such as your entire disco collection on one single disc! Over six full data CDs will fit on one single recordable data DVD, which works out to almost a thousand compressed digital audio files. The whole recordable DVD standard is very confusing. Several DVD formats are fighting for the lead position. We've got DVD-R, DVD+R, DVD-RW, and DVD+RW. Most recent DVD computer drives now read and write both DVD + and[md]formats. DVD-Rs tend to be a bit flakier than their CD-R brethren. I've had several cheap DVD-R discs completely fail after just a few months when optimally stored in dark, clean and temperate environments.

Internal Hard Drives

Most newer desktop computers come with at least 80 gigabyte internal hard drives, which is plenty of space for most compressed DJ music collections and the software needed to play them. Internal hard drives (Figure 9.1) are typically the fastest means of storage with the quickest access times. Faster is better in this business, because the faster your computer can access and process compressed digital music files, the less problems you'll have with embarrassing skipping situations.

Spindle speed, measured in revolutions per minute, is the most common standard measurement of a hard drive's speed. This represents how many times per minute the hard drive's platters spin per minute. Less expensive desktop hard drives spin at about 5,400 RPM, while standard hard drives spin at approximately 7,200 RPM, which is plenty fast for professional DJ applications. Serial ATA and SCSI hard drives are more expensive, and can spin at speeds up to 15,000 RPM. These drives are typically used for complex multitrack audio or video editing, as well as complex file servers for big company networks.

Laptop computers typically are sold with slower 4,200 or 5,400 RPM hard drives. In most situations, depending on how many programs you've got open at once and the disc resources required by those programs, 5,400 RPM laptop drives should provide fairly reliable performance in most DJ situations.

Hard drives can and do fail, usually as a result of power surges or excessive heat over an extended period of time. Laptop hard drives seem to fail more than desktop drives because they're banged around more when you move a laptop, and they can't dissipate heat as well as desktop drives. Hard drive backups are critical and should be done no less than once a month. It's a real pain in the butt to replace all the software, hardware, and music you'll spend hours collecting and compiling, so get into the habit of backing up your drives frequently.

Internal Hard Drive.

External Hard Drives

Basically, external hard drives are really just internal hard drives in a protective casing (Figure 9.2). Portable external hard drives have dropped in price and increased in speed storage capacity. With drives that can hold over 250 gigabytes, yes, gigabytes, one could potentially store tens of thousands of compressed digital audio files. Imagine having every song you own instantly available at your fingertips in a container no larger or heavier than a shoe box! An important factor when choosing a hard drive is the rate of speed in which the disc platter is spinning. Most hard drives spin at either 5,400 or 7,200 revolutions per minute ("RPM"). The faster the better. Conversely, the faster the drive spins, the more heat it produces, which may adversely affect its longevity.

External hard drives (see Figure 9.2) must be connected to the computer via USB, USB2, or Firewire. These special wires all have slightly different attributes. USB2 is supposedly a bit faster than Firewire in terms of bandwidth, but there are various considerations that I can't comprehend that cause USB2 to be close to Firewire speed. The original USB standard could work, but due to its very limited bandwidth, I wouldn't recommend using it with digital music files. If your bandwidth is too slow, you'll run into skipping problems because your computer can't read the data from the music file quickly enough due to the slow speed of the drive.

The advantages of external hard drives include a small size, affordability, easy plug and play installation, and they're available at virtually any electronics store in a variety of sizes. They're great for laptops with limited space. The disadvantages include the potential for loss, theft, or data corruption if you lose power even for a second. Corrupt data are incomplete data files that your computer won't be able to read. As a matter of fact, if you unplug the device without disconnecting it in your operating system first, the drive may still be writing to the disc. If the writing operation is interrupted, your data may not be fully written, resulting in data corruption.

External Hard Drive.

Solid State Memory Cards

Finally, there are solid-state digital music players on the market. These devices are usually battery operated, and store digital music files on some kind of portable memory card, such as a Compact Flash card, a Secure Digital card, or Sony's Memory Stick (Figure 9.3). My cell phone actually has MP3 files on it! They're great because there are no moving parts, and they're extremely small, easily fitting into your pocket. They do have limited capacity, meaning you'll need to carry lots of memory cards. Memory cards have been known to occasionally go bad, losing their data for no apparent reason, leaving you in a pickle. Most memory card playback devices are limited to MP3 files or Windows' WMA files.

Memory Stick.

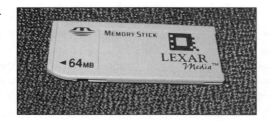

Sampling and Formats

Before we delve into some of the coolest DJ toys ever created, you'll need a basic understanding of how all this digital stuff works. Sure, it's complicated and boring, but a little schoolin' may help you solve some problems as you transition from the analog world into the digital domain.

A computer reads data which has been recorded as "binary" information. Oversimplified as usual, this means everything a computer reads, records, processes and reproduces is reduced to a series of 0s and 1s arranged in an order that the computer can easily process within a thousandth of a second. Music is stored on a computer's hard drive (also called hard disc or hard disc drive) as binary data. Data from songs or sounds are collected and "sampled" at various rates, forming a stream of data which represents an approximation of the frequencies collected during the sampling process. A sampling rate of 44.1 kHz, or 44 thousand samples per second, is collectively recognized as "CD quality." CD quality is far from a perfect sound reproduction, but it seems most folks have agreed this is a reasonably good reproduction suitable for personal use and public performance in DJ applications. The method of sampling an analog signal and converting it into those bits of 0s and 1s is known as Pulse Code Modulation (PCM).

Simple enough, right? Wrong. The other important component of a digital music file is its "bit depth." Usually, most DJs use music that's encoded with a 16-bit bit depth. This means that sixteen 0s or 1s are recorded for each of the 44,100 samples that occur each second while you're converting an analog signal to digital.

To summarize, a CD quality digital stream is 44,100 samples per second at a bit-depth of 16 bits per sample. If you were to look at the data from a CD quality sample closely, you'd notice a rather jagged curve with visibly defined corners rather than a smooth curve. The higher your sampling rate, the smoother the curve, and the closer the approximation to the true sound. The lower your sampling rate, the more jagged your curve, and you'll notice more digital noise. So why not just sample everything at 96 kHz at 64-bits per sample? Because the downside of higher sampling rates and bit depths is that they must store more information, resulting in even larger file sizes. The difference in your resulting sound quality isn't necessary in a DJ situation. Plus, the digital compression you'll most likely use would chop off a while lot of that super high fidelity information anyway.

The big step that made DJing digitally a reality was the evolution of digital compression. In the days of megabyte hard drives, storing uncompressed audio files was cumbersome and inefficient. Storing compressed audio files that are as little as ten percent of their original uncompressed file size made complete sense. Today, with hard drives racing into terabyte territory, compressed music collections can be virtually unlimited in size. Songs you might have left home to conserve space or weight can now become part of your everyday collection with no sacrifice.

Digital compression is usually "lossy," meaning that certain information from the original file is permanently thrown away during the compression process. Frequencies outside normal human hearing ranges are chopped off, and engineers figured out some other sneaky tricks that remove some other information they didn't think a file needed. When you're ready to listen to the resulting file, the file is uncompressed on the fly, and there's still enough of the original information available so that the sound is still recognizable at an acceptable quality. But instead of dealing with storing a 30 megabyte WAV file, you've got a much more manageable 3 or 4 megabyte file that sounds virtually identical to the original recording. It's a pretty amazing process.

Another term you'll see used loosely in the digital domain is "codec." Codec is short for compressor/decompressor, and refers to any compression and decompression software.

WAV

WAV files were developed by Microsoft as the first sound standard for Windows PCs. These pulse code modulated files are uncompressed, resulting in large files sizes that fill hard drives in a hurry. I remember toying with Windows' Sound Recorder back in Windows 3.1 in the early 1990s, recording sound effects with huge file sizes that I'd associate with my Windows startup or shutdown. Back in those days, hard drives were only a few hundred megabytes, and a minute of sound recorded at "CD Quality" in the WAV format was somewhere around 30 megabytes! My system would hang for a while trying to read the sound and then play it, but it was worth it. My coworkers were amazed that my computer made sounds other than dings and beeps.

AIFF

Apple Computer created their own standard called the AIFF file. Similar to Microsoft's WAV format, AIFF (or just .aif in Windows) files are not compressed and consume a lot of disk space. Many Macintosh based audio producers still favor this format when producing professionally recorded audio tracks.

MP3

Music's Digital Domain began with the emergence of the "MP3" digital compression created by a German company called Fraunhofer IIS sometime in the late 1980s. Fraunhofer developed something they call "perceptual audio coding" that was to be used in digital radio broadcasting, the next wave of radio. Fraunhofer developed a very smart mathematical algorithm that's formerly known as ISO-MPEG Audio Layer-3, or "MP3." Fraunhofer's MP3 compression can compress CD-quality digital sound files to about one-tenth of their original uncompressed size. This was critically important in the days of limited computer storage, when the average hard drive in a computer was in the neighborhood of 1 gigabyte (about 20 uncompressed digital audio files). The MP3 format made it possible to easily manage and store thousands of CD-quality songs on a plain old computer hard drive. You can store about 150 radio version songs, 10-11 hours of music, or about 11-14 complete traditional CDs of CD-quality music on one single recordable CD. An experienced DJ could conceivably bring two MP3 CDs to a party and program a full five hour party with nothing more than those two CDs. I've done it!

The most popular audio compression scheme is still MP3, although it's no longer the most efficient or the best quality. But it was the pioneering digital compression, and people are comfortable with it. Most digital music software and even newer CD players from professional to consumer level units now support MP3 files written on recordable compact discs. The software and hardware you choose must support the codec of your choice. Many DJs have converted their entire CD collection into MP3 files.

Most digital compression schemes will let you choose different qualities depending on your preference of the level of compression, known as a "bit rate." With a higher compression bit rate, more of the original song is kept, and you'll have a better resulting quality. FM radio quality is about 64-96 kbps (kilobytes per second), and are usually pretty nasty and noisy. CD quality is somewhere between 128 and 192 kbps, depending on the song. Some folks prefer 256- or even 320-kbps encoded MP3 files. Most DJs I know encode their MP3 files at 128 kbps to conserve disc space, and think they sound just fine in public performance situations.

There are two flavors of encoding, constant bit rate (CBR) or variable bit rate (VBR). Constant bit rate encodes a song at the same exact bit rate throughout the entire song. Variable bit rate is kind of smart encoding, where the bit rate varies depending on the complexity of the part of the song that's being encoded. During more complex passages, the bit rate automatically increases to retain more of the original information. The bit rate subsequently lowers during less intense passages.

Since MP3 files are purely digital, smart programmers allowed a few bits in the file to account for useful textual information such as artist, title, album, producer, comments, and even beats per minute information encoded in the song file itself. These comment fields are known as "ID3 tags." Their main benefit is that they allow DJs to index their music files. Most digital DJ software programs can extract ID3 tags and build searchable databases so you can quickly and easily find a particular song even in the largest music collections.

Several free software programs such as Winamp and MusicMatch emerged during the early days of the MP3, further entrenching the MP3 as the dominant compressed digital music format. Ironically, MP3 is not a free format. Licensing fees are collected by Fraunhofer for each piece of software that utilizes their encoding technology.

The other major benefit of MP3s is the evolution of the first practical solid-state music delivery systems. With some of the new portable digital playing devices, you can now play CD-quality music with no moving parts! That means no skipping, not to mention super extended battery life because there are no motors.

To learn more about MP3 encoding and Fraunhofer's latest developments, check out their website at www.iis.fraunhofer.de/amm.

MP3Pro

The MP3 is evolving once again into something even better and more efficient. Coding Technologies invented the MP3Pro codec. Some folks call MP3Pro a "super MP3." This codec promises better sound quality than MP3 at about half the size of an MP3. Plus, it's reportedly backwards compatible with plain old MP3 files. The trick with MP3Pro is a plain old MP3 file with an additional layer that includes previously discarded audio information, all at a smaller 64-kbps bit rate. Now, theoretically, you could fit up to 300 better sounding songs on one single 700-MB CD-R. Keep your eyes on this one at www.codingtechnologies.com.

Windows WMA

Microsoft created the Windows Media Audio codec (WMA) as their own digital music compression scheme. Similar to MP3Pro, the WMA codec boasts a smaller file size and better quality than plain old MP3 files. Plus, WMA's anti-hacker super-secret encoding algorithm often incorporates DRM (digital rights management) that restricts unlicensed copying or playing. The Napster service uses DRM encoded WMA files. Visit www.microsoft.com for more info and the latest WMA encoders and players.

Apple AAC

Apple's i-Tunes uses an MPEG-4 encoding algorithm called M4P. As Apple's answer to MP3 Pro, Advanced Audio Coding (AAC) is at the core of the MPEG-4 specification and is gaining popularity for Internet, wireless, and digital broadcasting. AAC provides audio encoding that compresses much more efficiently and at a better quality than older formats including MP3. AAC propaganda is readily available at www.apple.com/mpeg4/aac.

Real Audio

Real Audio, created by Real Media, was one of the first digital media players in the market. Real seems to be popular with "streaming" video and audio offered on the internet. Since DJs are rarely afforded the luxury of full-time high speed internet access during live gigs, Real Audio is seldom used by professional DJs. Visit www.real.com for more information on Real Audio.

Ogg Vorbis

There is a small group of programmers who created a completely license-free open standard known as "Ogg Vorbis." Weird name, cool concept. Like WMA and MP3Pro, OGG files are supposedly smaller and of better quality than MP3 files. Some popular consumer software programs like Winamp support this codec, but many professional digital DJ programs do not. Check to see if the program you choose to use supports it before going nuts with OGG. You'll find anti-establishment type people using OGG. Learn more at www.xiph.org/ogg.

Digital DJ Software

With the today's advanced computer technology, it's now feasible to incorporate an entire DJ system into one small, compact unit, complete with digital MP3 copies of your entire DJ music library. I've played digital music on a laptop as early as 1997 in front of a live audience just to prove that it was possible. In those days, due to processor and memory limitations, if you tried to do too much at once, the music would pause momentarily, allowing the computer to catch up. As you might imagine, that sucks in a DJ situation! Today with the amazing digital DJ hardware and software combinations on the market, you can run lights, video, and more all while mixing and playing two songs at once, with no pause in the music program. Digital DJing has come a long way in a few short years.

Let's look at a few of the leading digital DJ hardware systems on the market for professional DJs. If you're all gung ho to bust out your laptop's minijack and start jamming, hang on to your hard drives. Due to the volatile nature of the software industry, programs can change quickly and frequently. The following software has probably changed since this book went to print, so visit each of the companies' websites for the latest updates and feature descriptions.

Sound Cards and Latency

Before we jump into the software, we'll need to learn about something called "latency" and how it affects digital music. Latency is the measurement of the amount of time it takes a sound or instruction to be transferred from your hard drive through your computer's processor and finally delivered to your sound card. Although the process seems relatively simple, it's really quite inefficient.

Your computer's processor can only handle one task at a time. Processing a sound involves several separate individual processes. First, your software issues a request to find a particular music file on your hard drive. When it locates the music file, each bit of information is transmitted through the hard drive cables to the motherboard and then to your processor. Your processor must convert or encode the song data into a digital stream that your software understands. The trick is that in addition to running your DJ software, your processor is also simultaneously processing commands issued by your computer's operating system, your system clock, your internet connection, your network, your antivirus software, and probably about ten other processes your computer needs to function properly. Fortunately, your processor handles these tasks at the speed of light, and quite reliably.

Latency comes into play when you're mixing music. The moment you press the play button on your digital DJ software or hardware, you'll want the song to start as quickly as possible. A fraction of a second of a delay can cause your mix to be offbeat and sound terrible. Even simple actions like moving a volume or pitch slider adjusting an equalizer, or invoking a special effect will incur a bit of latency from when you issue the command to when the command is actually executed. The less latency, the quicker your computer's response time, and the more accurate your DJ show will be. The amount of noticeable latency is disputed. Some folks say about 12 milliseconds is the maximum latency a DJ would not notice.

If you're trying to run too many programs at once and your processor is stressed, you may run into latency induced problems. Digital skipping is an ugly sound that's simply unpleasant. Unlike analog skipping that is annoying but still understandable, digital skipping sounds like a pop, click, or just a garbled alien message.

Sound card manufacturers have solved this problem in most cases with a process known as "buffering." The buffering process reads ahead and stores some information in the computers memory, so the computer always has some data to work with, essentially avoiding disc reading errors. Ironically, buffering causes a bit of latency purposely! "Direct Sound," a component of Microsoft Windows' Direct X program, is a newer technology that helps sound cards handle more of their own processing to avoid getting stuck in a bottleneck situation while waiting for the computer's main processor to finish doing something else.

Since higher sample rates use up buffered information more quickly, latency decreases with higher sample rates. You can also avoid latency problems by closing any unused programs, defragmenting your hard drive, and making sure you have enough memory (RAM). Usually, 512 megabytes of RAM is sufficient for DJ applications.

Consumer Digital Music Software

There are several programs that play digital audio files ranging from simple consumer players to complex pro DJ software programs that can automatically beatmix remarkably well. Single deck digital audio players are the easiest to use, since they're targeted towards consumers. Don't be fooled by their ease of use[md]some of them pack quite a powerful wallop. I used quite a few of these programs during my first digital DJ experiences.

Windows Media Player

Windows Media Player comes bundled with Windows XP. This bad boy can play almost everything you can throw at it[md]audio, video, recorded TV shows, and more. The interface is a bit confusing at first, but becomes very intuitive as you keep messing with it. You can actually fade your music from one song into another with this single deck media player for a seamless jukebox-like playback. Since some songs are inherently louder than others, Windows Media Player's auto volume leveling attempts to equalize volumes across all tracks in a playlist.

The pros are its compatibility, and of course, it's basically free since it comes bundled with all later versions of Microsoft Windows. A downside might be that to a computer neophyte, this software can trick you into thinking you're rambling on playing your favorite tunes and videos with no repercussion. The truth is that if you don't switch this setting to off, your media player may anonymously report your listening or viewing habits to Microsoft. Microsoft collects your usage data, stuffs it into some database somewhere, and geniuses make sense of it all in an effort to improve upon their software. Microsoft tries to make usage reporting sound important by calling this process "The Customer Experience Improvement Program." The reporting process is basically anonymous. It doesn't send any personal or identifying information to Microsoft. But the whole big brother thing still freaks some people out.

Winamp

Winamp seems to be the most popular MP3 consumer software. Looking no more complicated than your average CD player interface, it's incredibly easy to use, but it's also surprisingly powerful. You won't be able to beatmix songs with it, but you could potentially DJ a mobile affair with nothing more than this program.

Winamp has a wide array of free features, upgrades, and special effects known as "Plugins." Plugins can be created by a professional company, or they might be created by amateur programmers or bored hackers. Plugins created by the latter are usually more fun. With plugins, your software won't become obsolete. There's usually a new plugin created for each new industry innovation.

There are also thousands of really cool front end themes known as "skins" that you can change to make your Winamp player look like anything from a high-tech metallic CD player to a stereo decked out with your favorite cartoon character.

The full version of Winamp is still free, and it supports other digital compression and uncompressed formats. You can also "stream" Internet audio with this player, meaning you can listen to live Internet radio broadcasts. Winamp supports WAV, MP3, WMA, CD files, and MP3Pro files with an optional plugin. For some reason, the folks at Winamp decided to allow their program to play compressed video files too. I've even found an unauthorized AAC/M4P (Apple I-Tunes) plugin that works pretty well. Visit www.winamp.com for more information or to download your own copy of Winamp.

MusicMatch Jukebox

MusicMatch was the first all-in-one CD ripper and digital music players I recall finding. I still use MusicMatch to rip my CDs to MP3. It's fairly easy to learn, and still relatively inexpensive. The basic version was still free the last time I checked. Their "Plus" version gives you a few more props including faster ripping speed and faster CD burning.

Simply insert one of your store bought CDs, and let MusicMatch rip the songs to WAV, MP3, or even MP3 Pro for you in the background. If your computer is connected to the internet, the CD database will probably pick up the song titles and artists, and name your files using that information automatically so you won't need to manually type all that information yourself. MusicMatch also includes a digital audio player that plays your digital music files on your computer along with streaming internet radio broadcasts; and will also let you create custom music playlists and burn CDs too.

MusicMatch also reports your listening habits unless you tell it not to. They state that they're doing research so they can provide you with customized music recommendations according to what they think you like based on the songs you've listened to in the past. You can opt out during registration, so read carefully. Check out www.musicmatch.com on the web for more scoop or to download MusicMatch.

Real Player

Real Audio was one of the first streaming internet formats. In the days of slow 28 kbps modems, Real's format allowed radio stations all over the world to broadcast their signals on the net. Thanks to the record industry and the advertising industry and their picky unions, you can no longer listen to your favorite radio station on the net. Real Audio's format has improved to a CD-quality stream with the advent of broadband internet connections, but isn't popular as a compressed digital music codec for live DJ performances.

Real Player also can report your listening habits if you don't smack it around and tell it who's boss. Just so you know. For more fun, visit www.real.com.

Professional Live DJ Software

If you're ready to trade your heavy duty wheels of steel for a mouse scroll wheel, chances are you'll need to get your hands on one or more of the following software titles. DJ software programs don't play by the same rules as standard hardware, so you can change things very easily as you go along. Software is always updated, making it more stable and constantly adding new features. Once you buy a piece of hardware like a turntable or CD player, you're pretty much stuck with it exactly the way it was when you bought it (although some pro CD decks are now shipping with upgradeable firmware). With software products, a quick trip to the software publisher's website can get you the latest updates and some tricks of the trade, usually for free.

You'll need to make several decisions before committing to one particular piece of software. How many and what types of special effects are you looking for? Will you need to beatmix, or is simple crossfading providing just the right amount of excitement in your life? Which external hardware controllers interface with which software programs? Which program will allow me to do all I want (or need) to do as a digital DJ? Try them all before you buy. Almost all of the digital DJ software publishers offer a free but limited demo program, which is usually enough to give you an idea how it works and if it fits your style.

PCDJ

Joe Vangieri, CEO of Visiosonic, told me how he was blown away when he saw a DJ using a laptop computer to play music at a wedding back in the late 1990s. At that moment, Joe V, a DJ himself, decided his calling was to help create a commercial digital DJ solution.

Jörgen Hedberg was working as a heavy duty financial programmer in Sweden during the day and DJing at night. Using his programming expertise, he created one of the first viable digital DJ programs. His first creation was called "Digital DJ," which he posted on the internet as a free download to get feedback from interested DJs. Response was strong, so he took his program to the next level and created "Digital 1200 SL." Hedberg wrote the program code so that his software could be controlled with standard midi controllers. Using a small synthesizer keyboard, he was able to perform various DJ effects.

In 1999, Laura Betterly and her husband were responsible for providing music for a wedding reception in Florida. Now that the MP3 format had taken off, they decided to attempt to DJ the reception *digitally*. Betterly asked her friend Vangieri if he knew a way to do this, and Vangieri told her he had seen Hedberg's program on the internet. Betterly was so blown away with Hedberg's software that she contacted him about a possible IPO opportunity, which eventually fell through. Eventually, Hedberg hooked up with Vangieri, and the cooperative effort that became Visiosonic was born.

Hedberg provided the software and programming expertise using his super stable Digital 1200 SL software, and Vangieri provided good ol' American marketing savvy.

Visiosonic's PCDJ Digital 1200 SL software could be called the granddaddy of the digital DJ industry, available in 1999 as a free download from the then wildly popular MP3.com website. Millions of people downloaded PCDJ and an industry was born.

PCDJ's software interface is very similar to a dual CD deck, providing instant familiarity and ease of use. Complete with a pitch slider, a digital display, two independently assignable decks and a built in crossfader, PCDJ Red was the first true professional DJ software to hit the market. It was fully functional and very stable considering how new this concept was. Any time a programmer writes code that must work with a foreign operating system on various types of unrelated hardware, there are usually problems. But Hedberg's program was so efficient, it worked almost everywhere flawlessly.

Hedberg has since left Visiosonic to pursue other digital DJ ventures (see Reflex), but Visiosonic continues to evolve with a new set of programmers and engineers.

Their latest product is the FX Family. FX's master tempo setting allows DJs to change the tempo of a song without changing key. You can speed up or slow down your slow songs considerably without distorting the pitch of the song. PCDJ FX also has a comprehensive software based mixer complete with adjustable cross-fading, three band EQ with kill buttons, and an adjustable compressor, just for fun. PCDJ has a unique way of organizing music that they call a record case. There are several ways to arrange your music so it's easy for you to find anything in seconds.

An important feature of PCDJ FX is its compliance with DRM protected music, purchased from online music retailers such as Napster. Many software programs did not yet support DRM when this book was written, but it's safe to assume they'll soon jump on the bandwagon if they haven't yet done so.

For more dirt on the PCDJ family, slide on over to www.visiosonic.com.

Traktor DJ Studio

Native Instruments' Traktor DJ Studio at first look can be as intimidating as trying to fly a commercial aircraft with no experience. But once you spend a few minutes with it, you'll realize it's fairly intuitive and massively powerful. Traktor includes graphic waveform displays, tempo recognition and automatic synchronization, real-time time stretching, up to 10 cue points and 10 loops per track, and a track

Visiosonic's PCDJ FX.

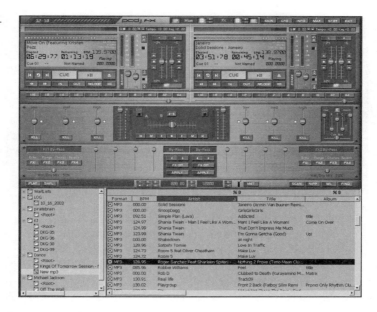

database with an ultra fast search function. My favorite feature is Traktor's "sync" function that analyzes the BPM of one song and matches the song in the opposite deck. You still have to know your eight counts to keep your mixes in synch.

Traktor's super phat time stretch function lets you adjust a song's tempo and pitch independently, so you can speed up or slow down tracks by as much as 100% without changing the key of the voice or song. It's pretty impressive technology. You can set the quality of the time stretch resampling manually, depending on the strength of your processor or computer system. To me, Traktor's time stretch algorithm sounded the best of all the time stretching algorithms I reviewed. I've sped songs up to 35% faster than normal and heard very few digital artifacts. For DJs who prefer to mix on key, this software is perfect. With the right music, you could feasibly mix an entire hour long set and appear to have played one single insanely long song.

Visit www.native-instruments.com for the latest information on Traktor DJ Studio.

Virtual DJ

One of my personal favorite digital DJ programs is Atomic Productions' Virtual DJ. It's incredibly intuitive, easy to use, yet filled with tons of killer features.

Virtual DJ's "beatlock" engine is simply the most amazing feature I've ever seen in any single piece of DJ software. Somehow, these French genius programmers figured out not only how to count BPMs, but also where the downbeat occurs. The beats are clearly illustrated in a visual waveform display at the top of the screen. Another neat function is that waveforms from both decks appear in the same window in different colors with their beat indicators overlapping perfectly when beatlocked. Even loops can be somehow stay in synch with the song no matter how beat deaf you might be. The waveform display alone is a powerful tool, and can be a huge aid in illustrating how beatmixing works.

Native Instruments'
Traktor DJ Studio.

The song structure visualization isn't a waveform as it's displayed in Traktor, but as a color bar. The color dims to indicate a drop in volume, like during breaks. It's not as accurate as Traktor's waveform, but still a pretty decent song structure indicator. Then there's the cool dual digital turntable displays, one for each deck, that you can actually grab with your mouse and scan, scratch, brake, or backspin with. And Virtual DJ also has a pretty darn accurate time stretch function too.

The coolest part of this program is its custom skins. I've seen skins on this thing that look and operate almost identically to hardware CD players, including Denon and Pioneer table top DJ models. You can download a few from Virtual DJ's website, but the real fun is finding the unauthorized skins designed by DJs who have way too much time on their hands.

Finally, you can set Virtual DJ to be a, well, virtual DJ. Wireless DJ completely blew my mind one night at a party as he seemed to randomly select about 10 different MP3 files and load them into Virtual DJ's playlist. He clicked a button and told me to watch. Without a single hiccup, Virtual DJ managed to perfectly beatmix each of those songs. Wireless DJ had clicked the AutoMix feature, which tells Virtual DJ to match BPMs, align the phase of the downbeats, fade from one deck to another during the end break of the song, and equalize the resulting volumes. Obviously, the AutoMix feature only works well with songs within the same genre, such as house, trance, or techno songs. Wireless DJ chose all trance and techno for his sneaky little demonstration.

The latest version of Virtual DJ has all kinds of sweet effects and plugins, including a really cool Karaoke player with vocal removing technologies, assignable sound effect buttons, and more.

Virtual DJ also seems to report information to the Internet. I'm not quite sure what information it's communicating, but each time I open the program, my firewall program tells me it's trying to communicate with some Internet location. I usually decline it, and everything seemed to work correctly. Wireless DJ assures me the Internet connectivity can be turned off in the program settings.

To learn more about the latest versions of Virtual DJ, bus' on over to www.virtualdj.com.

Atomix Productions' Virtual DJ.

BPM Studio

Germany's ALCAtech created BPM Studio to accompany its very sweet hardware controller units. However, the software can be used without the controllers. BPM Studio looks eerily like a Denon dual CD deck, but that helps it remain extremely intuitive to learn and easy to use.

According to Wireless DJ, BPM's key feature is its incredibly low latency resulting in the quickest response times in this category. ALCAtech programmers use a method called a "Kernel Driver" that allows BPM Studio to tap directly into the sound card rather than going through all the Microsoft stuff to get to the sound card.

It's got some cool features including master tempo, compressors, limiters, a dual band EQ, skins, and it even supports multiple users. It's pretty darn pricey compared to all the other programs. For more information and a complete list of features, visit www.alcatech.com.

MixVibes

MixVibes has a pretty cool looking layout and is fairly easy to use. They boast that they're the only software product that provides up to 16 individually controllable software decks. What in heck you'd use more than three decks for is beyond me, but there's probably some whiz kid somewhere who can use them all.

This program ships with many of the features found in other software including master tempo, scratching, automatic BPM counting, loops, real-time effects, and equalization. MixVibes supports several different hardware controllers including Hercules DJ, the DMC-1, DAC-2, and the XP-10.

For more information on MixVibes, hit up www.mixvibes.com.

BPM Studio
Professional.

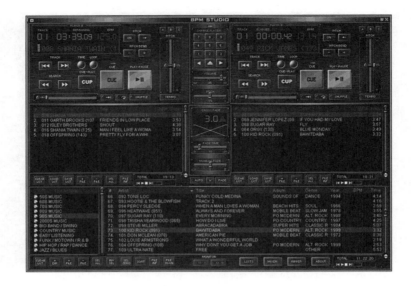

MixVibes Pro.

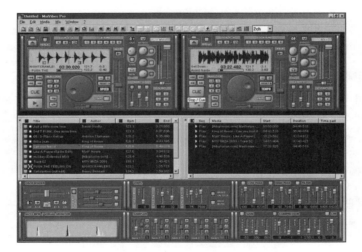

Ots DJ

Australia's Ots Labs (Figure 9.9) produces a software product called Ots DJ. This nifty little program allows DJs to set up fairly comprehensive playlists and will automatically fade songs from one into another as long as your computer has power supplied to it. It seems to be geared more towards radio station programmers than live mobile or club DJs. Pitch and tempo controls are included with this program, and it's got a single disc turntable effect that simulates vinyl scratching. There is also a software-based mixer in this program. It is fairly easy to use, and would suit interactive mobile DJs well. Ots DJ plays compressed MP3 or uncompressed WAV files.

See www.otsdj.com to learn more.

OTS DJ.

DJ Power

California's DJ Power (Figure 9.10) is popular software in bars and restaurants where these units are reportedly spectacular with seamless automation of libraries of thousands of songs, just like Ots DJ. But DJ Power offers several optional plugins or accessories, including Karaoke capabilities, video functionality, a music scheduler, and an optional beatmixing plug in, most of which are included when you purchase one of their pricey hardware solutions. A dual CD type remote controller is also available. The interface is kind of cheesy looking with pretty large buttons, probably because it was written for use with a touch screen controller. Big goofy fingers need larger targets. DJ Power is chock full of killer apps.

Mouse on over to www.djpower.com for more information.

DJ Power.

Reflex

Finally, leave it to the Bill Gates of the digital DJ frontier, Jörgen Hedberg, the original creator of the original PCDJ Red, the most widely used and stable digital DJ program, to create the most intense, functional, and stable digital DJ software ever created. Two hours before the deadline for this book, Wireless DJ finally coaxed Hedberg at Gizmo Labs to leak a tiny bit of the heavily guarded secret pre-production scoop on the coolest, most revolutionary digital DJ software the world has ever seen, known as "Reflex" (Figure 9.11) After Wireless signed a complicated iron-clad non-disclosure agreement (that I wasn't required to sign), we had a late night cell phone conference call and got permission to leak a tiny bit of this exciting new product that should be a worldwide legend by the time you get this book. Hedberg and company want to make sure this software is perfectly stable across any environment it encounters, so they're taking their time to perfect everything. Here are a few of the revolutionary key functions of the Reflex software scheduled to ship in late 2004.

* Two or three assignable full decks/players.
* Record case with automatic background scanning detecting the quality level on your tracks. BPM, location, and loudness are detected. Instead of normalizing or changing the track, it sets the player's volume to match the other on the correct side of player.
* Dynamic playlists that can be arranged in virtually any way you can think of.
* Auto Pilot with intelligent autocue, auto mix start, and auto mix end detection, all showing up in the wave window. If you like, you can move them.
* Built in beat mixing using only the list it was activated from, so you can turn it on and forget it. You can do track selection while auto play is running.
* Beat quantization and bar detection, with the correct first downbeat detected over 90% of the time. Loops can be quantized for seamless play, even if you have really bad rhythm.
* Automatic saturation, producing a virtually compressed, louder full sound without rampant DC noise that causes distortion and could damage speakers.
* An insane amount of independent pitch and tempo shift of up to +/- *900%* with a 100% tempo correct algorithm.
* Built in audio cache and cue cache to ensure 100% skip free playback even under periods of 100% processor utilization, with high priority auto-correcting buffer management for extremely skip free play. No tweaking necessary[md]it's all plug and play.
* Even more really cool stuff we aren't allowed to disclose just yet.

Features like Auto Pilot, fully automated mixing and tempo matching, could put some DJs out of business as five year olds and grandmothers begin to realize how easy this unit is to operate. "Grabbing" (one-button-push looping) and dynamic search capabilities this software and hardware package will blow your mind.

What's really cool is that Reflex is being engineer to work with several hardware based DJ controllers including Peavey's smokin' DAI, the phat EKS XP-10 units, Visiosonic's DAC-2, and Numark's DMC-1 modified with a Gizmo Labs firmware update chip. End users will have freedom to choose their favorite DJ controller.

Stay tuned to www.gizmolabs.net and your favorite DJ store for more information on what's sure to be an award-winning digital DJ software solution.

Gizmo Labs' Reflex,
Development Version.

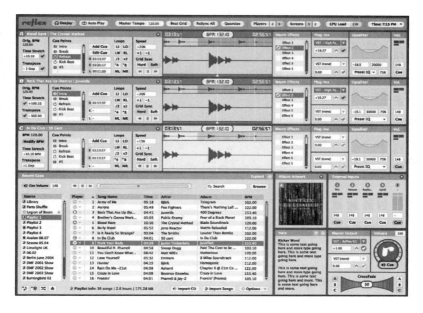

Digital DJ Hardware

The easiest way to convert hard-core old-school folk to the new school beat is to infuse the old stuff with the new stuff. Digital controllers with CD player type features have arrived. It all started with Numark's DMC-1 controller designed by a Swedish engineer named Kent Johansson.

Numark DMC-1

PCDJ's Jörgen Hedberg decided that in order to generate mass appeal for an emerging digital DJ market, they needed a physical controller device that would make the transition to the digital DJ frontier more easily accessible. Enter Kent Johansson, a super talented Swedish hardware engineer and friend of Hedberg. Johansson happened to have a Numark CDN-22 dual CD deck controller lying around. Using Hedberg's software along with midi controllers, Johansson gutted the CDN-22, replaced its innards with some electronics trickery, and got the controller to work with Digital 1200 SL. Little did he know that his modified device was about to change the entire DJ industry. Johansson met with the good folks at Numark and showed them his "modified" CDN-22. Numark loved the idea, and partnered with Visiosonic to manufacture the industry's first digital DJ hardware controller, the Numark DMC-1 in early 2001. DJs could now rack mount a computer with a controller and have instant physical access to thousands of MP3 files.

After Johansson and Hedberg left Visiosonic, they created their own firm called Gizmo Labs. One of their first projects was responding to an onslaught of requests from DJs wanting an upgrade to the DMC-1 so that it could work with other emerging digital DJ software. The boys delivered again. Gizmo Labs sells an easily installable chip that upgrades the firmware of the DMC-1, allowing it to be used with MixVibes, Virtual DJ, DJ Power, Traktor, and several other programs. A few other hardware issues were also resolved with Gizmo's updates. Check 'em out at www.gizmolabs.net.

CHAPTER 9

Visiosonic's PCDJ FX and DAC-2

Visiosonic's latest PCDJ program offers a newer dual CD-like controller called the DAC-2, that's basically a slight upgrade to the DMC-1. A jog shuttle wheel and pitch control slider with pitch bend buttons are included. The DAC-2's green backlit LCD display is limited to track number, elapsed or remaining time, and current pitch setting. That's really no biggie, since you'll be using your computer monitor for all that fun stuff anyway. I spent quite a few hours with the DAC-2 and found it to be very responsive using PCDJ FX and a few other programs.

The DAC-2 features a USB interface rather than a serial port interface, which is important. Many computers no longer have a serial port. Plus, USB is much faster.

Visiosonic's DAC-2 Controller.

BPM Studio

Germany's ALCAtech makes one of the coolest external controllers I've ever seen. BPM's kick butt $700 RCP-1001 remote control unit has the look and feel of a conventional dual CD deck. Its two function jog shuttle wheel lets you fast forward or rewind to locate a track or cue a particular part of a song, and determine the contents and scrolling speed of its gorgeous digital vacuum fluorescent display (VFD). The display is run by the BPM studio software and indicates the track number, elapsed or remaining time, BPM (if it has been included in the MP3 file's ID3 tag), current pitch setting, scrolling title and artist of the song, current play mode, and a cool 15 position horizontal tick mark bar that visually shows where you are in the song.

BPM's RCP1001 Remote Control Unit.

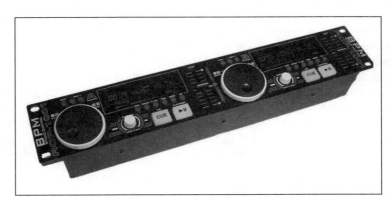

The RCP-1001's big brothers, the $1,199 RCP-2001A and RCP2001B, add several other functions to the remote control units including pitch bend, sample hotkeys, and a really cool feature they call "Set Key," which automatically sets the opposite deck to the same BPM of the song that's currently playing.

As of this printing, BPM's controllers wouldn't work with other digital DJ software programs, although there is a rumor that states they're about to change that. By the time you read this, BPM controllers will probably work with programs like MixVibes and Virtual DJ. For the latest scoop, visit www.alcatech-us.com.

PVDJ's DAI

Adam Lawson at Peavey Electronics and former Visiosonic engineer Kent Johansson, the brains behind Numark's DMC-1 and Visiosonic's DAC-2, developed Peavey's Digital Audio Interface (DAI). Digital DJs have been complaining about the confusion caused by using a mouse and keyboard along with a remote control unit. It seems you need to use both your hands and feet to perform anything truly creative with existing digital DJ hardware units. The DAI solves this problem with a touch-sensitive LCD screen, a multifunction jog wheel, and several multifunction buttons complete with all the controls DJs need for real-time mixing and remixing. The button functions have been smartly engineered to access as few layers as possible so that a DJ won't become stuck in several software layers he must escape before attempting to access play functions as his song is running out.

Four XLR balanced outs (left and right for each of the two decks) and a microphone input allow for connection to professional audio gear. A software based mixer comes standard with this unit, with its crossfader activated right on the LCD touch screen. Conceivably, you could connect this unit directly to powered speakers for the smallest fully functional pro DJ system ever created! A plain old USB 1.1 connection delivers all the controller's instructions and information to and from the software interface.

Peavey's DAI will probably ship with software also written by Jörgen Hedberg. Bookmark www.pvdj.com for the latest news on this groundbreaking controller.

Peavey's DAI.

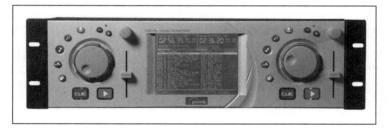

EKS XP10

EKS XP10 player is a Finnish-made USB device that plays MP3s off your computer. You might be thinking, "Yeah, so what? So do all the other hardware products." But MP3 playback is where the similarity ends.

The XP10 is the first real plug and play system for playing digital audio streams. Setup was quick and flawless, with no drivers to install. Each of the tiny 1" thick EKS XP10 units have a built in sound card, so there's no need to fool around with multiple or external sound cards. It has RCA outputs for connection to a mixer. And the coolest thing is that it's USB bus powered[md]no external power supply is necessary. You could pack your entire DJ setup into a laptop bag, take it to the beach, and run the whole darn thing from your laptop's battery.

The XP10 has a multi-function wheel. Tap on the metal plate on top of the wheel, and you can stop the digital sound for some cool stuttering effects. Touch the edges of the wheel with your fingers, and it's ready to shuttle your song to the cue point of your choice.

The XP10 unit ships with proprietary software called "Bison." Wireless DJ and I hooked two XP10s up to Virtual DJ as an experiment, and we were able to use this controller immediately. We remapped a few buttons and it appeared to be meant for Virtual DJ.

The audio quality of XP10 is extremely clean, with a signal-to-noise ratio of 105 dB. Response time with Bison and Virtual DJ was very good with no apparent latency issues on a 2.4 Ghz Celeron laptop with 512 megs of RAM.

For more information and American distribution, visit www.djresource.com.

EKS XP10.

Hercules DJ Controller

Guillemot Corporation's Hercules DJ Console is an all-in-one solution that includes everything you need to scratch and play MP3 and WMA files as well as CD audio. Complete with a bus powered USB connection, a built in mixer, and a built in four channel sound card, you can plug this in to your preamp and start bustin' out the jams.

Hercules DJ Controller features adjustable cue points, a looping function, a pitch slider to adjust BPM, and several other functions. The controller ships with MixVibes and Virtual DJ, but can be used with several other digital DJ software solutions.

Visit us.hercules.com for more information on this product.

Stanton Final Scratch

I thought this product was silly until I got my hands on Final Scratch. Man, was I wrong. It is definitely serious stuff! Final Scratch allows a DJ to pretend he or she is spinning vinyl, only you never have to change the records.

Basically, all you'll need are a couple turntables, a few specially encoded vinyl records; an electronic interface box that's connected via a plain old USB cable to your computer loaded up with funky tunes; and of course, Stanton's Final Scratch installed and ready to roll. Instead of plugging your wheels of steel into a mixer, you slam those cables into Stanton's "Scratch Box." This box takes the information from those special records and feeds it directly into your computer, and tells it what to do while playing your plain old MP3s, WAVs, or CD tracks.

Final Scratch is pretty easy to setup and use. It uses a special version of the powerful and practical Traktor DJ software, and incorporates Traktor's powerful time-stretching algorithms. Response times were virtually instantaneous. The only negative aspect of this program is that you will eventually wear out your specially encoded records if you're a heavy duty scratcher. Replacement records are readily available.

Scratch over to www.finalscratch.com for the latest on Final Scratch.

Stanton Final Scratch
with Traktor DJ.

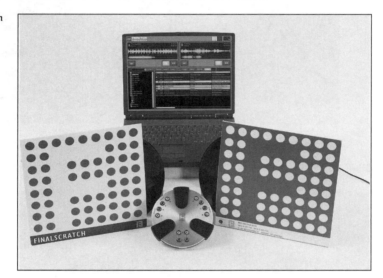

Rane Serato Scratch Live

Scratch LIVE from Rane and Serato, is another hybrid software and hardware solution that brings analog turntablism into the digital realm. Using your plain old analog turntables (or CD players) and Serato's specially encoded vinyl or CDs, you can scratch and mix files from your computer's CD or hard drive with the feel of manipulating vinyl.

The Scratch LIVE USB interface connects one or two standard vinyl or CD turntables to your computer via a small bus-powered USB audio device with two switchable phono or line inputs, a microphone input, two line outputs, and pass thru outputs for the phono/line and mic just in case you wanted to play real vinyl during your show without disconnecting the entire system. My favorite feature is the live microphone input. I could say a few words, create a sample from those words, then apply it to one of the decks and scratch the heck out of it. All the sudden, my voice was immortalized on simulated vinyl!

The software is fairly simple and easy to use, and includes a vertical waveform display that visually shows beats, breaks, and your scratching motions. The vertical display is smart because it allows more screen real estate for other functions.

Rane Serato Scratch Live.

For more information on Scratch Live, transform www.rane.com into your web browser.

Scratch Box PC Interface.

Complete Digital DJ Solutions

I own a computer store in Melbourne, Florida that just so happens to feature custom built Digital DJ systems. A coincidence? Hardly. I've found that most DJs are afraid of the digital frontier. They seem to want their systems pre-packaged, completely configured, and completely reliable. Sometimes, rather than creating your own disaster with a cheap laptop, it's better to leave it to the pros. So I leave it to the pros.

DJ RAK

The DJ RAK company is the innovator in hardware technology for the mobile and club DJ. DJ RAK builds custom compact, light-weight rack mount computers and complete digital DJ systems for several companies, and has systems installed all over the world.

What's really cool about the DJ RAK systems is their self containment. You've got your controller, your mixer, your computer, and your entire music collection all pre-wired and ready to roll, all in a package that weighs as little as sixty pounds. A single crate of vinyl can weigh that much! Add the ability to instantly locate a song with a few keystrokes, pre-arranged automated song lists, plus built-in video and karaoke capabilities, the option to choose your favorite digital DJ software and its optional controller, and you've got everything a mobile or club DJ could possibly ask for.

Most Windows based operating systems seem to be optimized for applications like word processors, spreadsheets, and Internet browsing. DJ RAK systems run on specially tweaked Windows computers that are specifically optimized for multimedia DJ applications. They've got multiple sound cards, so you have the ability to separate two independent channels as well as a third channel used for cueing, just like in a real hardware only DJ system. If you used your own off-the-shelf laptop, you would only have one stereo channel that would have to be split into left and right to get two independent channels - and forget about cueing. Additionally, DJ RAK systems have optional multiple video cards so you can visualize your mix while simultaneously showing a video to your audience on a separate video feed.

DJ RAK's Todd Sun won't let a product leave his lab until it's insanely stable and meets his incredibly stringent quality specifications. As a former engineer and DJ, Sun realizes the worst thing that can happen is a system failure during the middle of a paid gig, so his DJ RAK systems have several safeguards built in to avoid this. These systems are by far the most reliable and best sounding digital DJ systems I've ever used.

Learn more about DJ RAK at www.djrak.com.

DJ RAK Digital DJ Systems.

DJ Power

DJ Power also produces hardware custom tailored to their DJ Power software. I've only seen them at DJ shows, but I understand they have a pretty wide distribution in bars and clubs primarily as background music systems.

Portable MP3 Players

Marketing studies must have shown that folks like to take their music with them. It began with Sony's portable cassette tape Walkman back in the 1980s. Today, portables have gone digital, and are smaller and more powerful than ever. You'll have to choose your weapon carefully, because each of these players are different from one another and have advantages and disadvantages. Some of these players support MP3 files along with the popular WMA format, and some others prefer Apple's encoding. Remember that you'll still need a computer to create the digital audio files from your CDs, and to upload those tunes to your portable player.

Although not particularly suited as a primary device for DJ applications, a portable MP3 player could be used as a great backup device. Most of these devices also allow you to save pictures and documents too.

Apple iPod

Apple's iPod is probably the most widely known portable digital audio player. The pricey 40 gigabyte version can hold up to 10,000 songs. It easily syncs with Apple's Internet-based iTunes software, so you can use one single program to purchase new music and encode your existing CDs.

The downside is that there is a small hard drive inside this device. A sudden shock or jolt could potentially cause skipping or damage to the disc.

Creative Labs Nomad and MuVo

Creative Labs' Nomad Jukebox resembles a portable compact disc player. It also has a hard drive, but avoids most skipping situations with a seven second anti-skip buffer.

Creative Labs responded to active types with solid-state compact flash based audio players. With a 1 Gb model, you could store up to 16 hours of music, plenty of tunes to cover just about any type of private party or small bar gig in a pinch. You can even create a playlist on your PC and upload it to your MuVo for your own custom music program.

Other Portables

Dell sells a hard disk based unit called the "Dell DJ." Samsung produces a hard disk unit called a YP-910 that has a Napster interface for easy Napster music uploads. Rio Audio also has several various hard disc and flash memory models available.

Loop-Based Software

Most of today's well known DJs got to be well known not from their skills as DJs *per se*, but by having their name attached to a hit song either as an artist, remixer, or producer. So if you've got your heart set on becoming the next BT, you'd better get your songwriting skills in gear. I've been fooling around with songwriting for about a decade and I'm still waiting for my big break. Regardless, it's a lot of fun. Songwriting actually helps me relax.

Fortunately, the digital age has provided several solutions that make songwriting childishly simple. Instead of collecting expensive keyboards, synthesizers, and sequencers, software such as Sony Studio's Acid and Ableton's Live are affordable programs that run on just about any computer manufactured over the past few years. All you'll need to do is purchase some royalty-free drum, bass and synth loops, and you're off to the races. Once you become proficient with these programs, you can blow away audiences all over the world by producing music no one has ever heard and playing it live during your show.

The most popular music creation software for DJs is known as "loop-based" software. Short four or eight bar clips of instruments, bass lines and drum beats are sampled and perfectly quantized and clipped so they seamlessly repeat indefinitely. There are thousands of CDs available with loops you can use in your next production.

Sony Studios Acid

Sony Studio's Acid is by far the easiest loop-based music creation tool on the planet. With virtually unlimited tracks all arranged vertically on top of each other and scrolling naturally from left to right, I found Acid the most intuitive of any music creating software title.

Simply browse to the sample or loop you want to use, and Acid automatically matches the loop's beats per minute to match the rest of your project. Drag the loop on to a track, click and drag where you think that loop should be in your song, add a few more separate tracks for bass, drums, synth pads, and other special effects, and you've created a song. It is that easy.

Track adjustments, panning, and adding effects are also incredibly easy. Lay out all your tracks the way you want them, adjust the effects, panning and volume of each track, then mixdown to a final stereo MP3 or WAV file for further production or mastering, or just burn your new creation directly to CD. It's that simple.

Unfortunately, quite a few people I've talked to don't consider Acid to be a professional music making tool. Professional producers tend to sneer at products that don't take years of schooling to learn, regardless of the program's functionality. Well, pooh pooh on those snooty pros, because Acid works, and it works darn well. I created my first Acid hit in the late 1990s. I purchased a few royalty-free loops on the internet, and recorded some vocal samples in my studio. In less than five minutes, I created a less than flattering song about DJ Louie that became legendary in my club.

Paint mediasoftware.sonypictures.com on to your web browser for more scoop and a free demo version of Acid.

Sony Studios Acid.

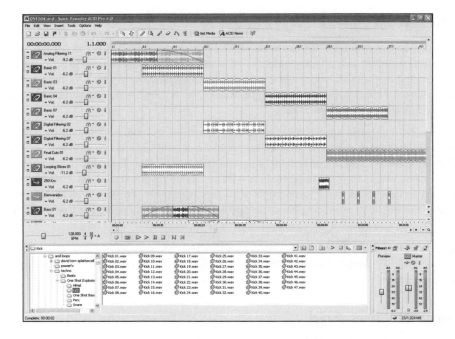

Ableton Live

Ableton's Live is another popular loop-based music creation software. It's not as intuitive as Sony's Acid, but it's much more powerful from a professional production standpoint.

Live appears to be better suited for studio use to create songs and compositions that you might play at your DJ gigs. Live itself appears to be a bit too complicated for most live DJ performance situations. Of course, if you took the time to learn this program and you wanted to look really cool at your next gig, you could bust out some Live in the middle of your show and play a few loops triggered by a keyboard or synth's midi controller while scratching to the beat on a plain old Technics 1200 or with another digital controller. I envision a projection screen monitor showing the audience your computer screen, so they can visualize your mastery of this program. This type of performance is very complex and usually reserved for top level professional touring DJs with paid entourages and stage crews. Regardless, it sounds like a lot of fun.

Tracks are arranged horizontally in something called Ableton calls "cells," which I personally found to be slightly fuzzy to follow after being jaded by Acid's horizontal "paint and play" and vertically stacked tracks. After a little more investigation, I was comforted to find that Live also has a "paint and play" mode in its arranger view which made more sense to me.

Cool Live functions include their famous "Elastic Audio" feature, which will enable you to physically adjust the timing of a loop or sample so that it fits into your project the way you want it to. You can also individually adjust track parameters including music key as well as volume, panning, and effect envelopes.

A big problem for me personally is that Live would not support MP3 files as of this writing, and all my songs and loops have been encoded to MP3 to conserve disc space. If I wanted to use Live for my DJ gigs, I'd need to load up my hard drive with large WAV files that are about 10 times larger than a compressed MP3 digital file. Then again, storage is relatively cheap today. If you're new and starting from scratch, you may decide to go uncompressed. Some DJs are reevaluating the need for compressed music.

For more information on Ableton's Live, visit www.ableton.com. There's also a great book titled *Ableton Live 2 Power* by Dave Hill Jr. (Muska & Lipman) that goes into extreme detail about song creation and actually DJing with Live.

Ableton Live.

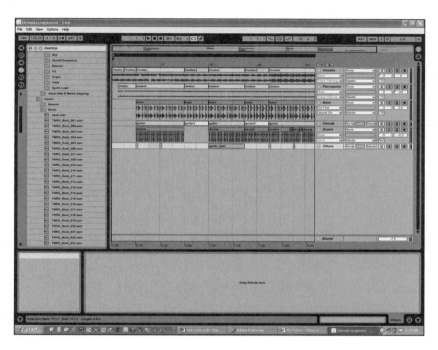

Propellerhead Reason

Propellerhead Software out of Sweden makes some very complicated but impressive programs specifically for music making. If you're in the trance and techno thing, you'll want to check out their ReBirth software. Propellerhead's software engineers managed to sample several older synthesizers and drum machines used to create many popular techno songs, and they've given you a second chance to get your hands on the funky sounds these machines once produced, only without the actual machines! ReBirth is a powerful program with a fairly steep learning curve.

If you're serious about music making, you'll definitely want to check out Propellerhead's Reason software package. Reason simulates a full production studio with a virtually unlimited rack system. Need a couple samplers? No problem[md]just click a few things, and they'll appear on screen. No need to wire anything, because the program does that for you. Want to see how your rack is hooked up? Flip the view to the back of the rack, and rewire the whole thing yourself with simply by clicking and dragging the cables with your mouse! To me, Reason seemed insanely complicated, but potentially insanely powerful. I'm still picking up pieces of grey matter off they floor after my head exploded trying to figure this thing out. Fortunately, there are several books and tutorials available that can help ease the learning curve for all Propellerhead programs.

Again, I don't see most average DJs using a program like this for live performances. This is definitely a studio program to create tracks that you'd burn to disc and play at your gigs later.

Visit their website at www.propellerheads.se for more information.

10
PLANNING FOR THE FUTURE

You've decided to get into an exciting, rewarding career. I spent 15 years of my life in this crazy business. I've made a pretty decent living and met quite a few thousand interesting people. And I can't count the thousands of dollars I saved on entertainment because I couldn't go out on weekends to spend any money! Most of all, I was out having fun while surrounding myself in music. And I never had the problem of having nothing to do on weekends. But there is life after being a DJ. I took some time to visit clubs all over the country and see what the rest of the world is up to. I didn't realize how much I'd missed by working every Friday and Saturday night all those years. This job is definitely a sacrifice, so you've got to love it. And those who love you have to understand your madness.

Radio DJ Career Paths

You can probably count the number of nationally known career radio DJs on one or two hands. I can only come up with five; Casey Kasem, Ryan Seacrest, Howard Stern, Rush Limbaugh, and Wolfman Jack. And Ryan Seacrest is a stretch! Quite a few radio DJs I've known faded into oblivion after uprooting their lives and moving ten or more times throughout their careers. What's really interesting is that most of them ended up in sales, either for radio stations, automobile dealers, or in some other field. Some radio veterans have capitalized on their local fame and became mobile private party DJs. And as more and more radio DJs are uprooted by tracking, expect to see more filter into the general population. If you're itching to broadcast, make sure you look into television, too!

Club/Bar DJ Career Paths

DJs who have survived the club circuit for ten or more years are usually on the back end of their careers, because club life is a rush and it's rarely forever. Many smaller bar and club jocks end up becoming mobile DJs, or filtering back into mainstream life doing something not particularly DJ related. The connections that a veteran big city club DJ has provides opportunities to enter the record industry, the promotion industry, or the club managing scene. In a way, being a club DJ is kind of like being in a country club-type prison; it's a prison you'd want to be in.

As club and bar DJs begin to gain experience, they gain valuable experience in all kinds of disciplines. Resumes will grow with titles such as "Event Coordinator" and "Music Director." Additionally, you'll meet people meet people from all walks of life, and non-DJ people like to brag that they "know the DJ." These fools, most with "real" jobs, just might refer you for a certain job at some point in your career. Regardless, nightclub and bar DJs gain valuable experience that can be applied to countless other professions.

Mobile DJ Career Paths

Forget about it—once a mobile DJ, always a mobile DJ. These dinosaurs have been around since the beginning of time, and will probably still be here millions of years after we're all gone. Get my drift? Mobile DJs tend to remain to be—nothing more than Mobile DJs. What's cool about this is the mobile DJ works two or three days a week, and makes an impressive hourly wage that makes radio people cringe.

Is this the best DJ job? Well, yes and no.

Yes, because you only work a few times a week, and it's fairly stable. Yes, because you can severely trim your music purchases, because most weddings are cookie cutter repeats of the last wedding. Yes, because your crowds are always different. And it's rarely the same place twice in a row.

No, because some people won't respond to your new hot dance music. No, because some weirdo will come up to you and ask for some John Denver, and you'll freak out.

Where Are They Now?

Nearly everyone who began their DJ career within a few years of me has moved on to something else. It seems the average DJ career lasts somewhere between 10-20 years, just enough time to completely destroy your hearing if you're not careful. Your mileage may vary.

Rich Huber, my first DJ mentor, moved to Nashville and took over some pretty big mainstream clubs. He worked his way up the ladder and eventually became a coveted *Billboard* Magazine reporter. His dream was to become a music producer. Last time we spoke, Richie was taking classes in music production. He's since disappeared somewhere between Philly and Nashville.

DJ J-Mo, or DJ Jose Miguel in his Latino incarnation, did clubs and bars for a whole bunch of years. A few years ago, he left the club scene and began to promote Latin nights in the underserved Philly area that were insanely popular. He's resigned himself to weddings and corporate affairs these days, mostly because he's "tired of working for nothing."

Marc Pears has toured the world on behalf of some of the world's largest adult bars, finally settling outside of New York City, where the big bucks are. He's got some great stories about his days in Iraq prior to the American invasion. He's embraced the digital revolution head on, and works with Todd Sun in promoting DJ Rak systems all over the country. Marc now performs at private parties along with his adult club duties.

Stewart Shocka had connections to die for, and always found his way into the most happening clubs in the Philly area. Why he was working at Touché, where I met him, I still don't understand. He dropped out of the DJ scene a few years ago to take over his father's construction trailer business.

Mel Toxic Taylor worked in the club scene for a few years until he got his radio break at WPST radio in Trenton, NJ. He ended up on WYSP in Philly, then on a few other Philly stations, and eventually settled into radio and newspaper ad sales.

I took a job with Time Life Music and left my club gig of over five years. I began to write and produce radio commercials for nightclubs all over the world. A few years later, I became a nightclub and bar consultant, teaching owners and operators how to manage and promote their bars, as well as helping other DJs find their grooves. I still do guest appearances once in a while to keep my feet wet, but there's no way I'd go back to working seven nights a week again!

DJ Burnout

I remember the first time I stepped into a real club as a DJ. It was the grand opening of a soon to be legendary nightspot in Voorhees, New Jersey called M-Street. I was young, single and the lead DJ in the club. Although I had only been doing clubs for a short while, I got to hire some of my heroes who were some of the hottest DJs in the Philly area at that time. Man, I was on top of the world! All I could think about was the moment I would put that brand new needle on a brand new record and fire up that brand new sound system for the first time while the crowd went wild. And it was good.

Three years later, I remember waking up one morning and actually dreading going into that club. I was doing Saturdays, and I had personally built one of the hottest Tuesday nights ever. Unlike weekend nights where all the clubs were busy, there was only one place to be on Tuesdays, and everyone who went out on Tuesdays went there. The strange part was the night was billed as a "Post Modern Tuesday," where we featured alternative rock music. The club owners thought I was completely insane, but Tuesdays were dead anyway, and they had little to lose. To everyone's surprise, including my own, we'd sometimes do more than 2,000 people on Tuesday nights.

But I had seen and done it all. I built the night from nothing, and proved I could make it happen. It just wasn't fun anymore. I was burned out and I didn't want to admit it.

How many times can you see the same people and play the same songs? Naturally, anything you do repetitively gets old. In the entertainment business, you've got to stay fresh or your show will suck, and so goes the whole bar. Be honest with yourself. If you're burned, do yourself and your bar a favor; voluntarily change your scenery. Don't just take a week off and assume everything will be peachy, because it won't. If you're dreading going to the job, move on.

DJ Burnout doesn't happen as often if you're a private party DJ, since your surroundings and audiences change frequently. But radio DJs and club DJs can suffer from severe burnout quickly. Here are my top four causes and solutions.

Cause #1: Too long in the same place (usually 18 months or longer).
Solution: You've been in that place too long. It's time to change your venue. When you become too comfortable at a bar, you lose sight of what you're supposed to be doing there. Some DJs start getting sneaky; hanging out behind the bar with hotties while playing pre-mixed compilation CDs. In this case, you're assuming you're at the club as a social event rather than a job. Begin looking for a new bar or club gig.

Cause #2: Too many shifts in the same place (usually two or more).
Solution: Cut back before you get fried. I know some guys who would work three or four *double shifts* a week, and that's just way too many shifts for the same person. I would do doubles on Thursday and Friday nights, and it was simply too long to be on your feet. A lack of energy in the later hours just makes the room seem too quiet and stale.

Cause #3: Working for the wrong reasons.
Solution: Some chicks simply dig DJs, but as I'm sure you already know, that's not the right reason to become a DJ. DJs sometime lose sight that they're in that booth to entertain and pump up the crowd, not pump up their hormones! And it always happens—they'll end up with a steady girl, and then this job really sucks.

Cause #4: Out of touch (failure to keep up with the "now").
Solution: As we get older, we tend to slow down. People stop going out as much. The problem is your crowd isn't getting older with you, so you're losing relevancy! You need to go hang out on the other side of the booth once in a while to see what's really going on. It's more fun out there anyway!

The Future of the Business

With the advent of the digital DJ and virtually unlimited access to both legal and illegal music downloads, it's easy to see why more and more people are becoming DJs. This is bad for the business, since you'll get people working for next to nothing, and these folks tend to bring your prices down too.

Try to aspire to that master level DJ who's the combination of a great MC, a decent mixer, and a killer promotions coordinator. I sincerely believe that this is the next step of club and bar entertainment. People are begging to be entertained, and they're very willing to give up their hard-earned dollars for quality entertainment. But it's up to you to make this industry recognize the star potential of this type of DJ. You've got to show the club and bar owners the potential of the master DJ. Only then will your earning potential increase to the star level salaries. With all the money these clubs and bars bring in, there's no reason you as a master level DJ, being the drawing figure to your room, shouldn't eventually get a big salary proportional to those big dollar sales. It's going to happen. Whether you want to be on that speeding train or not is up to you.

Whatever direction you choose, always remember not to pick your nose in public. Thanks to Howard Stern, belching and farting seem to be acceptable now, so go for it.

Index

N

Q-R

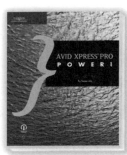